LEARNING TO TEACH SCIENCE

A Model for the 21st Century

Jazlin V. Ebenezer
University of Manitoba

Sylvia Connor
University of Manitoba

Merrill,
an imprint of Prentice Hall
Upper Saddle River, New Jersey   Columbus, Ohio

Library of Congress Cataloging-in-Publication Data

Ebenezer, Jazlin V.
    Learning to teach science: a model for the 21st century/Jazlin V. Ebenezer, Sylvia Connor.
        p.   cm.
    Includes bibliographical references and index.
    ISBN 0-02-331334-X
    1. Science—Study and teaching (Elementary)   2. Science teachers.   3. Elementary school
teaching.   I. Connor, Sylvia.   II. Title.
    LB1585.E187   1998
    372.3'5'044—dc21   97-30102
                                                                                    CIP

About the Cover: The cover photo was shot by Anthony Magnacca/Merrill, at COSI Columbus (Center of Science and Industry), a facility dedicated to providing hands-on science, learning, and fun. Manwell, the young man in the cover photo, is learning how he can depend on gravity while riding the high-wire cycle set up in COSI's Science Park.

Editor: Bradley J. Potthoff
Developmental Editor: Linda Ashe Montgomery
Production Editor: Mary M. Irvin
Design Coordinator: Julia Zonneveld Van Hook
Text Design, Composition, and Project Coordination: Elm Street Publishing Services, Inc.
Cover Designer: Linda Fares
Production Manager: Deidra M. Schwartz
Director of Marketing: Kevin Flanagan
Marketing Manager: Suzanne Stanton
Advertising/Marketing Coordinator: Julie Shough

This book was set in Galliard by Elm Street Publishing Services, Inc. and was printed and bound by R. R. Donnelley & Sons Company. The cover was printed by Phoenix Color Corp.

©1998 by Prentice-Hall, Inc.
Simon & Schuster/A Viacom Company
Upper Saddle River, New Jersey 07458

Photo credits: Anthony Magnacca/Merrill: pp. 7, 13 (both), 14 (both), 15 (all), 17, 36, 39, 53, 54, 76, 92, 93, 104, 142, 167, 168, 198, 243, 248, 250, 256, 350; Scott Cunningham/Merrill: 16, 71; Bart Smith: 282, 283; Kelly Pruden: 306.

Inside cover and National Science Standards margin notes: Reprinted with permission from *National Science Education Standards,* © 1996 by the National Academy of Sciences. Courtesy of the National Academy Press, Washington, D.C.

Printed in the United States of America

10 9 8 7 6 5 4 3 2 1

ISBN: 0-02-331334-X

Prentice-Hall International (UK) Limited, *London*
Prentice-Hall of Australia Pty. Limited, *Sydney*
Prentice-Hall of Canada, Inc., *Toronto*
Prentice-Hall Hispanoamericana, S. A., *Mexico*
Prentice-Hall of India Private Limited, *New Delhi*
Prentice-Hall of Japan, Inc., *Tokyo*
Simon & Schuster Asia Pte. Ltd., *Singapore*
Editora Prentice-Hall do Brasil, Ltda., *Rio de Janeiro*

This text is dedicated to members of our respective families: Thambakara and Jane Jabez, Sudesh and Dr. D. Luke Ebenezer, and Robin Connor for their encouragement, unfailing support, and academic expertise; to preservice teachers and practicing teachers who have given us their work without reservation for the education of future teachers; and to all the eager teachers and their curious students who together explore the domain of science.

Jazlin V. Ebenezer
Sylvia Connor

FOREWORD

You have in your hands a very valuable resource. As a beginning teacher of science at the elementary grade levels, you are most likely very anxious about the science instruction you will provide for young children. Part of the anxiety likely stems from your own experience in science classrooms, an experience that was, and still is typically a vocabulary laden one with the goal of learning the 'facts' of science. If you were fortunate, in the elementary grades you did activities and investigations. Most likely though, the activities and investigations were demonstrations of scientific knowledge and not inquiries into the structure and function of nature.

Science is a way of knowing. Science is a process of asking questions about nature and creating tools and techniques to listen to the answers. Science is working from evidence, data, observations, and measurements and creating explanations and models. More often than not though, individuals and groups reason to different and, at times, competing answers to questions and solutions to problems. Science is about arguing and evaluating methods used, goals sought, and knowledge obtained. Science is a way of knowing that seeks to bring about via negotiation and argumentation a consensus of opinion within the investigating community. You and the students in your classroom will form just such an investigating community.

Jazlin Ebenezer and Sylvia Connor have written a wonderful book grounded in contemporary research that sets out a variety of strategies you will use for creating and sustaining investigating communities. Importantly, the book sets out ways to manage the materials and activities of science lessons. More importantly though, and a distinguishing feature of the book, Jazlin and Sylvia provide you with a set of tools and strategies to manage and monitor the flow of information, language and ideas found in investigating communities.

Here, then, you have a first step, an introduction to the teaching tools and instructional techniques a teacher of science needs for developing a learning environment that promotes and values consensus building and the communication, reflection, argumentation and evaluation of ideas. The text is one I am sure you will want to make part of your professional library. My advice is to refer to it often in the years to come—as you gain experience working with children and their ideas you will learn to listen in new ways and hear new voices. When the new voices appear you will have begun to make the transition from a teacher of science to a science teacher.

Richard A. Duschl
Vanderbilt University

PREFACE

In recent years, science educators have been working on reforming science education. This reformation has been based on a vision of teaching and learning science in which all students have a greater opportunity to become scientifically literate. To reach this goal, educators must alter the way science is taught and learned. Therefore, the purpose of this text, *Learning to Teach Science: A Model for the 21st Century*, is to help you transform the way you think about teaching and learning science. This text will help you explore your prior ideas about teaching science, understand the true nature of science and scientific inquiry, and provide you with a teaching methodology in which you will learn how to help students construct meaning through scientific inquiry and discourse.

CONCEPTUAL HIGHLIGHTS OF THE TEXT

To realize the vision of science for all, we emphasize that a teacher must acquire an adequate background of science content knowledge, grasp and understand how children learn, and develop an underpinning of the theoretical aspects of teaching science. In addition, we assert that a teacher must learn how to engage in continuous reflective practice. Throughout the text we provide you with many opportunities to engage in personal and collaborative reflective inquiry about teaching and learning science. Thus, through interaction with this text, you will accomplish the following:

Develop an understanding of how learning occurs and how you may facilitate learning in science. We believe that incorporating children's ideas, beliefs, and questions about science concepts and related societal issues in meaningful science lessons is an effective way to teach science. To accomplish this, you must first seek children's science conceptions. Then you can learn to negotiate science ideas with children and conduct collaborative inquiry so that children will see the struggles and tensions that scientists go through as they invent scientific knowledge. In this manner, children will get a glimpse of the true nature of scientific inquiry.

Explore the nature of science. Modern as well as postmodern views about science presented in this text indicate how much has changed from the time of Bacon and Newton to the present day. However, the reason and logic of Bacon and Newton's day will continue to be practiced in school science, alongside the give-and-take of modern scientific discourse. Classroom discourse will enhance your construction of deeper meanings of scientific inquiry.

Examine curricular issues. Effective science curriculum includes planning for multicultural and gender equity, adapting activities for special-needs students, and utilizing technologies in science to create learning environments to meet the needs of all of your students. In this text, you will view science through a multiple-voice framework so that you may reach students with different backgrounds, interests, abilities, experiences, and motivations. A multiple-voice framework for science teaching enables you to develop learning objectives, review curricular materials, select teaching strategies and learning activities, choose assessment tasks, and engage students in a variety of ways to develop an understanding of science.

Enrich your science content knowledge. As an elementary teacher, you are most likely considered a generalist as you have probably taken only one or two courses in science before this methods course. You may be somewhat anxious about having a limited science background because you realize that to teach K–6 children you need a broad understanding of the major ideas in science. Thus, in this course you will be exposed to various science themes and the knowledge presented in them. You will also be taught *two learning tools,* Vee diagramming and concept mapping, to help you develop much-needed science content knowledge throughout your teaching career.

We do not expect you to have a deep understanding of all the sciences. Clarifying and deepening your understanding of science content, however, is part of your teaching responsibility. Hence, this is an area in which your knowledge can evolve through professional development activities even after you leave your university or college.

To have a sound foundation in science and an in-depth understanding, you must continue to seek scientific knowledge throughout your career. Participating in research at science workshops or field settings is a legitimate way to learn science and the nature of science. Why do we stress the importance of continuous learning of science? Teachers are ambassadors of the scientific community in the classroom. As ambassadors, it is important to present an authentic image of someone who engages in scientific inquiry, not someone who is a fountain of scientific wisdom.

Understand that your professional development is a continuous, active process for which you are professionally responsible. We suggest that once you begin your teaching career you seek professional activities that will provide you with sustained and contextual participation and reflection in integrating your content and curriculum knowledge, learning, and teaching skills. As researchers and reflective practitioners, preservice and practicing teachers can make significant contributions to the advancement of knowledge of teaching and learning. And through this course you will indeed develop theoretical and practical meanings to shed light on the problems of teaching. You will also develop the skills (journal writing and using audio/video recordings, peer observations, and dialogue) to conduct research in your classroom and carry out a reflective practice.

ORGANIZATION OF THE TEXT

This text is organized into three parts. Part One consists of three chapters. It considers different world views of science teaching and learning. Essentially, it argues for and leads to a conceptual framework of science teaching and learning labeled the "constructivist" approach. Under this umbrella, Part Two, consisting of five chapters, argues for collaborative learning for young science learners. Accordingly, it outlines a teaching and learning model called the **Common Knowledge Construction Model** that consists of four phases. Many examples and case studies illustrate parts of the model. Part Three consists of four chapters and focuses on the often neglected areas of the science curricula that contribute to the development of a scientifically literate person. This part of the text outlines a framework for a multiple-voice, integrated unit plan and gives a detailed example. It discusses how learning to teach is a career-long process and offers suggestions and tools for professional development and change.

SPECIAL FEATURES OF THE TEXT

To help you learn to teach science, we incorporated a number of pedagogical elements including:

- Preparatory teaching activities for reflective practice including journal writing and peer interactions
- Sample lessons and unit plan
- Instructions for creating Vee diagrams, concept maps, and hypercard stacks
- Case studies of preservice teachers from exemplary practicum science teaching experiences
- Contextual language that the teaching community and researchers use to exchange ideas
- Margin notes that include definitions of boldfaced terms, reflections on teaching strategies, and National Science Teaching, Assessment, and Professional Growth Standards

x PREFACE

Becoming an effective teacher is a career-long process. We hope, by reading this book and practicing suggested activities, you will feel adequately prepared to teach science. After extensive research with our own preservice teachers, we stand ready to develop your knowledge, understanding, and ability to teach science.

ACKNOWLEDGMENTS

Appreciation is extended to the 1991–1997 preservice teachers at the University of Manitoba for collaborating with us in preparing and sharing research-based lessons, activities, units, and strategies at the elementary level. The contributing preservice teachers' names are included along with their work throughout the text.

We offer a multitude of thanks to Jill Wharton, secretary of the Department of Curriculum: Mathematics and Natural Sciences, and Eileen Repeta of the Faculty of Education for giving us support on word processing. We thank Eddie Lau for helping us with computer graphics. Thanks are also extended to Tani Cyr and Carla Reilly for their assistance with this book.

Great appreciation is extended to our developmental editor, Linda Montgomery, for keeping in touch with us throughout the writing of this book, observing the methods classes at the University of Manitoba for three days and talking to our preservice teachers, and working with us on campus. Her hard work and enduring patience in editing this text will always be kindly remembered. The valuable suggestions made by 18 of our 1995–1996 preservice teachers at two group interviews conducted by our developmental editor for improvement of this text have been incorporated. These preservice teachers' input and time are greatly appreciated.

This text is the outcome of peer reviews by our American colleagues at different stages of its development. We sincerely thank our reviewers and support group for their helpful comments and suggestions: Joel Bass, Sam Houston State University; Glenn D. Berkheimer, Michigan State University; John R. Cannon, University of Nevada-Reno; Jacqueline A. Forbes, University of Houston; James J. Gallagher, Michigan State University; Jay K. Hackett, University of Northern Colorado; John Huntsberger, University of Texas at Austin; George T. Ladd, Boston College; Frances Lawrenz, University of Minnesota; Cheryl L. Mason, San Diego State University; Richard H. Moyer, University of Michigan-Dearborn; Michael Odell, University of Idaho; William A. Rieck, University of Southwestern Louisiana; Margaret Gail Shroyer, Kansas State University; and Douglas Zook, Boston University.

Special Acknowledgments

Special thanks are given to the program coordinator, Leslie Wurtak, and the teachers from the Fort Garry School Division #5, Winnipeg, Manitoba, Canada, who completed a survey questionnaire and were quoted with their permission in chapter 12. They are Shirley Adam, Mary-Ann Fast, Alan Holl, Sophia Munro, Ken Park, Barbara Maguire Shute, and Denise Weselake.

The authors are especially grateful for the contributions of the following individuals.

Preservice Teachers. Susan Atkins, Jacqueline Bays, Sasha Bergner, Lori Binder, Lisa Boch, Marla Brandt, Jane Couch, Donna Drebit, Sandra Ferguson, Cindy Ganz, Gerry Haines, Ron Harder, Brian Hargreaves, Diana Higgins, Michael Hlady, Judy Horst, Lisa Johnson, Brenda Klassen, Karen Anne Kristiuk, Heather Weins Kroeker, Phillipe Lajoie, Aileen Legault, Wraith Malik, Craig Milne, Kelly Pruden, Cheryl Resnick, Melanie Robinson, John Schrofel, Andrew Simons, Sharon Turner, Ingmar Wenzel, Teresa Wiens, Sascha Wohlers, Gloria Yaremkiewich, and Reina Younka.

Practicing Teachers. Mervin Haines, Bart Smith, and Joy Smith.

This text is also a by-product of many research projects that were financially supported by the Social Science and Humanities Research Council of Canada (SSHRCC 332-5501) and the University of Manitoba (Research and Development Office, Faculty of Education, and Communication Systems). Without the assistance of these institutions, this classroom-based research book may not have become a reality.

Jazlin V. Ebenezer
Sylvia Connor

BRIEF CONTENTS

CONTENTS

CHAPTER 3

Structuring Science Knowledge   44

PART TWO

The Common Knowledge Construction Model   71

CHAPTER 4

Constructing Common Knowledge   72

INTRODUCTION

☀ LEARNING TO TEACH SCIENCE: HEART TO HEART

TAMMY'S VOICE

This year's curriculum and instruction course opened up a new way of thinking about science for me. I must admit that, for the first half of the year, I was generally confused about what we were learning in class; it took some time to realize that we were actually participating in the constructivist approach to science.... I finally felt this course came together in the beginning to middle of February. I now believe I have an understanding of the relationship between science teaching and allowing children to better construct their own meaning of science concepts. I have learned this year that my own science conceptions will continue to be tested and revised in order to accommodate my new experiences and sense making.

What are your professional attitudes and disposition toward learning to teach science? Do you belong to the category of preservice teachers who search for right answers or become impatient when direct answers are not given? Do you agree with a group of preservice teachers who each stated to their science teacher educator in frustration, "Show it to me and tell me how to do it" (Stofflet, 1994)? How would you feel if you were asked to explore and assess your prior beliefs about science teaching? How do you react when you experience conceptual conflicts and your ideas are challenged? Your science teacher educator is cognizant of your problems and difficulties. Seek opportunities to engage in heart-to-heart talks with your educator about your stages of development as well as concerns that may arise as you become a teacher of science.

What are some of the stages you might go through in your preservice teaching? What might be some of your anxieties and concerns in science teaching?

FIGURE I-1

Successive stages in
preservice teaching

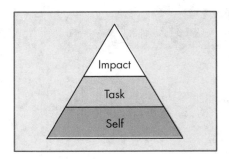

Possible Stages in Your Preservice Teaching

Professional Development Standard D

Guideline: Quality preservice and inservice programs are characterized by options that recognize the developmental nature of teacher professional growth and individual and group interests, as well as the needs of teachers who have varying degrees of experience, professional expertise, and proficiency.

Research shows that the preservice teaching period is marked by successive stages. The projection of *self* is first—the focus is on personal actions rather than students. For example, you might ask yourself, "How do I perform in class?" "How do others view me as a teacher?" The views of significant others—the science teacher educator, cooperating teacher, faculty advisor, principal, students, and parents—become most important. Inward-looking tendencies including the need for validation, affirmation, and confirmation about your role as a teacher may prevail. The next focus might be on the science *task*, the materials, and the best possible delivery of the activity. You might ask yourself, "How do I best present this science topic to my students?" Lastly, the focus moves toward the learner: "What *impact* do I have on the learner?" You begin to go beyond yourself and the activity and focus on what students are learning. Gunstone, Slattery, Baird, & Northfield (1993) point out that successful personal and professional development requires that the concerns at each level (self, task, and impact) be addressed in an integrated manner from the start of your teacher education.

Anxieties and Concerns

One major concern that you might have in your preservice period is the adequacy of your science content knowledge. This is understandable. This con-

FIGURE I-2

Integration of self, task,
and impact

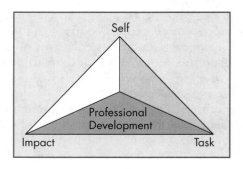

cern is expressed by those teachers who have and those who do not have a science background that includes successful completion of a number of science courses. Do not despair. Even teachers with a solid science background in biology, chemistry, or physics may have problems teaching other areas of science. One way of overcoming this problem is presented in chapter 3. Another way of looking at this problem is stated by Rose.

ROSE'S VOICE

I am now beginning to realize that an elementary teacher doesn't have to know everything about every subject he or she teaches. In fact, I think that a great deal of learning can occur for a teacher through the planning and implementing of lessons. I found that, before I taught my unit on clouds and precipitation, I knew very little about the subject. But, through the research that I did and the experiments also, I learned a lot about the subject with my students. My preconceived notion that the teacher must be the possessor of all knowledge has relaxed....

Professional Development Standard A

Guideline: Science learning experiences for teachers must build on teacher's current science understanding, ability, and attitudes.

You don't have to be an encyclopedia of science to teach science. Modifying your attitudes, beliefs, and values about science, science teaching, and science learning is important. Changing your behavior, however, involves investigating your personal conceptions of teaching and learning. Conceptions of teaching and learning are influenced by how you learned or how you were taught science. Thus, professional development can take place only if you are motivated to change and use reflection as a tool to bring about that change.

Teaching Standard B

Guideline: To guide and facilitate learning encourage and model the skills of scientific inquiry, as well as the curiosity, openness to new ideas and data, and skepticism that characterize science.

☀ REFLECTIVE INQUIRY

Becoming aware of yourself, becoming personally responsible for teaching and making decisions, carrying out personal reflections, and engaging in interpersonal interactions are necessary requirements in learning to teach science, but they are not easy. They are truly intellectually demanding.

To alleviate or overcome some concerns about engaging in reflective practice you will be given opportunities throughout this text to assess your own attitudes and beliefs about the nature of science and science teaching. You will create, negotiate, and recreate meanings through journal writing and peer interactions, through dialogue and intentional reflective inquiry. Your learning environment will resemble a research forum in which the collaborators share what they have done and what they claim to know to produce a joint teaching culture.

Professional Development Standard B

Guideline: Learning experiences for teachers of science must use inquiry, reflection, interpretation of research, modeling, and guided practice to build understanding and skill in science teaching.

Journal Writing

Journal writing is a tool that is often used in professional practice for reflection. Three questions about journals often arise (Connelly & Clandinen, 1988, pp. 36–37); they are presented in Figure I-3.

Active Self-Reflection

Professional Development Standard C

Guideline: Professional development activities must provide opportunities to know and have access to existing research and experiential knowledge.

Professional Development Standard C

Guideline: Professional development activities must provide opportunities for teachers to receive feedback about their teaching and to understand, analyze, and apply that feedback to improve their practice.

Engaging in a reflective practice means to intentionally make certain aspects of your practice problematic so that you may gain new insights into that practice (Clarke, 1994). Reflective practice involves conversing with your problem setting. When you openly and actively converse with yourself within a social context you generate personal knowledge (Erickson, 1986; Feiman-Nemser, 1986). Clarke (1994) conceptualizes this self-reflection as "the interplay between framing and reframing, experimentation and back-talk in the action setting."

To help you in this endeavor, seek ways to interact with students. Study their ways of sciencing, the decisions they make, and the actions they take so that this knowledge will help you assess your own prior knowledge and beliefs about teaching. Faithfully engage in journal writing to record the research you collect on your own teaching. This will allow you to stand back temporarily from your personal beliefs, acknowledge where they are inaccurate or incomplete, and reconstruct them. Take opportunities to work with role models—teachers who question and reflect on their pedagogical beliefs and teachers whose ideas and practices differ somewhat from your own so

FIGURE I-3
Three questions about journal writing

1. What should I write?

Write as much as you can in your journal. Describe your students, events, and your actions and reactions both while teaching and after you are finished teaching. Record the feelings you have about your teaching practices and the various events that happen. Be alert to past experiences that come to mind as you react emotionally and morally.

2. How often should I write?

Write regularly. Make an entry every few days or more frequently if you have time or if something notable occurs. To be a useful reflective tool, the journal needs to be an ongoing record of thought.

3. Do I go back and reread it?

It is helpful to reread your journal entries from time to time to try to make sense of the things that are important to you. As you read the entries, look for ideas to review. Read carefully to see if you can pick up any threads or themes that seem to recur. Keep an open mind and try to look for patterns. Keep comparing new ideas with those from before.

that cognitive dissonance will force you to question your personal beliefs and teaching practices. Without creating this cognitive dissonance, your learning about teaching will be shallow, technical, and imitative (Kagan, 1992).

✸ TEACHER EMPOWERMENT

When you engage in professional practice, you will shift from traditional classroom practices. Initially, you may frame your reflections in terms of "imitating" or "cloning" other teachers (Clarke, 1994). Later, you may reframe your reflections on your practice by probing into your own beliefs and making these explicit. We encourage you to reflect on your practice to become an empowered teacher (independent and autonomous). If you tend to replicate other teachers, you will evolve into a repetitive practitioner! Reflecting on your whole practice rather than particular aspects is important for defining a teaching practice that is effective.

To develop a practical philosophy for science teaching, you must seek opportunities to engage in reflective inquiry and to discuss salient principles and major issues of teaching. Additionally, you must be committed to examining ways of teaching through reading, contemplating, and researching. Committing to a novel way of teaching is easy when you become an active, collaborative partner with your peers and your science teacher educator in the inquiry of teaching and learning. Seek genuine opportunities for sustained, meaningful, and critical dialogue (Erickson, Mayer-Smith, Rodrigues, Chin, & Mitchell, 1994).

Professional Growth Standard C

Guideline: Professional development activities must provide opportunities for teachers to learn and use various tools and techniques for self-reflection and collegial reflection, such as peer coaching, portfolios, and journals.

PART ONE

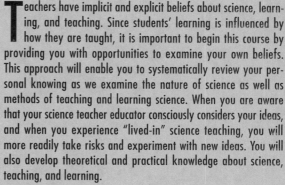

WORLD VIEWS OF SCIENCE KNOWING

Teachers have implicit and explicit beliefs about science, learning, and teaching. Since students' learning is influenced by how they are taught, it is important to begin this course by providing you with opportunities to examine your own beliefs. This approach will enable you to systematically review your personal knowing as we examine the nature of science as well as methods of teaching and learning science. When you are aware that your science teacher educator consciously considers your ideas, and when you experience "lived-in" science teaching, you will more readily take risks and experiment with new ideas. You will also develop theoretical and practical knowledge about science, teaching, and learning.

Chapter 1 explores your conceptions about the nature of science through the "voices" of preservice teachers. When you critically examine these conceptions, you may begin to question your own beliefs about modes of scientific inquiry. A brief review of *modern* (through evidence and logic) and *post-modern* (through social discourse) ways of "doing" science is given.

Chapter 2 explores your conceptions of science teaching and learning. Four lessons taught by preservice teachers are described and compared. The development of constructivist approaches will help you to understand contemporary views of science education.

Chapter 3 illustrates two learning tools—concept mapping and Vee diagramming—that will aid you in learning and structuring science content. These tools will help you to see the relationships among scientific ideas and to learn science content knowledge so that you will be able to teach science with greater confidence.

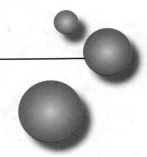

CHAPTER 1

Conceptions of Science

FOCUS QUESTIONS

1. How is scientific knowledge generated? Is there a scientific method?

2. How is scientific inquiry influenced by social enterprise?

3. What inquiry skills would be useful when discussing and negotiating a common understanding of science concepts?

4. How can teachers help children learn how to do science investigations?

5. What National Science Standards can be used as guidelines for developing new science curriculums?

Reflective Inquiry

SALLY'S VOICE
I believe there are ultimate truths about our physical world and its many scientific relationships. Everyone discovers these truths or absolutes to varying degrees. Because of our human limitations, none of us will ever fully understand our science world.

JOURNAL ACTIVITY

Exploring Personal Conceptions of Science

What is science?

What does it mean to do science?

How would I draw a scientist at work?

Write answers to the foregoing questions. Then meet with one other classmate and, after a brief discussion, write together what you understand about science. Next both of you meet with another pair of preservice teachers and collaborate on the same exercise. In this final grouping of four class members, come to some consensus about **conceptions** about science and report it to the rest of the class.

☀ THE NATURE OF SCIENCE

On the first day of class in a methods course, preservice teachers were asked to explain in writing what they understood science to be. Discussions revolved around two questions: What is scientific knowledge? What is scientific inquiry? Like Sally, a number of preservice teachers believed that scientific knowledge was absolute because of an independent existence of the natural world.

JOHN'S VOICE

I believe that scientific knowledge is absolute, and its existence is separate from the perceptions of humanity. The goal of people is to find ways to discover scientific knowledge. The work of science is similar to the work of a detective.

VALERIE'S VOICE

The nature of scientific knowledge is that it is a huge bank "waiting" to be discovered.

CARLA'S VOICE

Scientific knowledge gets formed by truths being exposed.

Conceptions are those sensible, personal understandings of a certain phenomenon. In this chapter, we examine conceptions associated with the social phenomenon of teaching and learning science.

For John, Valerie, and Carla, scientific knowledge is truth, waiting to be discovered. Metaphorically, this viewpoint may be described as the world's being operated by a built-in mechanism, the laws of which must be discovered through sensory experience and logic. In this view, the human mind is independent and separate from the "real" world. This suggests that the world is the same for every human being, detached from human inquiry and scientific objectivity. How do your perceptions about the world agree or differ from this idea? How then do you think scientific knowledge is developed? Do you agree with the following conceptions?

TAMMY'S VOICE

Science to me is an algorithm of exploration: hypothesizing a problem; observing the environment; proving hypotheses; observing results; and making conclusions based on those results.

Professional Development Standard B

Guideline: Learning experiences for teachers of science must address teachers' needs as learners and build on their current knowledge of science content, teaching, and learning.

JODY'S VOICE

In science our focus is often outside of ourselves—the world around us, the world we can sense.... Science, however, is not only focusing on the world but describing it through analysis, through interaction/exploration, through evaluation, through hypothesis.

For Tammy, science is rule-based exploration. Jody considers the physical world "outside" of human beings but perceived through "senses." These students have a "realist" perspective of the world. According to Bodner (1986), "the realist perspective assumes that we come into the world as discoverers who build copies or replicas of reality in our minds. This perspective leads to an iconic or picture-like notion of knowledge in which our mental structures somehow correspond to, or represent, reality as if they were direct copies or pictures. Therefore, it leads to the question of how well our knowledge corresponds to reality: something is true if and only if it corresponds to an independent, objective reality" (p. 874).

But is the human mind independent and separate from the real world? Are we not part of the world itself? How much is our world a product of our own mental processes?

Schrödinger (1958) writes that our world is a construct of our sensations, perceptions, and memories and it is convenient to regard it as existing objectively on its own. Yet he also reminds us that the outside world is "colorless, cold, mute" because color, sound, and sensations of hot and cold are our immediate sensations, made manifest to us only through the mind, so that each person's world picture is a different mental construct.

Modern physics tells us that the world is not some tame organism to be prodded, poked, and beaten into submission. It is a sensitive mechanism for which the very act of observing is a disturbance. Furthermore, the observer, the measurer, and the recorder are part of the apparatus. To perform an experiment, the experimenter becomes part of the system. How objective then is the outside world? In scientific inquiry we think we deal objectively; in reality, subjectivity is always present.

Professional Development Standard B

Guideline: Learning experiences for teachers of science must connect and integrate all pertinent aspects of science and science education.

Scientific Inquiry as a Social Practice

Understanding that the development of scientific knowledge is a subjective activity is not new to practicing scientists. In 1990, Longino proposed that the primary method of objectifying knowledge must be processes of interpersonal negotiations and social consensus. This mode of inquiry surmised that scientists work in a social context, answerable to and influenced by members of the larger society. For instance, the technological and social needs of a society often dictate what knowledge will be sought, what research will be done, and what research will be funded. Hence, science is a complex social enterprise.

The detailed anthropological study of scientists at work in the laboratory and the field (Latour, 1987), their discourse, their actions, their networks of allies, their support and nonsupport for competing ideas, reiterates that scientific knowledge resides in social practice rather than a rational, individualistic mind operating apart from the world (Jenkins, 1991). Science is a "socially constituted enterprise shaped at many levels by human values, beliefs, and commitments" (Kelly, Carlsen & Cunningham, 1993, p. 207).

For instance, even as early as 1905, with regard to the nature of science, Felix Mendeleev stated that "… statements of fact themselves depend upon the persons who observe them…. For this reason there will inevitably be much that is subjective bearing the stamp of time and locality—in every exposition of science" (p. viii).

And, in 1988, Richard Duschl defined the nature of science as "knowledge of both why science believes what it does and how science has come to think that way" (p. 57). These perceptions help us understand Kuhn's (1970) notion of a community of scientists and portray the establishment of a scientific paradigm as a social enterprise:

National Science Education Principle

School science reflects the intellectual and cultural traditions that characterize the practice of contemporary science.

> At the start, a new candidate for a new paradigm may have a few supporters, and on occasions those supporters' motives may be suspect. Nevertheless, if they are competent, they will improve it, explore its possibilities, and show what it will be like to the community guided by it … if the paradigm is one destined to win its fight, the number and strength of the persuasive arguments in its favor will increase. More scientists will be converted and the exploration of the new paradigm will go on. Gradually, the number of experiments, instruments, articles, and books based on the paradigm will multiply (p. 159).

Hence, identifying scientific problems, framing questions, seeking and providing evidence, and making knowledge claims are all determined by the social, political, and economic climates of a culture. Scientists' thoughts, language, and actions are governed by the multiple worlds in which they live (Martin & Brouwer, 1993): these worlds include the scientific network, family, and community. How might this have affected science historically? What implications might it have for exploring with students the nature of science? Like practicing scientists, science teachers and students should explore and integrate ideas as they try to make sense of the world around them. School science should account for the natural, technological, and social worlds of students in the science classroom, at home, and in the community. Science experiences at school should communicate to students the importance and excitement of "doing" science, the wonder of science, and the joy that is found in communal understanding. Engaging students in "doing science," in discourse as a part of inquiry, provides a foundation for developing scientific literacy.

Scientific Literacy

National Science Education Principle

Science is for all students.

The American Association for the Advancement of Science (AAAS, 1989) and the National Research Council (NRC, 1996) outline recommendations for developing scientific literacy, a more valid way to know how science works, a better sense of inquiry, and its dependency on human need and discourse. The following sections are consistent with the description of the nature of science in the American Association for the Advancement of Science report (1989, pp. 25–310) and science as inquiry standards in the National Research Council report (1996, p. 105).

Developing Skills for Inquiry

Collecting evidence, generating questions, and proposing and discussing explanations play major roles in scientific inquiry. These intellectual and communicative processes are integral to constructing and negotiating scientific knowledge. They create opportunities for critical thinking. And, although process skills should not really be an end in themselves or taught in isolation, they are basic to conducting scientific inquiry.

Teaching Standard A

Teachers of science plan an inquiry-based science program for their students.

Observing

Observing is the taking in of sense perceptions. It is an activity in which all of us, from infant to adult, are involved throughout our lives. What we should be doing in science lessons is assisting students in the art of scientific observation. Such activities as identifying rocks and minerals or studying drag on race cars require the use of content-specific observation

skills. What are the characteristics or qualities of good scientific observation? Observations are specific to a particular activity. For example, when identifying rocks, students must observe their texture, color, hardness, shape, patterns, and structure.

Classifying

Classifying is the process of arranging objects or events according to some property. Classifying is a basic skill and is at the root of all understanding. Human beings routinely classify phenomena into groups as they notice similarities and differences among objects. They also begin to learn how to use simple keys to aid in the identification of objects such as seeds or rocks.

National Science Education Principle

Learning science is an active process.

Measuring

Measuring is comparing things to a standard and begins early in preschool or elementary school with non-standard units and progresses to more refined stages using standard units in which greater precision is required. As science investigations in the upper elementary grades require more accuracy, students will use different units (such as Newtons) and different measuring devices

(spring scales), expanding their concept of measurement. A major goal of measurement is to learn how to select appropriate measuring instruments and read a variety of balances and scales.

Inferring

Inferring is interpreting or explaining what is observed. Learning to infer begins in infancy and develops into a sophisticated skill by the middle school years. Inferring is the process of carefully examining the observed data and suggesting relationships between objects or events. The value of inference is that it can lead to testable predictions. For example, a student can infer from the observed data that

the ice on a pond is very thin or that trees are preparing for winter.

Predicting

Predicting is forecasting a future observation by inferring from data that have been observed. You interpret your observations and suggest what will occur in the future. Students need to be aware that the reliability of their predictions depends on the accuracy and completeness of their observations. For the previous example, related predictions would be that the ice on the pond may break when a heavy animal steps on it, and the trees will lose their leaves as winter approaches. Predictions ultimately found to be incor-

rect are still valid and useful because they eliminate possible explanations and thus can point the way to better understanding.

Hypothesizing

Hypothesizing is based on observing and predicting but in addition requires an additional framework or pattern of evidence that indicates a relationship between phenomena. For example, one might *predict* that the ice on a pond would break if stressed but hypothesize that ice in early winter is very weak and dangerous for animals to walk on. The hypothesis therefore is based on an extensive accumulation of data.

Interpreting

Interpreting data is the ability to perceive patterns or trends in data. The data have to be recorded and organized into patterns, charts, or graphs so that interpretations can be made. Students who are skilled in interpreting data can identify trends and patterns, which can lead to inference, prediction, and further investigation.

Investigating

Investigating is the designing and carrying out of simple experiments. As students design or perform investigations, they should become increasingly aware of the wide range of variables. Understanding the idea of a *fair test* is recognized as an initial step in learning to do an investigation. Students learn to suggest the means for identifying and controlling relevant variables and build these ideas into their

investigations. They learn to review their investigations critically and to check their results by careful repetition. For example, in testing the solubility of substances, students must control the amount of substance, temperature, size and shape of containers, and time in order to have a "fair test" or do a proper investigation.

Fair Tests and Investigations

Teaching students how to control variables in conducting "fair tests" and investigations can be difficult and time consuming. Students will relate to the idea of "fairness" because it seems to be an intrinsic part of everyday childhood life and play. With some guidance they are soon able to discuss the fairness of a simple test *after* they have done it, and gradually they become able to think about fairness *before* doing a test. Taking the idea of fairness further by having them discuss the possible aspects of the investigation that may vary is a natural follow-up. Here is one approach a teacher used to help her students understand a fair test.

SALLY'S VOICE

> *How many of you girls and boys know what a **fair test** in science is? I'm certain that you know what being **fair** is—being sure that everyone gets the same amount of cake or ice cream at a party, or treating children in the same family the same way. That's being **fair**.*
>
> *A **fair test** is similar to that. Let's imagine a group of children riding their bicycles in a park. Two have new bicycles—Melaena and Ryan. They begin to argue. Both say that their bike is faster*

Melaena wins the race.
Does this mean that she has
the faster bike?

than the other's. They decide to do a trial ride to settle the
argument. With the help of their friends, they mark off about
55 m on the bike path. One person yells, "Start!", the two bikes
speed off, and the others stay at the finish line. Melaena crosses
the finish line first and declares that she has the faster bike.

However, one of the group—Carlos—says, "That wasn't a fair
test, because one of you may be stronger. We need to find out
which is the **faster bike**, not who can win the race while riding that
bike. Here's what we should do. Let's get a stopwatch and have
another person (not Melaena or Ryan) ride each bike as fast as he
or she can and time each turn. Then we'll know which bike is really
faster. We should try this several times to be sure we are right."

Do you agree with Carlos's suggestion? Is there any other way
that a fair test could have been done?

Let's think about what conditions are important for a **fair test**.
Using the bike situation as an example, we need to do the
following:

- Have each bike go the same distance
- Have the same rider for each bike putting out the same power
- Do the trials at the same time of day with the same
  temperature and road conditions
- Repeat the trials several times

Teaching Standard B

Guideline: To guide and facilitate
learning, challenge students to
accept and share responsibility for
their own learning.

Doing a *fair test in science* is much the same. You have to keep all the conditions the same except for the one that you are testing. A good example follows.

Two groups of children in the classroom wanted to find out which of two types of string was the stronger. Both tested each type of string.

One group tied the string to the back of a chair and tied bricks to the end of it until the string broke. They tested the other piece of string in exactly the same way and repeated their test several times with new pieces of string.

The other group tied the string between two chairs and hung the bricks from the middle of the string, adding bricks until the string broke. They tested the other piece of string in exactly the same way and repeated their tests for other pieces of the two types of string.

Both groups ended up with the same results. Both had done *fair tests*.

Investigations

After establishing the parameters of a fair test, students are ready to conduct *investigations* that will answer questions they have. Sally uses the following approach.

In order to prepare yourself to do some investigations, let's review the steps. Work in your groups and then we will get together, compare and discuss your answers, and decide as a class the steps we should take. (Here are the steps the class decided on.)

Teaching Standard E

Guideline: To develop a community of learners, nurture collaboration among students.

- Discuss the problem.
- Decide what question we wish to investigate.
- Do some exploring of the materials we may use.
- Make a hypothesis, that is, state what we think the results will be.
- Plan our investigation, including what measurements we will need to make.
- Gather our materials and equipment.
- Do our investigation, watching for any other factors we may need to control.
- Record our methods, our measurements, and the results.
- Repeat our trials several times.
- Compare our results with our hypothesis.
- Discuss our investigation and decide if it was a fair test.
- Report our results to people who might be interested.

Teaching Standard D

Guideline: Design and manage the learning environment by engaging students in designing their own learning environment.

Be sure to plan all investigations carefully, thinking about what you want to test for, and what conditions must be kept the same so that you will have a fair test. Some possible investigations are these:

- Find out which dissolves quicker in water, a sugar cube or loose sugar.
- Find out which kind of paper towel holds the most water.
- Find out which kind of sandwich bag keeps bread fresher.
- Find out which dishwashing liquid makes the most bubbles.

☀ **PEER INTERACTION**

Scientific Inquiry Processes

Select one of the following questions to discuss.

1. Examine two separate science activities. What kinds of scientific processes are called for in each of these activities?

2. Describe an investigation that will require children to carry out fair tests.

What About the Scientific Method?

Early philosophers were convinced that exploring the world and organizing their findings was a process, a scientific methodology that consisted of arriving at lawlike generalizations from observable data (observing the world through their senses). They confirmed such generalizations through further experimentation.

Even well into the twentieth century, Karl Pearson's single method for the generation of scientific knowledge was accepted. In his influential book, *The Grammar of Science,* written in 1892, Pearson convincingly argued for following specific scientific procedures to reach a scientific conclusion. These procedures have become known as the "scientific method" and embody four characteristics:

- Science has achieved a superior kind of truth.
- Science is characterized by progress.
- Science is in the possession of the only method of interrogating nature, namely the empirical-inductive or scientific method.
- This method can be simply described and easily taught. (Williams & Stinner, 1996, pp. 135–136)

Do you recognize Pearson's *scientific method* from the science you were taught in school? Even today curriculum guidelines, textbooks, and common practice all stress this way of doing science. Most science textbooks explicitly or implicitly tell students that there is/are scientific method(s) that involve procedures along the lines of Pearsonian science.

Recent reforms in science teaching methodology outline recommendations for developing scientific literacy and a more valid way to know how science works. For example, *Project 2061: Science for All Americans* (AAAS, 1989) models a better sense of scientific inquiry and its dependency on human need and human discourse.

THE SCIENTIFIC WORLD VIEW
- the world is understandable
- scientific ideas are subject to change
- scientific knowledge is durable
- science cannot provide complete answers to all questions

SCIENTIFIC INQUIRY
- science demands evidence
- science is a blend of logic and imagination
- science explains and predicts
- scientists try to identify and avoid bias
- science is not authoritarian

THE SCIENTIFIC ENTERPRISE
- science is a complex social activity
- science is organized into content disciplines and is conducted in various institutions
- there are generally adopted ethical principles in the conduct of science
- scientists participate in public affairs both as specialists and as citizens (American Association for the Advancement of Science, 1989, pp. 25–31).

☼ SCIENCE CONTENT STANDARDS

National Science Education Principle

Improving science education is part of systemic education reform.

As we have discussed in this chapter, using inquiry processes following a specific scientific procedure is not how real science knowledge is generated. In reality *there is no scientific method,* as no practicing scientists adhere to "the scientific method" of Pearson. Rather, science is conducted according to the procedures and methods established by communities of scientists based on the problems that they are seeking to understand. This is why science education researchers have been working to institute reforms in the way school science is taught. Reform documents such as *A Nation at Risk* (National Commission on Excellence in Education, (AAAS, 1983), *A Nation Prepared* (Carnegie Forum on Education and the Economy, 1986), *Project 2061: Science for All Americans* (AAAS, 1989), and *Benchmarks for Science Literacy* (AAAS, 1993) have led to the need to establish National Science Education Standards. Published in 1996, National Science Education Standards propose goals for administrators, curriculum specialists, and teachers to use when developing science education curriculum, programs, and practices.

Professional Development Standard D

Guideline: Quality preservice and inservice programs are characterized by clear, shared goals based on a vision of science learning, teaching, and teacher development congruent with the *National Science Education Standards.*

As you read, interact with, and reflect on the science teaching methodologies discussed in this text, familiarize yourself with the National Science Education Standards for teaching, professionalism, and assessment. Further, bear in mind the need, as a teacher, to engage students in the content standards outlined in the following few pages. These standards outline what the students should know, understand, and be able to do in a K–12 science program. They are as follows:

- Science as inquiry
- Unifying concepts and processes in science
- Physical science
- Life science
- Earth and space science
- Science and technology

- Science in personal and social perspectives
- History and nature of science (National Research Council, 1996, p. 6).

The National Research Council, which publishes the National Science Education Standards, emphasizes that this list of content standards is "a complete set of outcomes for students" and "what students should know, understand, and be able to do in natural science."

Science as Inquiry Standards

The science as inquiry standards consist of developing the "abilities necessary to do scientific inquiry" and "understanding the nature of scientific inquiry." Processes of science involve an intimate relationship between the inquiry process and constructing scientific knowledge for scientific reasoning (inductive and deductive) and critical thinking (arguing logically, recognizing patterns, and identifying sequences). Scientific inquiry enables learners to understand science concepts and the nature of science, appreciate how and what we know in science, and research the environment both independently and collectively.

Unifying Concepts and Processes in Science Standards

The unifying concepts and processes consist of the integrative principles that are the "big ideas" of science. These "big ideas" developmentally underlie K–12 science and include the following:

- Systems, order, and organization
- Evidence, models, and explanation
- Change, constancy, and measurement
- Evolution and equilibrium
- Form and function (National Research Council, 1996, p. 104)

For example, organisms and objects (both natural and designed) have forms and functions that enable human beings to survive in this world. Seeking evidence, models, and explanation are part of all scientific research.

Physical Science, Life Science, and Earth and Space Science Standards

These are the content disciplines framed by science concepts, principles, theories, models, and laws. Helping students construct domain-specific knowledge must be inquiry based. Science knowledge as factoids has been culturally handed down and often enshrined in basal science textbooks. Rather, science content can be fundamentally constructed by students if inquiry meets these criteria:

- Represents a central event or phenomenon in the natural world
- Represents a central scientific idea and organizing principle
- Has rich explanatory power
- Guides fruitful investigations
- Applies to situations and contexts common to everyday experiences
- Can be linked to meaningful learning experiences

Professional Development Standard A

Guideline: Science learning experiences for teachers must incorporate ongoing reflection on the process and outcomes of understanding science through inquiry.

Teaching Standard A

Guideline: Plan an inquiry-based science program by developing a framework of yearlong and short-term goals for students.

TABLE 1-1
Content Standards, Grades K–4

Unifying Concepts and Processes	Science as Inquiry	Physical Science	Life Science
Systems, order, and organization Evidence, models, and explanation Change, constancy, and measurement Evolution and equilibrium Form and function	Abilities necessary to do scientific inquiry Understandings about scientific inquiry	Properties of objects and materials Position and motion of objects Light, heat, electricity, and magnetism	Characteristics of organisms Life cycles of organisms Organisms and environments

Earth and Space Science	Science and Technology	Science in Personal and Social Perspectives	History and Nature of Science
Properties of earth materials Objects in the sky Changes in earth and sky	Abilities of technological design Understandings about science and technology Abilities to distinguish between natural objects and objects made by humans	Personal health Characteristics and changes in populations Types of resources Changes in environments Science and technology in local challenges	Science as a human endeavor

NOTE. Reprinted with permission from *National Science Education Standards.* Copyright 1996 by the National Academy of Sciences. Courtesy of the National Academy Press, Washington, D.C.

- Is developmentally appropriate for students at the grade level specified (National Research Council, 1996, p. 109)

Science concepts that are critical for every elementary student are identified in Tables 1-1 and 1-2.

As you examine these concepts, consider how the following inquiry examples could support learning and the eight standards described in this section.

- Conducting investigations with concepts such as heating and evaporation by observing, using measuring instruments, note taking, and graphing
- Directly experiencing living things, their life cycles, and their habitats
- Observing day and night by drawing the shapes of the moon each night for a period of time, and the movement of the moon's shadow during the course of the day, to identify sequences of changes and observe patterns in those changes (National Research Council, 1996, pp. 126–130)

The understanding of science concepts must be built on the intuitive notions of students rather than on requiring children to memorize technical terms and definitions. Major conceptual ideas such as energy (sound, electricity, light); physical and chemical changes; and the characteristics of organisms can be better developed through critical processes of science inquiry and content.

TABLE 1-2
Content Standards, Grades 5–8

Unifying Concepts and Processes	Science as Inquiry	Physical Science	Life Science
Systems, order, and organization Evidence, models, and explanation Change, constancy, and measurement Evolution and equilibrium Form and function	Abilities necessary to do scientific inquiry Understandings about scientific inquiry	Properties and changes of properties in matter Motions and forces Transfer of energy	Structure and function in living systems Reproduction and heredity Regulation and behavior Populations and ecosystems Diversity and adaptations of organisms

Earth and Space Science	Science and Technology	Science in Personal and Social Perspectives	History and Nature of Science
Structure of the earth system Earth's history Earth in the solar system	Abilities of technological design Understandings about science and technology	Personal health Populations, resources, and environments Natural hazards Risks and benefits Science and technology in society	Science as a human endeavor Nature of science History of science

NOTE. Reprinted with permission from *National Science Education Standards*. Copyright 1996 by the National Academy of Sciences. Courtesy of the National Academy Press, Washington, D.C.

The Science and Technology Standards

The science and technology standards link both the natural and designed worlds and cultivate decision-making capabilities in students. Raizen, Sellwood, Todd, & Vickers (1995, p. 12) distinguish between science and technology. (See Table 1-3).

The National Research Council (1996) suggests five abilities, listed on page 24, that make up problem-solving in the design process.

TABLE 1-3
Distinctions Between Science and Technology

Science	Technology
Originates in questions about the natural world	Originates in problems of human adaptation to the environment
Applies methods of inquiry	Applies problem-solving technology
Proposes explanations for natural phenomena	Designs, proposes, implements, and evaluates solutions to human problems of adaptation

NOTE. Adapted from Raizen, S. A., Sellwood, P., Todd, R. D., and Vickers, M. (1995). *Technology education in the classroom*, p. 12.

1. Identifying appropriate problems for technological design
2. Designing a solution or product
3. Implementing a proposed design
4. Evaluating technological designs or products
5. Communicating the process of technological design (pp. 137–138)

Problem-solving methodologies for science and technology are described in depth in chapter 10.

Science in Personal and Social Perspectives Standards

Science in personal and social perspectives standards provide students with decision-making skills to understand and act on personal and social issues as citizens. Students should be able to recognize and identify a personal or a social problem, to formulate questions, to examine alternative solutions, to make decisions based on available choices, to take a position, and to take action. This standard is elaborated on in chapter 7.

History and Nature of Science Standards

History and nature of science standards help students understand the origin and changing nature of scientific knowledge and inquiry. An understanding of cultural contributions to science, the development of cultures as a result of science, and science as a human endeavor is promoted by study of the history and nature of science.

The National Research Council notes that the descriptive accounts and tabular organization of the eight categories of science content standards should not be considered as science curriculum. According to the council (1996, p. 111), "curriculum is the way content is organized and emphasized, it includes structure, organization, balance, and presentation of content in the classroom." The National Research Council document that identifies and discusses the National Science Standards is not a curriculum; rather, it describes and discusses national standards that should be used as guidelines for developing curriculum.

Examples of exemplary curriculum developed with the support of the National Science Foundation are available. We encourage you to examine national, state, and district curriculum guides and recommendations, the National Science Standards, and the AAAS Benchmarks as you read this textbook to identify science concepts that mold curricular decisions. Further, we think that as you begin to better understand the nature of inquiry you will begin to picture yourself as a curriculum developer, particularly at the interface between you as the teacher and the students in your classroom. You will also grow as a teacher-researcher—you will struggle with the issue of "what science is worth knowing."

✺ CHAPTER REFLECTIONS

In light of preservice teachers' prior conceptions of science, we have explored the nature of science for elementary science teaching, as highlighted by the American Association for the Advancement of Science and the National Research Council. Our discussion of the contemporary nature of science points to several important implications for science education, which are elaborated on in the remaining chapters of this book:

- We should encourage children to inquire and construct imaginative theories to account for observable data (natural phenomena).
- We should enable children to be puzzle lovers and solvers.
- We should help children understand that science is not an isolated activity; rather, it is a *social* enterprise with socially informed, formulated, and accepted commitments in a given community.
- The underlying meaning of content should be understood from the children's contextual and experiential perspectives and previously learned theoretical frameworks.
- Science teaching should not necessarily focus on diagnostic work; rather, it should provide children with alternative theories (scientists' theoretical frameworks) to think about and use in developing personal meanings.

The discussions presented in this chapter set the stage for understanding the nature of science and challenge the way science has typically been taught. Teaching elementary science is not a matter of presenting, even in an active way, a collection of facts similar to the ones we all "learned" in school. Basic trends from the reform movement concerning the nature of science vividly show the difference between constructing an understanding of major science concepts and memorizing trivial facts.

Questions for Reflective Inquiry

1. Compare and contrast your present conceptions of the nature of science with accounts that are presented in this chapter.

2. With what science content frameworks are you familiar? Read selected parts of *Project 2061: Science for All Americans, Benchmarks,* or the National Science Standards and describe how they differ in philosophy from your school experiences.

3. What inquiry skills are you most comfortable with? What can you do to become more adept at using less familiar inquiry skills? Please be specific.

SUGGESTED READINGS

American Association for the Advancement of Science (1989). *Project 2061: Science for all Americans.* Washington, DC: American Association for the Advancement of Science Inc.

National Research Council. (1996). *National science education standards.* Washington, DC: National Academy Press.

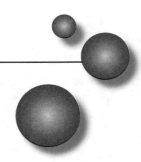

CHAPTER 2

Conceptions of Science Teaching and Learning

FOCUS QUESTIONS

1. Why are there so many views of how science should be taught and learned?

2. How can an interactive mode of science learning be developed in a science classroom?

3. What are the origins and advantages of a constructivist approach to teaching and learning?

4. How do the Learning Cycle and the Generative Model compare, and how do they relate to the constructivist approach?

5. What is a sociocultural approach to science teaching and learning?

Reflective Inquiry

KYLA'S VOICE

During my one-day-a-week practicum last year, I observed a classroom experience that suggested I question some science teaching practices.

My cooperating teacher was explaining to students, step by step, how electricity was generated by a water dam. To relate their understanding, students had to memorize the steps and recite them back to the teacher. Hearing the students recite the same identical passage to the teacher, it became obvious to me that the students did not understand how electricity was generated.

Truthfully, I had never thought to analyze the teaching of science before this experience. I never once thought that there might be a better way to encourage learning.

Prior to last year my opinions about science teaching were drawn from my own experiences in school. I thought back to my sixth-grade class, where the teacher did a number of demonstrated activities. Our job as students was to neatly write the correct words under the proper headings, draw labeled diagrams, and above all, follow the teacher's directions. Never having an opportunity to explore, I remained passive and submissive.

I do not think my science learning experiences were unique. I think students have long been taught that their ideas are unimportant and irrelevant to the science principles being taught. I think students were supposed to understand and learn from the science activities they did, but not question.

JOURNAL ACTIVITY

Perceptions About Science Education

What perceptions do you have from your own experiences in science classrooms or from classrooms where you observed science teaching? How might science be better taught?

Kyla's memories of the science taught in school are shared by many of us. Unfortunately, few of us had science teachers who encouraged our curiosity in ways that helped us better understand the nature of science or feel confident enough in our understanding of scientific knowledge that we considered pursuing a science-related career. Because it is our belief that teachers' actions are influenced by their own perceptions of how science should be taught and learned, we decided that in the first few days of methods class we would ask our preservice students to explore, first, their conceptions of science (chapter 1) and, second, their ideas for science teaching and learning.

REFLECTIVE PRACTICE

Teaching a Science Concept for Examining Personal Conceptions

Choose a science concept such as "air takes up space" or "light travels in straight lines." Prepare a science activity and teach several of your peers for about 15 minutes. Reflect on your teaching methods and your conceptions about science teaching and learning.

☀ MODES OF SCIENCE TEACHING AND LEARNING

Professional Development Standard C

Guideline: Professional development activities must provide opportunities for teachers to receive feedback about their teaching and to understand, analyze, and apply that feedback to improve their practice.

How do the following lessons fit in with the perspective that science is inquiry not independent of social enterprise?

A number of ideas and notions about science teaching have been perpetuated through the years as teachers have tried to find ways to present science to students. Through their reflective practice, our preservice teachers identified and used a wide variety of prior conceptions to illustrate what science teaching has entailed. What follows are preservice teachers' "voices" describing teaching and learning. How does your experience relate to theirs?

Retaining and Retrieving Facts

When asking preservice teachers what is important in science teaching, it is not unusual to find that many have learned that getting students to understand, retain, and retrieve facts is an important goal of science teaching.

LANNA'S VOICE

> I tried a method to present science concepts in which students investigated the characteristics of a variety of leaves. Students told me what they knew while I drew an actual diagram of this information. I guided students to the vocabulary that I wanted them to learn and recorded these words in the diagram. I then distributed a worksheet so students could utilize the vocabulary I introduced and be ready for a test on understanding and retention of facts.

Lanna was really keen on her students' learning the vocabulary of science and how to classify leaves. Thinking that this kind of teaching would prepare the students for tests, she also prepared a vocabulary sheet. See Box 2-1 for Lanna's lesson on types of leaves according to edge patterns.

BOX 2-1
Lanna's Leaf Activity

Lanna asked the children to explore the leaves that she had gathered.

Lanna then showed a chart in which she had drawn the leaves and labeled the types of leaves according to edge patterns: smooth, toothed, and lobed.

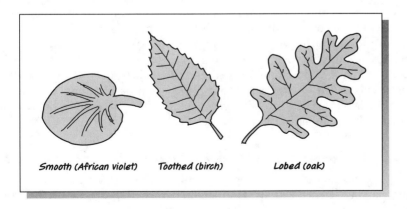

Smooth (African violet)   *Toothed (birch)*   *Lobed (oak)*

Lanna asked the children to group the leaves according to the teacher-given labels.

Like Lanna, many preservice teachers believe that if students are able to recall factual information they have learned and understood science concepts. That many teachers and preservice teachers model this practice is not surprising. We have all gone through science classes where a teacher first introduced the language of science so that we could fill in the blanks or match words to statements. We learned to spell the science words correctly, memorize the book definitions, and retrieve them for tests. However, this mode of inquiry is **transmissive**. Children are considered *tabula rasa,* or blank slates, on which knowledge bits can be written so that they can perform well on tests and examinations.

Learning the language of science is an important goal in science education. Without the language, students will not be able to converse with the teacher or comprehend their science reading materials. However, a premature introduction of science language may be a barrier to conceptual understanding. Children might get the idea that learning science vocabulary *is* science. Further, a premature introduction of scientific labels may lead students to believe that learning simple definitions alone is the same as understanding a concept.

It is preferable and more comfortable for children to be allowed the opportunity to discuss science ideas in their own words. Why? Many children hesitate to use words that are foreign to them. They often use labels they are accustomed to when attempting to explain something new. So what if students coin their own terminologies to explain a new science experience? Actually, children not only should use their own words to describe a new science event or experience, but they should be encouraged to do so. Scientific labels may be provided *after* children have been given opportunities to make meaning of the science activity.

Using Experts' Classification Systems

Many preservice teachers developed for students a classification system when first teaching science lessons. Cooperating teachers probably felt that this method was a "safe" entry into teaching for certain kinds of lessons. Sandy related her experiences with a grade 3 class.

A **transmissive mode of learning** involves receiving knowledge from the teacher and giving it back to the teacher on recall tests.

For example, let students explore different types of leaves in their community, maybe even giving them their own "fancy" labels before you provide them with the scientific labels (such as palmate, pinnate, alternate, opposite, network, serrated, lobed, and smooth) used to classify leaves according to shape.

Expert is defined here as any individual such as a teacher or scientist who appears to have greater science knowledge than do students.

SANDY'S VOICE

Before any investigation about the transmission of light, it is essential that all students clearly understand what is meant by **transparent**, **translucent**, *and* **opaque**. *With this in place, the teacher can then move on with the comfort of knowing that all students are starting their exploration on equal footing.... The teacher must also clarify terminology used by students to ensure they have a correct understanding.*

Sandy describes another transmissive mode of learning in which students categorize something following a teacher-given classification system. At the elementary level, teachers' directing students to classify everyday objects using teacher-given definitions is not uncommon. See Box 2-2 for Sandy's lesson on classification of everyday materials into transparent, translucent, and opaque categories. This activity involved establishing definitions of *transparent, translucent,* and *opaque.* After learning these definitions, the students were shown various materials belonging to each of the three groups.

BOX 2-2
Sandy's Classification Activity

Materials: Waxed paper, aluminum foil, cellophane, newspaper, flash card, clear plastic, colored plastic, frosted glass, clear glass

Activity: Classify the materials according to the given definitions. Use the chart.

Transparent	Transparent materials allow light to pass through.
Translucent	Translucent materials allow some light to pass through but scatter the light.
Opaque	Opaque materials allow no light to pass through.

Objects	Transparent	Translucent	Opaque
Waxed paper			
Aluminum foil			
Cellophane			
Newspaper			
Flash card			
Clear plastic			
Colored plastic			
Frosted glass			
Clear glass			

Sandy shows how she taught her students to classify materials into transparent, translucent, and opaque categories and states her views as to why giving definitions first is important. She believes that it is important to (a) have all students at the same level of knowing the teacher-stated definitions and (b) ensure that all students are clear about the concept before carrying on the investigation.

The core belief in this method of science teaching is that whatever the event may be, the teacher-given definitions and explanations must precede categorizing and/or carrying out activities. In this style of teaching the teacher's words are pronounced first and students must use these to validate their own knowledge. When we have students classify materials according to an **experts' classification system**, we teach them that new science knowledge is "acquired" and "applied" by first introducing scientific labels and defining them—by having the teacher drill students until they acquire the teacher-given ideas.

What might be some possible shortcomings of providing definitions first and having children classify according to the teacher-given definitions? This method of teaching does not give students the opportunity to explore, explain, or propose their own theories as to why materials are transparent, translucent, or opaque; why a mixture is a solution or suspension; or why a material is a conductor or nonconductor of electricity. In addition, it does not allow the teacher and students to carry out a meaningful conversation about the science concepts because the teacher has already given the explanations. All students have to do is to put the objects into appropriate teacher-made categories in a teacher-made chart to ensure that all students will have identical classification systems. Some teachers believe that developing a lesson this way puts all students on an equal footing with a similar level of understanding. What is inadequate about this assumption?

No matter how you teach, students will be at different levels of understanding a concept in science. There is no way to ensure that all students have correctly or clearly understood what you have stated. Construction of knowledge must be done by students so it is student owned. Hence, we must return the construction of knowledge to students.

Verifying Through Experimentation

Verifying through experimenting—inferring intended conclusions—is another science teaching experience preservice teachers described. This methodology, however, is another example of a transmissive mode of learning.

MONICA'S VOICE

It is the task of the teacher to convince students of false notions and this is best accomplished by having students discover correct information on their own by actively doing the experimenting.

An **experts' classification system** is a classification system that teachers or scientists have developed using specific criteria.

For instance, Sandy could have allowed her groups of students to examine the various materials to see to what degree light from the flashlight passed through them. Then she could have asked them to categorize the materials according to their findings. They could have shared their procedures and findings with the class as a whole to see whether they had reached consensus, explaining in their own words what they had observed from their own experiences. Only after this discussion might the teacher have introduced the scientific words.

Verifying means ascertaining or testing for the accuracy of some known data.

Verification rather than investigation has been the way "activity" science has been taught for a long time. Teachers expect children to come to implied conclusions based on concepts found in the curriculum guide or textbook. For example, Box 2-3 is a plan of Monica's lesson on plant growth. The purpose is to arrive at teacher-intended conclusions about plant growth through experimentation. The procedure for experimentation is clearly outlined. The students strictly follow the given procedure.

BOX 2-3
Monica's Plant Growth Activity

Activity Question: Under what conditions do plants grow?

Materials: Potting soil, marbles or stones, paper cups, spoons or scoops, eight seedlings, water (as needed)

Procedure: Divide the class into four teams. Provide directions for each team. Ask one team member on each team to record what happens. Direct each team to describe what happens to the seedlings.

Water Team
- Fill two paper cups with soil. Label cup 1 and cup 2.
- Plant one seedling in each cup 3 cm deep.
- Place both cups in a warm, sunny location.
- Give cup 1 25 ml of water each day for 10 days.
- Do not water cup 2.

Soil Team
- Fill one paper cup with soil and label cup 1.
- Fill the other paper cup with stones and label cup 2.
- Plant one seedling in each cup 3 cm deep.
- Place both cups in a warm, sunny location.
- Give cup 1 and cup 2 each 25 ml of water every day for 10 days.

Sunlight Team
- Fill two paper cups with soil. Label cup 1 and cup 2.
- Plant one seedling in each cup 3 cm deep.
- Place cup 1 in a warm, sunny location.
- Place cup 2 in a warm, dark location.
- Give cup 1 and cup 2 each 25 ml of water every day for 10 days.

Warmth Team
- Fill two paper cups with soil. Label cup 1 and cup 2.
- Plant one seedling in each cup 3 cm deep.
- Place cup 1 in a warm, sunny location.
- Place cup 2 in a cold, sunny location.
- Give cup 1 and cup 2 each 25 ml of water every day for 10 days.

From this activity, we assume that the students will verify that plants need water, soil, sunlight, and warmth in order to thrive. They will likely find that their results do verify these expected conclusions. However, they will not come away with an understanding of the concepts related to these phenomena. They will not grasp the concept that a complex combination of variables controls plant growth. In addition, they will gain a false impression of how scientists work. To have students discuss what they think plants need to survive and have them form groups to investigate the problem would be a more valid inquiry experience. For example: Do plants grow better in a cold or warm environment? Students could come up with their own designs to help answer their questions.

Exploring Children's Ideas

A few preservice teachers felt comfortable enough, after some experience in the classroom, to ask children what ideas they had about the subject they were about to be taught.

JUDY'S VOICE

In the first lesson, I showed students how two balloons get attracted by rubbing one of the balloons with wool material and bringing it close to the second balloon. The students observed the attraction of the balloons. Then I repeated the experiment while explaining what happened and labeled the force "static electricity." The explanation was premature, I think, because students had no questions; they had no time to reflect or learn from what they observed. A modification in the procedure that might stimulate inquiry would be to demonstrate static electricity without the explanation.

The second part of the teacher demonstration took place at the sink. A small stream of water was deflected by a charged glass rod. One student exclaimed, "Neat! How come the water did that?" Her curiosity made her question why. My initial impulse was to give her a "textbook" answer; however, that would have put an end to further inquiry. Instead I asked my students for their ideas. Several students were eager to give them. I learned that a teacher demonstration does not have to be teacher dominated.

Whereas many preservice teachers have experienced situations in which science teaching consisted of transmitting facts, using experts' classification systems, and verifying knowledge, Judy's reflections on her lesson illustrate a different approach. See Box 2-4 for an illustration of Judy's lesson on static electricity.

BOX 2-4

Judy's Static Electricity Activity

a. Materials: Two balloons, wool material

b. Procedure: Rub one balloon with wool.

c. Observation: Balloons are attracted to each other.

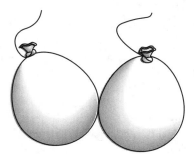

Like most preservice teachers, Judy starts by giving scientific explanations. However, she soon realizes that her explanation is premature. Furthermore, she talks about the time constraints on teacher reflections about the activity. From the first activity to the second activity, Judy changes her way of teaching. Although she does a teacher demonstration, she uses it as an opportunity to explore her students' ideas, changing her teaching pattern to be open to student questions and inquiry.

☀ A MORE INTERACTIVE MODE OF SCIENCE TEACHING AND LEARNING

An **interactive mode of science teaching and learning** is in direct contrast to a transmissive mode in that access to students' prior knowledge allows them to take an active part in acquiring new knowledge.

A more **interactive mode of science teaching and learning** indicates that the learner thinks about his or her own experiences, beliefs, and views and personally constructs meaning to acquire knowledge. "The most important factor influencing learning is that which the learner already knows. Ascertain this and teach him accordingly" (Ausubel, 1968, p. vi). Advocates of this perspective of learning believe that there is value in knowing and considering children's conceptions about the physical world and their unique ways of expressing these in science lessons (Driver & Erickson, 1983; Gilbert & Watts, 1983; Osborne & Freyberg, 1985). They see the artistry and craft of teaching from a psychological perspective of learning that matches the contemporary nature of science. They call this methodology for teaching **constructivism**.

History of Constructivism

Constructivism, in a simple sense, means constructing personal knowledge from experience.

A **constructivist** is one who believes that the learner is responsible for constructing knowledge and, therefore, the responsibility for learning must be returned to the child.

Information processing is another way of understanding how humans construct knowledge. Human thinking is likened to a computer processing information by organizing it into "chunks."

With the advent of computers, psychologists began to pay attention to the contribution of the human mind to cognition. Internal processing mechanisms called "schema" gave meaning to the incoming information. Early modern **constructivists** stressed the role of schema to the *exclusion* of all other variables. They viewed the mind as a processor of knowledge and viewed learning as **information processing**. For example, they believed the brain would take in and sort new information into categories it had already set up. If new information arrived that would not fit into previous categories, the brain would make new categories.

Constructivism goes back well before the 20th century. Its roots may be traced to the writings of a little-known 18th-century Neapolitan philosopher, Giambattista Vico, who stated that a learner knows only the cognitive structures he or she has put together (Glasersfeld, 1989). We build our own view of reality by trying to find order in the chaos of signals that impinge on our senses. What matters is that the knowledge we construct from the information we receive must function satisfactorily in the context in which it arises (Bodner, 1986). In other words, things have to make sense to us.

A Learning Theory for Cognitive Development

Jean Piaget (1973) researched the idea that knowledge is constructed in the mind of the learner. Through open-ended "clinical" (individual) interviews, Piaget developed a theory of *intellectual or cognitive development*.

   An important aspect of Piaget's theory of development is that he believed that the child's thought is not an imperfect copy of adult logic. Rather, the child's thought is logically consistent and *different from adult thought*. Piaget argued that children construct knowledge as they actively attempt to understand the world, and they construct this knowledge differently as they move through certain developmental stages or levels of knowledge. See Table 2-1.

TABLE 2-1

Piaget's Developmental Stages

Stage	Description	Examples
Sensorimotor (0–2 years)	The child interacts with the environment through his/her senses and muscle movement. As a result of this practice, the child controls action.	• The child reaches for a rattle because of an external stimulus. Through several attempts, the child reaches the rattle. In doing so, the child is able to establish a certain pattern.
Preoperational (2–7 years)	The child's physical actions are based on mental decisions. The representation function develops and the child thinks of his/her actions prior to doing them. In problem solving, the child tends to focus on only one variable at a time. Child is egocentric and animistic.	• The child thinks whether he/she can place a toy truck on a wagon before moving it. • The child centers on one aspect of an object when it is changed, such as length or width of a ball of modeling clay.
Concrete operational (7–11 years)	The child's thoughts are confined to what he/she perceives through experience. The child is able to classify or group objects and events according to observable properties, can engage in seriation activities, and is able to do reverse thinking and arithmetic operations. Child is able to locate relative positions in space and gradually attain conservation abilities.	• Child can classify objects such as leaves according to observable properties. • Child can order objects such as rocks in size from small to big and vice versa. • Child is gradually able to conserve substance, length, number, continuous quantity, area, weight, volume, space, and time.
Formal operational (12 years and over)	Child is learning to think abstractly, be reflective, and resolve problems in a systematic manner. A child can begin to handle multiple variables and conflicting ideas.	• Most adolescents reach this formal operational stage in some aspects of their life. They learn to control variables and reason deductively and inductively.

Bear in mind that although these stages generalize developmental thought processes, all individuals do not fall into prescribed categories and age-related stages. Seen in this way, the goal of Piaget's theory is not to sort learners, but to gain a general view of what it means to progress from a lower level of knowledge (novice) to a higher level of knowledge (relative expert).

The Construction of Knowledge

One especially important concept that Piaget identified in his studies is that two processes are involved in the construction of knowledge—**organization** and **adaptation**. Organization and adaptation are complementary functions. Information is taken in through the senses and organized as schema through adaptive processes. For example, a child may be able to mentally classify cat, dog, cow, horse, and tiger as animals.

Adaptation has two important components: **assimilation** and **accommodation**. Either knowledge is assimilated into cognitive structures or the structures are changed to accommodate new and different information. Knowledge is extended through *assimilation* but new knowledge develops and is made more complex through *accommodation*. Growing and accumulating higher levels of knowledge are then possible. For example, usually children consider organisms that have four legs to be animals. When a child considers higher levels of knowledge, the child may wonder whether the amoeba, cockroach, butterfly, earthworm, parrot, penguin, dolphin and shark are animals.

Both processes, assimilation and accommodation, are in a dynamic equilibrium that brings about coherent cognitive structures and organized ways of thinking. Structural wholes are then a defining characteristic of cognitive developmental stages. The child's mind, therefore, is not a blank slate. Rather, the child is constantly building, testing, and changing his or her mental models of the world on the basis of experiences.

Piaget used a biological process known as **equilibration** or self-regulation to explain this development of knowledge. A learner constructs knowledge when his or her stable state of mind is upset by a discrepant event. For learning to take place, a teacher must challenge the child with progressively more complex ideas. If the new knowledge is viable, the learner responds to the problem to achieve a new state of equilibrium. Successive equilibration results in further knowledge construction. Through a process of successive self-regulatory changes, each set of conceptual structures or models incorporates previous stages to generate a richer, more powerful mental system.

Piaget's developmental theory has had much influence in science teaching, learning, and curriculum development. The child-centered, hands-on approach; the discovery approach; and active learning are popular strategies acknowledging Piaget's principle of spontaneous knowledge construction. In the late seventies, science educators began to develop models of teaching and learning intended to better promote conceptual change and constructivist learning. Borrowing ideas from Piaget's work in developmental and cognitive psychology and from the philosophy of science, these educators

Organization is the mental structuring within the brain. A person internally organizes ideas into a more complex structure called a *schema*.

Adaptation refers to the interplay between a child's cognitive system and his or her experience.

Assimilation is the integration or interpretation of new information with existing mental structures. Thus, in assimilation, new input is changed to match existing structures.

Accommodation is the modification or changing of existing mental structures to account for new information and experiences.

Equilibration is a process that implies both stability and activity. Conceptual structures remain stable until a new event upsets the equilibrium.

have proposed certain teaching and learning models. One of these models is known as The Learning Cycle.

The Learning Cycle

There are many versions of learning cycles but we will describe the original one proposed by Karplus (1977) and expanded by Renner (1982), who proposed a three-stage cognitive model of learning as follows.

Concept Exploration

The teacher gives students materials related to the topic and encourages them to explore and phrase questions about things they do not understand. For example, the teacher might ask the children to test an assortment of objects (some that float and some that do not) in a tub of water. The objects are chosen so that children are given an opportunity to puzzle amongst themselves as to why some objects float and some sink. At the end of this stage, children might be asked, "Why do you think this object floats on water?"

Concept Explanation

Students explain their own understanding of the concept. The teacher guides this phase and supplies terms and supplements understanding through discussions. At the elementary level, the teacher might introduce and explain the concepts of weight, shape, and maybe water displacement to account for the phenomena of floating and sinking. At a higher level, the teacher might explain the concept of density.

Concept Application

The teacher helps students to apply the newly learned concepts to new situations. The students might try out their newly learned concepts to predict whether different objects will float or sink. For example, they might try to float both pumice and limestone. In a more practical way, students may determine why they might need an object to float and how to do so technologically. For instance, students may attempt to construct aluminum foil boats that would carry cargo (a certain number of coins, different plastic toys, etc.).

The Learning Cycle is based on Piagetian learning principles of self-regulation in which the learners develop new reasoning patterns as ideas are assimilated and accommodated. The students reflect on their ideas as they explore and interact with materials and with other learners. Learning is achieved by repetition and practice of similar explorations so that ways of thinking can become consolidated. Repetition and practice are thus recognized only as procedures—in this case, to improve cognition.

The Generative Model

Osborne and his associates were the first to espouse the idea of "children's science"—the views of the world and meanings for words that children tend to acquire before they are formally taught science (Osborne & Freyberg, 1985). Children's science develops as they try to make sense of their surroundings in terms of their experiences, knowledge, and language. Children's science differs from scientists' science in at least three ways: (a) children have difficulty with abstract reasoning—they see things from a self-centered viewpoint; (b) children are interested in specific explanations for individual events—they are not able to generalize over many situations and are not distressed when some explanations are contradictory; and (c) children have different meanings for words from those of scientists, and this may change with age and experience.

Osborne and Freyberg proposed the generative model of teaching, which took into consideration these views of children's science as well as a generative (constructivist) view about knowledge (Osborne & Freyberg, 1985). The generative model has the following four phases:

PRELIMINARY PHASE

The teacher ascertains students' ideas, classifies them, seeks scientific views, identifies historical views, and considers evidence that could lead to abandoning historical views.

FOCUS PHASE

The teacher establishes a context for science learning providing motivating experiences. The teacher then joins in the experience by asking open-ended, personally oriented questions. He or she then interprets student responses and elucidates students' views.

CHALLENGE PHASE

Critical to this model is how a teacher facilitates exchange of views. As a teacher ensures all views are considered, he or she keeps the discussion open. The teacher, at this juncture, may use demonstrative procedures if necessary, presents the evidence for the scientists' views, and accepts the tentative nature of students' reactions to the new view.

APPLICATION PHASE

Finally, the teacher contrives problems that are most simply and elegantly solved using the scientific view. He or she assists students in clarifying concepts for the new view, asking that they be used in describing solutions to all proposed problems. The teacher ensures students can verbally describe solutions to problems; joins in, stimulates, and contributes to a discussion on solutions. The teacher may observe students who need help in solving advanced problems and suggest places where help might be sought.

The generative model is widely used, especially in New Zealand, where it originated, and in Australia. It is user friendly and makes much sense to teachers. This model requires teachers to first determine children's ideas and to challenge students with activities that might promote conceptual change. Continuous interaction between the teacher and students is essential. Because problems may occur when a teacher's views of learning are at variance with those of the model's, a teacher must undergo a conceptual change with respect to how people construct knowledge. In addition, the emphasis on students' attaining the scientific view by the end of the topic is fraught with problems, as many of the students' ideas are found to be stable over time. Much time is needed for the planning and teaching of the units using this model, more than is often allotted in the curriculum.

Professional Development Standard C

Guideline: Professional development activities must provide opportunities to learn and use the skills of research to generate new knowledge about science and the teaching and learning of science.

☀ NEW PERSPECTIVES IN SCIENCE TEACHING

Constructivism implies that the starting point of scientific inquiry should be children's conceptions. When children engage in inquiry they will "describe objects and events, ask questions, construct explanations, test these explanations against current scientific knowledge, and communicate their ideas to others. They identify their assumptions, use critical and logical thinking, and consider alternative explanations" (National Research Council, 1996, p. 2).

This notion of scientific inquiry parallels the development of scientific theories through the ages. A fully developed theory, like Newton's theory of gravitation or the kinetic-molecular theory of gases, did not come easily or immediately. The question-and-answer procedure involved experiments and often used data selected on the basis of an incomplete theoretical background. The struggle to achieve a conceptual basis for such a theory involved a continual ordering and reordering of questions in response to experimental results and corresponding changes in deciding what the appropriate physical quantities must be. Likewise, it is imperative that students learn to explore their conceptions; identify their assumptions; use critical, logical, and creative thinking; and consider alternative explanations as they continue to study science.

Sociological Approaches to Learning Theory

O'Loughlin (1992) argues that active learning and a child-centered approach according to the developmental view do not take into account a *sociocultural approach* to teaching and learning. Learning, according to O'Loughlin, is situated in contexts such as the classroom, the playground,

Feldman (1980) and Carey (1985) suggest that we interpret Piaget's theory of intellectual development as the progression of a child from a novice to an expert in *each content area;* for example, in electricity, sound, or plant nutrition.

the family, the community, the ethnic background. Students use their subjective and cultural ideas to construct meanings in science.

The transmissive approach to science teaching, exemplified by three of the lessons taught by our preservice teachers, often does not consider the experiences and ideas that students bring to a topical issue or how these ideas develop in the students' minds as the lesson progresses. A more interactive, constructivist approach using a sociocultural framework seems to be more philosophically valid because **"common knowledge"** (Edwards & Mercer, 1987) is constructed via interpretive negotiation processes.

In the process of negotiating knowledge, some transmissive teaching must take place. For example, theoretical ideas such as cell theory or the kinetic theory of matter must be presented more directly to students in the higher grades. However, theoretical ideas become meaningful only when they are learned from children's perspectives (Driver, Asoko, Leach, Mortimer, & Scott, 1994). Similarly, methods of inquiry such as observation, interpretation, and conclusion are needed to develop theoretical meanings from children's perspectives. The development of these skills for transfer purposes should not, however, be the teaching focus. Inquiry skills change from context to context depending on the nature of knowledge and the specific problem.

In subsequent chapters we will build on this perspective and provide our own model of constructivist teaching: the Common Knowledge Construction Model.

Common knowledge refers to socially constructed and accepted knowledge. In common knowledge development, the teacher negotiates with his/her students to arrive at shared understandings.

☀ CHAPTER REFLECTIONS

We have examined preservice teachers' prior conceptions of science teaching and learning and investigated various approaches to teaching and learning. We introduced the constructivist view by briefly reviewing Piaget's developmental theory. We will continue to search for the answers to the questions: What does it mean to understand science? How should we teach in order to promote students' understanding of science? What implications do cognitive learning theory and constructivism have for learning school science?

Questions for Reflective Inquiry

1. What questions do you have about science teaching and learning?

2. How does the Generative Model compare with the basic ideas of the Learning Cycle?

SUGGESTED READINGS

Driver, R., Asoko, H., Leach, J., Mortimer, E., & Scott, P. (1994). Constructing scientific knowledge in the classroom. *Educational Researcher, 23*(7), 5–12.

O'Loughlin, M. (1992). Rethinking science education: Beyond Piagetian constructivism toward a sociocultural model of teaching and learning. *Journal of Research in Science Teaching, 29*(8), 791–820.

Osborne, R., & Freyberg, P. (1985). *Learning in science.* London: Heinemann.

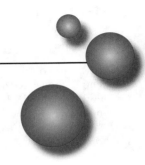

Structuring Science Knowledge

1. What is the advantage of meaningful learning over rote learning?

2. How can concept mapping be used to help structure science knowledge?

3. How would you teach concept mapping to your students?

4. How can Vee diagramming be used to help structure science knowledge?

5. What advantages might the use of Vee diagramming have over other means of preparing science content background knowledge?

Reflective Inquiry

> ### LIZ'S VOICE
>
> Although I had never heard of using concept maps or concept webs, one of my assignments for my science methods course was to make concept and Vee maps that spanned all the sciences and covered the elementary curricula.
>
> I began by developing a list of science activities. By the end of the term I had created 30 Vee diagrams and concept map combinations. The process took time, commitment, and research but I now have the practical and theoretical basis for 30 lessons covering a wide range of science topics. I know that each one can be modified and adapted to suit several ages and grades of students.
>
> By keeping an open mind to the process, I have developed a foundation for many future science lessons, a phenomenal resource that I can develop further later. Each map forced me to deepen my learning and see connections between scientific ideas that I had never pursued before.

JOURNAL ACTIVITY

Organizing Science Content

Reflect on procedures you have used to organize science content you are learning or preparing to teach. What thinking processes did you undergo? What note-taking or organizing tools did you use?

Professional Growth Standard B

Professional development for teachers of science requires integrating knowledge of science, learning, pedagogy, and student; it also requires applying that knowledge to science teaching.

A concept mapping–Vee diagramming combination is a philosophically sound strategy for lesson planning. It connects major theories, principles, and concepts; questions that may be asked about a particular science event; and the practical procedures needed to perform it. It is based on a theory called *meaningful learning*.

❈ MEANINGFUL LEARNING

Like Piaget, psychologist David Ausubel was interested in cognitive development. He proposed a theory (1968) that contrasts rote learning with more meaningful learning and considers prior knowledge. Rote learning involves memorizing facts and concepts, whereas meaningful learning involves understanding and integrating knowledge into one's cognitive structure. Ausubel stresses, however, that meaningful learning is not a dichotomy, but a continuum.

In line with Piaget, Ausubel's theory of meaningful learning presents learning as a process of assimilation where new knowledge is linked to existing cognitive structures. Meaningful learning thus depends on the prior existence of concepts in the learner's cognitive structure. New information is then linked to a main idea and could represent another example or an extension of that idea. The critical attributes of the original concept generally are not changed, but new examples are recognized as relevant.

New information may also be linked to a main idea in a way that it becomes a modification of the original concept, paralleling Piaget's theory of accommodation. In other words, newly acquired knowledge and the existing cognitive structures may be modified in the learning process.

Extending Ideas About Meaningful Learning

Elaborating on Ausubel's idea, Novak (1978) argues that the quality and quantity of relevant concepts and propositional frameworks are primary factors in new learning. These are *age-related,* primarily in an "experiential" rather than a "developmental" manner, as proposed by Piaget. Further, to create a deeper understanding of the nature of learning, Ausubel, Novak, and Hanesian (1978) expounded on what is meant by *meaningful learning*. Meaningful learning is the nonarbitrary, substantive, nonverbatim incorporation of new knowledge into cognitive structures. As the brain develops cognitive structures, knowledge forms hierarchically, with a major concept subsuming one or more subsidiary concepts. Elements of meaningful learning are illustrated by using concepts from a unit on matter for grade 1 in the following sections (Ebenezer, 1992, pp. 464–465).

Nonarbitrary Learning

Nonarbitrary means that a learner must choose to fit or relate new knowledge into the existing cognitive structure. If a student is learning what matter is, he or she should choose to relate this knowledge purposefully, not arbitrarily, to what he or she already knows, such as associating the term "matter" with solids and liquids.

Substantive Learning

Substantive learning occurs when the learner makes a conscious effort to identify key concepts for new knowledge such as in everyday materials. For example, if students relate that water is matter then they can correlate that water (liquid state) changes into ice (solid state) on freezing, and becomes water vapor (gaseous state) on boiling. As an additional example, students should identify concepts related to unique characteristics of matter. Solids have a definite shape such as a ball or toy car. Liquids take the shape of a container so orange juice can be poured from a pitcher into a glass tumbler. Gases fill any space into which they are placed, so it is possible to blow air into a balloon or pump air into a tire. Both nonarbitrary and substantive learning, therefore, require a conscious effort on the part of the learner.

Verbatim/Nonverbatim Learning

Verbatim learning occurs when definitions are memorized without stopping to consider the individual or combined meaning of each word in the definition. When the teacher writes or dictates the definition of matter—"matter is anything that takes up space and has mass"—and the students memorize this definition without putting forth any effort in thinking about what the emphasized concepts mean, the students are engaged in verbatim learning. At the end of the unit on matter, most students will be able to correctly define what matter is, causing the teacher to happily assume that the students have mastered the concept. However, within two or three days, the students are likely to have forgotten these rote-memorized definitions of matter. Nonverbatim learning is the product of nonarbitrary and substantive learning.

Rote Learning/Meaningful Learning

Rote learning is the opposite of meaningful learning. While teachers expect students to explain a given concept with appropriate terms, some students choose their own terminologies to communicate their understanding. The student might choose to define matter using different word sequences that are meaningful to him or her. For example, the student might say "matter is any stuff." It can be said that the student is on the continuum from rote learning to meaningful learning. As a student's ideas progress and as the student learns the language of science, he or she will progressively advance a substantively similar explanation to those which are widely accepted.

Meaningful learning involves developing knowledge structures of concepts. Concept mapping is a learning tool that aids in identifying main concepts and subconcepts and shows the interrelationships among these knowledge structures. The following concept map illustrates the key elements of meaningful learning. (See Figure 3-1.)

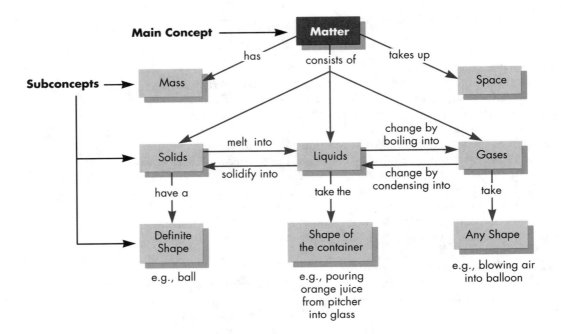

FIGURE 3-1
A simple concept map
on *Matter*

Knowledge Construction Tools

Based on Ausubel's theory of learning, Novak and Gowin (1984) invented two tools, *concept mapping* and *Vee mapping,* as visual lenses in which to promote new knowledge production and understanding. Thus, a concept map is a visual representation of a major concept subsuming one or more subsidiary concepts. For example, a "mixture—major concept" may be either "homogeneous—subsidiary" or "heterogeneous—subsidiary," following a hierarchy of knowledge construction. Further, Vee diagramming incorporates a concept map into the development of a plan for scientific inquiry. Usually knowledge structures are hierarchical. **Vee diagramming** shows how scientists' conceptual knowledge may be used as a lens to view our scientific inquiry.

In the last few years, much work has focused on the use of concept mapping and Vee diagramming as valuable tools for teachers to help organize and plan science teaching and learning. Teachers consider these strategies successful contributions to developing effective and meaningful teaching and learning, exploring children's conceptions, developing common knowledge through laboratory work, and assessing children's conceptions. Novak and Gowin (1984) claim that concept mapping and Vee diagramming help teachers and students to construct new and more meanings of science concepts and principles.

A **Vee diagram** is a visual representation that relates and connects scientists' ideas to a scientific inquiry.

Concept mapping and Vee diagramming are discussed in detail because teachers can use these knowledge construction tools in the *what* (curriculum organization) and *how* (scientific inquiry) of science learning.

☀ CONCEPT MAPPING

Concepts are an invention of the human mind, ways of organizing the world. Joseph Novak (1991) has defined *concept* as "a perceived regularity in events or objects, or records of events or objects, designated by a label" (p. 45). Leon Pines (1985) calls them "the furniture of the conscious mind" (p. 108), and he likens words to conceptual handles that enable people to grasp concepts and manipulate them.

> A **concept** is something conceived in the mind: a general or abstract thought, idea, or notion.

Concept maps can represent ideas about any topic. They are representations of interrelated concepts and provide a visual image of how the brain connects ideas. A simple concept map is illustrated in Figure 3-2.

A **concept map** is thus a semantic network showing the relationships among concepts in a hierarchical fashion. Concepts or ideas are linked with phrases that illustrate the relationships among them. How can one construct concept maps? A modified version of Leith's (1988) concept mapping activity sequence for teachers follows.

> A **concept map** is a schematic device for representing a set of interrelated, interconnected conceptual meanings.

Concept Mapping for Teachers

If teachers learn how to construct concept maps and use them for planning and assessing lessons, they will be able to teach students better how to make concept maps to organize their thoughts and ideas. Concept mapping is probably done better first in groups so that preservice teachers can interact with each other. Group members can then compare and debate the construction of their concept maps and subsequently compare their maps with those of other groups. Finally, individuals should construct and present their own concept map for a science lesson.

> **Teaching Standard A**
>
> **Guideline:** Plan an inquiry-based program by selecting teaching and assessment strategies.

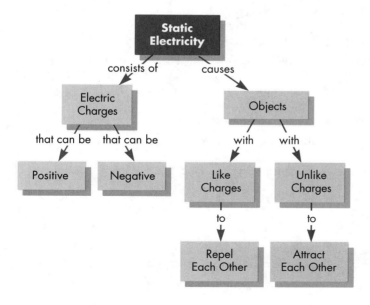

FIGURE 3-2
A simple concept map on *Static Electricity*

Use the following steps to construct a concept map (see Example 3-1).

1. Choose a passage from a science textbook.
2. Circle or underline the main concepts in this passage.
3. List all the concepts on paper.
4. Write or print the concepts on small cards or stickers so that the concepts can be moved around. If you prefer to use a computer-based semantic network, use SemNet, Learning Tool, TextVision, CMap, or Inspiration software (Jonassen, 1996).
5. Place the most general or all-inclusive concept on the top of the paper.
6. Arrange the concepts from top to bottom (from most general at the top to most specific at the bottom) so that a hierarchy is indicated. In constructing this hierarchy, place concepts next to each other horizontally if they are considered to have equal importance or value.
7. Relate concepts by positioning linking verbs and connecting words on directional arrows. Support the concepts with examples.
8. Have members of a cooperative group critically analyze the concept map to improve on and further extend your ideas.

EXAMPLE 3-1
CREATING A CONCEPT MAP

STEP 1   Choose a passage from a science textbook.

"A solution is a homogeneous mixture of two or more substances, the composition of which may vary within characteristic limits. The dissolving medium is called the solvent. The substance that dissolves is called the solute" (Metcalfe, Williams, & Castka, 1974, p. 223).

STEP 2   Circle or underline the main concepts in this passage.

"A <u>solution</u> is a <u>homogeneous mixture</u> of two or more substances, the composition of which may vary within characteristic limits. The dissolving medium is called the <u>solvent</u>. The substance that dissolves is called the <u>solute</u>."

STEP 3   List all the concepts on paper.

solution   homogeneous mixture   solute   solvent

STEP 4   Print concepts on cards or stickers.

solution
homogeneous mixture
solute
solvent

STEP 5   Center the most general concept on top of the paper.

homogeneous mixture

STEP 6   Arrange the concepts from top to bottom (from most general at the top to most specific at the bottom). Stick them in place when you are satisfied with their relationships.

homogeneous mixture
solution
solute   solvent

STEP 7   Relate concepts with linking verbs and connecting words to form sentences.

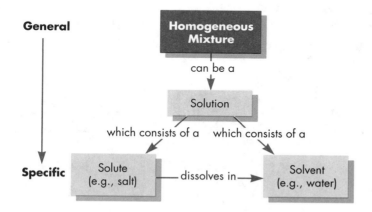

STEP 8   Ask people in a cooperative group to critically analyze your work.

Constructing a Concept Map from a Paragraph

Try gathering some of your own science-related paragraphs and practice creating concept maps.

Concept Mapping With Students

Concept maps can help students relate concepts they bring to the classroom or have learned from instruction. Students may know isolated concepts but not how they relate to each other. Students may write paragraphs about concepts but still not show that they understand how the concepts are interrelated. Concept mapping is a powerful strategy used across the curriculum that can help teach children the structure and meanings underlying a topic (see Figure 3-3).

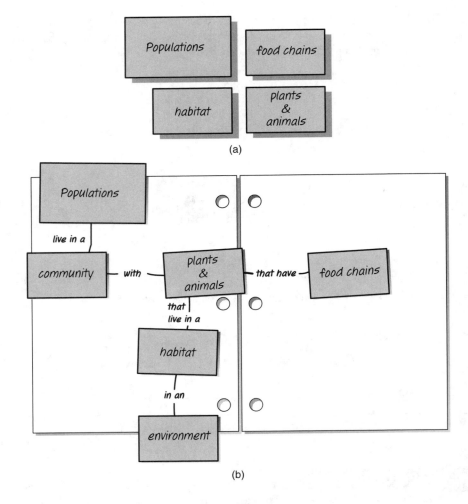

FIGURE 3-3
Child's concept map with cross-links on the topic *Populations.*

As soon as children can read, they can work with simple concept maps. Even before children can read, they can use picture concepts (Kilshaw, 1990; Cross, 1992). Kilshaw presented her 6- and 7-year old children with lists of words connected with the concept of *plant growth* after playing a word association game. She relates that the children worked on their own, beginning by copying the words on a sheet of paper. Then they were encouraged to draw arrows connecting the words and write other words to explain the connections. Kilshaw concluded that concept maps were an excellent tool for assessment but must be used in conjunction with discussion and questioning of children's understanding. Cross used picture cards instead of words, finding these more satisfactory for teaching his 5-, 6-, and 7-year-old children about *electric circuits* (Figure 3-4).

Concept maps can be constructed in the classroom using three different approaches:

FIGURE 3-4
Cross's concept cards used with young children (NOTE. From Cross, A. (1992).
Pictorial concept maps—putting us in the picture. *Primary Science Review, 21, 27.*)

- Students construct the maps using concept words supplied by the teacher.
- Students construct the maps identifying the concepts from an information source.
- Students construct the maps from their own personal knowledge.

We have taught 9- and 10-year-old children, in a single lesson, how to make concept maps. They constructed their concept maps after they had studied a unit on *Sound.* The method is outlined below:

1. **Preparing concept cards or labels.** We prepared a list of concepts and asked students to make a set of concept cards.
2. **Arranging concept cards in sequence.** We asked each student group to sort through the concept cards, tentatively ordering them in the way they believed the cards were related (see photograph).

3. **Negotiating to reach agreed-upon meanings.** We encouraged students to discuss their arrangements in small groups of peers and to come to a consensus (see photograph).

4. **Drawing relationships between and among concepts.** We asked students to write words on the lines between the concepts to show how they are related. We also reminded the students that the words on the lines should be connecting words or phrases that have verbs in them so that their conceptual links can be read from the top down and across (see the photograph).

5. **Justifying the position of concept cards.** We asked each group to show and explain its concept map, justifying the positions of the concept cards and the interconnecting sentences (see photograph).

One of the most critical aspects of making concept maps

is to make *appropriate links and cross-links. The relationships or linkages should read as sentences from the top down and across.* (Some educators have the sentences read from bottom to top, but it seems more logical to us to have them read from the top down.) Students should be given opportunities to practice with well-understood topics and concepts before they are given any that may be problematic for them.

Novak (1991) has cautioned that concept maps are no "magic bullet," as it usually takes considerable practice and feedback in order to teach students how to construct good concept maps. It also takes much teacher time to learn how to teach students to construct concept maps and how to criticize them constructively.

Presently, several researchers are using computer technology to help students make concept maps. A good computer program, such as CMap, Inspiration, and SemNet, can help students try out relationships, as they can be quickly displayed and modified.

Uses of Concept Mapping

Concept mapping can be used in a variety of ways while planning for and teaching a unit of study (Ebenezer, 1992, pp. 465–466).

A Big-Picture Look at a Science Unit

In the preparation of a unit, the teacher can construct a concept map to get an integrated understanding of the concepts involved. The teacher can also use concept maps as an advanced organizer to present the students with a big picture of a unit (see Figure 3-5). This will provide students with a visual representation showing the links among the concepts of a topic or lesson. After introducing a teaching unit in this manner, the teacher can draw back from the larger picture and focus students' attention on the details of a smaller segment of the unit.

Revealing of Prior Conceptions

Children can construct concept maps before beginning a unit of study in science to help identify their knowledge base or prior experience. For example, you can do either of the following:

- Demonstrate an experiment and ask students to think of all the concepts that pertain to this activity.
- Provide a list of concepts and have students link them and/or provide a topic and ask students to visually state the relationships among concepts.

The concept maps will not only identify the range of concepts and ideas that the students use but also reveal student conceptions that should be explored further. The teacher thus has an opportunity to become aware of students' conceptions of the topic under study. Students can also be made aware of their own understanding of a topic through concept maps. It then

Assessment Standard B

Guideline: Achievement data collected focus on the science content that is most important for students to learn.

FIGURE 3-5
A preservice teacher's
concept map on the science
ideas to be learned in a unit
on *Shadows*

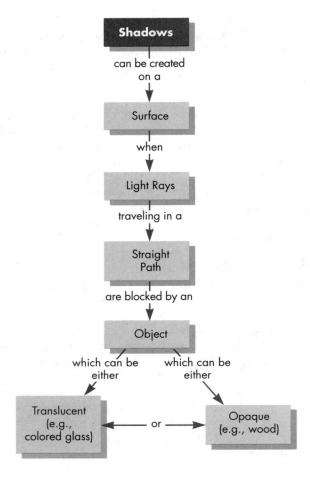

Assessment Standard B

Guideline: The opportunity-to-learn
data focus on the most powerful
indicators.

becomes easier to plan activities to either clarify students' thinking or elaborate on their ideas. In addition, motivation, attitude, and interest improve when students recognize that they already know something about the new topic of study when they construct a concept map.

Opportunity to Make Revisions

Teaching Standard C

Guideline: Guide students in self-assessment.

During the course of the unit, or as learning progresses, students can be given several opportunities to review their concept maps. The students should evaluate their maps in light of what they have been learning. With the teacher's help or even through conversation with their peers, students will be able to spot discrepancies between their maps and their new knowledge. In addition, more appropriate scientific terms and more enlightened examples might appear in children's revised maps (see Figure 3-6).

First attempt at concept map

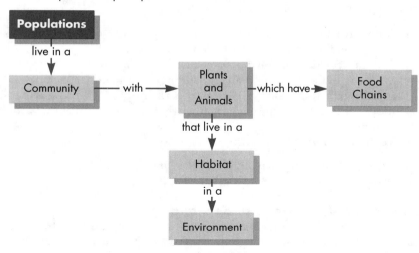

FIGURE 3-6
A fourth-grade student's
modifications to his concept
map on *Populations*

Second attempt at concept map

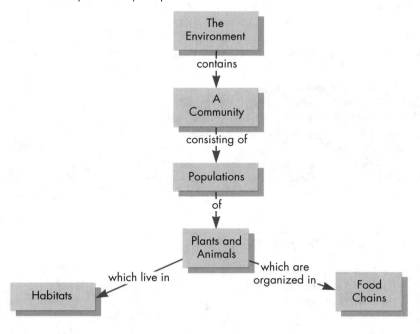

Development of Collaborative Relationships

A good relationship between the teacher and the student can be fostered
when they share the progression of science ideas that occurs when creating
concept maps. A recent research study traced student conversations as they

were negotiating science concepts to construct concept maps (Briscoe, 1993). This study's conclusions are as follows:

Teacher Standard B

Guideline: To guide and facilitate learning and orchestrate discourse among students about scientific ideas.

- A peer teaching-learning concept mapping activity engaged students in science discourse for an extended period of time.
- Social interactions involving peer assistance may enhance learning.
- Students negotiated new understandings of the concepts through social interaction, and were able to perform the task of building a more complete concept map together than any one of them was able to build alone.
- Teachers found that the group work enhanced students' learning.

Thus, shared meaning-making resulted in more and better results than did individual work.

Assessment of Children's Understanding

Teaching Standard C

Guideline: Analyze assessment data to guide teaching.

At the end of the unit, students can refine or correct their "*n*th" concept map. To assess student understanding in a science unit, a teacher might have the students present a portion of their concept maps to the rest of the class or explain their maps individually. We recommend that the students map their concepts without reference to any textbooks at this point to clearly reveal their thinking processes.

In this manner, concept mapping can be effectively used as a learning strategy that enables students to actively create content knowledge of science.

 PEER INTERACTION

Constructing a Concept Map on a Topic

In a peer group, select a science topic. Construct a concept map of this topic with the help, if needed, of an advanced-level science book. Choose a range of grade levels to which you might teach this topic; for example, grades 2–4. Identify clusters of concepts on which you will focus when teaching this topic.

❂ VEE DIAGRAMMING

Along with concept mapping, Vee diagramming is a heuristic device that can be used to visually organize science concepts and ideas. It was developed by Bob Gowin and can be used to illustrate key ideas regarding the *nature of knowledge* and *the process by which new knowledge is made in science investigations* (Novak & Gowin, 1984). It helps people to learn how knowledge is constructed and reconstructed. The Vee diagram allows students to consider their own conceptions of the natural phenomenon under study. The Vee diagram also helps one develop questions; plan, design, and conduct an activity; and interpret the results (Roth & Verechaka, 1993). In this manner, students can construct new meanings based on their own current

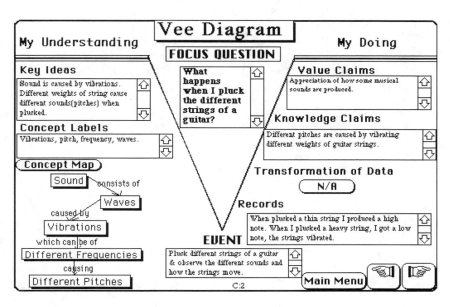

FIGURE 3-7
A Vee diagram on *Sound*

meanings. Finally, Vee diagrams allow students to link science to relevant personal needs.

A Vee diagram consists of two sides with a middle Vee. The left side is labeled "My Understanding" of scientists' key ideas (conceptual). The right side is labeled "My Doing" (methodological)—observations and statements of conclusions. See Figure 3-7 for a Vee diagram on *Sound*.

Vee Diagramming for Teachers

The following method has been used effectively with preservice teachers.

1. Place the term "Event" at the point at which the "My Understanding" side and "My Doing" side intersect (the tip of the Vee). This is the event that we will be studying or investigating. The event is the problem task. Everything revolves around it.

Professional Development Standard A

Professional development for teachers of science requires learning essential science content through the perspective and methods of inquiry.

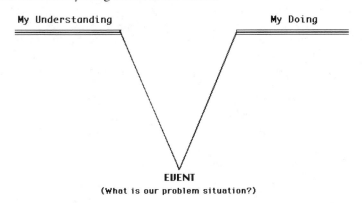

2. Observing the event, we ask ourselves, "What do we know about this event?" Or, "What do the scientists or experts say about this particular event?" In other words, "What are the key or major ideas?" Just below "My Understanding," we write "Key Ideas" because these ideas will guide our study of the event.

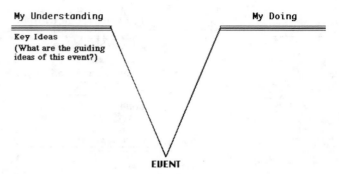

3. Observing the event, we ask ourselves, "What concept labels can we attach to this event?" Or, "What concept labels have the scientists or experts given to this particular event?" In other words, "What are the concept labels?" Just below "Key Ideas," we add the label, "Concepts."

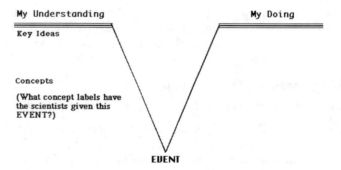

4. A concept map, developed separately, provides the concept labels.

5. Knowing the key ideas and concept labels for the event, we will now ask a question that focuses on the event. The term we use to describe this—"Focus Question"—is placed in the open mouth of the Vee.

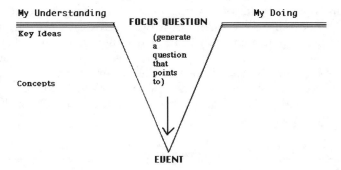

6. We set up procedures and conduct the investigation. We observe the results of the investigation. Then we systematically record the observations on the "My Doing" side, directly above the event. The label "Records" describes what we actually observed during the event.

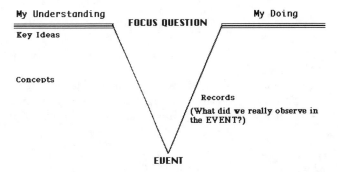

7. Our observations in some investigations can be easily reduced to a chart or graph. This is called "Transformation of Data," which is written directly above "Records" because we are reducing our observations for communication purposes.

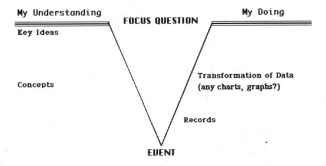

8. What general conclusions can we make about our observations? The term that we use for conclusions is "Knowledge Claims" because we have indeed generated knowledge that should match the experts' key ideas on the left side of the Vee. However, write these knowledge claims in your own words. Knowledge claims are yours. The "Key Ideas" section explains your knowledge claims in scientific language. State knowledge claims above "Transformation of Data" on the right side of the Vee.

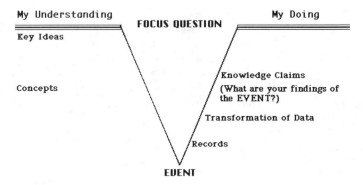

9. What is the value of this investigation for me and for my students? The term that we use to describe the value of the investigation is "Value Claims," which is stated above "Knowledge Claims" on the right side of the Vee.

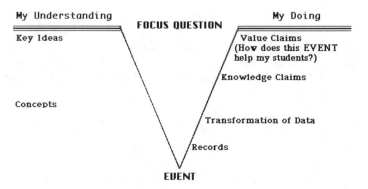

All the knowledge elements or components of the Vee diagram have been described and illustrated. Next, we will learn how to create a Vee diagram about a particular event. All the knowledge elements must relate to one another and to the event and focus question. Make sure you have actually answered the focus question on the Vee. The concept map that accompanies the Vee diagram must also answer the focus question. See Example 3-2 to see how a Vee diagram for a specific topic is prepared.

EXAMPLE 3-2

CREATING A VEE DIAGRAM

STEP 1   Choose an event or a problem context and write the procedures for the investigation.

You may develop your own event or borrow one from a science activity book. Write the procedures under the heading, "Event." A Vee diagram is a visual representation of the investigation that you have already carried out.

Event: *Erosion*
We put piles of sand into three cake pans (two piles of wet sand, one pile of dry sand). Air was blown through a straw across the dry sand to make wind. Ice cubes were melted on top of one wet pile and we watched as they melted. We formed a downhill trench on a side of the second wet pile to represent a river's path and poured a steady stream of water from a pitcher from the top of the pile down the trench.

STEP 2   What do you know about erosion?

Consult a secondary or university-level science text. What information is key to the event? Summarize the information under the heading "Key Ideas" on the left side of the Vee.

Key Ideas
The earth's features change over time. The agents that act to wear down the earth's surface include wind, water, and ice.

STEP 3   What concept labels about erosion do you know?

What concept labels can you pick up from reading about erosion? Again, consult a secondary or university-level science text. What are the key concepts that give meaning to the event? Write all the concept labels under the heading, "Concepts" on the left side of the Vee just below "Key Ideas."

Concept Labels
Erosion, mechanical/chemical weathering, glacier, glaciation, deposit, freezing, melting, friction, rocks, ice, sediment, wind, water, transport, redistribute

STEP 4   Since concepts are part of your Vee, create a concept map on another sheet of paper.

Please follow instructions in the "Concept Mapping for Teachers" section (see page 49–51) if you are unsure how to construct one. For a concept map on erosion, see Figure 3-8.

STEP 5   Based on your knowledge about the key ideas as well as concepts of erosion (the event), state the question you will ask to carry out the investigation or study the event.

Write this question under the "Focus Question" heading on your Vee diagram.

FIGURE 3-8
Concept map on *Erosion*

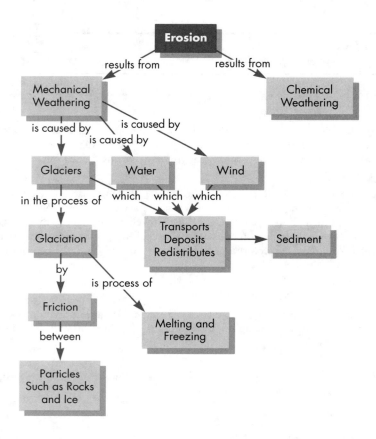

Vee Focus Question
What effects do wind, water, and ice have on land?

STEP 6   What did you observe when you conducted the investigation
          on erosion?

State it in your own words under "Records."

Records
The wind lifted and scattered the sand. The ice melted and picked up the sand
particles. As the ice melted more, it gradually moved down the pile of sand, collecting more particles and dropping them off. Water eroded the sides and the
bottom of the pile and carried particles down to the bottom, where they were
deposited. The trench became both deeper and wider.

STEP 7   Can you transform or reduce your records?

There are no charts or graphs to be made for this activity. So you might simply
write "N/A" under "Transformation of Data."

Transformation of Data
(N/A)

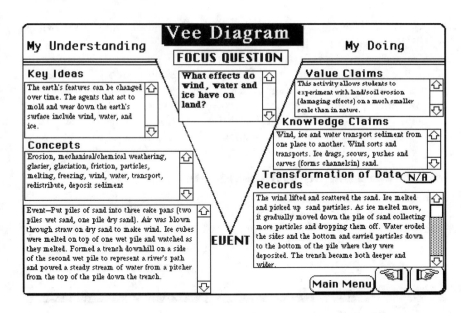

FIGURE 3-9
Vee diagram on *Erosion*

STEP 8   What general conclusions can you make about this investigation of erosion?

Write your conclusions under the "Knowledge Claims" heading on the right side of the Vee.

Knowledge Claims
Wind, ice, and water transport sediment from one place to another. Wind sorts and transports. Ice drags, scours, pushes, and forms channels in sand.

STEP 9   Is there a value for doing this activity on erosion?

Describe the value for yourself or children you teach. Write how worthwhile this activity was under the "Value Claims" heading on the right side of the Vee.

Value Claims
This activity allows students to simulate the effects of land/soil erosion on a much smaller scale than in nature.

All the elements of this Vee diagram are in place in Figure 3-9.

You have learned new ways of structuring and representing knowledge from the observation of events and objects. We attempted to answer two questions in science teaching: *how* (scientific principles) and *why* (theory). In asking and attempting to answer these crucial questions, we probe (on the left side of the Vee diagram) conceptual systems scientists have constructed concerning the nature of physical systems. In turn, these principles and theories are related to the right side of the Vee diagram, which consists of the

Teaching Standard A

Guideline: Plan an inquiry-based program by selecting science content and adapting and designing curricula to meet the interests, knowledge, understanding, abilities, and experiences of students.

methodological elements of knowledge-making. The right side also provides evidence and values for the activity.

We must stress the active interplay between what students observe or do in science and the evolving concepts, principles, and theories that guide scientific inquiry. The Vee diagram is a simple, yet powerful, heuristic that can promote this interplay. Visually, the Vee highlights the relationship between the "my understanding" and the "my doing" sides of a scientific event, directing attention to and explaining the event—the point at which theory and practice coincide (Ebenezer, 1992).

Vee Diagramming With Students

Students as young as 9 or 10 can be taught to make Vee diagrams with help from the teacher. Middle school and junior high students can make Vee diagrams on their own after instruction. A case study follows.

3-1: Vee Diagramming With Students

Wraith Malik

This activity was done with my *grade 5* students, who were studying the topic *Chemical Change*. We had done several lessons on physical and chemical changes. To teach them Vee diagramming, I chose to use one of the simplest investigations about chemical changes, mixing vinegar with baking soda to create carbon dioxide gas. The focus question for the Vee diagram was, "What happens when you add baking soda to vinegar?"

I approached teaching the Vee diagram as a data management tool for the students, from which they could easily interpret their observations and results. We did the Vee diagram as a group, not individually. I felt that was a good way to begin with this strategy. I put the drawing of the Vee on the overhead projector, and the students helped me fill it in as we went along. We began with the focus question, the event, the key ideas, and the concepts involved. We made a concept map from these concepts. The students had already made concept maps in Language Arts, so this was not new to them. We then performed the experiment and filled in the rest of the diagram using the appropriate data (Figure 3-10).

I think that the biggest and best thing I learned from this experience is that I should never underestimate the potential and ability of the students. This strategy worked very well at the grade 5 level. I also learned that not

Professional Growth Standard B

Guideline: Learning experiences for teachers of science must address teachers' needs as learners and build on their current knowledge of science content, teaching, and learning.

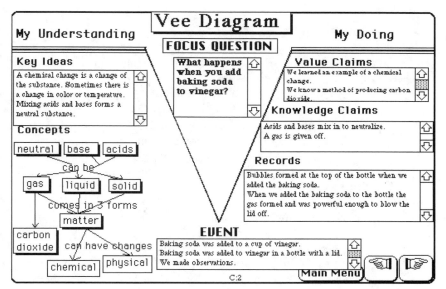

FIGURE 3-10
Vee diagram on
Chemical Changes by
grade 5 students.

only is the Vee diagram an essential tool for lesson planning, but it can also act as a great tool for students' learning. For the teacher, the Vee diagram requires a complete understanding of the lesson; for the students, it provides a management tool for the write-up or can serve as an alternative to notes.

 REFLECTIVE PRACTICE

Constructing a Concept Map and a Vee Diagram

In collaboration with your students, draw a Vee diagram for a science activity. For the same science activity, together with your students, list all the science concepts. Then have students develop a concept map in peer groups. (Go through the steps listed in "Concept Mapping With Students" (pages 51–55.) Write a two-page reflective report.

CHAPTER REFLECTIONS

Pedagogy built on adequate theoretical perspectives, such as Ausubel's (1968) learning theory, can provide a sound foundation for learning science. Concept maps and Vee diagrams can help teachers and students explore students' prior knowledge and thus plan a large mental map of how a unit of science could be presented. They also help to link students' ideas with science concepts, develop collaborative social skills, clarify children's meanings, and assess children's understandings.

Questions for Reflective Inquiry

1. Construct a Vee diagram–concept map combination for one of the following activities:
   - Soak a few popcorn kernels in water. Roll up a paper towel and place it in a jar. Put the soaked popcorn kernels in various positions between the paper towel and side of the jar. Add enough water to moisten the towels. Put the jar in a warm place. Observe the direction of root growth.
   - Attach a small balloon over the mouth of an empty glass bottle. Place this bottle in a container of hot water. Observe the balloon.
   - Rub a plastic comb with wool. Then bring the comb close to a thin stream of water from a faucet.
   - Use a magnifying glass to observe and describe the physical properties of sugar, salt, baking soda, baking powder, and powdered chalk. Heat a teaspoon of each of the substances. Observe. Test each of the substances by adding it to water. Observe. Test each of the substances by adding it to vinegar. Observe. Be sure to include your observation chart under "Transformation of Data" in your Vee diagram.

2. Choose a unit of study from the following list:
   - Light
   - Heat
   - Magnetism
   - Static electricity
   - Current electricity
   - Sound
   - Properties of matter
   - Changes in properties of matter (physical changes and chemical changes)
   - Plant growth
   - Life cycles
   - Adaptations
   - Weather
   - Air and air pressure
   - Force and motion

   Carry out a number of exploration activities connected with such a study and create a number of Vee diagrams and concept maps for your teaching resource files.

SUGGESTED READINGS

Ebenezer, J. V. (1992). Making chemistry learning more meaningful. *Journal of Chemical Education, 69,* 464–467.

Jonassen, D. H. (1996). *Computers in the classroom: Mindtools for critical thinking.* Englewood Cliffs, NJ: Prentice-Hall.

Novak, J. (1991). Clarify with concept maps. *The Science Teacher, October,* 45–49.

Novak, J. D., & Gowin, D. B. (1984). *Learning how to learn.* Cambridge: Cambridge University Press.

Roth, M., & Verechaka, G. (1993). Plotting a course with Vee maps. *Science and Children, 30*(1), 24–27.

PART TWO

THE COMMON KNOWLEDGE CONSTRUCTION MODEL

In Part One, we examined the nature of science as well as science teaching and learning from preservice teachers' points of view. We presented two learning tools, concept mapping and Vee diagramming, as aids for structuring science content knowledge and for organizing curriculum.

In this section, we will discuss a model for developing children-teacher common knowledge: the Common Knowledge Construction Model. Based on this four-phase model, we will suggest several ways of exploring children's conceptions; indicate many strategies for common knowledge construction, translation, and extension to everyday life; and describe how common knowledge can be assessed.

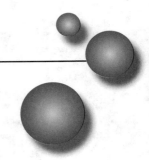

CHAPTER 4

Constructing Common Knowledge

FOCUS QUESTIONS

1. How did Ron explore his students' conceptions about air and air pressure?

2. What strategies did Ron use to begin to construct common knowledge with his students?

3. What factors other than classroom science teaching may influence children's science learning?

4. How can a teacher use Vygotsky's notion of "scaffolding"?

5. What types of personal knowledge may a child have?

6. What is the relationship between a teacher's academic knowledge and children's personal knowledge?

7. How is common knowledge constructed? (What is the Common Knowledge Construction Model?)

Reflective Inquiry

RON'S VOICE
Instruction must be a systematic procedure where prior knowledge is used. If you can access prior understanding, it creates some comfort and confidence. Then you can stretch the student mind more easily.

JOURNAL ACTIVITY

The Effect of Previous Knowledge on Your Learning

Reflect on what you knew about teaching and learning before you began this methods course. How has it influenced your present views of how to teach science?

Common knowledge refers to knowledge that is accepted by the scientific community. It also refers to the meanings that teachers will negotiate with their students to arrive at shared understanding.

Ron alludes to the importance of using children's ideas in teaching. Ron's ideas reflect those of a famous educational psychologist, Ausubel, introduced in Chapter 3. Recall his philosophical statement: "The most important single factor influencing learning is what the learner already knows. Ascertain this, and teach him accordingly" (Ausubel, 1968, p. vi). What Ron said—that students' ideas must be incorporated into teaching—was very significant. We will use this preservice teacher's experiences to explore the practical aspects of developing **common knowledge** between the teacher and students in a science classroom.

Ron's work was chosen because he was part of our research group and his lesson plans illustrate his attempts to develop common knowledge with his students. Throughout this chapter, we will pause at different points in Ron's lesson development to critically analyze his work so that we may learn from it. Then various aspects of common knowledge construction will be considered so you will begin to understand our teaching model for science instruction (Common Knowledge Construction Model).

☀ RON'S APPROACH TO SCIENCE TEACHING

How Does Ron Prepare to Teach a Science Unit on Air and Air Pressure?

Ron states that he prepares to teach this unit in five ways:

1. He gathers information and resources on air and air pressure.
2. He researches the content of the topic of air and air pressure by reading science books and textbooks, carrying out some of the experiments, and drawing a concept map (Figure 4-1).
3. He reads key articles to find out what researchers have stated about students' understandings of air and air pressure.
4. He gathers additional resources—activities and materials from the curriculum, textbook, other related books, and journals such as *Science and Children* and *Science Activities*.
5. He chooses age/experience/topic–relevant methods and strategies to explore children's conceptions about air and air pressure, keeping in mind that the goal is to establish categories of children's meanings and not to diagnose their understandings. He develops a Vee diagram for that lesson (Figure 4-2).

How Does Ron Explore Children's Conceptions?

In his science methods course, Ron has learned how to explore children's ideas. He remembers that an appropriate activity is important to focus children's attention on the chosen science topic. So Ron chooses the "dancing penny" activity to elicit children's thinking about air and air pressure. In fact, Ron's group in the methods course used the very same activity to explore their individual partner's ideas of air and air pressure.

Ron states that his role is simply to run the activity, provide an opportunity for the students to reflect, and then gather the students' ideas as they

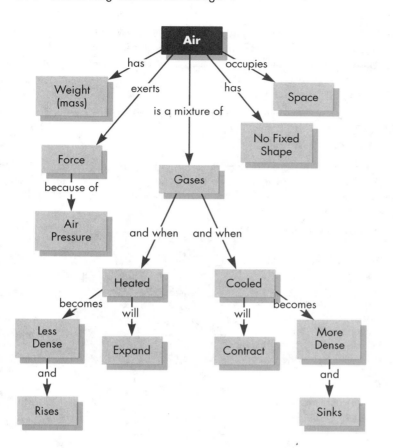

FIGURE 4-1
Ron's beginning concept map for a unit on *Air and Air Pressure*

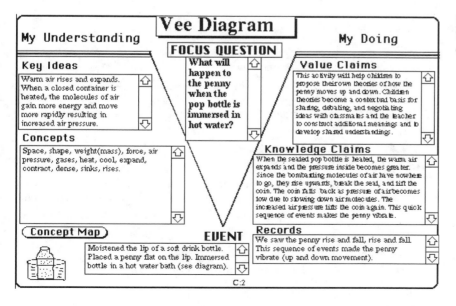

FIGURE 4-2
Ron's Vee diagram for the exploration activity

Teaching Standard D

Guideline: Design and manage the learning environment by creating a setting for student work that is flexible and supportive of science inquiry.

surface. When Ron states his main task is to gather children's ideas, he means that he will not intervene in their thinking by teaching them or leading them to a particular answer during exploration. Ron's exploring lesson is related in his own words in Box 4-1.

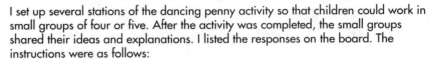

BOX 4-1

Ron's Exploring Lesson

I set up several stations of the dancing penny activity so that children could work in small groups of four or five. After the activity was completed, the small groups shared their ideas and explanations. I listed the responses on the board. The instructions were as follows:

1. Dab the soapy water on the bottle-top rim. Then place a penny over the opening of the bottle. (See Figure 4-3.)
2. Predict what will happen when the bottle is placed in the warm water.
3. Put the sealed bottle into the water to test the predictions.
4. Write one or two sentences telling what is happening and why it is happening.
5. Share ideas and explanations as the teacher lists the responses on the board.

I concluded my exploration by asking the question, "As a result of your new observations, what more can you tell me about air?"

Ron's analysis of the students' responses to the exploration activity follows.

How Does Ron Make Sense of Children's Conceptions?

Ron recorded all the children's ideas on the board. Then, after class, he tried to group the ideas into meaningful categories. How did Ron group children's ideas? Here are the steps that Ron and his peers were taught in their methods course:

1. Color-code similar ideas.
2. Cut out the ideas that have the same color.

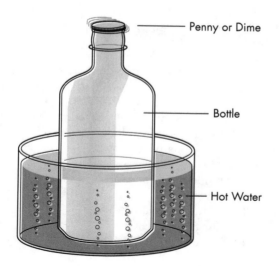

Penny or Dime

Bottle

Hot Water

FIGURE 4-3
Diagram of the dancing
penny activity

3. Put all of the ideas that have the same color into a pile.
4. Decide on a label that reflects the concept in each pile. This label is referred to as a "teacher-made category."
5. Write the teacher-made category labels on your page, leaving room for the examples that best indicate the label.
6. Write one or two of the best examples under each teacher-made category label.

The label must reflect students' ideas, not curricular words.

Ron's Sense-Making

I explored children's ideas in my cooperating teacher's class and my cooperating teacher supported me in my reflective practice. It was a great opportunity for me to be able to explore children's ideas and reflections in the real classroom situation. This is my first attempt at exploring as well as making sense of children's ideas. I sorted their comments for the exploration activity in the following way.

- Air does/does not occupy space.
  - "It's nothing."
  - "It's everywhere."
  - "It's *not* because sometimes things are empty and nothing's in them."
  - "It's all around us."
  - "There is nothing inside, so it's just like magic."
- Wind and air are one/separate thing(s).
  - "You need it to fly a kite."
  - "That's wind."
  - "So, that's windy air."

- "Wind is moving air."
- "Moving air can move objects."
- Air is steam.
  - "The hot water made steam inside that pushed the penny up."
- Air can exert force.
  - "The air inside wants to get out."
  - "We blew through the straw and it pushed the ball around."
  - "I think the whole thing will explode."
  - "Air made the penny go up and down."
- Hot air rises.
  - "They use fire in hot-air balloons."
- Air does not have any weight.
  - "You can't feel it. It's just there."
- Air is needed by humans.
  - "We breathe it."

Ron's Reflections

The third-grade students struggled at times trying to explain what air actually is. This is not surprising, since air is invisible, odorless, and colorless. Therefore, what students know about air is often related to what they hear rather than see, as in, "That's a breath of fresh air," "Air out your sleeping bag," and of course "Air Jordan shoes help you jump high." Roger Osborne and Beverley Bell (1983) note that "... everyday language of our society often leads children to have a view distinctly different to the scientists' view. Such views may not change as the child grows older, or they may even become, with time, increasingly different from scientists' science" (p. 3).

Also, what children can see, and therefore share, is what air is in relation to objects. Many of the children's reflections referred to how air moves objects like a Ping-Pong ball or how moving air keeps a kite flying. For many students, air is best described as "nothing—the space between myself and another object." This is a sensible conclusion, given its ability to elude some of our most depended-upon senses. At this age level (grade 3), there is also a connection between what cannot be seen and magic.

In their article, "Knowledge of air: A study of children aged between 6 and 8," Borghi, De Ambrosis, Massara, Grossi, and Zoppi (1988) note that "children ... do not have an awareness of the presence of air in the environment in which they live." For example, when I conducted the dancing penny experiment, a number of children thought that I was performing a trick. After watching the dancing penny experiment, Charles stated, "There is nothing inside [the bottle] so it's just like magic." Other students were a little more astute as they struggled to explain what was happening using logic. Mickey, for example, spent a long time thinking about what had happened to make the penny dance. He said quite slowly and deliberately, "The air inside wants to get out and is pushing up the penny."

Perhaps the "magic" theory could be dispelled by (a) helping students think about other possible explanations and (b) demonstrating the classic "balloon on the neck of the bottle activity" (pages 93, 94).

When examining students' ideas, it seems they have had many experiences they can draw on to understand the properties of air. Perhaps the focus of these lessons should be helping students to make connections between the specific properties of air and what they already know about how air works. In other words, if Susan states that "leaves fall off when its windy," she is expressing her knowledge that when air moves, it exerts a force. Helping Susan make the connection between these two statements is the process of making sense of, revealing, labeling, expanding on, bridging, identifying, and so on, which is a vital part of science education.

> **Teaching Standard A**
>
> **Guideline:** Plan an inquiry-based program by selecting science content and adapting and designing curricula to meet the interests, knowledge, understanding, abilities, and experiences of students.

 PEER INTERACTION

Analyzing Ron's Questions

What questions do you think Ron asked as children observed the dancing penny activity? How did students respond to him? How did Ron's questions probe children's ideas? Preservice teachers tend to begin or end an exploratory activity with a general question, such as, "What can you tell me about air?" Ron asked a similar question at the end of the activity, when he asked, "Can you tell me more about air?" Which of the following questions might have elicited better responses? Why?

"What do you think is in the bottle?"

"Have you ever seen something similar happen?"

"What might happen when what is in the bottle is heated?"

"What might happen when what is in the bottle is cooled?"

In his reflections, Ron points out how children use everyday language to describe something. He quotes researchers who propose that everyday language influences our thinking and everyday meaning often differs from scientific meaning. These researchers are referring to two distinct worlds: the world that children are a part of and the world of scientists.

What we often fail to remember is that children move into the scientists' community when they study science just as we know that scientists are part of the same main community as children. So, it is not unlikely that in their everyday normal talk, scientists resort to non-special language like every other individual. Thus what is important is developing an awareness of "contextual talk" or "relational talk" in children. Getting children to be comfortable using conceptual ideas when they explain their ideas about science events is a key to bridging the gap between the perceived world of scientists and the everyday world of science we all observe and try to explain.

☀ RELATIONAL LEARNING

Ferrence Marton, a Swedish psychologist, takes into account the uniqueness of the cognitive process of a child, although not in the same ways proposed by Piaget or Ausubel. Marton (1981) does not subscribe to the idea of successive mental structures forming a powerful whole or growing into an elaborate network. Instead, Marton argues for **relational learning**—that the child's thinking is related to and determined by his or her complete environment, including the object of perception.

Relational learning involves studying the contextual link between the subject and the object.

Children's experiences and values are determined by cultural, religious, and social experiences. Within the same child, responses may vary because of contextual experiences. There are differences in the contexts in which the child learns the content of the subject matter. For instance, when we study light and shadows, some children say that God created shadows. This is a common view expressed by children who are taught that God created everything. Other children will say that the shadow is part of them and that their shadow follows them wherever they go. This reasoning might arise from the child's experience, for example, from reading the Robert Louis Stevenson poem, "My Shadow." Still others might say that a shadow is caused when light is blocked. In each of these contexts, the *content* (shadows) is the same, but a child may experience the *concept* of shadows from one, two, or all three perspectives.

The task for the teacher is to listen to and analyze children's expressions for the distinctively different ways in which children relate themselves to various aspects of their world. The teacher speculates on the sources of children's ideas. The main approach, then, is to focus on the *relations* between the child and his or her world and the content. In contrast to Piaget and neo-Piagetian thinkers, Marton states that the basic images of our environment are not in the conscious mind, but are reflected in the way we organize an event according to some purpose (1981). Marton focuses on child-context relationships rather than on individual perceptions.

Marton argues that thinking is always thinking about something. We can observe our own thoughts when we can describe what we are thinking. As teachers, our primary goal in the classroom should be to attempt to understand what our students are thinking. Children's thinking can be observed by understanding the characteristics of their speech. According to Marton, the aim of teaching is to consider variations of children's meaning when they describe things. An example is how children describe their concept of shadows made from shining a flashlight on an opaque object.

Our secondary goal in instruction is to look for "invariance" in a set of varying conceptions. Experience in research tells us that as we explore our students' conceptions we will find a limited set of conceptions: produced within a content area (subject matter), context (the environment in which the subject matter is studied), and children who have had similar experiences. The teacher can then learn to reveal the underlying scientific structure. We will look at this more closely when we return to Ron's case study.

For now, consider this example: "A vacuum cleaner sucks the dirt." This description seems to make sense in everyday talk, even to a teacher and a scientist. In the science class, we would translate that idea by saying that the vacuum cleaner works on the principles of air pressure.

The main point of departure between Marton and some constructivists is that students have well-established mental structures or schema that need to be accounted for in teaching. Marton believes that these mental structures are *fluid and not static* and used in different combinations to study the content, depending on the context.

In summary, Piaget's theory of cognitive development and Ausubel's theory of meaningful learning focus on established mental schema and on assimilation and accommodation of conceptual structures. Both Piaget's and Ausubel's theories stress the importance of children's prestructured, existing knowledge. Marton's relational theory does not contradict Piaget's or Ausubel's but goes one step further by suggesting that these structures are not in the conscious mind. The structures are brought together on the basis of variations in the experiences of the child, and the content and context in which the child has had those experiences. Marton's idea of learning implies that we as teachers should encourage children to construct *multiple meanings* based on purpose and function.

> **Professional Development Standard B**
>
> Professional development for teachers of science requires integrating knowledge of science, learning, pedagogy, and students; it also requires applying that knowledge to science teaching.

☼ SCIENCE LEARNING AS A COMMUNAL ACTIVITY

Marton (1981) looked at the relations between the cognizing agent (who) and the event (what). Although Marton alluded to the sociocultural aspects of learning, he did not fully characterize exactly what he meant by "relations." Bruner (1986) offers one way of characterizing relations, and that is through language. He states that "language imposes a perspective in which things are viewed and a stance [is taken] toward that view" (p. 121). Bruner's idea is that *language is a tool* and the standards of its use perfect the mind and the hand. Without language, the mind and the hand alone cannot construct knowledge about the world. This is why we recommend including "speak-on" (or talk-about) science with hands-on and minds-on science.

We know that language and its use are embedded in culture. Therefore, our direct experiences are subject to the interpretation of cultural ideas; in our case, that culture is the culture of science. What we mean here is that our personal constructions and puzzlement about the physical world are assigned interpretations from the science world. For instance, children's personal talk about "air is nothing" is assigned for further interpretation in science class. It is the fusion between our personal worlds and the science worlds through a process of discourse and negotiation using scientific language that eventually forms our *knowing*. What we believe and what we think is true are *negotiated* with those around us. In the science class, those around us are the textbook authors (who speak indirectly, through their textbooks) as well as the children. Thus our personal construction is never our own; it is always conforming to some set of ideals formed by the culture. Bruner reminds us that culture comprises ambiguous text that is constantly in need of interpretation by those who participate in it. Therefore, the constitutive role of language creating social reality becomes important. The question is, What is the origin of a science "concept"? The perceiver's head? Interpersonal negotiation? Where does it get formed?

The meaning of science concepts is a result of scientists reaching agreement through creating, recreating, interpreting, arguing, negotiating, and sharing. Science concepts are formed in the science cultural forum and are bounded by its rules. Hence, the child in the science classroom does not occupy the central position, as in the child-centered, traditional (Piagetian) view. The child becomes a part of the negotiatory process by which his or her personal understandings of the science world are recreated. The child does not become a knowledge inventor on his or her own (discovery learning); rather, knowledge is constructed through a process of personal-cultural negotiations.

Science learning is a *communal activity,* a sharing of the science culture. Therefore, science teaching should be characterized by the spirit of a forum, in which the members (students and teacher) negotiate and recreate meaning through a process of reflection. This indeed will produce a joint culture, or shared meaning, in the science class. When the child learns to reflect, then the child controls, selects, and guides knowledge from within rather than having knowledge guide the child from the "outside in."

Professional Growth Standard C

Guideline: Professional development activities must provide opportunities to learn and use the skills of research to generate new knowledge about science and the teaching and learning of science.

 REFLECTIVE PRACTICE

Science as a Communal Activity

Bruner emphasizes *collaborative* learning for the creation of common knowing. Reflect on Ron's use of collaborative learning. For what purposes did Ron use it?

☀ ZONE BETWEEN STUDENTS' KNOWING AND SCIENTIFIC KNOWLEDGE

Believing in the developmental nature of content knowledge and the role of language in human development, Vygotsky (1978) states that higher knowledge will transform the meaning of lower concepts. This process of conscious or reflective learning in a science class happens as a result of the expert-novice (Ron-students) relationship, where the expert (Ron) helps the novices (students) reach the higher ground in a particular knowledge domain. We may liken this to scientists helping their graduate students reflectively learn higher knowledge structures not by simply telling them but by assisting them with problem-solving activities.

Let us translate the scientist–graduate student metaphor to school science. The teacher is the expert and the students, who are the novices, collaboratively learn with the teacher. Children are the research associates in solving a problem that both they and the teacher have defined. The teacher's function is to help children move from their level of problem solving to a higher level of problem solving. The distance between the learner's level of problem solving and the predetermined goal level has been called the **zone of proximal development** (Vygotsky, 1978). For Vygotsky, "Human learning presupposes a specific social nature and a process by which children grow into the intellectual life of those around them" (1978, p. 88). Vygotsky uses the term *scaffolding* to describe the process by which the teacher helps the child to grow intellectually.

We must not mistakenly believe that Vygotsky's scaffolding process is one of traditional transmission, where the teacher puts the pieces of knowledge into the child's head. Scaffolding refers to the "negotiable transaction" between the teacher and children. Children must be willing to examine their views from the "other" or expert perspective. In order to do that, children need help understanding the language and culture of science. To progress across the zone of proximal development, the students-to-teacher discourse must be carefully played out and most children must be *assisted*. In class, therefore, children need more than science learning centers. They must be provided with the procedures and tools of science and the processes and exploration of science activities.

The classroom social support system (small-group discussion such as provided in Ron's lesson), through the medium of language, is essential to traverse the zone of proximal development. Science language has a cultural past and a generative present in that science knowledge is being generated and negotiated all the time. Through classroom discourse, science language may be used for clarifying, elaborating, and transforming or giving new meaning to one's personal understandings of or description of the world.

The many worlds of meaning can only be created, not discovered. Negotiation is the process of creating multiple meanings for the science culture of which we are part. For science learning to occur, we must be part of the science communal life. This will enable us to understand science cultural patterns, symbolic systems, language, and discourse modes. Hence, Bruner's emphasis on classroom discourse and Vygotzky's scaffolding process for intellectual development make sense. Teaching becomes community centered rather than child centered.

> **Zone of proximal development** is the distance between the learner's level of problem solving and the teacher's goal for the student.
>
> Constructivist teaching does not equate to leaving students on their own to construct meaning. Constructivist teaching involves community-centered (teacher-students and peer-peer) negotiated, learning.

 REFLECTIVE PRACTICE

Bruner's and Vygotsky's Assumptions

Identify how Ron's first lesson reflects Bruner's and Vygotsky's assumptions of intellectual development.

✳ CHILDREN'S PERSONAL KNOWING

A Concern: Infinite Expressions and Finite Conceptualizations

HEIDI'S VOICE

> *As a professional I have now developed a more positive, sound view of science teaching. I always knew that it was important to use children's ideas but was never sure how to go about doing it. The children have so many ideas. How do you narrow it down and choose the appropriate ones? I was afraid that 20 different ideas on the same topic would be too confusing for students and the teacher alike. The constructivist approach gave me the answers to my questions.*

Over and over, preservice teachers ask, "How does a teacher deal with the many conceptions of different students?" or "The children have so many ideas. How do you choose the appropriate ones?" Indeed, you may find that children express many views (seemingly *infinite expressions*) on a topic, but on careful analysis, as suggested by Marton's "invariance", you will generally find that these may be gathered into a limited number of categories (*finite conceptualizations*) (Ebenezer, 1995, pp. 100, 101).

Remember how Ron made sense of children's conceptions and grouped them into meaningful categories? Can this be done for all the science topics we are called upon to teach? Yes! Consider now this seemingly insurmountable problem.

Piaget (1973) and Marton (1981) point out that although the linguistic expressions of the conceptions of a phenomenon may be numerous, beneath them are *limited conceptualizations*. For example, people would never call a desk that is placed against a wall a chair, although the desk has four legs and the wall can be used as a chair back. There is some perceived regularity in our concept of chair, by which an individual knows that a chair is a chair. Yet describing all chairs in a generalized way would be difficult.

Similarly, any physical system is bounded by its own distinct features. For example, studies show that the two main student conceptualizations of sugar/salt dissolving in water are as follows:

- Sugar/salt melts into its liquid form.
- The solution process involves a chemical change (Prieto, Blanco, & Rodriguez, 1989; Ebenezer & Erickson, 1996).

Thus there is *consistency* in individuals' responses to certain phenomena because of certain perceptual constraints.

Human thinking is contextually determined and people's conceptions of reality are specific to a particular context and to problems raised within that context (Säljö, 1988). Children also bring cultural meaning to their perception of a system (Gabel, 1989). For example, when referring to sugar dissolving in water, children often say that the sugar is melting, perhaps because of the language we use to describe a candy being sucked. Human thinking is also perceptually bound (Driver, 1985). What children see is what they say. For example, sugar appears to turn into a liquid because the resulting solution is in the liquid state.

From the foregoing argument, one ought to remember that the number of conceptions is limited because the ways in which an individual construes the world are dependent on that individual's physical and social world, both of which are finite (or limited).

Types of Personal Knowledge

Children's personal knowing is their sensible understanding of certain phenomena. That knowing may be the same as or qualitatively different from the understandings accepted by the scientific community. Personal knowledge may be *perceptual, metaphorical, episodic,* and/or *cultural.* Let us consider Ron's students' ideas about air in the context of the dancing penny activity and his general question, "What can you tell me about air?" (See Figure 4-4.)

It is useful and important to recognize these distinctions so that the teacher can speculate on the sources of children's ideas. When teachers analyze and categorize children's ideas, they should consider what types of personal knowledge are being exemplified and where their ideas are coming from. This information will help to guide planning for teaching.

The teacher should be empathetic toward children's experiences and plan suitable activities to incorporate children's meanings such as "It's not because sometimes things are empty and nothing's in them" (see Ron's first lesson to follow). A science sense must be given to children, but children's episodic and metaphorical talk must be entertained in a science class because they are indeed attaching everyday language to the science sense developed in the science class. Moving back and forth from the children's world to the scientists' world should be an important aspect of science teaching.

Perceptual meaning occurs when a child says that "it's [air] everywhere" because he or she thinks that air is all-pervasive.

"Air inside wants to get out" is a *metaphorically* guided statement.

"We saw them use fire to make the hot-air balloon go up" is *episodic;* that is, based on a remembered episode.

"You need air to fly a kite" is *cultural* and universal; that is, something the child has heard a grown-up say.

FIGURE 4-4

Examples of children's perceptual, metaphorical, episodic, and cultural knowledge

Children Constructing Meaning

Much research has been done on children's meanings about the world, and science education literature is replete with documentation of children's conceptions of physics, biology, and chemistry topics. In the area of physics, studies have examined topics such as light, shadows, vision, color, sound, heat, and flotation. Children's conceptions of animals, photosynthesis, and cell growth are examples of the biology topics that have been described. In the discipline of chemistry, children's conceptions of matter, states of matter, physical and chemical changes, chemical equation balancing, and solution chemistry have been described. Children's ideas about how the world works based on these concepts are often very creative and logical. One student mused, "The higher you go up, the stronger the gravity is until you get out of the atmosphere." His reasoning came from his experience of jumping from a high tree and falling harder than when jumping from a small step.

A few examples of children's conceptions about specific topics have been summarized in the following section. Many others are described in detail in Driver, Squires, Rushworth, and Wood-Robinson (1994).

Biological Topics

Living. Young children (4–7 years) have little biological knowledge and do not develop this understanding until ages 9 or 10. Little children believe that things that are active and move (including cars and the sun) are alive. They believe that animals are living because they move, but most young children believe plants to be nonliving (Carey, 1985; Stavy & Wax, 1989).

Growth. Several studies of young children's concepts of growth indicate that growth means "getting bigger" and "one gets bigger on one's birthday" and "eating birthday cake makes one bigger." Children do believe that eating is a necessary condition for growth but don't realize that the food taken in is transformed into other materials the body needs. Other research indicates that some children believe that an animal grows or stretches in order to accommodate the food that it wants to eat (Carey, 1985; Russell & Watts, 1989).

Physical Science Topics

Density. Some children of ages 5 to 7 may describe an object as "heavy for its size." Prior to that children seem to have separate concepts of size and weight. Weight and density are not differentiated but are included in the idea of "heaviness." Even at age 11 most children have misunderstandings about volume that could present problems in understanding the concept of density (Rowell, Dawson, & Lyndon, 1990; Smith, Carey & Wiser, 1984).

Solids, Liquids, and Gases. Children as old as 5 and 6 consider any stiff material to be a solid, and pliable materials, such as jelly or a cloth, to be something between a solid and a liquid. Children identify anything that pours (such as powder) as a liquid. Their beliefs about gases are fascinating. Some children as old as 11 years believe that gases have "negative" weight and, when added to a vessel, will cause the vessel to become lighter (Leboutet-Barrell, 1976; Stavy & Stachel, 1984).

Evaporation. Children ages 5 and 6 believe that evaporated material just disappears. Not until they are between 8 and 10 do they suggest that the evaporated material must go someplace. By the age of 12 to 14, children begin to form a conception of conservation of matter related to evaporation (Bar, 1986).

Electricity. Many children as old as 12 hold views about electric circuits different from recognized scientific ideas. Nearly 40% believe that the current flows outward from the two terminals of the dry cell. About 50% believe that the current is used up by the light bulb and there is less current going back to the dry cell. Less than 10% believe that when current flows through a circuit, its strength returns undiminished to the dry cell (the correct view) (Osborne, 1983; Shipstone, 1984).

Light. Many children as old as 10 and 11 do not recognize light as an entity (electromagnetic radiation) existing between the source and the eye. Their drawings often show light rays coming from the eye to the observed object (Guesne, 1985; Watts & Gilbert, 1985).

Terminologies for Children's Ideas

The terminology used for discussing children's ideas varies according to what educators believe about children's conceptions. They may be referred to as "preconceptions" (Novak, 1977), "alternative conceptions" (Driver & Easley, 1978), "intuitive ideas" (Hawkins, 1978), "misconceptions" (Helm, 1980), "children's science" (Gilbert, Osborne, & Fensham, 1982), "alternate frameworks" (Gilbert & Watts, 1983), "prescientific ideas" (Bruner, 1986), "primitive science" (di Sessa, 1988), "untutored beliefs" (Hills, 1989), or "episodic knowledge" (Bloom, 1992). For example, the term "misconception" refers to conceptions that are wrong from the curricular point of view; thus, the teacher would attempt to *correct* the children's misconceptions to achieve scientists' conceptions. The term "untutored beliefs" is used when an educator appreciates children's ideas but attempts to *change* them to the scientist's viewpoint. For example, many children still believe well into the teens that humans are not animals, but of a separate category, and that trees and yeast are not plants, because they do not look like the typical green plant.

The common underpinning identified in the literature describing children's ideas is the belief that one helps children make transitions from their perspective to scientists' perspectives—one of the present goals in science education. We think a better term for children's utterances may be "children's meanings" or "children's conceptions" because *children's talk characterizes contextual meanings, and in a science class it is essential to provide them with science contextual meanings.*

Moving from children's talk directly to scientists' talk should not be the main goal of science education. Practicing this methodology is one reason why we have failed when we have attempted to replace children's ideas with scientists' ideas. Instead of trying to replace children's everyday ideas, let us add ideas from the science point of view and help children negotiate their own meanings about the science ideas. To find out how to do this, we explore new teachers' and students' roles in science learning.

☀ TEACHERS' ACADEMIC KNOWING

Historically, a teacher's role in the classroom was to present sequentially laid out, prescribed curricular materials to students. This was the **teacher's academic knowing**. That is, the teacher entered the curricular world first and saw the student from that perspective. Subsequently, students' worlds of knowing were bypassed, and students were instead expected to step into the teacher's realm of meaning making. The drawing of students into the teacher's world is still at the heart of most teaching. A student's success depends on the extent to which he or she can be included in the teacher's world. Correspondingly, students expect the teacher to provide them with academic knowledge and to search out teacher meanings to acquire basic knowledge.

A commonly used method of conveying academic knowledge in science class is having the class work through a science investigation with the teacher, who takes the students through a series of sequential steps to find the solution. The teacher usually provides a definite procedure for investigating the problem. As the class works through the problem, the teacher carefully points out the steps in the procedure, which may be used in solving other problems of this sort.

While the teacher presents this academic knowledge, the students for the most part play a silent role or say something only when asked to. In this way the students' contributions are directly constrained by the teacher's questions and by the normal requirement that any answer to a question be relevant, appropriate, and informative. In trying to evaluate the students' replies, the teacher often repeats and recites, and in so doing provides confirmation and shapes the meaning of what is said in the desired direction toward the desired outcome. Thus the teacher controls what conclusions are reached and what interpretations are given to a particular science activity. This type of teacher authority has been commonly understood and accepted by students.

In the foregoing method of teaching, students often suspend what they know about the subject matter. Because the students have to give the academic or "right" meaning that the teacher desires, they feel compelled to leave their world and enter the teacher's world. As a result, there is usually a disparity between students' personal knowing and their teacher's academic knowing. This restrains the students from communicating effectively with the teacher.

Edwards and Mercer (1987) suggest that we should view education as the creation of *common knowledge* because it is an intrinsically *social communicative process*. Instead of the term "knowledge," we have used "know-

Teacher's academic knowing consists of their knowledge about the content of the topic to be studied by the children.

ing," as in "preservice teachers' knowing." "Knowledge" refers to the conceptual aspects of learning, but "knowing" is an action word. It refers not only to the conceptual but also to the experiential.

We must live in the students' experiential worlds to develop rich insights about their worlds. Therefore, in teaching, we *begin* a lesson *from a student's point of view* rather than confront them with a "conceptual conflict" or "discrepant event." For example, when children say sugar is melting in water, we teach them what is meant by melting with a number of examples and activities, maybe even student developed. Then we give them examples of dissolving. If we simultaneously show similar examples of melting and dissolving, such as an ice cube in water and a sugar cube in water, this will indeed create conceptual conflict. A conceptual conflict such as this may be useful *after* developing the ideas of melting and dissolving separately. Discrepant events are definitely useful in the "constructing and negotiating meaning" phase of teaching.

The nature of this social communicative process depends on the teacher's beliefs about effective teaching strategies. That is, the teacher beliefs and the school culture in which he/she works determine how the subject matter is taught and what roles the teacher and students play. Common knowledge may indeed be achieved through a transmissive mode, inductive mode, or personal-social constructivist mode. But the choice of mode determines how a teacher teaches, how students learn, and what relationships the teacher and students have. A personal–social constructivist approach indeed suggests a symmetrical relationship between the teacher and students. This relationship is essential for the process of common knowledge construction that we are talking about. Let's return to Ron's class and see how Ron uses his academic knowing to help his students develop common knowledge about a basic science concept.

What Is Ron's Source of Academic Knowing?

Ron explores the curriculum guide. His academic knowing includes the curricular structures outlined in the guide or textbook. He is accountable for teaching these concepts to his children. The following are scientific ideas about air and air pressure found in his Science Curriculum Guide for Grade 3.

AIR AND AIR PRESSURE
1. Air occupies space.
   – Cold air occupies less space than warm air.
   – Air can create resistance.
2. Air has weight.
3. Air exerts force.
   – The force of air can move objects or cause them to change their direction.
4. Warm air rises and cold air sinks.
5. Air is composed of gases.
6. Air does not have a fixed shape.

Looking at the curricular ideas, we may guess why Ron chose the dancing penny activity for his exploration activity, as well as why he asked the general question, "Can you tell me about air?" The dancing penny activity encompasses curricular ideas 1, 3, and 4. No wonder Ron asked a more general question to see whether students would talk about other ideas listed in the curriculum guide.

What Does Ron Do With Children's Knowing and His Academic Knowing?

Assessment Standard B

Guideline: Achievement data collected focus on the science content that is most important for students to learn.

Ron and other preservice teachers were concerned as to how the curriculum could be "covered" if students' ideas were interjected into lesson sequences. To resolve this problem, Ron thinks that it is sensible to find relationships among children's conceptions, his personal knowing, and goals that reflect the local science curriculum. He has depicted these relationships in Table 4-1. This table helps him to plan for subsequent teaching, keeping children's conceptions in mind.

Across the conceptual structures "Air has weight" and "Air is composed of gases," Ron states "scientific ideas that must be covered." This suggests that the exploration activity, which in this case was the dancing penny, may have focused and perhaps *constrained* children's thinking. This is to be expected, and this is why we say children's talk is very contextual.

Ron decided that the following children's ideas relating to their understanding of the first concept, "Air occupies space," needed to be addressed in the first lesson because this is a very basic idea that underpins the whole unit.

- Air cannot be felt. ("You can't feel it; it's just there.")
- Air is nothing. ("It's nothing.")
- Air pressure is magic because there is nothing there, yet something is happening. ("There is nothing inside so it's just like magic.")

TABLE 4-1

Relationships Between Teacher's Academic Knowing and Children's Personal Knowing

Teacher's Academic Knowing	Children's Personal Knowing
Air occupies space.	"It's (air) everywhere." "It's (air) all around us."
Air has weight.	
Air exerts force.	"The air inside wants to get out." "Wind is moving air." "Moving air can move objects."
Warm air rises. Cold air sinks.	"Air made the penny go up and down."
Air is composed of gases.	
Oxygen is a gas used in respiration.	"We breathe it."

These three ideas are related to the notion some children have that there is no air in the jar if it is empty. It is perceptual meaning-making. Since this notion—"Air is nothing"—also appears in the literature, Ron incorporates this idea in his first lesson.

What Is Ron's First Constructing and Negotiating Lesson?

Ron prepared five lessons to incorporate children's conceptions into his teaching. (We will relate only Ron's first lesson, which has two activities, to indicate some of the fundamental features of constructing and negotiating meaning. See Box 4-2.)

BOX 4-2
Lesson 1: Constructing and Negotiating Meaning

Title: Is Air Nothing?

Objectives:
A number of students have expressed ideas that suggest "air is nothing" or exists separate from the space around us—"Things are empty and nothing's in them." The purpose of this lesson will be to provide experiments and an opportunity for students to reflect on and discuss the presence of air. By the end of this lesson students will be able to:
- identify air as being present all around us, even inside objects that appear to be empty.
- understand that air can create a resistance to another force applied in the opposite direction.

The verbs *identify* and *understand* are used in the student learning outcomes to help the teacher focus on the ultimate understandings a student may have.

Materials and Resources for Each Group:
- One clear glass
- One large bowl or plastic tub almost full of water
- One plastic 2-liter pop bottle (empty) for each pair of students
- One balloon for each pair of students
- (An awl or hammer and nail for the teacher to make holes in the plastic bottles)

Activities and Procedures:
Activity One
1. The teacher begins by getting the students, carrying pencils and science journals, to huddle around the large tub of water. Their journal notes will form the basis for a teacher-students discussion.
2. The teacher asks the students to draw what they think will happen when he inverts the empty glass into the water (see photo). See Figure 4-5 for Ron's Vee diagram for this activity. The teacher puts the headings "Before" and "After" on the board to direct students' drawings.

3. The teacher gives the students time to explain their drawings as well as share their written ideas with one or two other students. Then they meet in a large group to engage in a teacher-students interpretive discussion to explore how they will answer their questions using the materials of the activity.
4. The teacher proceeds with the demonstration, having one student invert the glass and push it under the water.
5. This activity will likely confirm some students' earlier predictions and cause some students to begin to question what they saw.

FIGURE 4-5

Ron's Vee diagram for Activity One: The not-soggy paper

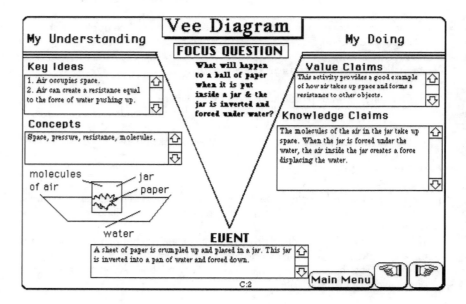

Activity Two

1. The students are grouped put into pairs and each pair is given a 2-liter plastic pop bottle and one balloon.
2. The teacher instructs the pairs to put the balloon inside the bottle and secure the opening of the balloon over the mouth of the pop bottle (see photo). The teacher demonstrates this procedure as well.

3. When all students are ready, the teacher tells the students to blow up the balloon.
4. Before the students get too frustrated, the teacher asks, "Why can't you blow the balloon all the way up?" A brief discussion takes place as the students identify the difficulties they are experiencing.
5. The teacher asks, "How could we solve our problem so that we are able to blow the balloon all the way up inside the bottle?"
6. The various ideas are tried and, if no one has already thought of it, the teacher suggests putting holes in the bottom of the bottle.
7. The teacher circulates to each group, putting holes in the bottom of each bottle with the awl or hammer and nail.

It is advisable that only the teacher use the awl or hammer and nail to punch the holes in the bottles.

8. The students are given time to try again to inflate the balloon. They should be encouraged to feel the bottom of the bottle as they do so.
9. All the materials are cleaned up, and the teacher begins a discussion to help relate the following concepts to children's explorations:
   – Air occupies space all around us and inside of things even if they look empty.
   – Air can create resistance (which keeps water from rushing into the glass or the balloon from filling the sealed bottle).

Assessment:

Listen to the students as they work and assess their understanding by giving them a handout with two pictures of pop bottles, each one under a "Before" and "After" heading. On that sheet, instruct students to draw a picture of the activity they just did and label all the parts, including the bottle, balloon, air, moving air, trapped or resisting air, and holes. Then have the students answer the following question at the bottom of the sheet, "What was similar about the two investigations we did today?" The teacher can then compare the drawings done at the beginning of the class with the final drawing and comments done at the end of the class.

> This lesson is not a final, comprehensive study on the concept "air occupies space." The teacher will likely want to expand this concept further in future lessons. Here is a follow-up idea: Air does not have a fixed shape. Fill a plastic bag or balloon half full of air and seal it. Now feel its shape!

☀ PEER INTERACTION

Analyzing Ron's Lesson

Trace every step Ron took to teach Lesson One.

What are his intentions for this lesson?

What teaching strategies is Ron using? Identify them.

☀ CHILDREN'S-TEACHER'S COMMON KNOWING

In his preparation to incorporate children's conceptions into his teaching and to reach common or shared understanding, Ron considered four worlds of meaning-making:

- The students' world (he explored children's ideas)
- The teacher's world (he explored his own ideas by drawing concept maps and Vee diagrams)
- The curricular world (he referred to the school district's curriculum guide and followed up with extensive preparation)
- The physical world (the dancing penny activity simulates what happens in our environment—the expansion of air, the rise and fall of air)

Ron developed his content knowledge; then he explored children's ideas, and finally he incorporated children's ideas to develop children's-teacher's common knowing. For example, after Lesson One, Ron's students may have arrived at the common meaning that air does occupy space even though a container looks empty.

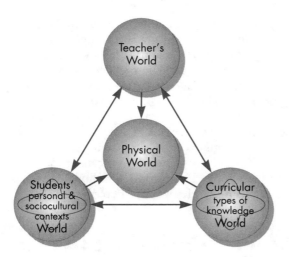

FIGURE 4-6
Interconnections among the
four worlds of meaning

The teacher's world, the students' world, and the curricular world constitute the socially constructed world. The social beings within these worlds create meaning for the physical world (in this instance, expansion of air). Individuals create meanings about their own social world as well as interpretations of the physical world. Individuals' interpretations, bounded by sociocultural canons (for example, curricular ideas) convey complex multifaceted meanings, which are often ambiguous. Hence, teaching becomes rather complicated, and it requires the ingenuity of the teacher to interpret the students' worlds and connect them to the curricular worlds. This is the role of the constructivist science teacher.

The four worlds of meaning-making are all interrelated (see Figure 4-6). In this figure, the worlds are depicted as circles, and the lines represent conceptualizations. Look at the *students' world*, which is represented by many subworlds. These subworlds represent various beliefs and practices of the culture to which the student belongs. The students conceptualize the *physical world* from their own perspectives and experiences. For instance, you noticed how students' experiences and perspectives were played out in Ron's exploration activity on air. The question is, "What are some student sociocultural beliefs about air?" Some children talked about using fire in hot-air balloons, meaning hot air rises. Some children talked about explosions because of the buildup of pressure inside the bottle. Both these examples are experiential, based on human-cultural inventions.

Now let us move to the rightmost circle, which is the *curricular world*. Depending on the subject matter, the curricular world consists of different types of knowledge structures. If we open a science textbook, we see many forms and representations of knowledge: line diagrams, artistic drawings, symbols, formulas, mathematical and chemical equations, analogies and metaphors, propositions, and procedures. These forms of knowledge are culturally formed and comprise the cultural precepts of a given discipline. In addition, many minds shape the science curriculum. For example, Ron used a prescribed curriculum guide for grade 3 students. The specific curricular propositions that Ron used to compare his students' ideas about air (see Table 4-1) are designed by curriculum experts after much discussion and deliberation as to what should form a grade 3 curriculum on air and air pressure. Elementary science books are often illustrated with everyday examples of the effects of air. However, we will not find highly specialized scientific language and mathematical symbols in a book meant for grade 3 children because they are not cognitively appropriate for this age level.

We move now from the four worlds of meaning-making to the teaching model that will incorporate these worlds. We hope you see the connections here to all the learning theories we have described.

☀ A TEACHING MODEL FOR COMMON KNOWLEDGE CONSTRUCTION

Marton's "relational" theory, Bruner's "cultural symbolic" theory, and Vygotsky's zone of proximal development accommodate the idea that *scientific knowledge is relative, contextually constructed, and requires meaning-making at the personal and social levels in qualitatively different ways.* Therefore, we envision teaching and learning as "constructing meaning"— helping children interact with science phenomena or socioscientific issues. This implies that children are allowed to use everyday talk but encouraged to use context-dependent science talk at different levels of complexity in their science classes. In the exploratory phase, we do not try to fit children's expressions to scientific norms. Instead, we search for the qualitatively different meanings children attach to a phenomenon. In class, we do not focus on attempting to *change students' beliefs,* but develop in students *additional meanings* so that they may use newly constructed meanings in personally, relevant contexts.

These three theoretical frameworks, elaborated on in detail in this chapter, tie in with the four worlds of meaning—the students' sociocultural world, the physical world, the teacher's world, and the curricular world. Using these frameworks and the four worlds of meaning, as well as the theories about science learning that we have previously described, we have developed a teaching model for developing **common knowledge** between teacher and students.

This Common Knowledge Construction Model has four interconnected phases, namely: exploring and categorizing, constructing and negotiating, translating and extending, reflecting and assessing. These phases are described in detail in subsequent chapters. The interrelated nature of each phase of the Common Knowledge Construction Model is depicted in Figure 4-7. The dashed lines indicate that the reflecting and assessing phase is integrated in all other phases.

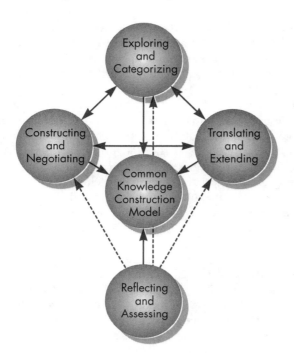

FIGURE 4-7
Common Knowledge
Construction Model

Exploring and Categorizing

In this phase, children's conceptions, beliefs, and attitudes are explored and categorized using one or two related, simple, everyday "systems," tasks, or phenomena. For example, Ron explored children's ideas about air and air pressure with the dancing penny activity. Ron carefully recorded his students' verbal as well as written expressions. Given this pool of children's expressions, Ron looked for commonalities in meanings and developed teacher-made categories. The conceptions are not attached to an individual or group of children, although this would be possible if one of the aims were to trace conceptual development for one child. Indeed, tracing a child's conceptual development is often a goal in science teaching and in science education research. Chapter 5 discusses effective strategies to elicit children's ideas, group these ideas into categories, and compare and contrast them with curricular structures. This process provides a basis for subsequent lesson planning for constructing and negotiating meaning.

Constructing and Negotiating

This phase consists of constructing meaning using the students' ideas in negotiating curricular ideas with them. Ron began with a simple, commonly found, teacher-made category of meaning—"air is nothing." Ron created

Teaching Standard B
_____

Guideline: To guide and facilitate learning, focus and support inquiries while interacting with students.

This exploring and categorizing phase, in which children's conceptions are explored and grouped into meaningful categories, is an essential foundation for the teaching of a science unit.

Teaching Standard B
_____

Guideline: To guide and facilitate learning, orchestrate discourse among students about scientific ideas.

Suppose a group of students reaches a conclusion that is clearly false. Perhaps, through observation and intense work, they conclude that the moon does race through the sky at intervals or that it is truly larger in size and volume when seen at the horizons. The guiding constructivist teacher should present the established ideas without extending a series of inquiries ad infinitum. But one should always be careful not to short-circuit the scientific inquiry. Provide meaningful experiences so that students will come to grips with their understandings. Give sufficient time for the inquiry to fulfill its purpose.

The constructing and negotiating phase leads naturally to the translating and extending phase and vice versa because, while teaching, the teacher will automatically give examples from everyday life.

During the translating and extending phase, the teacher will continue to make meaning and negotiate with students for common knowledge development.

Reflecting and assessing are ongoing authentic learning experiences as, throughout each phase, students become intrinsically involved in critical-thinking and problem-solving activities.

two more activities to study this particular idea. Although Ron chose the activities for his first lesson, children may design their own activities to test their ideas. Students will usually come up with possible tests for their science ideas in a spontaneous fashion. They might have suggested that we show that air has force by blowing up a balloon until it bursts.

During the teacher-children and peer discourse, more meanings might be generated; these meanings may even accommodate children's original conceptions, elicited in the exploration phase. Children's ideas must be incorporated into future teaching as the unit progresses. Chapter 6 describes teaching and learning strategies such as journal writing and using analogies that will help you to negotiate meaning with children.

The strategies used are suited to the topic to help children make relational or contextual meanings. The teacher acts as a mediator but is not a fountain of knowledge. Extensive use of oral and written classroom discourse before, during, and after a practical, collaborative science activity is a powerful tool to help children negotiate meanings. The purpose is to provide children with additional meanings. In this discourse, children are proposing multiple meanings, weighing alternatives, testing their hypotheses, thinking about their own thinking, and using a variety of materials within varied contexts. When the teacher and children become collaborative meaning-makers, searchers, sharers, and negotiators, an attitude of collaborative scientific inquiry for the construction and validation of contextual knowledge exists.

Translating and Extending

In this phase, children are given many opportunities to relate/translate their knowing to everyday contexts. They may even extend their activities into other disciplines or societal issues. Extensions may arise sooner, during the exploring or constructing phases. For example, Ron's students' idea that "we need air to breathe" should be the starting point for integrating science with technology and society. Health issues such as the effects of air pollution may be studied through research and practical inquiry.

Reflecting and Assessing

In this phase, both reflecting and assessing occur. Reflecting suggests that we encourage students to think about their own thinking. Assessing can be student or teacher driven, but both forms must occur throughout all the phases. Reflecting and assessing are continuous, integral parts of our relational, personal-social, constructivist process. Ron assessed his students' ideas before he started the unit (by exploring and categorizing children's ideas), during the unit (see the end of Lesson One), and at the end of the unit (see the lesson's culminating assessment). He reflected upon children's meanings through a process of analysis.

Reviewing students' recorded conceptions of science ideas as they progress through the unit encourages them to reflect on the growth of their ideas. For example, journal writing was used in the exploration activity in which Ron asked his students to write their observations and explain why the penny danced. Then, in Ron's first lesson on air, he asked students to use their journals to draw pictures as well as to record their sense-making of the activity. Additionally, throughout the unit, teachers and students will share their "thinking about thinking" by their verbal and nonverbal expressions and actions. Careful reflection and assessment of these written, verbal, and nonverbal student actions can be a guide to further instructional needs.

Ron reflected on an idea that could be included as part of the culminating assessment in his unit on air and air pressure: To assess the students' understanding, the teacher could have students fill out a concept map on air and air pressure. The teacher could provide a worksheet showing a barebones concept map with short quotes underneath each space. For example, under the space intended for "air has weight," the quote would be, "This property of air broke the ruler." Constructivist teaching will lead to a higher level of student involvement, affording the opportunity to assess higher levels of thinking.

Teaching Standard C

Guideline: Analyze assessment data to guide teaching.

☀ CHAPTER REFLECTIONS

Using Ron's ideas and experiences, we focused on three aspects of science teaching: (a) children's personal knowing, (b) the teacher's academic knowing, and (c) the children's-teacher's common knowing. We also presented a teaching model that emphasizes relational conceptual change. We used Ron's exploratory activity, his Lesson One, as well as his ongoing and culminating assessment to illustrate the Common Knowledge Construction Model. Can you now see the importance of valuing and considering children's personal knowing in science teaching? Can you visualize yourself in a classroom in which the teacher and students lead a communal life and take on new roles—students and teacher working together as a community of meaning-makers?

Questions for Reflective Inquiry

1. Analyze whether the following children's responses exhibit perceptual, metaphorical, episodic, or cultural types of personal knowledge. State reasons for your choices.
   - "The wind wants to make the candle go out."
   - "We always cut our candle wicks very short so they won't smoke."
   - "Beeswax candles smell very nice."
   - "We used a special string to make our candles."

2. Review the Common Knowledge Construction Model and the four worlds of meaning. How do they relate to each other?

3. Try to observe an elementary teacher teaching science. In this teacher's practice, what learning theories are obvious? Give examples.

SUGGESTED READINGS

Bloom, J. W. (1992). The development of scientific knowledge in elementary school children: A context of meaning perspective. *Science Education, 76*(4), 399–413.

Bruner, J. (1986). *Actual minds, possible worlds.* Cambridge, MA: Harvard University Press.

Driver, R., Guesne, E., & Tiberghien, A. (Eds.). (1985). *Children's ideas in science.* Philadelphia: Open University Press.

Driver, R., Squires, A. Rushworth, P., & Wood-Robinson, V. (1994). *Making sense of secondary science: Research into children's ideas.* London: Routledge.

Ebenezer, J. V. (1995). *Reference for students' conceptions.* A HyperCard stack. Winnipeg: The University of Manitoba.

Gilbert, J. K., & Watts, D. M. (1983). Concepts, misconceptions and alternative conceptions: Changing perspectives in science education. *Studies in Science Education, 10,* 61–98.

Hills, G. (1989). Students' untutored beliefs about natural phenomena: Primitive science or common sense? *Science Education, 73*(2), 155–186.

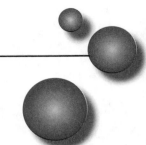

CHAPTER 5

Exploring and Categorizing

FOCUS QUESTIONS

1. Why is it important to explore children's conceptions of science topics?
2. How does one go about exploring children's conceptions?
3. What are several useful strategies for exploring children's conceptions?
4. What are some guidelines for exploring children's conceptions?
5. How can you relate children's conceptions to scientific ideas?

Reflective Inquiry

JOURNAL ACTIVITY

Exploring Your Own Conceptions of Natural Phenomena

1. Heat one end of a metal rod with a candle. What are the possible mechanisms for the movement of heat?

2. Add sugar or salt to water. What do you think might be happening to the sugar or salt in the water? Draw a picture to illustrate what you imagine happened.

3. Why does it get dark at night? Explain your ideas through diagrams or by using styrofoam balls.

4. What makes it cold during the winter? Explain your ideas through diagrams or by using styrofoam balls.

Reina explored her grade 6 ESL (English as a Second Language) children's conceptions about the shape of the earth. She then followed up with the question, "How would we convince people that the earth was spherical?" Reina used a teaching strategy called *interactive discussion* to explore her students' ideas. This is one of the strategies we will describe and explain in this chapter.

☀ EXPLORING CHILDREN'S CONCEPTIONS

As we discussed in previous chapters, social, cultural, political, and/or religious influences shape children's conceptions and play an important role in determining the kinds of questions they ask. These influences also affect the observations, inferences, and conclusions children use to consciously or unconsciously make meaning of natural phenomena in the world around them. Thus, the conceptions children form become the rudimentary foundation of their scientific knowledge. However, this knowledge may be very different from scientifically acceptable ideas.

As you explore children's conceptions, you will find some that are misconceived but loosely held and you will have great satisfaction when you hear, "Aha, I get it!" during a classroom investigation. In contrast, some children's conceptions are deeply seated, and children will hold on to them tenaciously because they are strongly rooted in their own belief and perceptual systems. Such conceptions are resistant to change despite effective teaching. For instance, Lisa, one of our preservice teachers, wanted her grade 3 students to understand that "shadows are formed as a result of the blocking of light." Despite the many activities that Lisa carried out to contradict the belief that "shadows are part of you," children continued to believe that their shadows sleep with them and go wherever they go.

Such strongly held beliefs and inclinations may interfere with classroom learning. It is not that children do not want to change their conceptions,

Making shadow figures is often a spontaneous activity of young children.

but cultural, linguistic, and perceptual meanings and reasoning eclipse teacher explanations. Children might write the teacher-given explanations to pass tests, but they find personal comfort in their *own* meanings as these remain logical, reasonable, and sensible. The scientists' ideas in this case lead to a conflict of values and beliefs. However, children should be taught to distinguish between their reasoning and the scientists' point of view. It should be stressed that science provides another way of thinking.

Reasons for Exploring Children's Conceptions

Exploring students' conceptions before teaching a unit is therefore important for several reasons:

- To identify the qualitatively different meanings children attach to a natural phenomenon or socioscientific issue.
- To shape and reshape a teacher's thinking, decision making, and actions, and thus the curriculum.
- To reinforce to children that their ideas are important. Children gain feelings of personal worth when their ideas are valued by their peers and the teacher.
- To increase interest in the subject matter. When children see the relevancy of subject matter to concepts they already hold, they are more eager to become intrinsically involved.
- To encourage children to take control of their learning right from the beginning. Children are more apt to do this if they are shown how to work toward finding solutions.

Children need to take ownership of ideas. They must feel responsible for outcomes. As they continue to search for ways of resolving conceptual conflicts, they will experience new ideas and even birth new conflicts. For these reasons, it is essential to explore children's ideas carefully and thoroughly. It is the first important step in using the Common Knowledge Construction Model for teaching.

Guidelines for Exploring Children's Conceptions

We suggest the following guidelines for the exploration of children's ideas:

- Choose a relevant activity for exploring children's conceptions.
- Keep the initial exploration simple.
- Provide a supportive environment.
- Respect children's ideas.
- Take time to make sense of children's conceptions.
- Reflect upon children's ideas with conceptual empathy.

Choose a Relevant Activity for Exploring Children's Conceptions

Choosing a relevant activity for exploring children's ideas before a unit is very important. This activity must reflect the key physical or biological

Teaching Standard D

Guideline: Design and manage the learning environment by engaging students in designing their own learning environment.

Choose an exploration activity that will cover most of the concepts in a unit. After you have covered a few lessons in a unit, there will be a need for another exploration activity. Sometimes each inquiry might begin with a brief exploration phase. You will notice that you as well as your students are constantly checking their understanding as you carry out this unit.

Construct a Vee diagram for heating of an ice cube to explain the key ideas of the physical processes involved.

concepts and processes of the topic. Therefore, an important step is to identify the concepts and processes and draw a concept map. Then you can see how concepts are related. For example, in a unit on matter, the key concepts are solid, liquid, and gas. The physical processes are freezing, melting, and evaporating. A simple activity that illustrates these three concepts is gently heating an ice cube. A starting question could be, "What happens to the ice cube when it is heated?" Subsequent questions might include, "Where is the water?" "What happened to it?"

Keep the Initial Exploration Activity Simple

Teaching Standard D

Teachers of science design and manage learning environments that provide students with the time, space, and resources needed for learning science.

Plan a simple activity or two that sustains interest and lasts only 20 to 40 minutes, depending on the topic and the age of the children. Have students focus on this activity, which might be a science investigation, a demonstration, some pictures, or video clips.

During your activity, ask open-ended questions and, based on students' responses, develop further questions. Your questions must be carefully worded, using language that children can understand. Allow the conversation to take a natural course. Do not jump from question to question. Develop some *key questions* before the exploration lesson and use them where appropriate. Keep the line of inquiry flowing for each question until it comes to a natural conclusion. Refrain from just asking such questions as, "What do you mean by *sound*?" or "What can you tell me about energy?" Students are often intimidated by these questions and assume that you are asking for textbook knowledge. Some suggestions follow:

- What do you notice about this?
- What do you think will happen?
- Why do you think that happened?
- Can you think of other reasons?

Teaching Standard D

Guideline: Design and manage the learning environment by creating a setting for student work that is flexible and supportive of inquiry.

Sometimes children's ideas may intimidate us and make us feel inadequate because of our lack of understanding of the science concepts involved. We must still be willing to explore children's ideas. This is why we encourage you to develop your science content knowledge by constructing concept maps and Vee diagrams.

Provide a Supportive Environment

For children to be open and honest and to express their ideas freely, we ought to provide them with a learning environment that encourages and values their contributions. With such a classroom atmosphere, children will come to realize that all their ideas are acceptable and won't worry if their ideas do not appear logical to others. Children's ideas will open up whole new avenues of thought and action from both students and teacher, producing some very rewarding results and interesting inroads.

Respect Children's Ideas

Children may have ideas contrary to our beliefs and ways of thinking. It is quite common and natural to want to intervene right away and express our views, but patience and suspension of judgment are two imperative attributes we need to exercise. However, during the constructing and negotiating phase of our Common Knowledge Construction Model, we should strike a balance between waiting for conceptual change to occur naturally and helping students reach the zone of proximal development, as pointed out in chapter 4. Premature intervention, however, is not appropriate.

Take Time to Make Sense of Children's Conceptions

The first activity of a new unit or lesson you set up for your class is exploratory, done only to access children's prior conceptions/knowledge. Our experience informs us that we should *not* mix this pre-unit exploration activity with activities designed to develop common knowledge. *Teachers need time to reflect upon children's ideas before any constructing and negotiating of meaning, the second phase in our Common Knowledge Construction Model.*

Reflect Upon Children's Conceptions With Conceptual Empathy

It is important to examine children's ideas and reflect upon them with conceptual empathy. These ideas should not be explored with a view to determine what children know or do not know about a topic. As teachers, we are not trying to determine how much factual information children have stored in their memory, but to find out students' "ways of seeing."

If we explore children's ideas to judge their worth, we may overlook the meaning children attach to a natural phenomenon. The role of children's ideas in the teaching/learning process is undermined when our mission is simply a matter of altering "misconceptions." Our goal should be to make sense of students' conceptions and to provide meaningful experiences that will allow them to explore qualitatively different explanations for a given phenomenon.

☀ STRATEGIES FOR EXPLORING CHILDREN'S CONCEPTIONS

Research provides a number of useful methods to explore children's ideas. It is worthwhile to examine some of these strategies through preservice teachers' direct experiences. When we explore children's ideas as part of our teaching, we become both researchers and learners about what children are thinking. Not only may we learn or construct meaning during a lesson, but we may also learn some science concepts as we explore our own understandings.

Once children's conceptions have been obtained, it is necessary to examine them closely to see if they form any patterns. All their responses should be taken into account and categories made. How these categories fit the objectives in the curriculum can then be examined. Children's ideas should be the basis for planning for teaching.

Two main strategies for exploring children's conceptions are the POE strategy and children's classification systems.

Our preservice teachers have found it very useful to make an audiotape or videotape of an exploration lesson, then analyze a transcript. This exercise offers powerful insights into what children are thinking and the language they use to communicate their understanding. It also reveals a teacher's questioning techniques.

Teaching Standard E

Guideline: To develop a community of science learners, display and demand respect for diverse skills, ideas, and experiences of all students.

Professional Development Standard B

Guideline: Learning experiences for teachers of science must occur in a variety of places where effective science teaching can be illustrated and modeled, permitting teachers to struggle with real situations and expand their knowledge and skills in appropriate contests.

See chapter 4 for a method of categorizing students' ideas.

108 PART TWO   The Common Knowledge Construction Model

Prediction, Observation, and Explanation (POE) Strategy

Prediction means making intelligent guesses, observation means seeing through the use of all our senses, and explanation means advancing theories about a phenomenon.

One strategy a teacher can use to explore children's ideas is the **prediction, observation,** and **explanation** (POE) method originated by White and Gunstone and described in their book, *Probing Understanding* (1992). In the POE technique, children are presented with a system and asked to *predict, observe,* and *explain* what happens when an activity is carried out. For example, they can be asked to predict, observe, and explain what will happen when physical or chemical change occurs. The general POE format is as follows:

In this activity the tablet is an acidic substance. The liquid is a solution of phenolphthalein indicator in water. This activity is appropriate for students grades 3–4 and can be used to explore their concepts in solubility and solutions.

1. **Ask students a question about an event about to happen.** For example: "What will happen if I place this white tablet in the glass of liquid?"
2. **Have students make a prediction.** Either have them make an open-ended prediction or have them choose from one of several you have listed. These can be obtained from predictions students have given previously. For example:
   a. It will dissolve.
   b. It will crumble when water touches it.
   c. It will sink to the bottom.
   d. It will disappear.
3. **Ask students to give a reason for their prediction.** For example, if they picked (c), they might write, "The tablet is heavy."
4. **Have students write down their observations as the event happens.** For example, "The tablet completely dissolved and the water turned pink."
5. **Have students try to explain what happened.** For example, "The tablet consists of a substance that makes the water pink."

The correct answer is that the tablet consists of an acidic substance and dissolves in an indicator that turns pink when an acid is present.

An important aspect of the POE strategy is that students must decide on the explanation they will apply to the event. Their explanation may not coincide with initial ideas expressed in their prediction, so they must use new reasons to explain and interpret the event. You can record the children's initial ideas on paper for immediate and future reference. Another method is to have students write their ideas in "think" journals. An initial step might be a teacher-students conversation, followed by the children's committing their ideas to writing. Yet another POE method is individual or group exploration of a natural phenomenon, with the children then writing their ideas in their science "think" journals and sharing them with the teacher or the whole class. You may want to respond to students' journals.

Preservice teachers' ways of exploring children's ideas should not be perceived as expert examples. Case studies are primarily reflections about preservice teachers' observations and interpretations.

Teachers have found all these POE combinations useful. The following case studies illustrate variations of preservice teachers' use of the POE strategy with curricular topics at different grade levels to explore children's ideas.

5-1: Exploring *Grade 4/5* Children's Ideas on *Dissolving*

Cheryl Reznick

Preservice Teacher Practice

Prior to placing a few Kool-Aid crystals in a glass of water, I asked my students, "What do you think will happen when these crystals are added to water?" Some students predicted, "They will disappear," "They will melt," and "They will dissolve." It is interesting that quite often when students are asked to clarify what they mean by "dissolve," they say the "substance melting into the water."

I then proceeded to add the Kool-Aid crystals to the water while the students observed. I asked the students to explain (orally and in writing) what happens to the crystals when added to water. Here are some of their responses:

TEACHER: What has happened to the crystals?

TRACEY: They dissolved.

ALAN: Some went to the bottom and sank. Some went into the water, and a bit went to the top because you didn't stir it yet.

TEACHER: What happened to the crystals that went into the water, Alan?

ALAN: It melted and changed the water color.

TEACHER: What do you think happened to the crystals, Jimmy?

JIMMY: The crystals dissolved.

TEACHER: How? Can you explain what you mean by that word *dissolve*?

JIMMY: They went smaller and smaller and smaller and then went away.

Children's Work

Here are some of the children's journal accounts with regard to Kool-Aid entering the water environment:

- They melted into the water and the powder change [changed] the water colors to clear to red pink. Because when sugar crystals tuch [touch] water it melts and turns into liquid and the powder turns the water colors.
- The crystals dissolved into colors. The presher [pressure] in the water melted the crystals.

The chemical process in a unit on solutions is *dissolving*. Cheryl has chosen an activity to depict this process.

- The crystals melted. When a solid tuchs [touches] a liquid it transforms into a liquid because the solid touched the liquid.
- The water soaked threw (through) the crystals and melted.

Personal Reflections

From a careful study of children's ideas, I was able to create two categories of children's ideas on the dissolving aspect of Kool-Aid crystals in water:

1. The crystals *melted* because:
   a. they touched the water and turned into a liquid;
   b. of water pressure;
   c. when a solid touches a liquid it turns into a liquid;
   d. the water soaked through them.
2. The crystals *dissolved* because they went smaller and smaller and smaller and then went away.

Using these categories as an aid for planning my subsequent lessons, I focused on the processes of melting and dissolving. I thought that it was necessary to provide the children with various experiences dealing with both melting and dissolving, and to help children understand the qualitative differences between these two processes.

A common conception that children have is that the Kool-Aid crystals melted. Children often explain dissolving as a process of melting because the resulting solution is in the liquid state. Hence, subsequent scientific inquiries should focus on the physical processes of melting and dissolving and distinguish between the two. Now, if you do not have sufficient chemistry background to know the difference between these two processes, construct a Vee diagram for the same activity that Cheryl conducted with her students. Also draw a concept map that relates the chemical concepts in this activity.

In this lesson, we are attempting to progress through the zone of proximal development by scientific inquiry through investigations and science communal talk.

BOX 5-1

A Lesson to Distinguish Between Melting and Dissolving

To show the difference between *melting* and *dissolving,* melt ice, wax, and butter. Add sugar, salt, Kool-Aid, and other substances that dissolve to water. Establish that when *melting* takes place, the solid is transformed into its liquid state. In *dissolving,* a solution is formed when a substance (sugar) is added to another substance (water). A solution appears the same throughout—you will not see distinct parts as when, for example, you put sand into water and the sand settles at the bottom of the container. Also, the substances can be mixed in any proportions.

After students understand the difference between melting and dissolving, carry out the following assessment: Have children in small groups pour the same amount of water into two glasses. To one glass, add a cube of ice. To the other glass of water, add a cube of sugar. Have children conduct peer discourse about their observations. Then have children share their findings with the rest of the class as you lead the discussion to distinguish between melting and dissolving.

5-2: Exploring *Grade 3* Children's Ideas of *Heat*

Phillipe Lajoie

Preservice Teacher Practice

I explored my students' ideas of *heat* with the following activity. I placed a wax bead on one end of a steel rod. I supported the rod in the middle by a stand. Then I placed a candle flame under the other end of the rod. The students recorded their predictions in their "science learning log" and then shared their ideas with the class. Then they viewed the demonstration and wrote down what they observed. A short discussion followed, in which the students shared their ideas as to why the wax bead fell off the end of the rod.

The children's predictions regarding what would happen when the metal rod with the wax bead was heated are summarized in Table 5-1.

Children's Work

After the experiment, the wax was seen to fall off the rod. The children wrote in their learning logs an explanation for what they had seen. The reasons the children gave for what they had observed were as follows:

* The heat made the wax sweaty and it fell off the rod.
* The wax melted and fell off because the rod got hot.
* The rod turned black because it was hot.
* The heat from the candle traveled through the rod and melted the wax.
* The wax got hot and fell off.

This exploration activity helps students to inquire about the materials that are good conductors and bad conductors of heat. If you want to focus on the nature of heat or how heat travels, then the following activity should be done and suitable questions asked: Heat the end of a rod with a candle. Ask your students, "How does heat travel? How does it get hot?"

TABLE 5-1

Grade 3 Children's Predictions About Heating the Rod

Children's Predictions	The Number of Students Who Responded (Total = 21)
The rod will get hot and the wax will melt.	5
The wax will melt.	4
The flame is going to burn out.	8
The rod is going to turn colors.	2
The wax is going to fall off the rod.	2
I think that the middle of the rod is going to light up.	2
The rod is going to get hot and burn the wax.	2

Personal Reflections

Most of the students' responses dealt with the melting of the wax. The majority of students thought that the wax melted because of the hot rod. Only one student took this explanation further, suggesting that the heat traveled through the rod to melt the wax. I planned my future lessons to help students understand that metals are good conductors of heat and wood and plastic are bad conductors of heat. I also developed lessons on the everyday applications of conductors and insulators.

CASE STUDY

5-3: Exploring *Grade 5* Children's Ideas on *Chemical Reactions*

Heather Wiens Kroeker

Preservice Teacher Practice

This is a good activity to explore children's ideas about chemical reactions because bubbles are produced. Chalk consists of calcium carbonate. When a dilute acid (vinegar—acetic acid in water) is added to a carbonate, carbon dioxide is liberated. To develop your content knowledge, read about changes in matter, particularly chemical changes. What can you substitute for chalk in this activity to produce the same results?

I wanted to find out what my students' ideas were about how rocks are changed by chemical reactions. I showed them a piece of chalk and a glass one-quarter filled with vinegar. I asked for their prediction: "What do you think will happen to the vinegar, the chalk, and the glass?" Students were asked to choose from a list of several predictions that a previous group of students had suggested. Their predictions are found in Table 5-2.

TABLE 5-2

Grade 5 Predictions About Chalk Added to Vinegar

	Number of Students
Acid (vinegar)	
It will turn white.	12
It will evaporate.	2
It will bubble.	8
Chalk	
It will crack or break.	6
It will dissolve.	12
It will expand.	4
Glass	
It will have a white residue in it.	10
It will stay the same.	12
It will shatter.	0

Children's Work

Examples of children's reasons for their predictions given in Table 5-2 follow:

ACID (VINEGAR)

- The vinegar would turn white because when you put the chalk in the vinegar and crush it up, the vinegar will turn white.
- All liquids evaporate. I think the chalk will speed up the process.
- I know the vinegar causes a lot of things to bubble. In grade 2 we put baking soda in vinegar and it bubbled.

CHALK

- The chalk will break because the water puts pressure on it.
- Vinegar is a stronger substance than the chalk, that's why vinegar dissolves it.
- The vinegar will get into the air holes in the chalk.

GLASS

- The glass will get white stuff on it because the chalk will dissolve and stick to the sides.
- My Mom uses vinegar to wipe her windows, so I know it doesn't break the glass. The chalk can't make the glass dirty because vinegar takes away the dirt.

Some of their observations of the activity were as follows:

- I saw the chalk get eaten by the vinegar.
- At first the chalk cracked, then broke down and dissolved and the vinegar bubbled.
- The chalk made bubbles and then broke.

Students were then asked to explain the reasons for their observations in a journal report. Some of them follow:

- Today we put chalk in vinegar. From this I learned that vinegar makes a chemical reaction with the chalk and that's why it forms bubbles.
- We poured vinegar in a glass and dropped in the chalk and watched what would happen. The stuff in the vinegar changes when it comes in contact with the chalk.
- I learned that chalk and vinegar have opposite qualities, when they are put together they clash forming bubbles. My teacher told me the bubbles were carbon dioxide.

Personal Reflections

By using the POE strategy, children develop a greater understanding of their personal ideas. Conceptual reorganization takes place as the students have to provide reasons for their predictions and then explain what happened. It is more than doing an experiment or absorbing lectured information. The students have to take responsibility for their learning when asked to give reasons. Journal writing within the POE strategy has tremendous

Professional Development Standard A

Guideline: Science learning experiences for teachers must incorporate ongoing reflection on the process and outcomes of understanding science through inquiry.

benefits. Students are required to figure things out in their own way and are not penalized for not getting the "right" answer.

One problem with the strategy was that some children had difficulty giving reasons. They said, "... because it just happened." What surprised me were the questions they asked. Many were well thought out and reflected a desire to learn. I felt as if I had motivated them to learn more. From their questions, I was able to design follow-up lessons. Their questions were as follows:

- What other stuff will acid break?
- If there is acid in the rain, will it damage statues and buildings?
- How fast will rocks and minerals get weak from acid?
- Why do bubbles come up from the chalk when you put it in the vinegar?
- What is chalk made from?
- What makes an acid an acid and a base a base?
- Where do you find limestone?
- What exactly is a chemical reaction?

Discussion of the POE Explorations

All three preservice teachers had chosen activities in physical science to illustrate key physical processes: *dissolving, heat,* and *chemical reactions.* Preservice teachers developed their science content knowledge by reading high school textbooks and constructing concept maps and Vee diagrams. As a result, they were able to choose appropriate activities for developing children's ideas.

The POE strategy was good for exploring children's conceptions of these physical concepts because all three events are from children's experiential worlds. Otherwise, children will not be able to predict. So we learn from these teachers that POE activities must be from children's everyday experiences.

The teachers demonstrated the activity after having students make their predictions. In Case Study 5-1, the teacher held a discussion about their observations and had them write their observations in their journals. In Case Study 5-2, the students recorded their predictions in their journals and shared their ideas with the class. Then, after children observed the wax on the hot rod, the teacher asked them to write in their science learning logs.

In Case Study 5-3, students were asked to choose from predictions that a previous group of students had given. Then they had to write the reasons for these predictions as well as for their observations.

In all three case studies, children were expected to express themselves in written language as well as in class discussions. What we learn here is that journal writing is a reliable way of gathering children's ideas. Further, more than one source of data is important for validation of children's ideas.

The preservice teachers could have asked children to conduct the exploration activity in small groups and to answer focus questions in their journal. They could then have had students report their journal entries to the larger group. In this method, the teacher should ask questions such as, "What do you mean by *dissolving, melting?*" "How do you think heat travels?"

If the teacher conducts the POE activity, he or she can immediately ask students what they mean by certain expressions and have them give examples. The lesson we learn here is that children's ideas should be explored in different ways.

Science Teacher Educators' Comments

White and Gunstone (1992) propose that prediction, observation, and explanation (POE) is an excellent strategy to help students illuminate their beliefs. The teacher-students discussion that follows a POE activity should help reconcile any conflict created when the result did not coincide with student predictions. The teacher should not give scientific explanations at this time but hold back until the constructing and negotiating phase, when many more experiences will be provided for further scientific inquiry.

A POE strategy falls within a constructivist tradition because it seeks predictions and explanations for a given phenomenon. Although careful observation is a necessary condition for POE, students often use only their perceptual reasoning to govern their explanations. And, too often, what students "see" contradicts scientific explanations. For example, when children observe a charged plastic comb picking up tiny bits of paper or sawdust, they often say that the comb acts like a magnet and it is able to attract objects. This knowledge comes from their experience with magnets.

We should not, however, expect children to construct or "discover" by themselves theoretical entities such as atoms, positive charges (protons) and negative charges (electrons), induction, and transfer of charges. Such technical vocabulary may not be necessary at the elementary level, but understanding of these concepts may be developed through appropriate analogies and by "humanizing science" through drama activities.

We have observed that preservice teachers who practice a constructivist approach for the first time are dismayed when they do not hear children uttering the discipline-based, specialized language found in textbooks. When specialized language is not part of children's vocabulary—when preservice teachers do not hear what they expect to hear—they tend to classify such children as not knowing anything or naive. We believe that constructivist teaching does not begin with the notion that children are naive due to lack of scientific vocabulary. Constructivist teaching also does not expect children to construct all of the theoretical entities on their own. Children as novice learners must learn the cultural givens from the teacher-expert. Personal meaning-making within a social medium enhances common knowledge construction.

We suggest some cautions and conditions when using a POE strategy:

- Students must understand the nature of the event that is to happen. It should not be a *trick demonstration* or a *magic show.* Allow them to ask questions to clarify their understanding of the materials and procedures to be used.
- Be sure all students have *written down* their *predictions* and their *explanations,* as students should commit themselves to a position. Encourage students not to say "I don't know."
- Be sure all students *write down* their own *personal observations,* as different students may see different things. Other students may convince

them that they did not see what they said they did if they have not committed their observations to paper.

- Students may have difficulty explaining the discrepancy between what they observed and what they predicted. Encourage them to consider all possibilities, as these will reveal their understandings.

PEER INTERACTION

Reading the Literature for Exploration Activities

You now know how preservice teachers explored children's ideas. For the same or different topics, read science education journal articles to find out how experts explore children's ideas. Describe their activities. State their questions. List their findings and provide examples of children's expressions and diagrams. What have the experts learned as a result of their study with children? Share this information with your peers in class.

Interactive Discussion

Interactive discussion is an integral part of the prediction and explanation stages of a POE strategy. In this pattern of discourse, the teacher allows students to discuss their ideas and puzzle over them. The teacher must learn to question subtly in order to bring out students' ideas in a climate of acceptance.

Erickson (1992) relates how a science study group has devised some basic ideas to help develop skills for carrying out interactive discussion during an exploration activity. Students must believe that they all will be heard, that their opinions will be respected by both their teacher and their peers, and that constructive disagreement will be respected. Students must understand the value of listening and reacting to other students' ideas. The rules this group established are as follows:

- Delay judgment.
- Increase wait time between questions and answers and between statements by participants.
- Listen to what everyone says and, if necessary, check your understanding of their meaning.
- Use encouragement lavishly (Erickson, 1992, p. 1).

In the following case study, the preservice teacher holds a lengthy interactive discussion with her students after conducting a POE-style demonstration.

Professional Development Standard B

Guideline: Learning experiences for teachers of science must use inquiry, reflection, interpretation of research, modeling, and guided practice to build understanding and skill in science teaching.

5-4: Exploring Children's Ideas About *Flotation*

Gloria Yaremkiewich

Preservice Teacher Practice

I explored my *grade 2* students' ideas of *flotation* through a demonstration using a glass bowl placed in front of the chalkboard and a 1-cm-long paper clip. I used the POE strategy, carrying on a conversational-type exploration with the students and recording their ideas on paper. The following is the transcription of the part of my exploration activities that I audiotaped:

TEACHER: I would like to find out what each one of you thinks will happen if I put this paper clip into this bowl of water. Put your thinking caps on and think hard.

LYNN: I guess it'll sink.

TEACHER: Lynn, what do you mean by "sink"?

LYNN: It will go to the bottom.

TEACHER: How many of you agree with Lynn? If you do, show me by lifting up your hand. Okay, let's count: 1, 2, 3, … 19 of you agree that it will sink.

JUSTIN: I think it'll float.

TEACHER: Justin, what do you mean by "float"?

JUSTIN: Well, you know, stay on the top of the water, like, like I do when I swim.

TEACHER: Good for you, Justin. How many of you agree with Justin? (No one agrees.)

TEACHER: Well, that's all right, Justin, scientists don't always agree with each other. They know that there is never a wrong nor a right way to do things. Just remember, when we do these experiments no one is right or wrong. Does anyone have any more ideas or guesses? No one has any more ideas? Well, then, does anyone know what we can call these guesses or ideas? (3-s silence)

TEACHER: We could call them "predictions." That means all of us were just predicting what might happen. Now we should try it, or, like the scientists say, "test it."

KITTY: Can I drop the paper clip into the water?

TEACHER: Are we ready to see what will happen? Okay, Kitty, you may drop the paper clip whenever the whole class is ready. (Kitty drops the paper clip into the water.)

TEACHER: What happened to the paper clip?

CLASS: It sank, it sank, we were right.

TEACHER: Good for you, but remember what I said about right and wrong. (Because of the disappointment in Justin's face, I realized that the first lesson must be to prove that he, too, could be right.)

TEACHER: Okay, now that we tested it, let's think why the paper clip sank.

NEIL: It's heavy.

TEACHER: Does anyone else have any other explanation why it sank?

LYNN: It is made of metal and metal is very heavy.

TOMMY: Because it is made from metal and metal can't float.

TEACHER: Any other explanations to add on this paper? We're going to keep these chart papers up so that we could always look back to them if we need to.

GARRY: It has a hole in it.

JOHN: Wait! Boats can float.

TEACHER: Why are you saying boats can float? What does that have to do with what we're talking about?

JOHN: Because a boat if it has holes, it'll sink, but if it doesn't have holes, it doesn't sink.

TEACHER: Thanks, John. Do you have any other ideas you'd like to share with the class? (He shakes his head and remains puzzled.)

ARTI: The paper clip isn't made from metal—it is made from wire, and wire is thin, so it sinks.

LORI: It has a funny shape.

ASHI: It's small.

MARK: It doesn't weigh anything—see? It's light.

TEACHER: So if it's light and not heavy, would that make a difference?

MARK: No. Maybe yeah. I don't know. Uh, light things should float.

KATE: It sank because it has holes in it and the water goes through it.... My dad has a boat. We go on the lake a lot. It's made from metal and my dad can hardly push it off the trailer. It can float—how come?

TEACHER: What do you think?

KATE: Well, Tommy said—see at the top (pointing to the chart paper)—metal is heavy and that's why the paper clip sank. I don't know.

DANIEL: A washer is made from metal and I saw a washer float.

MIKE: What is a washer?

DANIEL: You know, it screws on a bolt.

TEACHER: Daniel, would you like to explain to the whole class
what you saw?

DANIEL: One day I was in the garage with my dad—you know, he
works in a garage, he is a mechanic. He was fixing a car and he
asked me to pass him a washer. I dropped it into a can of oil. I
got real scared, but it stayed on top so I just pulled it out.

TEACHER: Why do you think that the washer stayed at the top and
didn't sink? It has a hole, it is made from metal.

DANA: Because it, it doesn't look like a paper clip, it's round and a
washer, uhhhh, is flat.

TEACHER: So do you think that if I took the same thing, say the paper
clip, would it sink in the oil like it sank in the water?

LISE: Yeah, it would sink because oil and water are kind of the same.

TEACHER: Does anyone have any other explanations why the paper clip
sank? Okay, then, now I'd like to go over all the different
explanations and see how many of you agree with them.

Children's Work

At this point in our discussion, I proceeded to take a count to see how many
agreed with the ideas given by others (see Table 5-3). We tallied the fre-
quency distribution and recorded these ideas.

TABLE 5-3

Grade 2 Children's Ideas About *Flotation*

Children's Ideas About Why Things Float	N = 20
It's heavy.	5
It is made of metal and metal is heavy.	14
It is made from metal and metal can't float.	4
It has a hole in it.	15
Boats can float.	18
Because a boat, if it has holes, it'll sink, but if it doesn't have holes, it doesn't sink.	16
It is made from wire and wire is thin so it sinks.	13
It has a funny shape.	18
It's small.	13
It doesn't weigh anything—see? It's light.	8
Light things should float.	11
It has holes in it and the water goes through it.	20
My dad's boat is made from metal. He can hardly push it. It can float.	6
A washer is made from metal and I saw a washer float.	2
It (paper clip) would sink (in the oil) because oil and water are kind of the same.	16

Personal Reflections

I taped the entire lesson as well as wrote the students' ideas on the chalkboard. Thus I had two sources for children's ideas. It was a difficult process of transcribing the audiotape, as it takes at least 3 to 4 hours to transcribe a 1-hour-long tape. However, it was very useful for me to have done this because now I can see the richness of my conversation with the students. I can judge whether I asked appropriate questions, note how I can improve on my questioning techniques, observe how I responded to girls as well as boys, note whether I was giving fair turns to all students and whether I remained neutral or gave praise by saying "good" when I hear what I like to hear. Also, I could analyze how much I talk as compared to the students' talk.

The students had many different ideas about flotation. They believed that the following factors related to the ability of objects to either float or sink:

- Lightness/heaviness
- Holes/no holes
- Type of object (e.g., boats float)
- Shape
- Size
- Material (e.g., metal, wire)

Interactive discussion was very useful for me as an exploration device. I was very surprised at what the students knew, and the richness of the interaction was very enlightening. For the lessons to follow, I would have to provide activities to help them sort out each of these factors, one at a time.

BOX 5-2

A Small-Group Exploration Activity for Flotation

Ask children to bring six objects from home that they want to test for floating. Have them test each object based on the following criteria:

- I think it will float.
- I wonder if it will float.
- I think it will sink.
- I wonder if it will sink.

Be sure to tell students that the objects cannot be any bigger than their hands, or you might be in for a surprise when Jonny walks in with a close-to-life-sized boat!

In this activity, place children in heterogeneous groups of six. Give each group a tub of water and each child a teacher-prepared "flotation" journal. Ask children to test each one of their objects to see whether it will float. After testing their objects, ask children to do the following:

- Draw what they saw in their journal.
- Write a few sentences to tell what happened to their objects.
- Write why the object was able to float or sink.

Journal Writing

Children's writing was used to explore students' prior conceptions in several of the POE lessons. Writing helps children think about their ideas and clarify their thinking. In the following case study, **journal writing** is used in conjunction with a picture, questions, and a problem-solving scenario.

Journal writing is children's free expression of their feelings or thoughts.

Various types of journal writing are described in detail in chapter 6. In this section, we will just examine one preservice teacher's example of journal writing done in the exploratory phase of teaching.

CASE STUDY

5-5: Exploring *Grade 6* Children's Ideas About the *Nature of the Earth*

Gerry Haines

Preservice Teacher Practice

In my *grade 6* class, we were beginning a unit on *Earth, Moon, and Stars.* I wanted to find out what my students' conceptions were of the horizon and the spherical nature of the earth. I showed them a picture of a horizon. I asked students to think about the following questions:

- What is the horizon?
- What objects are close? Far away?
- How can you tell?

Then I gave them the following statement: "The earth is flat." I told them to respond to this statement in their diaries. Then I directed a short investigation as follows:

1. Have students look at eye level along the flat surface of a table. Give them each a toy boat, and have them move this toy boat slowly away from themselves and describe what they see. Have them record their observations in their journals.
2. Have students look at eye level at a globe. Repeat the same procedure as before, moving the toy boat slowly away, around the globe. Have students record their observations in their journals.
3. Engage students in a discussion of their observations in both situations. Have students record their understanding about the horizon and the shape of the globe.

Children's Work

The students seemed to already have grasped many of the concepts with which I was concerned (Figure 5-1).

FIGURE 5-1
A child's journal writing

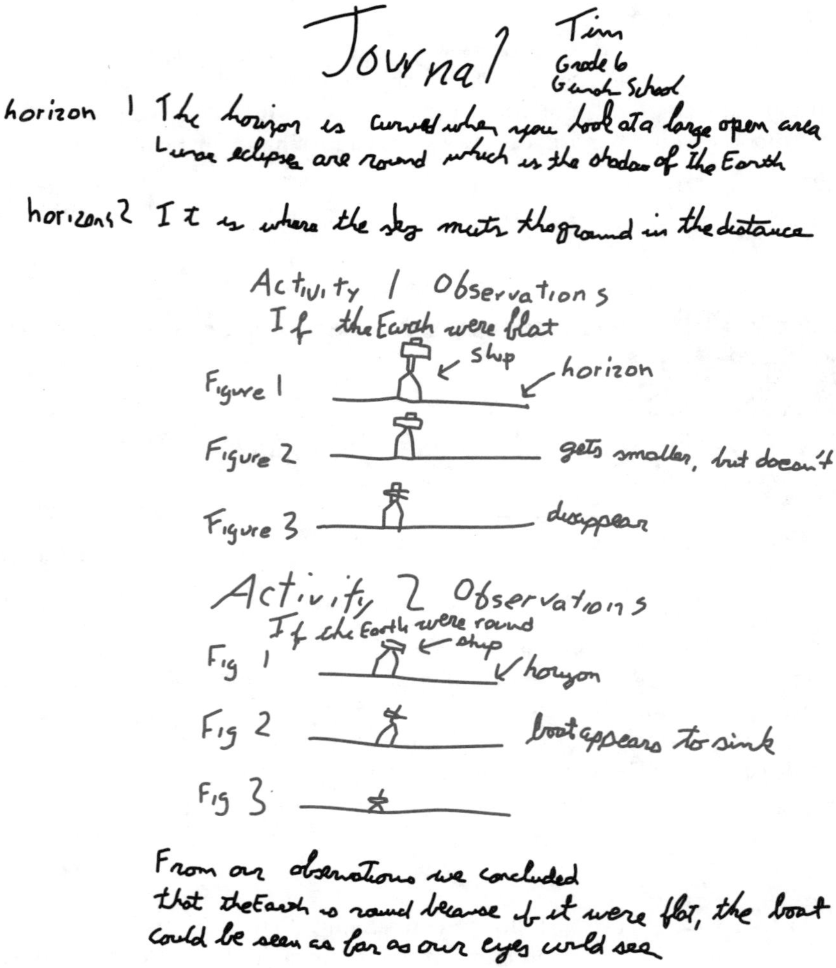

Journal   Tim
                                           Grade 6
                                           Gench School

horizon 1 The horizon is curved when you look at a large open area
Lunar eclipse are round which is the shadow of the Earth

horizons 2 It is where the sky meets the ground in the distance

Activity 1 Observations
If the Earth were flat
Figure 1 _____ ship   horizon
Figure 2 _____ gets smaller, but doesn't
Figure 3 _____ disappear

Activity 2 Observations
If the Earth were round
Fig 1 _____ ship   horizon
Fig 2 _____ boat appears to sink
Fig 3 _____

From our observations we concluded
that the Earth is round because if it were flat, the boat
could be seen as far as our eyes could see

Personal Reflections

Journals (or learning logs, as some call them) are a great way of having students become active learners in their classroom. Students should be encouraged to put their own personal responses in their journals. Teachers can gain valuable information about students' beliefs from their journals. Journal entries completed before performing a science activity or lesson allow teachers to assess children's prior knowledge about a certain concept or topic. Once children record predictions for the activity, these journal entries should be shared with peers through discussion. During this time, the teacher must be carefully listening to what the students are saying to gain an understanding of the children's ideas.

Journal analysis can give the teacher insight into the affective issues relating to the students. The teacher should be able to sense students' general disposition toward science in general or a particular science topic. Journal writing allows students to take ownership of their learning. I was surprised at the ease with which the children seemed to accept doing journal writing. I was very surprised to find out that they had not had any experience with journals, so I expected some difficulties with their responses. They were amazed when I told them that I wanted to know how they felt about these science topics.

Some students do have difficulty in expressing themselves. Therefore, you should be cautious in relying solely on journal responses for assessing student knowledge. However, for my class, using journal drawings proved a valid way for students to predict and explain their observations.

Children's Diagrams

Most children enjoy making drawings, and these provide an excellent basis for discussion with peers or the teacher. Children's drawings can assist a teacher to "see into the mind" of a learner, particularly learners who have difficulty expressing themselves verbally.

Several educators have used children's drawings to explore children's conceptions about the solar system. This involves a number of related conceptual areas and the understanding of spatial aspects of the earth, conceptions of day and night, and seasonal changes. For example, Jones and Lynch (1987) from Tasmania described a study investigating children's views of the shape, size, and motion of the earth, moon, and sun. They collected data by interviewing the children using various shapes such as spheres, hemispheres, circular discs, etc. They found that grade 3 to grade 6 children's understanding fell into the five distinct concept systems shown in Figure 5-2: the earth-centered magic model, the spinning earth-centered model, the earth-centered model with orbiting sun and/or moon, the sun-centered model with orbiting earth and/or moon, and the sun-centered model with orbiting earth and with moon orbiting earth.

The sixth-grade children chose the last (correct) model more often than did the third-grade children. Their understanding of the shape of solar system objects fell into three categories: two-dimensional shapes, a mixture of two- and three-dimensional shapes, and all spheres. Most grade 6 children were correct, but less than half of the grade 3 children were. With respect to the relative sizes of the solar objects, less than half of the grade 6 children were correct, and fewer still of the younger ones were. Jones and Lynch said that these beliefs are the result of the interaction among children's concepts derived from the perception of natural phenomena and science presented by teachers, textbooks, and the media.

FIGURE 5-2
Children's models of the relationships of the earth, moon, and sun and their relative movements during one year (NOTE. From Jones, B., and Lynch, P. (1987). Children's conceptions of the earth, sun, and moon. *International Journal of Science Education, 9*(1), 47.)

Model 1: Earth-centered magic model

Model 2: Spinning earth-centered model

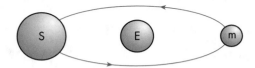

Model 3: Earth-centered model with orbiting sun and/or moon

Model 4: Sun-centered model with orbiting earth and/or moon

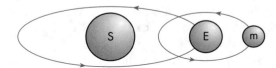

Model 5: Sun-centered model with orbiting earth and with moon orbiting earth

These findings are not surprising considering that most young children view the world from an earth-centered perspective, as did early astronomers. It took many centuries of mathematical and theoretical studies for the sun-centered view to be widely accepted. When Galileo, following the ideas of Aristarchus and Copernicus, proposed a sun-centered solar system, he was disgraced and excommunicated for his views. However, children's drawings do help to illuminate their personal knowledge in order to plan the teaching procedures we will need to use to help negotiate meaning with our students.

CASE STUDY

5-6: Exploring *Grade 5* Children's Ideas About *Gravity* in Relation to the Earth

Susan Atkins

Preservice Teacher Practice

I had the students draw pictures to help express their ideas about how they believed gravity operated to hold objects down to the surface of the earth. First we talked about the shape of the earth, and then I asked them to draw a picture of the globe and show in what direction the force of gravity acted on it.

Children's Work

The children's diagrams (Figure 5-3) revealed some of their thinking about how gravity related to the sphere of the earth.

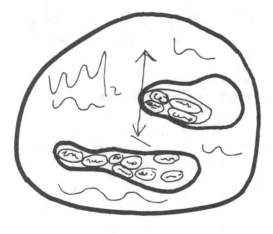

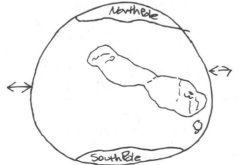

FIGURE 5-3
Children's drawings of gravity and the earth

The arrows in the diagrams indicate the force gravity exerts both vertically and horizontally on the earth.

Personal Reflections

My students' diagrams help explain some of the discussion we had previously. It was difficult for some to put into words what they understood about gravity and the direction in which the force acted. Many students found it much easier to make diagrams than to describe what they thought. Future lessons would be planned to clarify and expand their notions about gravity and how it is related to the center of the earth.

 REFLECTIVE PRACTICE

Focusing on Gloria's Exploration Activity (Case Study 5-4)

1. Analyze the interactive discussion between the teacher and Justin in Case Study 5-4 to find if there is a pattern to the teacher's technique. What might the teacher have said to Justin to allow him to feel "safe" in being wrong again?

2. Suggest an alternative activity for exploring children's ideas about floating and sinking.

3. Using Gloria's final small list of categories on children's ideas about flotation, develop activities that will help students' understanding about the characteristics that contribute to an object's ability to float or sink.

Teaching Standard C

Guideline: Use student data, observations of teaching, and interactions with colleagues to reflect on and improve teaching practice.

Children's Classification Systems

The second main strategy for exploring children's conceptions is using children's classification systems—encouraging children to devise their own system to classify objects or pictures into groups. In other words, we expect children to use their own ideas to categorize. This strategy is used mainly with young children to help them explore the nature of physical objects through hands-on inquiry. It differs from the POE strategy in that it is used mainly to help children see similarities and differences in such objects as animals and plants; POE is better used for physical science topics. It also differs from the POE method in that no investigation is carried out.

In this process, children explore the nature of various objects (pictures, toy animals) set out before them, freely examining, touching, smelling, and playing with the objects. The children then group the objects according to classifications of their choice. In this activity, children make their own categories rather than use teacher-defined categories (such as mammals, birds, etc.) with specific characteristics. What we are advocating here is that children create *their own category schemes* and that the teacher, along with the students, then try to improve these schemes and, when appropriate, assign concept labels.

5-7: Exploring *Grade 2* Children's Ideas of *Living* and *Nonliving*

Jane Couch

Preservice Teacher Practice
I used three activities to help explore my students' ideas about living and nonliving.

Activity A: Children's Exploration and Talk
Students talk about and handle 15 objects put in front of them. That is, students may use their senses and their science sense to "play" with objects. Students are asked open-ended questions about objects.

Activity B: Children's Classification Systems
Students are encouraged to group the objects according to their own criteria. This process is done mainly through open-ended questioning.

Activity C: Children's Diagrams and Writing
Students are given worksheets to draw examples of living and nonliving objects and to justify in writing why those objects are living or nonliving.

MATERIALS
Actual objects for exploration include a stuffed toy, a bag of soil, a flower, a rock, a dead leaf, a glass of water, a pen, and a carrot. Students are given a picture of the following: a cat, a house, people, a fish, a tree, a cloud, and a fly (see Figure 5-4). A tape recorder is used to tape the children's and my suggestions.

METHOD
1. Spread objects out on table. Let children explore and play with objects.
2. Interview (ask open-ended questions) students about objects. Ask students questions about the objects and how to group the objects (see "Key Questions").
3. Record on the chalkboard the groups of objects students make.
4. Interview students again to see if they want to change anything they have classified. See if students can add more objects to the groups they made.
5. Ask students to draw pictures of living and nonliving objects. On the same sheet, have them explain their pictures.

KEY QUESTIONS
1. What is this (to clarify that students know what all the objects are)?

FIGURE 5-4
Worksheet picturing objects
for exploration activity

2. Do you know where this comes from? If so, where?
3. What do we do with this?
4. Tell me something interesting about this object. What are its features/characteristics?
5. What other things here have similar features?
6. Are there objects here that you could group together?
7. Find objects that you think have similar features or go together and make groups.
8. Why did you put those objects together?
9. Are there any differences between the objects in each group?
10. Can you create names or titles for each group?
11. What other objects can be added to each group?

All responses were uncritically accepted from all students. The purpose of the questions was to guide the students to form categories, rather than lead them to believe that all objects can be classified as living or nonliving. This exploration activity serves as a way to find out the students' understanding of living and nonliving objects.

Children's Work

The children responded to the grouping task in Activity B by making the following initial groupings:

- cat, stuffed toy, fish, fly
  - *reason:* "All animals can be together."
- house, people, dead leaf, tree, pen
  - *reason:* This category began with "people" with the intent of being "things that act like people". However, the children needed a place for the other objects in the category, so this group became "things in or around your house."
- soil, flower, glass of water, cloud, carrot, rock
  - *reason:* "the flower and the carrot grew in the soil." "You pour the water over the garden." "Clouds make water." When asked about the rock, "I don't know" was the response. Then they rearranged all the categories.

Final grouping of objects (with others added):

- *Animals:* cat, dog, bunny, tiger, lion, bird, fly, koala, bear, hyena, guinea pig, kookaburra
- *Family:* people, fly, cat, dog
- *Growing:* tree, flower, people, carrot, vegetables
- *Water:* fish, clouds, sharks, glass of water
- *Nonliving:* garden (soil), house, stuffed toy, rock, dead leaf, pen, dinosaur, baby birds (in egg), wood, bricks, bed, picture, doors, lights, telephone, blinds, cup, forks, and knives

For Activity C the children drew examples of living and nonliving objects and justified why they placed the objects in this category. (See examples in Figure 5-5.)

Personal Reflections

An analysis of the students' responses to Activities A, B, and C reveal the following categories of meanings about living and nonliving:

- Living organisms can exist in families.
  - "You can have a family of dogs, a family of cats, a family of people, and they're all alive."
- Eggs are nonliving until they hatch.
  - "Baby birds ... when they're in eggs are not living."
  - "When the egg breaks, it [the bird] is alive."
- Living organisms move.
  - "A dog can run and walk."
- Living organisms have organs.
  - "It [a living object] has a heart and lungs."
  - "It has a brain."
- Living organisms need air.
  - "The person is alive because she breathes."

FIGURE 5-5
Examples of children's classifications and reasons

- All living organisms breathe in oxygen.
  - "The growing things all need oxygen."
  - "In order to live, you breathe oxygen."
- Living organisms need food to grow/exist.
  - "Growing things need the right kind of food."
- Plants require an environment with food and water in order to grow.
  - "If you put the carrot in the dirt and put water on it, it will grow up."
  - "You can put the carrot in the water [referring to glass of water] and it will grow."
- Nonliving objects do not affect living objects.
  - "Dinosaurs got old and died, and now we don't need them."
  - "The leaf doesn't help us. It's dead!"

After exploring children's ideas, I believed they had experience with the topic of living and nonliving from grade 1. For example, they described living organisms as "growing," "breathe oxygen," "heart," "lungs," and "brain." Wurtak (1990) explored grade 1 children's ideas about living and nonliving. The responses of these children to the question, "What does it mean to be alive?" are as follows:

All the children identified *movement* and *nutritional needs* as the main characteristics of living things. Most used *growth* as a third criterion, but only in relation to plants, not in reference to human beings and other animals. Half the children used the presence or absence of *facial features* as a criterion for distinguishing between living and nonliving objects. *Respiration* was used by three children when identifying the fish as a living thing (Wurtak, 1990, as cited in Ebenezer & Connor, 1993, p. 300).

When I asked my students for reasons to their suggestions, their answers were typical to the Wurtak study. I think the students are ready to explore the objects in our exploration activity in a real-world context.

I know that the children are able to classify objects and work together well in a group. They understand that one object can be part of more than one category, such as "people" being part of the "family" group as well as the "growing" group. The children were able to group the objects in the exploration activity in a variety of ways, such as using associative characteristics (fish, clouds, sharks, and the glass of water can all be associated with water, so the children made this a group). Also, the idea of origin was explored when the children initially categorized house, people, dead leaf, tree, and pen as "things in or around your house." It was also interesting to see one functional category or category of organisms with similar needs arise—the "family."

Exploring children's ideas indicated to me that teachers need to assess students' understanding before teaching can effectively begin. This is the most logical starting place for planning activities. Knowing what children understand and find interesting about living and nonliving things can help in choosing suitable activities for exploring new ideas. I can develop a clear, concise unit just for the students, and it serves as an introduction to *Living Organisms in the Environment* in the grade 2 Manitoba Science Curriculum. (See Table 5-4 for how the children's ideas relate to the scientific ideas in this curriculum guide.)

TABLE 5-4

Connections Between Grade 2 Children's Conceptions of Living and Nonliving to Scientific Ideas in the Curriculum Guide

Children's Conceptions	Scientific Ideas
• Living organisms exist in families.	The world of life depends on a system of interactions between living organisms.
• Living organisms move.	Living organisms have life functions within them.
• Living organisms have organs.	
• Living organisms need food to grow/exist.	
• Plants require an environment with food and water to grow.	Living organisms need different environments in which to exist, depending on their needs.
• All living organisms breathe in oxygen.	Life functions are metabolism, growth, responsiveness, and reproduction.
• Eggs are nonliving until they hatch.	Every living organism experiences a birth and a death, whereas nonliving organisms do not.
• Nonliving objects do not affect living objects.	Valuable interactions take place between living and nonliving organisms.

Due to the conceptions of living and nonliving brought forth in the exploration activity, I think it would be beneficial to review the interactions between the living and nonliving and the significance those interactions have on the environment. The exploration activity revealed that the students understood that certain objects can interact with others. However, one student verbalized the idea of putting a carrot in soil, giving it water, and watching it grow, but did not pursue the idea that the result of this process is food for living organisms. Thus, I wish to explore "real life" using practical activities with students to ensure that they know how to apply their scientific knowledge.

CASE STUDY

5-8: Exploring *Grade 1* Children's Ideas About *Animals*

Lisa Boch

Preservice Teacher Practice

Before I told them what the task was, I encouraged the children to look at the different pictures and think about what they knew about each animal. A discussion among the students took place. They talked about the names of the different animals, foods the animals ate, animal habitats, and which animals were enemies of other animals. I was surprised that the students thought of so many topics to discuss, simply by looking at the pictures. I then told them that their next job was to place the animal pictures into different groups. I was worried that the students would not understand what I meant, for they had never been asked to groups things based on classification systems of their own before. Within a few seconds, however, they were eagerly forming ideas and classifications that made sense to them. Sean, for example, mentioned to another student, "This guy [referring to a tiger] is going to eat the other one. That's because he's a meat eater." This encouraged the students to form meat-eater and plant-eater groups. One student mentioned the possibility of starting an endangered animals' group. That idea was quickly forgotten, for it seemed that the rest of the students were unsure what the term "endangered animals" really meant. The students then began to form a category of animals that swim. They eventually formed five groups. After these groups had been made, I asked them how they could record their work. One student suggested that we could tape the animal pictures onto chart paper with the proper headings.

Some students have a lot of background knowledge about some topics (for example, animals) because of prior experiences with pets, family outings to the zoo, television, movies, etc. Children who have had language-enriched experiences will have greater prior knowledge and much to share.

Children's Work

The categories formed were the following:

Bird Group:	Golden eagle, toucan, kingfisher, turkey, flamingo, penguin, owl, woodpecker, hummingbird
Plant-Eater Group:	Zebra, giraffe, rhinoceros, donkey, camel, monkey, kangaroo, goat, elephant
Meat-Eater Group:	Bear, mountain lion, lion, snake, tiger, wolf
Swimming Group:	Fish, crocodile, snake, frog, turtle, octopus, squid
Insects:	Grasshopper, ant

Personal Reflections

After completing these activities with the children, I reflected on how capable they were of actually creating their own categories. Allowing them to do so gives teachers the opportunity to observe how students form these categories and what criteria they use to do so. I was able to listen to them discuss their justifications for their criteria. A few disagreements did occur in regard to specific animal placements. For example, Matthew believed that snakes were insects, whereas Sean thought that they would fit better in the meat-eater category.

After the children had finished their groupings, I asked them if they could group these animals differently. They suggested they could group them based on "where the animal lives, by their enemies, as zoo animals, and endangered animals."

Questions that arose while doing the classification activity were these:

- "Where should the flamingo go?"
- "Is an elephant a meat eater or a plant eater?"
- "Is the frog an insect? What about a snake?"

Students have to learn to work cooperatively. This was difficult for two of my students, who thought that the categories that had been created were "theirs" and no one else could tell them which animals should be placed in "their group."

Discussion of Children's Classification Systems

Real objects or pictures can be used in this exploration strategy. The first teacher (in Case Study 5-7) used real objects and pictures, and the second teacher (in Case Study 5-8) used pictures as a stimulus for classification. The grade 2 teacher was very informal with her students, allowing for play-type activity. She used 16 objects familiar to the children. In groups of four, children were allowed to informally interact with these objects. Children were also encouraged to talk to each other about the objects. She noted her students' behavior with the objects. She also moved around, asking them informal questions. Teacher monitoring of and participation in play-type activities is extremely important for this practice to be successful.

PEER INTERACTION

Follow-up Lessons

How would you plan your next lessons based on the children's responses to:

- the living and nonliving exploration lesson?
- the animal classification lesson?

✸ ASSESSMENT OF CHILDREN'S CONCEPTIONS

Assessment Standard A

Assessments must be consistent with the decisions they are designed to inform.

Assessment of children's understandings about their physical world begins in the exploring and categorizing phase in an informal manner. Teachers use assessment data for "improving classroom practice, planning curricula, and developing self-directed learners" (National Research Council, 1996).

Improving Classroom Practice

Students' conceptions form the initial assessment data before a unit of teaching begins. These assessment data improve classroom practice by helping teachers make adjustments to their teaching and lesson plans.

Planning Curricula

Teachers use students' conceptions to plan curricula. Do you see yourself as a curriculum planner? Students' conceptions form the basis for selecting content activities for scientific inquiry. Data on students' conceptions form an integral part of a unit or a lesson. Assessment data help in selecting science content activities and examples that are developmentally appropriate and interesting to students so that desired learning outcomes may be achieved.

Developing Self-Directed Learners

When you explore children's ideas, they feel the need to reflect on their own scientific understanding. They take opportunities to clarify their meaning. They begin to trace their own conceptual changes. Self-reflection becomes a natural part of learning. Children recognize their abilities to do science and feel that they can do science.

Teachers no longer *instruct* science. Rather, teacher and students *converse* about science. Students are teachers' "intellectual friends." Within this supportive medium of learning, students will provide evidence of their own understanding of a science concept through writing, oral discussions, and scientific inquiry. Students will take risks to make suggestions, ask challenging questions, and provide reasons for conclusions.

☼ CHAPTER REFLECTIONS

Are you convinced that the exploration process is an essential and critical step in teaching students science? Have we given you a sufficient variety of exploration strategies to help you begin to explore students' conceptions? By first exploring children's ideas about the world, we promote learning that involves children making sense of their world. For students to understand that what they learn in science class they use in everyday life, major science concepts must be integrated with children's own ideas about the world and how it functions.

We have presented just a few of the many strategies that can be used to explore children's ideas. Each has its own positive and negative attributes. We should consider the students' age, experience, and ability carefully when choosing a particular strategy. We encourage you to experiment with some of the exploration strategies that we have identified through our own research and consider researching others so that you might endeavor to create your own.

Exploring children's conceptions is not a waste of teaching time or effort. This assessment helps to determine initial understandings and abilities, to monitor students' progress, and to provide parents with grades reflecting their children's science achievement. We will discuss assessment in detail in chapter 8.

Questions for Reflective Inquiry

1. The following is an excerpt of interactive discussion of *grade 4* students' ideas about *rocks*. What teacher-made categories can you create from her dialogue with children? What sense do you make of these categories?

TEACHER: Now that you have had the opportunity to observe and examine rocks, what are some of the characteristics of rocks?

JOHN: Rocks are all different sizes and shapes.

MELODIE: Rocks are weird shapes, and I think they are all different. Not one rock in the whole world is the same as another.

LEROI: They can be one color or many colors.

MARLENE: Some rocks have, like, cracks or holes in them.

MIKE: I think rocks are breakable.

MELODIE: When I rubbed the rock, little bits of sand fell onto my desk. Our rock is like a big piece of sand.

TEACHER: Okay, those are some great observations. Now, how do you think rocks are formed? Who can give us one suggestion?

MELODIE: They are formed when sand hardens together.

JOHN: I think that rocks are formed by lots of minerals together, like iron and copper and stuff.

ALAN: Rocks are formed from dinosaur eggs. I know this from a book I saw it in, and I saw dinosaur tracks.

SHAMMI: I agree with Melodie, that stone hardens together.

2. Choose a science topic for your unit. Review at least one major article on exploring children's ideas about your topic. Develop an activity to explore children's ideas. State questions that you will ask. Describe the methodology you will use. Share these with your peers in class as well as your science teacher educator to refine your ideas about the exploration activity.

Explore a group of children's ideas on your topic. Categorize these ideas (see chapter 4). Compare your findings with those of the article you reviewed. Share your findings and examples of children's work and diagrams with your peers.

SUGGESTED READINGS

Driver, R., Guesne, E., & Tiberghien, A. (Eds.). (1985). *Children's ideas in science.* Philadelphia: Open University Press.

Jones, B., & Lynch, P. (1987). Children's conceptions of the earth, sun, and moon. *International Journal of Science Education, 9*(1), 43–53.

Osborne, R., & Freyberg, P. (1985). *Learning in science: The implications of children's science.* London: Heinmann Educational Books.

Shapiro, B. (1994). *What children bring to light: A constructivist perspective on children's learning in science.* New York: Teachers College Press.

White, R., & Gunstone, R. (1992). *Probing understanding.* New York: Falmer Press.

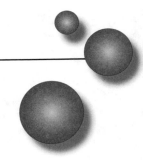

CHAPTER 6

Constructing and Negotiating

1. Why is cooperative learning so important to inquiry and problem solving?

2. Why are scientific activities and investigations so important for constructing and negotiating scientific knowledge?

3. What role does language play in constructing and negotiating meaning?

4. What are several strategies useful for constructing and negotiating meaning with children?

5. What role can journal writing play in children's science learning?

Reflective Inquiry

LISA'S VOICE

One of our main goals in science teaching is to construct, or arrive, at common meanings together with our students. This is obviously achieved through language use. Sometimes, however, we are deceived by thinking that teachers and students attach the same meanings to concepts in science, just because they are using the same terminology. This is an inappropriate inference. Different individuals often have divergent understandings of a certain concept due to the particular way they have constructed their knowledge based on past experiences and present stimuli.

JOURNAL ACTIVITY

Multiple Meanings in Science

Make a list of 10 words that have specific scientific meanings but may be used more commonly in everyday life. Here are a few words to start you off: energy, cell, solution, force, reaction.

How do you think these words' meanings could become discrepant? Choose one word and consider how you could help students arrive at a common meaning.

When teachers explore children's ideas, both parties become aware of the meanings students associate with specific terminology. When this is the case, we can consciously (rather than unintentionally) connect ideas in our teaching and thus be more successful in our attempt to arrive at common understandings. A number of teaching methodologies support the development of common knowledge and the constructing and negotiating of meaning among students.

☀ SCIENTIFIC INQUIRY AND PROBLEM SOLVING

Arriving at common knowledge is a collaborative affair. As students engage in scientific inquiry and problem solving, they come to some common understanding about what they observe and what they can infer from their observations. They do this through the medium of language.

Scientific Inquiry

Teaching Standard A

Teachers of science plan an inquiry-based science program for their students.

In school science, *scientific inquiry* refers to how students attempt to develop knowledge and understanding of scientific ideas. Through activities, students learn how scientists go about studying the world, communicate with one another, and, through consensus, propose explanations for how the world works. This is a major goal for science teaching projected by the National Research Council (1996, p. 23):

> Inquiry is a multifaceted activity that involves making observations; posing questions; examining books and other sources of information to see what is already known; planning investigations; reviewing what is already known in light of experimental evidence; using tools to gather, analyze, and interpret data; proposing answers, explanations, and predictions; and communicating the results. Inquiry requires identification of assumptions, use of critical and logical thinking, and consideration of alternative explanations. Students will engage in selected aspects of inquiry as they learn the scientific way of knowing the natural world, but they also should develop the capacity to conduct complete inquiries.

Problem Solving

Problem solving is also an important strategy for constructing and negotiating meaning. Science education literature reports a number of problem-solving frameworks. For Good and Smith (1987), a problem-solving process includes defining the problem in a resolvable form, obtaining data, organizing data, analyzing data, generalizing and synthesizing the data, and decision making. Pizzini, Shephardson, and Abell (1988) developed a four-step, cyclical model—Search, Solve, Create, and Share (SSCS)—that allows for reentry into the various stages of the model during the problem-solving process. See Figure 6-1.

An important aim in science education is safety, and knowing how to store, use, and care for materials and organisms in the science classroom. This aim should be emphasized in all scientific inquiries and problem-solving methodologies.

We will not discuss these specific problem-solving models at length in this book. However, we have provided similar problem-solving models in chap-

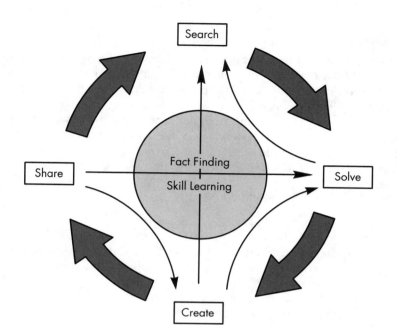

FIGURE 6-1
The SSCS problem-solving cycle (NOTE. Adapted with permission of NSTA Publications from "Rethinking Thinking in the Classroom," by E. Pizzini, S. Abell, and D. Shephardson, from *The Science Teacher,* December 1988, published by The National Science Teachers Association, Arlington, Virginia.)

ter 7 and chapter 10. Problem solving, like scientific inquiry, lends itself to collaborative learning opportunities.

☀ COOPERATIVE LEARNING

Constructing meaning via scientific inquiry and problem solving requires all parties (teacher, students, parents, community, experts) to work together to create common knowledge and shared understanding. Collaboratively working with peers to achieve mutual common knowledge can be the fundamental basis for constructing meaning in science classrooms. Collaboration implies interaction and discussion in small cooperative groups.

Use of small cooperative groups allows students to interact with and learn from one another as well as from the teacher and significant others. Whether working in pairs or in groups of four or five, students in a cooperative learning setting build on one another's ideas and experiences to learn more effectively. Having students reflect on their ideas in light of the views of others is an important part of the development of common knowledge.

Numerous studies (see Johnson, Johnson, & Holubec, 1993) have demonstrated that cooperative learning can help students achieve higher academic levels, solve problems more effectively, improve their thinking skills, and develop both a positive attitude toward the subject matter and a greater motivation to learn. Students involved in cooperative learning are also said to develop stronger feelings of self worth, an acceptance of differing points of view, greater responsibility for their learning, and attitudes such as respect for others, helpfulness, and empathy. The important elements of cooperative learning that are associated with high achievement according to Slavin (1990, 1995) and Johnson and Johnson (1989) are: positive interdependence/group awards, individual accountability, equal opportunity for success, collaborative skill instruction, and learning strategy instruction. However, cooperative learning does not always lead to positive academic outcomes. Some teachers' attempts at cooperative learning have failed miserably. Careful preparation of the students as well as lesson planning is necessary for a positive outcome. (See Appendix A, Managing Cooperative Learning.)

The main characteristics of cooperative group learning are:

1. *Interdependence.* Cooperative group activities are structured in such a way that students work together to support each other's learning. Students achieve this interdependence by setting and working together toward common goals as they complete their individual work responsibilities.

2. *Individual accountability.* Each team member contributes to the success of the group. They support, assist, and encourage each other.

3. *Cooperative skills.* Social skills for working successfully in a group have to be learned. Young children need to learn to be active listeners and contributors to the group. Cultural and developmental norms need to be taken into consideration.

4. *Face-to-face interaction.* Students need to interact with one another, discuss ideas, and help each other solve problems together.

This cooperative group of students is involved in face-to-face interaction in trying to solve a problem by observing and recording animal behavior.

5. *Group reflection.* Group members need to reflect on whether they have achieved the group goal and how well they have functioned as a team. They need to analyze their problems and after reflection, propose solutions to the problem.

Collaborative learning is an instructional strategy that encourages students to work together to accomplish shared goals. However, it also requires an active teaching role. Two key elements of your role are *careful observation* and *supportive intervention.* These are critical to making cooperative learning work. You must determine students' needs, plan appropriately, and facilitate learning. When approaching a group that needs assistance, a few minutes of observation may enable you to supportively intervene. You might need to encourage some members to express their feelings, or to make suggestions and pose questions that will encourage students to consider possible solutions to their difficulty.

☀ PEER INTERACTION

Cooperative Learning

Select a topic in science (for example, classifying rocks or shells, solving an ecological community problem, building a model kite) that would be appropriate for collaborative learning. Describe how you would plan for students to work in groups and collaborate on their learning.

Appendix A elaborates on defining roles and setting rules for managing cooperative groups.

☀ SCIENCE INQUIRY STRATEGIES

Science inquiry activities are fundamental for every science program. Children need such direct experiences to help them explore their ideas, communicate with their peers about their observations, argue and debate their ideas, and rethink their interpretations of the phenomena they observe. We will look at three different types of science activities (stations, demonstrations, discrepant events) through the experiences of preservice teachers. Science investigation, another type of inquiry, was discussed in chapter 1.

Activity Stations
Description
The station format consists of science activities set out on tables around the room. Each station has a specific objective, and the students move from station to station as they finish each activity.

Uses
Activity stations allow students to do directed, hands-on activities and respond to questions about them. These stations are excellent when there is not enough science material for the whole class to work on the same activity at once.

Science investigations are activities that may be done in pairs, groups, or even individually, depending on the materials available. The most satisfactory type of investigations are those in which students attempt to answer questions they themselves have generated. Less satisfactory investigations are teacher-directed and use step-by-step procedures to reach a foregone conclusion.

Teaching Standard D

Teachers of science design and manage learning environments that provide students with the time, space, and resources needed for learning science.

6-1: Using Activity Stations for Constructing Meaning

Lisa Johnson

Preservice Teacher Practice

I used stations with *grade 5* students who were studying *Force and Motion*. The activities were set out in three stations, with small groups of students working through the stations. The stations were as follows:

Station 1:   Students will construct a maze from construction paper, tagboard, scissors, and glue. When done, they will cause a Ping-Pong ball to travel through the maze without actually touching it.

Station 2:   Using the pictures provided, students will determine which type of force is being illustrated.

Station 3:   Students will find magazine pictures that depict a force. They will identify the force and the object the force is applied to, then give the reason for their answer.

Students will share their work, trying each other's mazes and questioning each other about the forces in the pictures.

Children's Work

Children constructed various types of mazes and answered questions for stations 2 and 3.

Personal Reflections

The stations gave me the opportunity to monitor the students' understanding of how forces push and pull. I observed them and listened to their conversations as they tried to apply force to their Ping-Pong balls. One student said, "I'm making the ball get pulled by sucking the air around the ball with a straw. It makes a vacuum and the ball gets pulled." This student displayed knowledge of some terms related to forces but was not sure of their meanings. The maze station took a long time to complete, whereas the other two stations were completed fairly quickly. There was much discussion as the station activities were performed, and it was possible for me to get a good sense as to how students were progressing in their construction and negotiation of meaning.

We recommend that you set up several stations at which children try out different forces. These stations should take children approximately the same time to negotiate. Allow sufficient time for conducting station activities, such as the maze activity.

Considerations

The biggest drawback to this strategy was the amount of time required for the students to work through the stations. It was necessary to set aside the whole afternoon. The advantage of using stations was that a minimal amount of equipment was needed, as students worked in groups and did different activities from the other groups. Overall, I felt that the stations were a useful strategy for the construction and negotiation phase.

Teacher Demonstrations

Description

A teacher demonstration is an activity that involves the teacher showing or illustrating a principle, concept, or phenomenon. The outcome is known to the demonstrator.

Uses

Teachers often use demonstrations when there are insufficient materials for the class, the cost of materials or equipment is prohibitive, the management of multiple materials in individual or group settings could be problematic, or the activities may pose safety hazards, such as when using boiling water or steam. If they involve the students in observing and questioning, occasional demonstrations can illustrate a point, pose a problem, help solve a problem, serve as a climax, promote inquiry and meaning-making, and act as a review.

Teaching Standard D

Guideline: Design and manage the learning environment by ensuring a safe working environment.

CASE STUDY

6-2: Using Demonstrations for Constructing Meaning

Aileen Legault

Preservice Teacher Practice

The activity I did with my *grade 3* students was called *"Leakproof Fabric"* and dealt with the concept of *surface tension* in a unit on water. Surface tension stops water from pouring through the tiny holes between the threads of woven fabrics such as cotton or gauze. I filled a bottle with water and fixed the gauze over the top with a rubber band. Students were asked to predict what might happen when I turned the bottle upside down. Then they were asked to observe carefully what happened when I did so.

Children's Work

My students were very interested in the demonstration and carefully attended to what happened. One student's prediction was: "When you touch the piece of material, all the water will come gushing out." After the demonstration was performed, students had many questions, such as the following:

What if you shook the bottle? Would some water come out?
Would this work with a paper towel?
Why doesn't the water leak through?
What if you put oil in the water?
Is this why my Mom tells me not to touch the tent when it is raining?
Does the water leak only through the part that was touched?
Would this work with a pail or just a small bottle?

These questions suggested that further investigations about surface tension were necessary.

Personal Reflections

It is important to try out the demonstration before class to be sure that it works. I also learned that a teacher demonstration alone is not a sufficient activity for a science lesson. Students were itching to do the experiment themselves. On reflection, it would have been nice to have enough equipment for groups of students to each take a problem to try to solve and report their results back to the larger group. Many questions arose out of this demonstration, and I was shocked at how some of the students responded to some of the questions asked and how insightful some of the questions were that came up. I guess I wrongly assumed that the students' level of understanding was lower than it actually was. One student stood up and exclaimed that the water was *not* running/leaking through the fabric because the water was sealing all the little holes like glue. This little Einstein didn't know the specific term but was definitely on the right track. Another shock to me was the student who made the link from this experiment with a tent on a rainy day. The ideas which surfaced from our discussion convinced me that I did a good job of introducing this concept to the children.

Considerations

The advantages of using this strategy are that the teacher can monitor the learning and be sure that all students are focused on the concept. Demonstrations are usually easy to organize and can save time and equipment. The disadvantages are that this strategy is teacher centered and controlled, with students not having a hands-on experience. It also may be difficult to keep all students' attention if they are too far away to have a clear view of the demonstration.

Discrepant events can be used very successfully in the meaning-making phase. You'll remember that in chapter 4 we cautioned about using this type of conceptual conflict situation in the early stages of teaching a unit. We must begin our teaching using students' ideas and viewpoints, then gradually expand our teaching to introduce different points of view to our students.

Discrepant Events
Description

Discrepant events are situations that display unexpected or unusual results. They pose conflicts, differences, or inconsistencies for the observer.

Uses

Discrepant events provide excellent learning opportunities for students. They are interesting and puzzling and thus motivational. Discrepant events get students to ask questions that will help them make meaning about a scientific event. Situations that contradict existing ideas create a state of imbalance or disequilibrium in one's mind. Observing discrepant events often creates an imbalance between what is known and what is unknown. To resolve the imbalance, students' understandings must grow.

Teaching Standard B

Teachers of science guide and facilitate learning.

See Appendix B, Using Discrepant Events in Science Lessons.

CASE STUDY

6-3: Using Discrepant Events for Constructing Meaning

Andrew Simons

Preservice Teacher Practice

This discrepant event was carried out before my *grade 3* students, who had been studying *Floating and Sinking*. The investigation involved testing whether steel needles would float. My lesson began with my showing students a steel needle and asking them, "Does steel float?" They wrote down the problem and their hypotheses. Then they all gathered around a worktable, where we tried out various combinations. I had brought two steel needles, one thin and light and one thicker and heavy duty. I also had a small and a large container of water. I put the lighter needle in the big container of water. It floated. Then I tried the heavy needle and it sank. I asked what would happen if I did the same thing using the small container of water. When we tried them, the same thing happened as with the large container.

The teacher could ask questions such as, "Why did the lighter needle float on water? Why did the heavier needle sink?"

Children's Work

Children recorded the procedure and observations in the format given by the teacher (Figure 6-2).

Personal Reflections

This activity was very engaging for students, and they were fascinated with the possibilities. They especially liked the discrepant event aspect.

Considerations

The discrepant event has to be related to experiences with which children are already familiar. It must promote puzzlement and wonder. And, particularly important, *all students must be able to clearly see the event*. It is important that

Ideas for managing discrepant events are presented in Appendix B.

FIGURE 6-2
Student observation report about a discrepant event

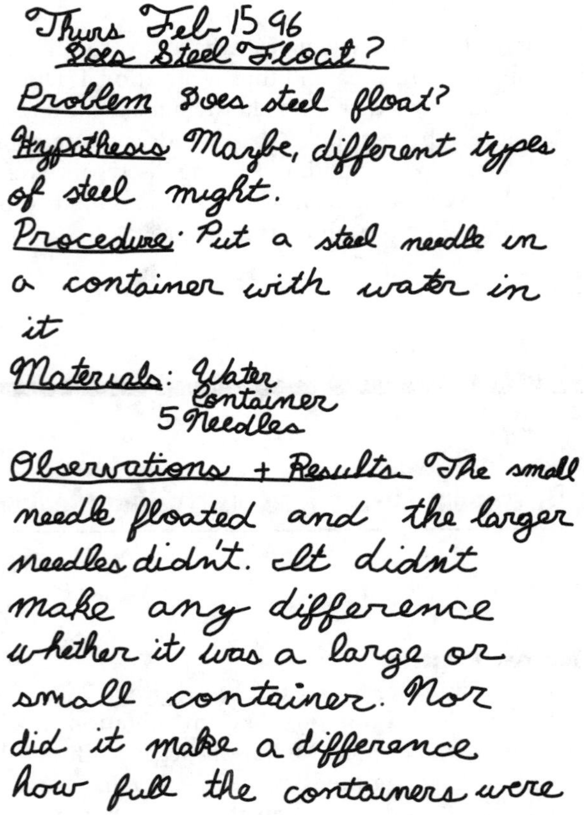

> Thurs Feb 15 96
> Does Steel Float?
> Problem Does steel float?
> Hypothesis Maybe, different types
> of steel might.
> Procedure: Put a steel needle in
> a container with water in
> it
> Materials: Water
>   Container
>   5 Needles
> Observations + Results The small
> needle floated and the larger
> needles didn't. It didn't
> make any difference
> whether it was a large or
> small container. Nor
> did it make a difference
> how full the containers were

students discuss and write observation reports about the event and try to come to some personal meaning-making.

☀ THE POWER OF LANGUAGE FOR CONSTRUCTING AND NEGOTIATING MEANING

In this section, we explicitly connect science to language arts.

Language is a powerful interpretive medium in scientific inquiry and problem solving. It forms a bridge between the phenomenon and the perceiver(s). Emmitt and Pollock (1991, p. iv) describe language as a "pane of glass through which we can view our thinking." Scott (1993, p. iv) suggests that "language is the servant of science," a tool that must be mastered to commune with the natural and social world. As students of science learn science through language, they also learn language that is peculiar to the science culture.

Classroom Discourse

"It seems to me that words do not just inform, they persuade" (Sutton, 1992, p. 3); therefore, a teacher deals in persuasion, whether subtle or not so subtle. With respect to human thinking and its relationships to linguistic expressions, Sutton grapples with the questions of where pupils get their ideas from and how they manage to elicit thought in someone else. Sutton investigates the linking of thoughts and words, concluding the following:

- The words chosen by any speaker or writer help to crystallize his or her thoughts and subsequently steer that person's perceptions. For example, Mike, a grade 5 student, said, "Vinegar makes baking soda react because it is an acid. It is not a strong acid that eats holes in your clothes like some do, but it is still an acid."
- Sometimes—but not always—one person's words elicit a corresponding shift of perception in somebody else. For example, Kim observed, "The baking soda bubbled over the cup because of the pressure of the vinegar." After she listened to Mike's statement, Kim said, "Vinegar has pressure because it is an acid." Thus, Mike's idea caused a shift in her perception.
- Thoughts of this kind are invariably accompanied by some aspect of feeling, which is no less important than their intellectual effect (adapted from Sutton, 1992, p. 3). For example, with much excitement and emotion, Michelle exclaimed, "Oh! It is up and bubbling over like a volcano!"

Classroom discussion is an essential part of children learning science. All parts of the Common Knowledge Construction Model depend on children talking and exploring, probing, questioning, doubting, and perhaps concluding.

Two functions of talk, exploratory and presentational, have been identified by Barnes (1988). Exploratory talk occurs when children talk about their ideas, and presentational talk occurs when they report on what they have found out. If we want children to construct their own meanings in a scientific inquiry, we must put a greater emphasis on children talking (peer science talk). How can we encourage thoughtful discussion in the classroom?

Erickson suggests the following tactics to keep the discussion thoughtful and within reasonable limits:

- When a student brings up an important but unrelated point, ask him or her to hold the point until discussion on the present topic is finished.
- When a student presents a clearly expressed point of view, be sure to recall other related comments and help students link them together.
- If a student presents a clearly expressed view, ask other students if they agree or disagree with this point and to explain their reasons.
- If you get several points of view, you may wish to ask other students to take a stand and commit to one point or another.

Teaching Standard B

Guideline: To guide and facilitate learning, orchestrate discourse among students about scientific ideas.

FIGURE 6-3
Classroom discourse
management skills (NOTE.
From "Some Suggestions for
Running an Interpretive
Discussion," by G. Erickson,
1992, *[SI]² Network
Newsletter, 5* (1), p. 2.)

- Encourage students to finish comments.
- Encourage group discussion rather than one-to-one talk with the teacher.
- Repeat the comments of a quieter student who cannot be heard by all.
- Have small groups report their views.
- Announce an order of speaking if several students try to talk at once.
- Allow students to express themselves without put-down or interruption.

- You may want to keep the discussion going until you have obtained the range of student views, or you may want to end the discussion if you wish to use one of the expressed ideas as the basis for further exploration.
- Alternatively, if group members have reached an impasse, you may have to clarify what you want them to resolve by suggesting an investigation or activity that may assist them.
- You may wish to summarize what has been discussed and then perhaps later divide students into small groups to investigate and discuss the issues further (summarized from Erickson, 1992, pp. 1–2).

To carry out effective classroom discourse, consider the management skills suggested by Erickson, shown in Figure 6-3.

Analogies

Analogies have long been used in the classroom as explanatory tools to help facilitate understanding because they are commonplace in communication.

Description

An *analogy* has been defined as "a process of identifying similarities between two concepts" by Treagust (1993, p. 293). One concept, which is familiar, is referred to as the *analog*. The other concept, which is unfamiliar, is called the *target*. Usually the target relates to the scientific concept; the analog is often from everyday use. The two concepts should have *shared* attributes. Treagust points out that the analog and the target may have many attributes that are not shared. Most of the analog features should be the same as the target features; for example, we can compare a water pump to an electric battery, as in Table 6-1.

Do you notice where the analogy breaks down? There is no analogy between the water pump and the battery with respect to the flow through the circuit and the source of the energy. Most analogies break down at some stage. None have a perfect 1:1 correspondence. They can be used only to facilitate understanding and provide an opportunity for discourse.

TABLE 6-1
An Analog Comparison Between a Water Pump and an Electric Battery

Analog Attributes Water Pump	Comparison of Analog Attributes	Target Attributes Electric Battery
moves water	compares	drives flow of electrons
water travels in a pipe	compares	electricity (flow of electrons) travels in a wire
cut the pipe and the water keeps flowing out	does not compare	cut the wire and the current of electricity stops
source of energy is external (gasoline or electricity)	does not compare	source of energy is internal (chemicals in battery)

Uses

Teachers commonly use four models of analogies: verbal, pictorial-verbal, personal, and practical.

Verbal. The teacher presents the analogy. The students reach conclusions about the target upon exploring the similarities between the analog and the target. For example, a teacher might say plants and trees grow just as we grow taller and wider, and we both need nourishment and water to contribute to that growth.

Pictorial-Verbal. The teacher highlights the characteristics of the analogy using a pictorial representation, followed by verbal explanations. This visual representation is useful to reduce unfamiliarity with the analog. For example, we can use water wave motion to study the phenomenon of sound waves, as in Figure 6-4.

Personal. The teacher relates abstract science concepts to the students' real world. Students can be either physically or mentally involved. Research suggests that "personal analogies cause better learning of concepts and this learning approach is enjoyable; however, personal analogies can cause students to give intuitive feelings to inanimate objects and concepts" (Treagust,

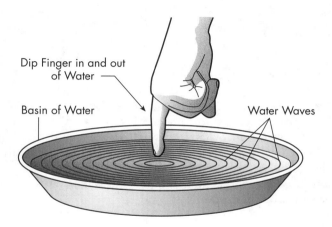

Dip Finger in and out of Water

Basin of Water

Water Waves

FIGURE 6-4
A pictorial-verbal analogy using water wave motion as an analogy for sound waves

1993, p. 295). Here is an excellent example: After running in the gym, some kindergarten children were asked by the teacher to find their pulses and describe what they felt. One child asked, "What is a pulse?" Before the teacher could respond, a 5-year-old replied, "It's like a piece of your heart in your wrist."

Practical Model. A teacher may make a model to represent something in the physical world, such as an atom or the solar system. One must be very cautious in doing this, as many misconceptions can arise. For example, in teaching about the earth, moon, and sun, a teacher used a basketball to represent the earth, a flashlight for the sun, and an orange for the moon. Although this was a good simulation of light and shadows, the objects used misled the students about the proportional sizes of the actual earth, moon, and sun. Instead, the teacher might have drawn on the floor a circle with a radius of 1.5 m to represent the size of the sun, a bead with a radius of 2 mm (for the moon), and a bead with a radius of 5 mm (for the earth).

CASE STUDY

6-4: Using Analogies for Constructing Meaning

Diana Higgins

Uses

Analogies can help facilitate understanding if students are familiar with the analog but unfamiliar with the target concept. Analogies are a part of children's worlds and can play a powerful role in the children's making sense of something. It is important for teachers to analyze children's analogies to determine what types of sense they are making about science concepts and their physical world.

Preservice Teacher Practice

I used analogies with my *grade 3 and 4* students when I was introducing them to *how sound travels*. Since the students could not visually see how sound waves travel, I decided to compare this with another science concept with which they were already familiar: water waves. I constructed the analogy and placed a copy of the analogy map on chart paper (Figure 6-5) so the students could see how an analogy worked and where we were making comparisons. As we experimented with making water waves, we discussed the comparisons to sound waves.

Analog Feature (Water)	Comparison	Target Feature (Sound)
Water wave motion	compared to	Sound wave motion
Direction of water wave motion	compared to	Direction of sound wave motion
Outward movement of water waves from source	compared to	Outward movement of sound waves from source
Causes of motion	compared to	??????????

FIGURE 6-5
Water wave/sound wave analogy

Children's Work
With help, the children developed an analogy (Figure 6-5).

Personal Reflections
It is more effective to use analogies with other meaning-making strategies than alone. I used analogy with discussion and demonstration. I also learned that when using analogies, it is a good idea to have physical materials relative to the analogy in the same lesson. Seeing the analogy map on the chart really helped the students to understand what we were doing, and being able to refer back to it was also beneficial to them. Overall, I found it to be a very useful strategy.

Considerations
Sometimes the use of analogies as a teaching strategy can be fraught with danger; if both teacher and student do not make the same meaning from the analogy, the analogy will confuse rather than teach. Young children may have trouble using analogies, particularly teacher-created analogies, as they may understand the analogy less well than they understand the concept.

Analogies can make sense to some people because some people have had personal experiences that others may not have had. Some cautions about using analogies are given by Treagust (1993):

- Students may take the analogy too far and may be unable to separate it from the content being learned.
- Students may remember only the analogy and not the content under study.
- Uncritical use of analogies may generate alternative conceptions when unshared attributes are treated as valid or when learners are unfamiliar with the analogy (Treagust, 1993, p. 296).

PEER INTERACTION

Evaluating Analogies Used in Textbooks

Evaluate analogies from a student science textbook using the guides for analogical reasoning in science given in the previous section.

Metaphors

The two-way effect is a feature of how metaphors work. It may actually cause a shift in the meaning of the word used as a metaphor. In the phrase, "clouds blanket the earth," the meaning of "blanket" has been expanded.

We use metaphors all the time in everyday life without giving a thought to their meaning. Metaphors are an example of using language to extend ideas; they involve comparing two things not usually compared. This can be done by putting together words that would not normally be linked, such as "blanket of clouds," or "windows into the mind." Note that, when used in a metaphor, the two words take on slightly different meanings.

Sutton (1992) alerts us to some concerns. He says the difference in the two words of a metaphor creates a *two-way effect* (p. 18). We can examine some common metaphors, such as "hole in the ozone layer," "computer virus," and "magnetic field," to see how they help or hinder our students' understanding of the underlying concept. So much of our language is metaphorical that it is important to stop and consider how appropriate our metaphors are to science learning. We have to know the implicit purpose of the metaphor. We need to establish common meanings for the metaphor and the words therein, or the metaphor will not be useful.

PEER INTERACTION

Searching for Metaphors

Locate as many examples of metaphorical language as you can in newspapers or science literature such as journals and magazines. Suggest other metaphors that might be appropriate.

Journal Writing

We should teach children to think through writing and to write for thinking.

Science writing is not merely a description of what we see. Instead, it is an *interpretation* of what we see. More aptly put, "Writing encourages active involvement in learning.... Writing forces organization.... Writing helps students become metacognitive" (Santa & Havens, 1991). We write to communicate our ideas, and we write to learn. It is the latter that we want to pay more attention to in this chapter. Writing to learn is more appropriately referred to as "thinking on paper" (Howard, 1988, p. 88): an opportunity for generating a personal response to something, for clarifying ideas, and for constructing knowledge. Journal writing is probably the most common example.

I think the Strawberry basket didn't Sink because it's made out of Plastic and there are holes all over on the basket So the Water can't pull it under.

FIGURE 6-6
A student's journal entry about floating and sinking

To scientists, journal writing is personal persuasion. Much journal writing involves informal writing and scribbling done before formally writing for publication.

Journal writing should be an integral part of inquiry in school science. In the science class, journal writing can become a highly personal activity in which students can write about things that confuse them, ask questions, come up with conjectured answers, and use their own words or pictures to explain concepts they are learning (Tompkins & Hoskisson, 1991).

Journal writing involves students' recording and/or reacting to what they have learned in class. It gives students the opportunity to state their own ideas for solving a problem, record their observations, draw inferences from possible solutions, make decisions and choices, and reflect on their problem-solving procedures and consequences. Journal writing also enables students to reflect on the information they have received, to find out where they are still lacking knowledge, and to connect new material to previous learning and experience (Pradl & Mayher, 1985; Tompkins & Hoskisson, 1991). See the example of a student's journal in which she reflected on what she had seen and came to a conclusion (Figure 6-6).

Journals may be used to make predictions or hypotheses about a natural phenomenon, to record observations over a period of time, to summarize and react to the results of an experiment or demonstration, and to share findings with others. In essence, journal writing enables students to assume the role of scientists and experience similar mental processes—writing down intuitive ideas, gut reactions and feelings; drawing pictures and diagrams to illustrate theoretical frameworks, expressions, confusions, pitfalls, and tinkering. An example of a student coming to a new insight is related in the journal entry in Figure 6-7.

I learned that air has chemicals. I learned that you don't smell air, you smell the pollution + stuff that's in they air.

FIGURE 6-7
A student's insight about air pollution

Teaching Standard B

Guideline: To guide and facilitate learning, challenge students to accept and share responsibility for their own learning.

The following types of questions may help children put their ideas into writing:

What did I do?
What happened?
What did I observe?
What was puzzling?
What if I change this variable?
What other questions arise out of this activity?
What was the most interesting thing that happened today in science?

Having students write daily in their journals about the events of their science class and their reflections on what they are learning encourages them to think about their learning and helps teachers see what meanings students are constructing.

Sustaining Interest in Journal Writing

At first students are eager to write in their journals, but eventually this interest may wane. Blough and Berman (1991) have many suggestions on how to keep this interest strong. Some of the ones that pertain more to science follow:

- What did you think of today's activity/video/discussion? Did you learn something?
- Explain these new ideas as if you were explaining them to a younger child.
- Find similarities between what you learned today and what you already know.
- Explain step by step how you propose to solve the problem.
- Draw a picture or a diagram that helps you understand today's activity.
- Reread last week's log and write a reaction to what you wrote (Blough & Berman, 1991, pp. 64–65).

Types of Journal Writing

Simulated Journals

This type of journal writing involves children's writing from another person's perspective (Tompkins & Hoskisson, 1991). For instance, in studying early astronomers, children could take on the role of Galileo (Kagan, Ozment, & Turner, 1987). What thoughts would characterize a man who faced much opposition for his belief in a Copernican system where the sun and not the earth was the center of the universe? This simulated journal activity could help students empathize with the feelings of men and women who have shaped science, thereby bringing a human dimension into the study of science.

Learning Logs

Learning logs are a written expression of children's understanding of an investigation or event. They help students apply their newly learned knowledge. This is a great way of teaching students a way of thinking for themselves. Teachers can get a sense of what students are learning.

6-5: Using Learning Logs for Constructing Meaning

Lori Binder

Preservice Teacher Practice

I gave each *grade 1* child a chocolate chip cookie and asked them to mine all the chocolate chips from their cookies and put them in a pile on a paper towel. I then asked them if they could put the cookie back together. I discussed their comments and introduced the word *reversibility*. I asked students what it means and how it applies to the cookie. We then moved into a discussion of objects that show reversibility. I asked students to record the activity in words and pictures in their journals. I put some of the key words and starting phrases, such as, "What I learned …", on the chalkboard. As some were very nervous about spelling, I made it clear to them that they were to spell as best they could and just sound out the words they wanted to use.

Children's Work

Many children were able to make drawings and describe what they learned (Figure 6-8).

Personal Reflections

I have learned a lot from using journal writing in my science classroom. First, journal writing is a great method of having students apply their newly learned knowledge as well as their previous knowledge. Students are not being asked to respond to a question with only one answer, but to reflect and write on what they learned in the lesson. I was very reluctant to use journal writing with my grade 1 class. However, by asking them to use pictures and words on the sheets of paper I gave them (half blank and half lined), I found that all responded with words and pictures.

Considerations

Be sure that children feel free to write what they think and don't worry about spelling and grammar. Encourage them to use diagrams as well as

FIGURE 6-8
A student's ideas about reversibility as applied to cookies

words. Give young children prepared sheets of paper with a blank space and ruled lines. Establish a feeling of comfort and confidence in the classroom. Use journal writing regularly.

Freewriting

Freewriting is yet another style of writing that can be incorporated into journal writing. In freewriting, students simply begin to write and let their thoughts flow from their minds to their pens.

This strategy helps alleviate the "blank page syndrome" and can be used to elicit students' ideas on a particular science topic. Freewriting can also be used to identify students' knowledge about a topic and encourage them to relate personal experiences about it, which stimulates interest. Freewriting can be used again at the end of a science unit and the two freewritten entries compared to reveal children's conceptual growth. The difference between learning logs and freewriting is that freewriting is even more personal and may take place in the absence of teacher questions. A student might have to be really motivated to do this type of freewriting.

Here are some examples of topics that would encourage students' freewriting:

What happened to me when the Martians came into my bedroom.
The most unusual animal I have ever seen.
How I can make the most scary shadows.
What I would do if I were a Monarch butterfly.
Travels of a water drop.

Values of Journal Writing

The values of journal writing are as follows:

- Freedom to write personal opinions without fear of being penalized
- Active involvement in figuring things out as opposed to memorizing
- Visible progress in learning
- Focus on ideas, not on looks, of the write-up
- Valuing of students' ideas (Kuhn & Aguirré, 1987, pp. 269–271)

Another value of journal writing is its ability to help students think critically and lead them to higher level thinking skills such as application, analysis, synthesis, evaluation, and metacognition (Edwards, 1991/1992). A further benefit of journal use in the classroom is the direct link it provides between teacher and student. Teachers are given a good indication of how a child is doing—the child's frustrations, confusions, understandings, questions, and conceptual development. Moreover, journals can make teachers aware of any changes that need to take place in teaching strategies. As Sanders (1985) states, "They provide a simple 'educational pulse'" (p. 7).

What is important about journal writing is that when children have enough practice in how to write this way, they become engaged in the scientific inquiry just as scientists do. Journals enable children to be active thinkers rather than accepters of scientific knowledge. By writing down their thoughts, students experiment with the written language and try to make sense of what they think.

Teaching Standard B

Guideline: To guide and facilitate learning, recognize and respond to student diversity and encourage all students to participate fully in science learning.

Teacher Aids for Encouraging Journal Writing

In incorporating journal writing into science teaching, several factors should be considered.

Teaching and Modeling

It is important that journal formats be clearly taught and modeled and their purpose explained by the teacher. For example, to encourage clarity, the teacher may ask students to write their journals as if they were writing for someone who knows nothing about the content. Or the teacher might encourage the student to write from another perspective, as if the student were a drop of water or a sound wave. This allows the students some freedom of choice even when the topic is constrained. It is not enough to tell students simply to write down their thoughts; students need to be guided until they master the art of journal writing.

Collaborating and/or Writing Independently

Journal writing can begin as a structured class collaboration, move to a group activity, and finally become an independent exercise (Edwards, 1991/1992; Tompkins & Hoskisson, 1991). Eventually, students may be given the freedom to select the format they prefer if the situation lends itself to this.

Sharing Journal Entries

Sharing of journal entries should be encouraged; through sharing, questions may be raised about specific points. Through sharing and peer response, children gain feedback that will help improve the quality of their writing. Sanders (1985) states, "Several times weekly students can share excerpts of their entries with the class. They can discern similarities and differences in one another's learning experiences, as well as difficulties and attitudes" (p. 7). Sanders is of the opinion that teachers, too, should write and share their entries. This will help children see that teachers also are continually learning and have personal sense-making, queries, and reactions with regard to science ideas and phenomena. Children will not so easily view journal writing as only a student task.

Diagrams in Journal Responses. In the early school years, drawing will often show conceptual development more clearly than writing. For beginning writers, invented spellings can supplement their drawings.

Providing Word Lists

Word lists can be posted to help children in their writing.

Students' Dictating Their Ideas

Because the verbal skills of beginning writers tend to be much ahead of their writing skills, allowing them to dictate their ideas (to a tape recorder or the teacher) is likely to make the journal experience easier and more enjoyable for students (Tompkins and Hoskisson, 1991).

Teachers' Assessing and Giving Feedback

Informative feedback for students' journal writing is essential in order to help students improve the quality and completeness of their responses (Pradl & Mayher, 1985). Through teacher assessment and positive feedback, students can be made aware of components that need to be addressed. Teachers may remind students to write using their own words or to relate information to personal experience. Moreover, assessment should not focus on mechanics, nor should it take a hard right/wrong view when considering responses unless specific content criteria were asked for. Grading student journal pages squelches children's freedom to express their

Children may wish to write to their teacher or their peers through electronic means (for example, via e-mail and Internet Relay Chat—IRC).

ideas about a science activity or topic. We have to realize that children require time to understand and accept the scientific viewpoint (Tompkins & Hoskisson, 1991).

If we use journal writing as a medium for helping to share viewpoints, attitudes, and dispositions appropriate to scientific enterprise (such as curiosity, honesty, openness, tolerance, and reflection); methods of inquiry such as prediction, observation, interpretation, and conclusion; and team skills such as collaboration, communication, and responsibility, the science skills we wish to cultivate in our students should come to pass. This is not to say that semiformal or formal lab reports cannot be presented by older students. However, extensive journal writing must precede formal lab reporting, just as scientists spend most of their time developing their thoughts in their journals. Our classrooms must be a place for personal inquiry; as such, journal writing rather than formal reporting should be the main concern.

Other Writing Strategies

Several writing strategies other than keeping science journals can be used for concept development in science. The important point is to encourage your students to *write about science*.

Cubing

Cubing is a writing strategy that encourages students to consider a topic from various angles. A cube is merely a six-sided device made from paper.

Description. Cubing involves writing six dimensions on the six sides of a cube. Children can begin to use this technique by constructing a model cube with their ideas written on each side. These six dimensions (modified from Tompkins & Hoskisson, 1991, p. 214) are as follows:

Describing:	What are the characteristics?
Comparing:	What is it similar to or different from?
Associating:	What does it make you think of?
Analyzing:	Tell how it is made or what it is composed of.
Translating:	What can you do with it? How is it used?
Arguing:	Take a stand and list reasons for supporting it.

An example of how to place these dimensions on the faces of a cube is illustrated in Figure 6-9.

Uses. Using these six categories to guide their exploration of a science topic will help students view science topics from different angles and thereby gain a more complete understanding. Moreover, cubing "encourages students to become more flexible in their thinking" (Tompkins & Hoskisson, 1991, p. 215). It will be easier for elementary-level students to work in groups. The teacher can also provide a set of questions specific to the topic under consideration and based on the six dimensions of the cube.

FIGURE 6-9

A model of a cube with six dimensions (NOTE. Adapted from *Language Arts: Content and Teaching Strategies* (2nd ed.), by G. E. Tompkins and K. Hoskisson, 1991, New York: Merrill, p. 215.)

Describing (What are the characteristics?)

Comparing (What is it similar to or different from?)

Analyzing (Tell how it is made or what it is composed of.)

Associating (What does it make you think of?)

Translating (What can you do with it? How is it used?)

Arguing for or against (Take a stand and list reasons for supporting it.)

CASE STUDY

6-6: Using Cubing for Constructing Meaning

Sharon Turner, Brenda Klassen

Preservice Teacher Practice and Children's Work

Several teachers used cubing in their classes to explore and develop children's meaning. As an introduction, they reminded students about cubes from mathematics and then used model cubes with the dimensions written on them (Figure 6-9) as a motivator for explaining the method of cubing. They went through an example with the whole class (see Figure 6-10) before asking students to do their own work. One preservice teacher (Sharon Turner) adapted the cubing technique for the study of animals (see Figure 6-11).

Personal Reflections

The strategy of cubing is very useful if used in a context with which students are familiar. It causes the students to think about the activity from various angles. This broadens their perceptions of the idea. We will certainly use cubing as an alternative writing strategy in our science classrooms one day. The nice thing about cubing is that it can be used across the curriculum.

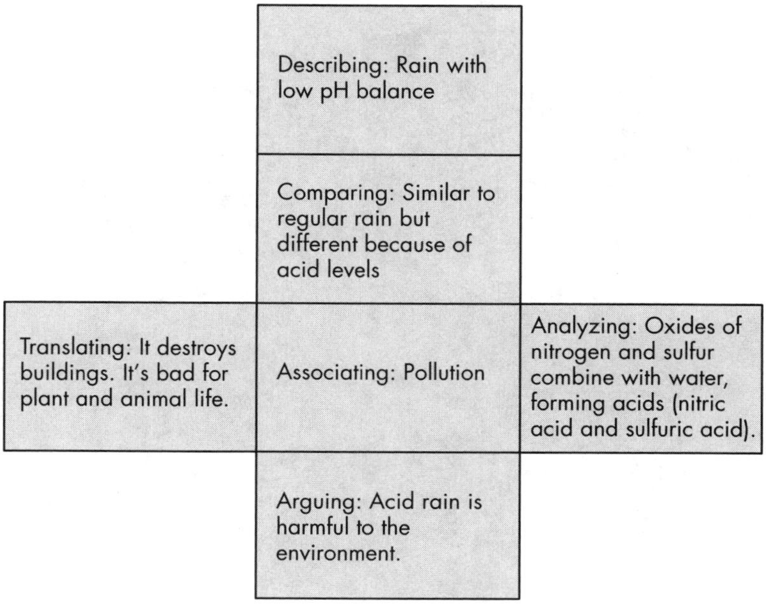

	Describing: Rain with low pH balance	
	Comparing: Similar to regular rain but different because of acid levels	
Translating: It destroys buildings. It's bad for plant and animal life.	Associating: Pollution	Analyzing: Oxides of nitrogen and sulfur combine with water, forming acids (nitric acid and sulfuric acid).
	Arguing: Acid rain is harmful to the environment.	

FIGURE 6-10
Example of cubing:
Acid Rain

1. I am (description—what you look like).

2. I live (habitat —where you live).

3. I eat (foods—herbivore, carnivore, omnivore; predator or prey).

4. My favorite thing to do is _____.

5. Other interesting things about me are _____.

6. I would/would not like to be this animal because _____.

FIGURE 6-11
Example of modified
cubing: *Animal Study*

Considerations

Cubing is a good strategy to use occasionally. It is important to explain the strategy carefully and go over the method at least once using a science example.

Cartoons and Comics

Cartoons and commercial comic strips are occasionally used to make a point on a topic, but most teachers have not availed themselves of the potential of

FIGURE 6-12
Student-developed comics

these humorous drawings for students' exploring and consolidating their ideas about a topic. Using cartoons and comics as a meaning-making strategy may be a technique you will find useful. Some have.

Description. Cartoons are the humorous representation of one situation or event. Comics are series of events that represent a person's thoughts, both pictorially and in writing. Student-written comics have a sequence—a beginning, middle, and an end—and can be modeled after actual published comic strips.

Uses. Teachers can incorporate cartoons and comics into science lessons as a way to determine prior knowledge, monitor development of student's understandings, and assess students' learning. Teachers can also use cartoons and comics as a way to teach new concepts or reinforce old ones. Comics convey what students have learned so that further clarification can take place. Cartoons and comics reveal the level of students' understanding and how the student is progressing. (See Figure 6-12 for a student's view of what plants need to survive.) These devices enable children to be active thinkers about what they are learning and may also be used to motivate student learning. Cartoon and comic writing can help students who have a difficult time writing. Because cartoons and comics offer a chance for students to communicate through drawings as well, students may feel free to illustrate their meaning.

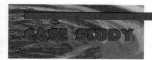

6-7: Using Cartoons for Constructing Meaning

Teresa Wiens

Preservice Teacher Practice

My *grade 2* students experimented with many objects constructed of varying materials to determine which objects are sinkers and which are floaters, and then categorized the objects as one or the other. The purpose of this lesson is to determine whether students have developed an understanding of what makes a sinker and what makes a floater. They will then use this knowledge to turn a sinker into a floater. I first reviewed a chart students made from a previous lesson containing their characteristics of what makes a sinker and what makes a floater. I then asked for predictions about what would happen when a lump of clay is placed in a basin of water. The students placed the lump of clay in the water and observed that it sinks. I then asked them to change the sinker into a floater. After they created a floater they were asked to draw a cartoon that will reflect the process they went through to create a floater from a sinker. I showed them a *Calvin and Hobbes* example that contained some ideas about floatation.

Children's Work

These grade 2 students communicated their ideas on how to illustrate sinkers and floaters, as shown in Figure 6-13.

Personal Reflections

I learned that this was an interesting way for students to reflect on their science activity and to present what they had learned. Many students feel restricted by having to do journal writing and tend to write very little. Constructing comics or cartoons provides them more freedom to express their ideas through pictures and limited dialogue. I was very surprised to find the ideas my students had. You get a different perspective on their ideas when they take a different form. Creating cartoons was very motivating for my students. They were very excited about it. When asked to create the cartoons, they didn't hesitate, and showed no reluctance or resistance to begin their drawings. The students demonstrated a willingness to participate because they were communicating in a form they were comfortable with, had some prior knowledge of, and were assured that they could successfully transmit their ideas.

FIGURE 6-13
Students' views of sinkers
and floaters

Considerations

Encourage students to focus on the ideas rather than the appearance of their comics. It will take practice for students to draw comics with an intent. It is better to have students draw cartoons immediately after an investigation or a discussion of a science concept. This enables both the student and the teacher to relate the comic to the activity at hand as well as assess how the concept has been developed and interpreted by students.

Brochures

Brochures are short booklets or pamphlets about a specific topic. Examples obtained from business, industry, and the arts can be shown to students.

Description. Short descriptions about a specific topic are written by students to provide others with information in booklet form.

Uses. Brochures can be used as a motivational tool to help students consolidate their knowledge about a certain topic. This can be a very effective strategy for constructing meaning if used occasionally. Making brochures helps students organize and explain their ideas. Brochures can be shared with other classes and grades to advertise work students have done.

Brochures proved to be the ideal format in which to present students' research on planets.

6-8: Using Brochures for Constructing Meaning

Michael Hlady

Preservice Teacher Practice

I used brochure development with my *grade 6* students, who were studying *Earth, Space, and Time.* Students were allowed to work in pairs or individually. Each individual or group was given a planet and asked to make a travel brochure for that planet. Incorporated in this brochure were such headings as Introduction, History, Position, Physical Characteristics, Conclusion, and Bibliography. Students had the freedom to add additional headings if they wished. They researched information about their planets and then decided how they would construct their brochures. After the brochures were completed, the students were to come up with a sales pitch and present it to the rest of the class in an attempt to persuade others to visit their planet. Attempts varied from role-playing to presenting a commercial.

Children's Work

These brochures present science ideas in a novel manner.

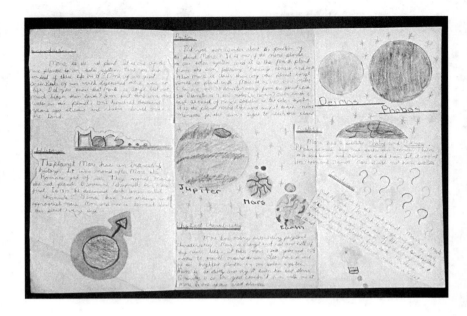

Personal Reflections

Teaching Standard A

Guideline: Plan an inquiry-based program by selecting science content and adapting and designing curricula to meet the interests, knowledge, understanding, abilities, and experiences of students.

I discovered there were many important outcomes from designing brochures. I have come to the conclusion that constructing meaning in science can be fun and doesn't have to be dry and mundane. Also, because the students were actively involved in "real-world" and hands-on tasks, they were more motivated and teaching/learning was easier and more enjoyable. Many students were better able to build and develop concepts when presented with a visual/tactile experience to complement the auditory experience.

Considerations

Certain aspects of the activity surprised me and worked well, and others did not. What surprised me was the level of enthusiasm generated by this activity. At time the enthusiasm got a little out of hand and off task, but a quick reminder brought them back to work. The degree of creativity was outstanding, with the ideas for the brochure and sales pitch nothing less than excellent. However, many had not finished on time, as there were the usual school interruptions. I had not anticipated how long it would take some students to research the material, design and make the brochure, and plan their presentation strategy.

Letter Writing

Letter writing can encourage thinking through writing; as a result, meaning-making may follow.

Description. Short letters in correct format are written to help students reflect on their activities and reveal their understanding of the concepts studied.

Uses. Letter writing can be an alternative to journal writing as a follow-up to an activity lesson. Letter writing can make the science topic more meaningful.

6-9: Using Letter Writing for Constructing Meaning

Sasha Bergner

Preservice Teacher Practice

I used letter writing with a combined group of children from *grades 1 to 4*. The lesson was focused on the *different needs of animals*. First we had a discussion on the different things that animals need in order to survive. A game dealing with the need of deer for food, water, and shelter followed. After we discussed the game, I explained the letter-writing process. I asked students to write me a letter, pretending that I am one of their friends who was not in school today. They had to write me a letter describing what we did, what they learned, and what they thought about the activities.

Children's Work

Children were inspired to write about their science lesson in this novel format (see Figure 6-14).

Personal Reflections

I honestly think I can say that the entire lesson went over extremely well. The children behaved well, accomplished their tasks, and learned something.

Considerations

When I do this again I think I would get students to write rough drafts of their letters first and then better copies. I also think that I would get students

FIGURE 6-14
A child's science letter

Dear Miss Bergner,   Feb. 23
Today I learned about all about
the things animals need to survive
Some of the things are
- food,
- water,
- shelter,
- attention (for pets)
   We played a game. We were deer
and we had to find either food,
shelter or water. I learned that
the deer population can be big and
small. It all depends on how much
food, water and shelter theyhave.
It was alot of fun
                    From,
                         Chandra

to write to a person employed by a wildlife or conservation authority. This way I believe students would be more conscientious about the content of their letter, because it would be more "official" sounding. It would probably also reveal the kinds of questions students thought about as they explored the topic of animals.

Poetry
Poetry is another excellent medium for promoting meaningful learning.

Description. The type of poetry used for science writing is usually short verses that fit a formula.

Uses. Using poetry in a science class may seem like a novel idea, but pre-service teachers found that children enjoyed researching the ideas for the poems and came up with some excellent examples.

6-10: Using Poetry for Constructing Meaning

Melanie Robinson, Sandra Ferguson, Karen Anne Kristiuk

Preservice Teacher Practice

We decided to use poetry to help our *grade 2* students arrive at or construct common meaning together. Since this is achieved through language, we thought poetry would be an excellent choice. Furthermore, we love poetry and feel that it should be integrated across the curriculum in order for students to take it seriously. We have never seen poetry used in science, and were curious to see how the students would respond. The reactions toward poetry were interesting! The students were studying *adaptations of animals,* and we decided asking students to write animal poems would be an excellent way for them to expand the topic. The format we provided for the students was as follows:

Line 1: Name the animal.
Line 2: Describe the animal.
Line 3: Name an adaptation of the animal.
Line 4: Describe its habitat.
Line 5: State a feeling about the animal.

We also used poetry when students were studying the five senses. This particular lesson was on *the sense of smell.* The children tasted some foods and then discussed why they couldn't distinguish what they were when their noses were plugged. We brainstormed for words we had used in the investigation and reviewed rhyming patterns. After they finished their poems, we held conferences with them and helped them edit their pieces.

Children's Work

Polar Bear
A teddy bear, one big teddy bear
Thick white beautiful fur
Playing and dancing under Northern lights
I love Polar Bears

Smell and Taste
They aren't a waste
Smell is good for knowing
What you are going to eat.
Taste is good for eating
Like, smelling cheese
And eating peas.

I can taste
and I can smell
I can smell very well
And I can taste well too.
I like to taste things
Like popcorn is good.
I like to eat it, I would
It's really a good snack.

I like to smell things
From really far away
Hay, hay, hay!
I like to smell.

Personal Reflections

What surprised us about this activity was the creativity many students showed. The knowledge students had about the animals surprised us too. Some students knew even more than we did. However, we believe that is of value when teachers and students explore knowledge together.

Considerations

Poetry and science are difficult to combine. Poetry does not have to rhyme, but the scientific topics that would suit this strategy are limited. Science terms and explanations are often lengthy and unfamiliar, which poses a problem to students writing a poem. A decision has to be made on whether the poems will describe a topic, explain a phenomenon, discuss the result of an investigation, or interpret what was observed. It would also be helpful if you first teach how to write poetry before incorporating it into a specific topic lesson.

Students thought doing poetry in science was strange, so it was necessary to model this type of poetry writing to help them get going. But we believe that the more poetry is used in all subject areas, the more confident students will become.

Teaching Standard E

Guideline: To develop a community of science learners, display and demand respect for diverse skills, ideas, and experiences of all students.

PEER INTERACTION

Using Writing Strategies in Science

Select a science topic and, after reviewing the suggested writing strategies, discuss where and how they might be used in the unit. Can you think of any other writing strategies that might be useful for constructing meaning?

Dramatization and Role-Playing

Common knowledge may be developed through drama and role-playing.

Description

Drama can involve reading, writing, experimenting, demonstrating, cooperating, improvising, expressing, communicating, and analyzing. Drama creates an environment where students are free to explore ideas. It provokes thought and allows freedom of imagination and expression. Creating meaningful life experiences for the children through role-playing deepens children's understandings and connects real feelings and actions to historical/biographical facts, science inventions, and discoveries. It can also allow children to act out the feasibility of a scientific idea or debate a controversial science topic.

Uses

The teacher may initiate a role-play situation, creating a problematic scenario that will challenge students. For example, the teacher might initiate a scenario in which someone has forged a check and ask how to find the culprit. This involves such scientific activities as fingerprinting and chromatography. The students act as co-workers, lab assistants, or other colleagues working in a technological field of society. The teacher may serve as the main character throughout this activity, modeling scientific thinking processes and behaviors for the students. The teacher becomes a collaborative research partner in the activity. This activity motivates and inspires students because the character that the teacher takes on is a scientist with a problem that needs solving. The students take on the role of fellow scientists who share common goals, commitments, and concerns in the research endeavor. On the other hand, the teacher may play the role of the expert scientist and the students may become experts in the field by being guided and tutored by the expert (via a scientist–graduate students relationship).

Children can put on plays about historical events or characters using their understandings of concepts.

Teaching Standard E

Guideline: To develop a community of learners, nurture collaboration among students.

Teaching Standard E

Guideline: To develop a community of learners, model and emphasize skills, attitudes, and values of scientific inquiry.

6-11: Using Drama for Constructing Meaning

Reina Younka

Preservice Teacher Practice

Children may explore the ways in which great inventors of our time manipulated science and technology to benefit society. For example, students may study about one of the greatest scientific inventors of our time, namely,

Thomas Edison, by dramatizing his life history as in the following play we wrote. This gave my *grade 6* students insight into the nature of scientific exploration. The students will associate real-life feelings, ideas, attitudes, and actions with this historical genius. The students collaborate to interpret and perform Edison's story. The students will further enhance their science learning by considering the scientist as a tangible reality rather than a hypothetical entity, and they will be able to relate to the real-life sensibilities of the scientist. Moreover, when science is taught by depicting the life story of a scientist and his work, the science concepts connected to the theoretical framework of the scientist have much more meaning.

The following is the dramatic play titled "He Gave Us Light," designed to depict the character of the scientific genius Thomas Edison. Some ideas on the life of Edison were obtained from Ellis (1980).

Characters:
Narrator, Tom Edison, Mrs. Nancy Edison (mother), Mr. Sam Edison (father), schoolteacher, railroad worker, townspeople, schoolchildren

Place:
Milan, Ohio, in 1879

Act I, Scene I
Setting:
Dark stage with spotlight on narrator

NARRATOR: Do you like to see a dark room light up? Do you like to play records? Do you like to go to the movies? If you do, you might be interested in the man who is responsible for bringing these inventions into our lives. It all began with a very curious boy named Tom.

(Curtain opens and Tom Edison is sitting on goose eggs in the barn.)

MOTHER: Thomas, what on earth are you doing? You're going to break all of our goose eggs! What has come over you?

TOM: (all flustered) But Mom, I've seen a goose sit on eggs to hatch them—why can't I sit on eggs and hatch them too? I must find out how eggs hatch!

MOTHER: Thomas, you are always trying to figure out why things happen and why things work, but you cannot sit on the gooses' eggs or you will break them! Now get off them and go and play with your friends. It seems that you never want to play with them.

TOM: Mom, I have books to read and things to learn. I must find out about everything and I have no time to play those silly games. You just don't understand.
(Stage darkens.)

NARRATOR: Tom learned that by asking questions and reading books, he could find answers to his questions. In fact, the first time he ever saw a library, he said he was going to read every book on the shelf.

FATHER: Tom, it's time for you to go to school. Get off the eggs and get yourself to school! Oh, and try not to bug the teacher so much today!

NARRATOR: Never had any boy or girl in school ever asked so many questions.

Scene II
Setting:
Tom in school

TEACHER: Now, class, today we will learn our *ABCs*—*A* is for apple, *B* is for... (Tom rudely interrupts.)

TOM: (very curious) But why? Why is *A* for apple?

TEACHER: That's the way it is, Thomas—stop interrupting the class! That is very rude and I have told you a hundred times that if you continue to be a disturbance, I will tell your parents!

(Other students in the class giggle and cause a small disruption.)

TOM: Why couldn't *A* be for alligator—Why just for apple?

(Teacher shrugs and shakes her head.)

NARRATOR: While Tom was so busy thinking about his questions, his teacher couldn't handle him anymore and, after three months, she called his mother into the school.

TOM: What is *addled*? My teacher says I'm too addled to stay in school.

MOTHER: (sighs) To be addled is to be mixed up, Tom.

NARRATOR: That was the end of school for Tom, but not the end of learning.

MOTHER: From now on, Thomas, I will teach you at home.

(Stage darkens and Tom and his mother are at the table. Mother is frantic with Tom because she can't keep up with his knowledge.)

MOTHER: Thomas, what am I going to do with you? I don't think there is anyone on the face of this earth that could teach you—you just learn too fast!

Scene III

NARRATOR: When Tom was 12, he decided he wanted to study chemistry, but he had no money to buy chemicals. Therefore, he went to work on the trains. Tom read and experimented while working on the train and sometimes got himself into trouble.

Setting:
On a train car. Train worker finds Tom in trouble.

WORKER: Oh, my goodness!! What are you doing, lad? Help! Help! Fire—there's a fire in here!! (starts stomping out fire that Tom accidentally caused in a make-shift laboratory)

TOM: I just wanted to see what would happen if I mixed these chemicals together. I can't help it—I have to know things.... It was an accident ... I'm sorry ... so sorry!

WORKER: I'm sorry, Tom, you are just too curious and cannot work on the train anymore. It's too dangerous. (motions his hand toward the train car door for Tom to leave. Tom drops his head sadly and steps out of the train.)

NARRATOR: Then Tom got a job as a telegraph operator—until he was discovered sleeping on the job because he was so tired from reading all the time. For the next years of his life, he was always thinking about ways of making things and faster ways of doing things. Tom opened his first workshop and met his wife, Marie. He could finally work on his own inventions and improve the inventions of others.

Setting:
In Tom's lab

MARIE: Tom, please come home for dinner. It's getting late.... You can't spend day and night in this place—it's not good for you and it's not good for our marriage!

TOM: I can't, Marie … I'm onto something really big. I think I've improved that thing Alexander invented so people can hear each other without shouting—you know, that newfangled thing called the telephone. I think I've made it better—this one's really going to get his goat!!

NARRATOR: Tom went on to create in his lab (long pause) the phonograph …

TOM: (talking into a speaker) Mary had a little lamb.…

NARRATOR: The light bulb …

TOM: (switching the light bulb off and on) Let there be light!

NARRATOR: The electric distribution system …

TOWNSPEOPLE: (standing outside admiring their houses) Every home in town has electricity! That Tom is amazing!

NARRATOR: Thomas Edison died at the age of 84. The "wizard" had changed the lives of people all around the world with his inventions. Since his death, others who are trained in science have invented strange and wonderful things, and there will be still others. But there will be few who, like Thomas Edison, gave so much to the world!

The End

Personal Reflections

When used appropriately, dramatic activities and role-plays such as the one on Thomas Edison can be effective motivational tools and vehicles for student expression and concept development. The activities will serve to heighten students' sensibilities and understandings of the subject matter. The science teacher must skillfully craft and implement the activities according to the students' progression through a subject area and their background characteristics.

Preservice teachers should research scientific ideas and the history of the scientist before writing dramatizations.

Debate and Argumentation

Both debate and argumentation are excellent strategies to help students clarify their ideas and take a stand relative to their belief systems.

Description

These strategies can take the form of informal arguments about a topic or a formal debate.

Teaching Standard E

Guideline: To develop a community of learners, structure and facilitate ongoing formal and informal discussions based on a shared understanding of rules for scientific discourse.

Uses

Both argumentation and debate can be used to help students clarify their ideas about a topic and extend their knowledge. Formal debate would require a more timely and deliberate preparation of a topic than informal classroom argumentation.

CASE STUDY

6-12: Using Debates for Constructing Meaning

Donna Drebit

Preservice Teacher Practice

The *grade 3* students in my class were studying *Earth, Sun, and Moon*. They had made up their own UFO diaries as part of the unit. While they were writing in their diaries, they had to answer many questions about what UFOs are and whether they believed in them. I used this as a basis for my strategy of debate and argumentation. We had a debate as to whether we believe in UFOs.

Before the debate, the class talked about what they thought a debate was and how it works. Students decided which side they would be on. Then I gave them 10 minutes to plan their case.

Children's Work

The pro side briefly stated why they believed in UFOs and then someone from the con side was given a chance to counteract the pro side's ideas. The debate continued like this for about 25 minutes until we ran out of time. There was no consensus reached because it is a topic that scientists can't resolve.

Personal Reflections

What I learned while doing this activity is that my students have very wild imaginations. I also learned that many are very acute listeners to their peers and follow the latest news reports about UFOs.

Considerations

During the debate the students talked in turn at first, but once they got excited about what someone else said, they started blurting out their points. Other than that, the students cooperated very well. Some students didn't enter the debate at all. Perhaps the size of each team should be limited, rather than splitting the whole class into two teams. The nondebate group could act as the audience and vote as to which side best presented its arguments.

Using Textbooks

Ideally, we would design our students' lessons not from textbooks but from our understanding of pedagogic and science content knowledge as well as from reference books and resource materials. Practically, we, as teachers of many subjects, are constrained by time and energy in searching for the ideal activities to meet our students' particular needs. Therefore, we may be inclined to rely more on student textbooks if they are available and suitable.

Textbooks outline theories, principles, concepts, experiments, and discussion questions in science from the expert or the cultural perspective. Although students' personal knowledge often conflicts with the scientific information presented in the textbook, most textbook authors have not yet incorporated children's conceptions in their textbooks with the intention of addressing them. Roth (1991) vividly illustrates the conflict between children's and the expert point of view by considering the concept of *photosynthesis*. Many children believe plants obtain food through their roots. This personal reasoning conflicts with the textual version: In the presence of sunlight, plants make food from nonfood materials such as water and carbon dioxide.

Since textbooks do not challenge students to consider their belief system in relation to the scientific explanation, as illustrated by Roth, students will need structured experiences that help them confront the discrepancies between their views and those presented by the text. One cannot expect students to read a textbook with the task of reconstructing their personal ideas. Therefore, teachers must provide students with strategies for maximizing their use of textbooks. How, then, do we use the textbooks, or what role should the prescribed textbooks play?

We must explore students' ideas before introducing the textual material so we are able to anticipate the areas where there may be conceptual conflict. Often it is useful to help students generate questions and problems they would like to solve *before* the textual reading is attempted. This will give them a purpose for reading and will help them focus on the concepts related to the problem. For conceptual modification to occur, students have to be able to realize that their beliefs are often in conflict with scientific explanations because their beliefs are incomplete, inadequate, or at variance with the accepted explanation. They need opportunities and time to consider the explanations in the text.

Roth (1991) suggests discussing with students the essentials of how to use the textbook for conceptual development and teaching students how to monitor their use of the text. Roth's strategies follow:

- Focus on a few critical issues.
- Ask questions to elicit and challenge students' thinking.
- Probe students' responses and give students clear feedback about their ideas.
- Represent text explanations in different ways that make explicit the contrast and connections between scientific concepts and students' ideas.
- Select activities to create conceptual conflict and to develop conceptual understanding.
- Ask questions that give students repeated opportunities to apply text concepts to explain real-world phenomena (modified from Roth, 1991, p. 57).

CASE STUDY

6-13: Using Textbook Reading for Constructing Meaning

Sascha Wohlers

Preservice Teacher Practice

The strategy I researched and conducted is textbook reading for conceptual change. I conducted this study with a *grade 5* class on the topic of *Static Electricity*. Although there are a number of ways in which textbook reading can be made more effective, I chose to focus on one. My procedure was as follows:

1. I explained that we would be studying about electricity, reading a portion from the textbook, and answering a few questions.
2. I began a short discussion with the students about static electricity and asked them a few questions in order to give them a purpose for reading the textbook. They wanted to find answers as well as learn more because of my questions. This method helped them focus on the concepts and activate their prior knowledge about the topic.
3. Next, students read the pages in the text.
4. I then tried to represent the text explanations in different ways on charts in order to help them make connections between the text and their ideas. For instance, I linked text concepts with real-world concepts.
5. We then did a few investigations that demonstrated what was in the text.
6. Students answered a question sheet.

We should point out that using text prematurely, exclusively, or to "verify" facts on an investigation should not be considered an authentic science experience.

While researching this topic, I came upon a wide variety of activities one can do to provide focus and purpose before and after reading textbooks.

One activity is to put students in cooperative reading groups and have them take turns reading a section and explaining the text to the others. This strategy allows students to share conceptual knowledge constructs and negotiate meaning of the concepts in the text.

Reflecting on my activity with the students, I have learned that if students have a purpose for reading and a focus on the concepts because their prior knowledge has been activated, they can benefit from reading textbooks.

✵ CHAPTER REFLECTIONS

Scientific inquiries and problem-solving activities as well as classroom discourse are the vehicles for active construction of meaning in science. Language can be used to clarify and explain conceptual ideas. Words are the instruments of understanding, and their power must be fully appreciated. Learners explore ideas through active inquiry, oral discourse, and writing as the negotiation of meaning takes place. Ways of seeing, ways of knowing, and ways of interpreting textbooks are influenced by students' ideas. Words represent our thoughts and the thoughts of those who have come before us.

Questions for Reflective Inquiry

1. Select a topic and describe how you would incorporate several of the chapter's teaching/learning strategies in a three-lesson sequence.

2. Develop a strategy for construction of meaning that has not been listed in this chapter and that incorporates music or art.

3. Select a section of a student textbook and state how you would use it to help clarify and incorporate children's ideas about a topic.

4. In a classroom setting, practice one of the strategies described in this chapter. Write a reflective report of 3–5 pages outlining your activity, strategy(ies) used, and examples of children's work to support your strategies and findings. Briefly comment on what you have learned, what worked and what did not work, what questions came up, what surprised you, and other aspects of the experience. Include grade level(s) and a complete bibliography of all the resource materials used.

SUGGESTED READINGS

Blough, D., & Berman, J. (1991). Twenty ways to liven up learning logs. *Learning,* July/August, 64–65.

Chaille, C., & Britain, L. (1991). *The young child as scientist: A constructivist approach to early childhood education.* New York: HarperCollins.

Friedl, A. E. (1991). *Teaching science to children: An integrated approach.* New York: McGraw-Hill.

Glynn, S. M., & Duit, R. (Eds.). (1995). *Learning science in the schools: Research reforming practice.* Hilldale, NJ: Erlbaum.

Good, R., & Smith, M. (1987). How do we make students better problem solvers? *The Science Teacher, 54,* 31–36.

Harlen, W. (1985a). *Taking the plunge.* London: Heinmann Educational Books.

Harlen, W. (1985b). *Teaching and learning in primary science.* London: Harper and Row.

National Research Council. (1996). *National Science Education Standards.* Washington, DC: National Academy Press.

Pizzini, E., Abell, S., & Shephardson, D. (1988). Rethinking thinking in the science classroom. *The Science Teacher, 55*(9), 22–25.

Roth, K. J. (1991). Reading science texts for conceptual change. In C. M. Santa & D. E. Alvermann (Eds.), *Science learning: Processes and applications* (pp. 48–63). Newark, DE: International Reading Association.

Sanders, A. (1985). Learning logs: A communication strategy for all subject areas. *Educational Leadership, 42*(5), 7.

Treagust, D. F., Duit, R., & Fraser, B. J. (Eds.). (1996). *Improving teaching and learning in science and mathematics.* New York: Teachers College, Columbia University.

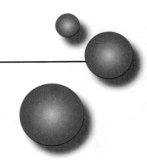

CHAPTER 7

Translating and Extending

FOCUS QUESTIONS

1. How are science, technology, and society interconnected?

2. What are some teaching models that incorporate science, technology, and society?

3. How can lessons incorporate these science/technology/society connections?

4. How can qualitative reasoning be translated into quantitative problem solving?

5. How can students' everyday experiences be used in science lessons?

MIRANDA'S VOICE

I was pleasantly surprised to see that the level of excitement in "snow dumping" had increased significantly. The students seemed eager to participate in the group discussion. The students are moving away from this being a small problem. They are starting to see that it is big and affects many things, such as wildlife, the environment, etc. Although the students see that this is a problem, they have no clue as to how to solve it. This aspect may require some guidance from the teacher and assistance from out-of-school sources.

JOURNAL ACTIVITY

Environmental Concerns

"Snow dumping" is an environmental concern in several northern cities. What environmental concerns are prevalent in your community? Create a list that you can in the future incorporate into science units.

What activities could students engage in relative to any topics on your list? Choose one of these and consider how far you could allow students to go in investigating this problem.

One goal of any well-developed science curriculum is to naturally connect science concepts to relevant real-world experiences. Therefore, the third phase of the Common Knowledge Construction Model is translating and extending students' understanding of science concepts to real-world problem solving and responsible decision making. For example, Miranda's students, through their science class experiences, decided they needed to be concerned about where the city dumped dirty snow plowed from city streets. They viewed this issue as a major environmental concern in their community. Miranda's students were making the connections among science, technology, and society, most popularly known as STS. The following science educators have written at length about STS connections: Aikenhead (1987, 1988), Bybee (1985), Cutcliffe (1989), Fensham (1988), Solomon (1988), Yager et al. (1988).

☀ SCIENCE, TECHNOLOGY, AND SOCIETY CONNECTIONS

Science educators refer to teaching STS connections as "authentic science"—interdisciplinary science education that can be made relevant and accessible to all schoolchildren (American Association for the Advancement of Science [AAAS], 1989; Orpwood, 1984; Rutherford & Ahlgren, 1990). STS education places science in a larger social context—an environmental, economical, political, cultural, and historical context. Science education research shows that teaching STS issues enables students to identify a problem, analyze data, make rational choices among alternatives, and take appropriate actions and is necessary for citizens to be considered scientifically literate (Aikenhead, 1980; Bybee, 1985; Yager, 1984; Zoller, 1987). The relevance of STS education, therefore, lies in its ability to help students understand and make value judgments about societal issues at the local, national, and global level.

Associated with value-based learning, STS education leads to the development of necessary democratic decision-making and informed action-taking capabilities that include identifying problem contexts, understanding

 REFLECTIVE PRACTICE

Technological Products

Think of a product that has made an impact on the everyday lives of people (toothbrush, perfume, carpet, machinery, computers, etc.). Do a little exploring on your own and try to find answers to the following questions:

- Who created/invented the technology?
- On what scientific principles does this technology work? Use diagrams as appropriate to explain.
- What are the social benefits, limitations, and disadvantages of this technology?

the problem, framing questions, generating possible investigations, gathering and analyzing data, sharing and evaluating findings, drawing possible solutions and suggestions, planning and assessing proposed courses of action against relevant criteria, and choosing and implementing actions (Jackson, 1985).

The Relationship of Students to Science, Technology, and Society

Through an STS approach, "students tend to integrate their personal understanding of the natural world (science content) with both the man-made world (technology) and the social world of the students' day to day experience (society)" (Hofstein, Aikenhead, & Riquarts, 1988, p. 358). Technology leads students to consider practical aspects of scientific knowledge. Societal connections raise important personal and social issues for investigation and discussion. The relationship among science, technology, society, and the student is diagrammed in Figure 7-1. The dashed arrows represent the connections made in STS teaching materials, and the solid arrows represent student sense-making of science content. In this way, curriculum knowledge and personal knowledge are bridged in a meaningful context.

Science/Technology/Society Emphases

Hofstein et al. (1988) recommend thinking of STS issues with a more holistic view rather than a reductionist approach. Hence, the learning situation should be made relevant to students via less emphasis on issues that are content specific and more on how science influences social life and social life influences science.

Bybee (1985) has compiled a list based on rankings from surveys assessing STS themes in science education. Populations sampled in these surveys included college students, science teachers, an international group of science educators, scientists, and engineers. The STS themes perceived to be most important were air quality and the atmosphere, world hunger and food resources, war technology, population growth, water resources, energy

Teaching Standard D

Guideline: Design and manage the learning environment by creating a setting for student work that is flexible and supportive of science inquiry.

Teaching Standard E

Teachers of science develop communities of science learners that reflect the intellectual rigor of scientific inquiry and the attitudes and social values conducive to science learning.

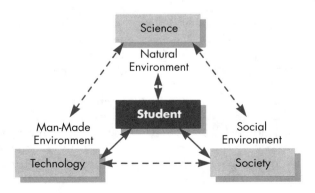

FIGURE 7-1
The relationship among science, technology, society, and the student (NOTE. From "Discussions Over STS at the Fourth IOSTE Symposium," by A. Hofstein, G. Aikenhead, and K. Riquarts, 1988, *International Journal of Science Education, 10*(4), p. 358.)

shortages, hazardous substances, human health and disease, land use, nuclear reactors, extinction of plants and animals, and mineral sources, but the possibilities are actually limitless.

Strategies for teaching STS are limitless as well. They can encompass "simulation games and role playing, forums and debates, individual and cooperative group projects, letter writing to authorities, active research field work, guest speakers and community action" (Hofstein et al., 1988, p. 362). You might keep in mind that STS instruction is particularly effective when it is adopted and adapted to suit local needs, problems, and concerns (Waks & Barachi, 1992). The teaching goal of STS education is to provide intellectual, social, and moral development and a natural forum for developing problem-solving skills.

 PEER INTERACTION

The STS Approach

Select a major science idea from your science program. How would you translate this to the everyday world of children in your classroom using an STS approach?

Problem-Solving Models for STS Teaching

A five-stage organizational model for STS education was developed by a practicing teacher (Verstraete, 1990) doing postgraduate study, using two models (Jackson, 1985; Yager et al., 1988) as a basis. He used his model as a basis for developing a teaching unit and conducted a collaborative research study with another classroom teacher, who actually taught the unit. The five steps of this model are as follows (see Figure 7-2).

1. **Issue Identification and Selection.** The STS program begins with the identification and selection of a socioscientific issue drawn from real life.
2. **Issue Clarification/Initial Research.** In the second stage, students critically examine the issue. Together with the teacher, they compile and study the available information, determine what further data might be needed and how it will be obtained, and collect relevant information through a variety of means including investigations, media sources, field trips, contacts with officials, interviews, etc. At this stage the issue is examined and clarified against a backdrop of knowledge. Scientific concepts and skills are developed and strengthened in the research process.
3. **Strategy/Action Proposals.** Once the facts are in and the issue is in clear focus, action plans or strategies are generated. In this phase, students seek answers to the question, "What can be done about the problem?" On a more personal level, this translates into, "What can *we* do about it?"

Teaching Standard D

Guideline: Design and manage the learning environment by identifying the use of resources outside the school.

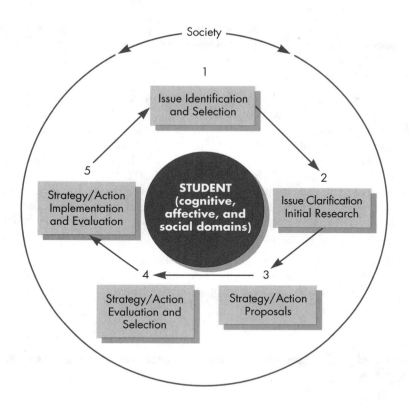

FIGURE 7-2
An STS organizational model (NOTE. From *Issues-Centered STS (Science-Technology-Society) in the Elementary Classroom: A Case Study,* by L. Verstraete, 1990. Unpublished master's thesis, University of Manitoba, Winnipeg, Manitoba, Canada, p. 40.)

Proposed actions may have wide-ranging implications. At one end of the spectrum, solutions or resolutions might be forthcoming. At the other end, students may realize that there is little that can be done or that much more information or expertise is needed. Between these two extremes lie other possibilities of social action: publishing an information newsletter about the issue, organizing debates or interviews to increase public awareness, building models that illustrate the problem or possible solutions, writing letters to officials, organizing an assembly for the whole school, writing and performing in an issue-related play, etc.

4. **Strategy/Action Evaluation and Selection.** In the fourth phase, action plans are evaluated for feasibility, effectiveness, social appropriateness, relationship to the issues that initiated the process, and other criteria defined by the group. The most plausible strategies are selected and implementation procedures identified.

5. **Strategy/Action Implementation and Evaluation.** In the fifth stage, the selected action plans are implemented and monitored. Continual evaluation provides feedback for the students and teacher and may provide opportunities for related issues to be examined (Verstraete, 1990, pp. 38–39).

Teaching Standard D

Guideline: Design and manage the learning environment by structuring the time available so students are able to engage in extended investigations.

Another similar and less elaborate five-step problem-solving procedure has been described by Kanis (1990), and we suggest it as a possible way to begin problem solving in the science classroom. The five steps of this simpler model are as follows:

1. **Define the problem.** Recognize that a problem exists and state the question you want answered.
2. **Devise a plan.** What knowledge do we have about the problem? What investigation will we conduct to help answer the question? What materials will we need? How will we know when we have solved the problem?
3. **Implement the plan.** Gather the data and organize them.
4. **Analyze the data to see if there are patterns.** If the question is not answered, refine and clarify the problem and repeat the procedure.
5. **Make a decision.** Decide if the answer to the question will lead to action (Kanis, 1990, pp. 24–25).

Three case studies are described on the following pages. One follows the Verstraete model, a second uses a model similar to that of Kanis, and the third uses computer-based simulation programs to help solve problems.

CASE STUDY

7-1: Issue-Based Problem Solving for *Grade 6*

Marla Brandt, Donna Drebit

Description
Our *grade 6* students were studying a unit on the *Environment*. We wanted them to translate and apply some of the concepts they had learned to make them relevant to their lives.

Preservice Teacher Practice
We used the five steps of Verstraete's STS organizational model (see Figure 7-2).

Children's Work
Students worked in groups and followed the format. Their question was, What can we do about water pollution and water resource management? After a verbal report by each group on research studies, the class concluded that water pollution was caused by acid rain from industry, oil spills, wastewater from homes and industry, and farm chemicals. The class then went on to suggest what can be done about water pollution and what they could do about water pollution. The class list was as follows:

We can stop pollution by slowing down the factories.

Don't put chemicals like gasoline in water.

Don't put garbage in the water.

Try to stop ships from going to hit big rocks.

Don't leave water running when you're brushing your teeth.

Don't use too much water.

Don't change the water in the bathtub when another person in your
family is going to have a bath.

Take short showers.

Personal Reflections

Issue-based problem solving is an effective way for young children to look at
large issues in society. It allows children to become aware of what they can
do about problem situations. Children can also learn about technology and
how science has developed products and techniques to help minimize, for
example, water pollution. By studying this topic, the students were able to
develop scientific knowledge and concepts regarding acid rain, the use of
chemicals, industry, and waste matter.

Dividing the class into small groups was a good time-saver. Each group
was able to come up with a number of good strategies and action plans to
stop water pollution. Later, many of the students said that they were implementing some of the strategies and action plans that were proposed. Most of
the students said their water-saving strategies were working out well. They
had made a commitment to implement several of the more personal steps
they had identified (such as improved garbage disposal and water usage) and
were pleased with the results of their study.

Considerations

The procedures worked well, but in preparation for this lesson, one major
question came up. My cooperating teacher thought that I should teach the
lesson using a set of three or four guppies in separate bowls. She thought
that as the children learned about water pollution, they should pollute each
guppy's water with a different kind of water pollution and watch the guppies
die. Could I kill animals to prove to children that water pollution kills fish?
I felt that although these were only guppies, this was an animal rights issue.
We certainly would not feed a dog poisonous food to prove that poison kills
dogs. I think that we cannot make animals suffer and die just to prove to
children what science has already proven. Doing this activity could also
result in negative feedback from parents and society. I felt that this suggested activity was inappropriate and told my cooperating teacher I would be
uncomfortable doing the activity.

References

Microsoft. (1994). *Ocean and oceanography*. Encarta Funk & Wagnalls
Corporation.

Microsoft. (1994). *Oil spill clean-up*. Encarta Funk & Wagnalls
Corporation.

Teaching Standard B

Guideline: To guide and facilitate
learning, encourage and model the
skills of scientific inquiry, as well as
the curiosity, openness to new ideas
and data, and skepticism that
characterize science.

Microsoft. (1994). *Polluted river.* Encarta Funk & Wagnalls Corporation.
Microsoft. (1994). *Water pollution.* Encarta Funk & Wagnalls Corporation.

7-2: Issue-Based Problem Solving for *Grade 2*

Brian Hargraves

Description

We can frame problems relative to students' lives in such a way that students are challenged to try to solve them. For example, I used this problem-solving strategy with a *grade 2* class that had been studying a science unit on *Flotation*. The problem of how to transport a set of materials across a body of water was posed to students in this manner: "You need to move a load of materials from one point to another, and there is a body of water in the way. You cannot go around it, so you must figure out a way to travel on it, through it, or over it. How could you do that?" By framing the question in such a way, students are forced to solve a real-life problem for shippers of goods today.

Uses

Teaching Standard D

Guideline: Design and manage the learning environment by engaging students in designing their own learning environment.

This strategy can be very effectively used to help students translate the science concepts they have learned into real-life situations and to extend their knowledge. By relating the intended activity to a real problem that humans encounter, students can then take ownership of their learning, as well as become more interactive with the material and the content matter. From the introduction of the initial problem, the students can then be guided through a small series of activities that will enhance meaningful learning. This type of problem solving can be used for all types of students, not just those of above-average ability.

Preservice Teacher Practice

Students were given the practical situation of creating a boat that would transport a load (some fishing weights) over a body of water. The initial goal was to make a boat that would float from a 1-ft square of aluminum foil. They then loaded their boats with the weights and found that the boats sank. The question "Why did your boat sink?" was posed to the students, and their responses discussed. These ideas were used as starting points for a second activity. Based on their observations and discussion, they were all able to build better boats that would hold more weight than their first ones. The initial and final boats were preserved as a means of comparing the initial and final outcomes of the students' knowledge of some of the basic principles of flotation. At this point, the students were asked to discuss why their second attempts were more successful than their first tries. I then asked, "What kinds of forces are acting on a boat when it is placed on a body of water?" Student responses were in line with their ages and abilities.

This problem-solving exercise consisted of exploring and meaning-making as well as translating and extending activities.

Children's Work

In the discussion that took place between the testing of the first boats and the production of the second, the students suggested reasons for the lack of success of their boats. Summarized, they were as follows:

- Uneven weight distribution in the boats
- Lack of strength in the bottoms of the boats (most of the boats folded in half when they sank)
- Sides that were not high enough to allow for the increased displacement of water caused by the added weight of the cargo
- Designs that were not stable when the weight was added

Students' responses to the question as to what forces act on a boat focused on the weights pushing down on the boat. They also mentioned buoyancy and gravity, weight distribution in the boats, water surface conditions, surface contact of the boat hull, and the amount of displacement the boat had. Second graders may use these terms because they have heard of them, but one should not assume that they understand their scientific meaning.

One final issue that was discussed was how their increased knowledge about boat design was useful or relevant. They were able to generate responses such as how to design extra-huge ships such as supertankers and cargo ships, as well as more efficient hulls and boat types.

Personal Reflections

I learned several things as a result of conducting this activity. It is very important to connect the materials that the students are studying to their world and to their interests. Students were highly motivated and were critical thinkers, as this activity gave students some ideas as to why and how boats come to be shaped like they are, and what happens to a boat as it sinks. Much discussion occurred during the activity, and there was ample time for meaning-making discourse to take place.

Considerations

There were very few problems with the activity, but a few suggestions follow:

- Try out the activity before class.
- Use weights that are uniform in size, such as coins and fishing weights.

- Use weights that are not too heavy for children to handle.
- Be sure the body of water is deep enough that the boats do not touch bottom when the weights are added. (A kindergarten-type water table is excellent for this activity.)

☀ QUALITATIVE REASONING FOR QUANTITATIVE PROBLEM SOLVING

Thus far, we have been reading case studies on STS issues. What follows is an example of another type of problem solving—how a preservice teacher developed students' conceptual ideas of forces and simple machines before she carried out mathematical applications.

In most science classes, problem solving that focuses on mathematical quantities or outcomes often involves the following steps:

1. The teacher begins a topic, such as *Force and Machines,* by naming and defining the scientific terms (for example, *force, acceleration,* and *mass*).
2. The teacher follows up with illustrative examples of force and writes the definition and a formula or gives an algorithm to solve a problem involving force on the chalkboard or overhead.
3. Students are then taught how to work out one or two problems involving force, using a formula.
4. For more practice, students are asked to solve the end-of-chapter problems. The unfinished classwork becomes homework.
5. The next day's lesson begins by going over the previous day's in-class and homework problems. That day, a new topic may also be introduced.

Zoller (1987) refers to this cycle of problem-solving instruction as "exercise solving"—instruction that requires students to solve problems merely by applying a known procedure to obtain the teacher-known, correct solution. This type of problem solving emphasizes mathematical formalism to promote scientific precision and predictive power (Reif, 1981), and by introducing technical terms, suggests that "scientific knowledge resides in technical terms rather than in underlying understanding and concept formation" (Arons, 1981, p. 22). For example, after stating the definition of a type of simple machine such as a lever, the teacher may introduce the formula ($f_1 \times l_1 = f_2 \times l_2$) to work out word problems involving a lever. In this case, a relatively simple problem—namely, the quantitative description of a simple machine—is presented in class. We expect students to "discover" the quantitative generalization, or, failing that, to "see" the generalization when pointed out. Such instructional strategies do not adequately promote the kind of problem solving envisioned by science educators and outlined by curriculum developers nationwide.

What *does* count as authentic problem solving in science? More specifically, what evidence do we have that students have constructed the quantitative generalization themselves rather than just memorized it?

We will relate, in detail, a research study in which Anna Landry Marchetti applied authentic problem solving in a science unit. During her first 5-week block of student teaching, Anna taught a unit on *Forces and Simple Machines* to a class of *grade 6* French Immersion students in an urban school. Anna's study indicates a way of helping students go from their personal knowledge to "common knowledge" using a constructivist problem-solving approach.

Anna employs a constructivist approach to problem solving in order to foster common knowledge—the school science knowledge that becomes established as a part of the student's understanding through activities and discourse. Anna accomplishes this by generating students' personal knowledge and incorporating this knowledge into a sequence of nine lessons on Forces and Simple Machines. Common knowledge then becomes the contextual basis for further communication and learning of the discipline. This chapter reveals the importance of first establishing common knowledge and understanding between the teacher and students for meaningful communication to take place. In order to develop an argument for fostering common knowledge through problem solving, we illustrate the lesson in which Anna elicits her students' ideas of simple machines. We follow that with the second lesson, in which Anna develops common knowledge about the workings of a lever, and finally, a third lesson, in which Anna helps students shift from qualitative reasoning to quantitative reasoning.

Anna's lessons on Forces and Simple Machines were constructed on the basis of students' qualitative descriptions given in the exploring and categorizing phase (first lesson, not reported here), as well as their newly developed ideas in the ongoing lessons. What we describe as Lesson 1 was actually the second lesson in her unit, in which Anna attempted to build on the meanings that students had reached at the end of the first lesson: that levers work best when the resistance is close to the fulcrum and that levers make our work easier. In addition, Anna attempted to help students understand the workings of the lever through quantitative analysis—by changing the magnitude of the force in the downward direction.

Anna uses model seesaws so that students may experiment and observe how a seesaw behaves and how this relates to the behavior of a lever. Anna notes that, seeing the materials she had brought into the classroom, students were very excited to find out what they might do. The materials for the seesaw activity (Cross, 1992) are heavy blocks, light blocks, a plank, a pivot for the planks, levers, weights, and a spring scale.

Anna asks students if they remember being on a seesaw when they were younger. She also asks them, "If you were on the seesaw with someone who wasn't your size, how did you manage to balance the seesaw?" Following are some of the answers that students give:

Teaching Standard A

Guideline: Plan an inquiry-based program by selecting science content and adapting and designing curricula to meet the interests, knowledge, understanding, abilities, and experiences of students.

FIGURE 7-3
Model seesaw used in Lesson 1 (NOTE. Adapted from "A Balancing Act," by B. Cross, 1992, *Science and Children, 29,* p. 17.)

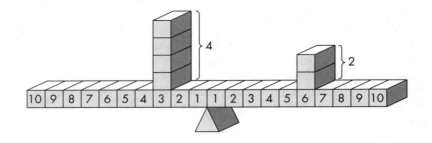

JANE: One person had to move closer to the middle.

NILA: Yes, that's right, but I can't remember who moved—the bigger person or the smaller person.

The whole class agrees that this is what they used to do—move around on the seesaw until they found a balance. This concept is probed mathematically. Each group of three students assembles a model seesaw using a heavy block marked in four sections (which they label 4), a light block marked in two sections (which they label 2), a plank numbered 10 on each side of the pivot, and a pivot to place in the center of the plank (Figure 7-3).

With the heavy block on a particular number, Anna asks the students to predict within their groups where they would place the light block in order to balance the seesaw. Anna encourages them to experiment with the model seesaw. They could place the heavy block anywhere on the plank—this was their point of reference. The focus question was, "Where must you place the light block in order for the seesaw to balance?" Sample student recordings of balance readings are given in Figure 7-4.

The number patterns that students observed when the beam was balanced are (a) the heavy block was always on one half the number of the little block; (b) the little block was always on the larger numbers; and (c) the heavy block was always closer to the pivot. According to Anna, no student recognized the scientific proposition that the weight on one side, multiplied

Teaching Standard D

Teachers of science design and manage learning environments that provide students with the time, space, and resources needed for learning science.

FIGURE 7-4
Students' recordings of seesaw balance readings

Balanced

4 on 5 - 2 on 10

4 on 3 - 2 on 6

4 on 4½ - 2 on 9

2 on 8 - 4 on 4

by its distance from the pivot, is the same as the weight on the other side, multiplied by its distance from the pivot. Anna states this propositional knowledge to students, who are surprised that they hadn't recognized this pattern by themselves. Note students' remarks in the student-student discourse that followed:

ALAN: I get it now—the small block and the longer part of the beam are equal to the heavy block and the short part of the beam.

TOM: If we move the small block further away on the beam, it lifts the large block.

BRET: Does that mean that to move our boulder, we would have to find a pretty long plank?

TARA: Well, it couldn't be short, that's for sure.

JIM: Look, we just proved our point again: If we think of the boulder as being the heavy blocks, and we are the little blocks, the resistance is still closer to the fulcrum, so we would need less force to move it. I guess the farther away we get from the fulcrum, the easier it would be.

This "aha!" experience conveys a powerful message. Herein is the difference between a constructivist and a conventional approach to problem solving. In the constructivist approach that Anna uses, she develops students' understanding about levers until they are ready to receive a propositional statement from the teacher. In other words, Anna develops the idea of levers first, makes it a part of students' conceptual structure, and eventually pronounces the scientific precept. Hence, there are children's remarks of surprise and acceptance of the proposition. In the conventional method of teaching levers, however, children would be made to plunge into the definition, equation, and mathematical expressions, with the result that there is no meaningful "aha!" experience for students. Successive procedural experiences of the latter type in the science class promote boredom, vigorous copying of answers from one another (no ownership of learning), and negative attitudes in children toward science and math (Ebenezer & Zoller, 1993).

In this lesson, the students build on their conception: Not only did the load have to be closer to the fulcrum, but the length of the plank mattered as well. They observe that the closer the larger block (on the model seesaw) is to the pivot, the farther away the little block has to be in order for the seesaw to balance. A student takes this one step further by suggesting that if they moved the small block farther away, it would actually lift the large block. This observation leads the students to conclude that the farther away the small block is from the large block, the easier or the higher it would lift the large block, which, in turn, leads the students to believe "the longer our plank was, the easier it would be to move the boulder."

It is amazing to see how students relate their hands-on experiment to their original hypothetical problem. "It is obvious to me," notes Anna,

Teaching Standard D

Guideline: Design and manage the learning environment by creating a setting for student work that is flexible and supportive of science inquiry.

Students try out their ideas about where one needs to sit to balance the seesaw.

"that the students are using their previous knowledge to make new assumptions and conclusions. As well, whenever one student makes a comment, it is like a chain reaction—many different ideas would emerge from the one." Anna wants to continue to build on students' ideas:

- The fulcrum has to be close to the load (first variable).
- The length of the plank is important (second variable).

Anna notes that although students have mentioned "weight" (third variable, and a primary focus of this lesson), so far they have not dealt very much with it. The students gather in the carpeted area of the classroom, forming a semicircle facing a round table. To find the relationships among the position of the fulcrum, the length of the plank, and the weight, students use a 2-m, 5 by 10 cm plank marked in four equal lengths and a bathroom scale (Streitberger, 1978).

Teaching Standard E

Guideline: To develop a community of learners, nurture collaboration among students.

Student A holds one end of the 2-m plank, and the other end rests on the edge of a table that serves as a fulcrum. Student B, who weighs about 40 kg, sits on the plank. The class predicts where student B would have to sit so that student A can hold student B and the plank with the least effort. The answer is unanimous—student B would have to sit "as close as possible to the table, on the first mark." The students test their collective prediction and find that it is not hard to hold student B and the plank when student B sits close to the first mark on the plank. Then student B inches her way toward student A, who is holding the plank. Students predict that it will be progressively more difficult for student A to hold student B as she moves toward student A. Their predictions are right—the effort needed to hold student B and the plank increases as student B inches her way toward the student holding the plank. Everyone in the class takes a turn to try this.

"Students make the same observations with each student, but it is important that each child gets a turn sitting and holding the plank," Anna comments. At the end of the activity, students make these observations:

TARA: Some people were able to hold the plank longer than others.

KATY: The closer the people on the board got to the people holding the board, the harder it was to hold the board.

ALAN: It was always easier to hold the board when the people on the board were farthest from the people holding the board.

TEACHER: Does this resemble anything we learned the other day about levers?

KATY: We learned that the closer the resistance was to the fulcrum, the easier it was.

TEACHER: If that's true, where's the fulcrum in this case, and can we even call this a lever?

JIM: Well, it was easier when the people were near the table, so the edge of the table must be the fulcrum.

TOM: This must be a lever, or we wouldn't have done the experiment.

TEACHER: What's different about this lever than the other ones we saw?

TOM: The other ones had the fulcrum in the middle. This one has the fulcrum at one end.

Anna then asks students how much effort is needed to hold up the plank. She points out to students that the distance from the effort (student A holding the plank) to the fulcrum is four spaces, and the distance from the load (student B sitting on the plank) to the fulcrum is one space. Anna suggests to the students that the ratio of these two distances is 4 to 1, and the effort must be less than the resistance. Anna adds that if they multiplied the weight of the load times ¼, they would find the effort required to hold up the plank and student B. The students are anxious to see if this is right.

To measure the force required, Anna uses a bathroom scale to hold up the effort and the plank. The bathroom scale is adjusted to zero with the plank resting on it to eliminate the weight of the plank. Anna asks student B, who weighs about 40 kg, to sit on the plank. Anna purposely chooses a student whose weight is easily divisible by 4. Student B sits on the first mark, and Anna asks someone to check the recording on the bathroom scale. The bathroom scale points to about 10 kg. Anna asks students to make predictions as to where student B would have to sit on the plank so that the effort needed to hold up the plank and student B would be one half of her weight. A few students reply very quickly that student B would have to sit two spaces from the fulcrum. For the sake of all students, Anna writes the following information on the board:

Load weight	Load distance	Effort weight	Effort distance
40	1	10	4

The students experiment with a few more students and record the results on the chart. The students note that the effort weight is always one quarter of the student's weight if the student sits on the first mark and one half of the student's weight if the student sits on the second mark. They are amazed that they could actually measure the amount of force required to lift something.

A student then suggests that they could probably calculate how much force they would need to move their imaginary boulder. Anna encourages the whole class to try solving the boulder problem. Anna helps students by reviewing what they know about the boulder problem and by writing the information on the chart: The weight of the boulder is 500 kg. The students want the boulder to be as close as possible to the fulcrum. This means the boulder must be one space away from the fulcrum. When Anna asks, "How much effort do we want to use to lift it?" some students suggest 50 kg. Ultimately, their chart looks like this:

Load weight	Load distance	Effort weight	Effort distance
500 kg	1 space	50 kg	10 spaces

Other students suggest using 10 kg of effort to move the boulder. That means the effort would have to be 50 spaces from the fulcrum. "From here on," Anna states, "it is a matter of calculating how much force they would need to move our hypothetical boulder depending on how far the boulder was from the fulcrum and how far we were from the fulcrum ($500 \times 1 = 50 \times 10$)."

For this lesson, Anna sawed a "life-sized" plank and made appropriate grooves so that her giant homemade lever would work sufficiently well to illustrate the relationship between the length, weight, and force. Although it takes time and effort, Anna provides the children a very valuable experience of lifting each other using the homemade lever. This experience enables children to become more convinced of the theories they had set forth concerning the position of the fulcrum in relation to the resistance. Furthermore, some students actually try to solve their imaginary boulder problem mathematically by finding the length of plank they would need and by determining how much effort they would want to use. We note that Anna provides a real-life problem situation about the effort needed to move the boulder. This approach requires the learner to integrate knowledge and ideas from a variety of sources.

So far, Anna has been setting up many novel problems to expose her students to the workings of levers. These choices enable students to combine their bits and pieces of knowledge in an integrated whole that eventually allows them to translate their new knowledge to the original boulder problem. Anna's experience may be seen from the perspectives of di Sessa (1988) and Driver (1989). These authors argue that children do not have organized theories about the world, but possess a large number of fragments. Transition to scientific theories then involves the systematic organization of children's fragmented knowledge. Anna's story helps us to recall Driver's recommendation that students are provided with several experiences within an area of study and encouraged to organize and interpret those experiences systematically and coherently.

Anna developed an orientation/exploration lesson as well as a problem-solving approach in lessons 1 and 2. She consciously built on students' personal and collective ideas. In the teacher/students' dialogue, we note that one student's idea gives birth to a chain of ideas. By expressing their ideas orally, students are comparing, contrasting, and interrelating their ideas. This process seems to spawn further questions and ideas. It must be pointed out, however, that each time the student "throws the ball," Anna seems to be the first person to catch it. In other words, it is the teacher who bounces the idea back and forth to the student in the teacher-students' dialogue. However, Anna seems to be able to create simple problem contexts before she tosses the question again, thus enabling her students to think of solutions for moving the boulder.

Anna's decision to give students time—a limited resource in the school structure—to think about solving the problem is noteworthy because she seems to recognize that verbal interaction alone is not sufficient. Furthermore, she realizes that the creation of new ideas takes time and interpersonal dialogue. She gives her students the freedom to work by themselves in groups without her direction and intervention, thus giving students ownership of the problem. In turn, because of the time given, students take on the responsibility to spend more time to explore the problem. The students may have recognized Anna's effort to explore their ways of reasoning. The preceding characteristics are essential for successful problem solving as well as for creating common knowledge. Anna seems to work on an idea pointed out by Vygotsky (1976): that all higher cognitive functions originate as well as come into play in complex and multitudes of forms when interpersonal relationships among students in the classroom are established and encouraged. We argue that group work within the classroom environment also leads to personal development.

For Anna, problem solving is the heart of science teaching. Problem solving stimulates and encourages children's thinking in the science classroom. Too often in science classes, when a middle-years student is confronted with a problem, he or she searches for the answer the teacher might have. Perhaps the student might be asking, "How does the teacher want me to solve this problem?" The student rarely asks, "What might be different ways of solving this problem?" The sorts of problems that Anna presented the students seem to be real problems growing out of firsthand experience. They can be solved in more than one way or have more than one acceptable solution. Anna's type of problems cannot best be solved by remembering an algorithm. A procedural component may eventually be necessary to derive

Teaching Standard C

Teachers of science engage in ongoing assessment of their teaching and of student learning.

Teaching Standard E

Guideline: To develop a community of learners, model and emphasize skills, attitudes, and values of scientific inquiry.

Teaching Standard E

Teachers of science develop communities of science learners that reflect the intellectual rigor of scientific inquiry and the attitudes and social values conducive to science learning.

This investigation strongly suggests that the manipulation of concrete materials before formulas are given can lead to a genuine understanding of the principles involved.

the numerical answers, as exemplified by Anna's third lesson. However, the use of an algorithm comes about only after the problem is solved conceptually. From a constructivist viewpoint, Anna's creations of active problem solving are at the heart of meaningful knowledge construction.

If problem solving is viewed as the core of science and if our primary reason for teaching science is to help students understand this way of knowing, then problem solving should constitute the central goal of science education (Good & Smith, 1987). Teachers ought to encourage their students to explore, test, manipulate, propose hypotheses, take detours, reach dead ends, trace and retrace their steps, make mistakes, and recognize and correct their own initiatives rather than having them quickly search for teacher-given solutions. Science curriculum and instruction must place problem solving in a more central position in science education. Bruner (1966) has pointed out that in order to use Anna's type of problem solving to foster common knowledge, the teacher has to want it, encourage it, and provide materials that make it possible. The result is increased student motivation, persistence, and learning intensity (Pizzini, Shepardson, & Abell, 1989).

☼ CHAPTER REFLECTIONS

We have illustrated that the translating and extending phase can be implemented in several ways—by using an STS problem-solving approach, issue-based problem solving, computer-based simulations, and qualitative and quantitative problem solving. Throughout the translating and extending phase, many aspects of the other phases appear.

Questions for Reflective Inquiry

1. What qualities must a teacher have to teach an issue-centered unit?

2. Ideally, what skills do students need to participate in an issue-centered unit?

3. What factors should you consider when implementing an issue-centered approach?

4. What might be the advantages and disadvantages of an issue-centered approach?

SUGGESTED READINGS

American Association for the Advancement of Science. (1989). *Project 2061: Science for all Americans.* Washington, DC.

Bybee, R. W. (1996). *Reforming science education: Social perspectives and personal reflections.* New York: Teachers College Press.

Cross, B. (1992). A balancing act. *Science and Children, 29,* 16–17.

Fensham, P. J. (1988). Approaches to the teaching of STS in science education. *International Journal of Science Education, 10*(4), 346–356.

Good, R., & Smith, M. (1987). How do we make students better problem solvers? *The Science Teacher, 54,* 31–36.

Pizzini, E. L., Shephardson, D. P., & Abell, S. K. (1989). A rationale for and the development of a problem solving model of instruction in science education. *Science Education, 73,* 523–534.

Rutherford, F. J., & Ahlgren, A. (1990). *Science for all Americans.* New York: Oxford Press.

Solomon, J., & Aikenhead, G. S. (Eds.). (1994). *STS education: International perspectives on reform.* New York: Teachers College Press.

Waks, L. J., & Barachi, B. A. (1992). STS in U.S. school science: Perception of selected leaders and their implications for STS education. *Science Education, 76*(1), 79–90.

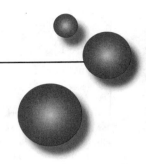

CHAPTER 8

Reflecting and Assessing

1. How does assessment within a constructivist framework differ from assessment within a traditional framework?

2. What do we mean by "authentic" assessment?

3. How can one evaluate the quality of science assessment?

4. What assessment goals have been developed by the National Science Education Standards?

5. What are several performance assessment strategies?

6. What is the difference between continuous and culminating assessment strategies? What are several unique strategies of each type?

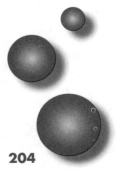

Jacqueline's Voice

I believe that it is important for a teacher to keep an ongoing account of the development of children's conceptions in science. That is why I included assessment strategies throughout my unit plan. Science journals and charts allow children to express their ideas in written form. A teacher can collect this work and record children's levels of understanding. The performance tasks really helped me get a better sense of what students were able to do in science.

JOURNAL ACTIVITY

Reflecting on Assessment Procedures

For what purpose(s) should teachers use assessment?

What might be an innovative but effective means to assess students' science knowledge?

☼ ASSESSMENT WITHIN A CONSTRUCTIVIST FRAMEWORK

Assessment involves the procedures and techniques teachers use to gather information about students' understanding of and attitudes toward the subject matter.

Using a constructivist approach to teaching—exploring and categorizing student concepts; providing students opportunities to negotiate and create shared common knowledge; and translating and extending students' science concepts into relevant, everyday situations—may mean that **assessment** of children's learning will look very different from traditional assessment methods. Traditional assessment methodologies that require student regurgitation of bits of information or one right answer do not best serve as effective assessment practices for constructivist teaching.

Additionally, traditional science tests that include multiple-choice, poorly constructed true/false, or fill-in-the-blank questions are often problematic because there is only one acceptable response for each question. Children can respond only to the options given. An example provided by Murphy (1994) illustrates this point: A child is taking his first test and is asked to identify what rabbits eat. He is offered three choices—lettuce, dog food, or sandwiches. But he knows that rabbits eat carrots, so he draws a carrot in the margin.

Nonnegotiable tests such as these do not enable children to show what they know. Test-taking techniques that set up a "guess what the teacher wants" scenario focus on right or wrong answers and thus have a profound effect on teaching and learning, limiting classroom science activities and student ownership and involvement.

Assessment Standard A

Assessments must be consistent with the decisions they are designed to inform.

Teaching Standard C

Teachers of science engage in ongoing assessment of their teaching and of student learning.

Because we know that children do not simply drop their personal ideas and adopt the ideas presented by the teacher, and because children's ideas tend to develop over a period of time, assessment must of necessity be *continuous*. The information obtained from an ongoing monitoring of the development of children's ideas can reveal areas where children are struggling with concepts so that additional or remedial instruction can be initiated. In this sense, assessment procedures become diagnostic and more valuable as teaching tools.

This is not to say that there is no appropriate time or use for traditional assessment instruments. Some commercially prepared tests, tests devised specifically for state departments of education to assess science proficiency, and carefully constructed tests created by well-informed teachers can and should be used to evaluate cumulative student knowledge and the effectiveness of science programs. However, it is not our goal in this chapter to teach you how to use or create traditional assessment instruments. There are well-written tests and measurements books that can do that far better than we can. It *is* our goal to inform you of an assessment process that complements ongoing and continuous assessment and a constructivist teaching perspective.

Reflective thinking enables teachers to break away from habitual ways of doing things. Although many preservice teachers' school experiences include the completion of worksheets and fill-in-the-blank questions, reflecting about past experiences can help us implement better assessment practices. We learn by reflecting on our experiences. Reflective practice is a component of teaching, and it is essential classroom practice. For assessment practices to change, reflection must occur.

When we adopt a constructivist perspective, we reflect on the fact that knowledge is actively constructed by children on an ongoing basis; thus, assessment should no longer be a recital of facts and memorized concepts in an end-of-unit set of questions or periodic quizzes and tests. Rather, we embrace the premise that assessment is an *integral part of the teaching process*. Emphasis is more on day-to-day observation and sense-making of children talking, doing, reasoning, problem solving, writing, and thinking.

Assessment should not be conducted for the sole purpose of providing grades. It must be used to explore children's ideas, determine how much of the teaching has been effective and with which children, and identify what concepts need to be reexamined and explored further. The National Center for Improving Science Education (quoted in Raizen & Kaiser, 1989) suggests that teachers ask the questions shown in Figure 8-1 when they evaluate the quality of current classroom assessment.

Assessment Standard A

Guideline: Assessment procedures are internally consistent.

Assessment Standard A

Guideline: Assessments have explicitly stated purposes.

- Are there problems that require students to think about and analyze situations?

- Does the test feature sets of problems that call for more than one step in arriving at a solution?

- Are problems with more than one correct solution included?

- Are there opportunities for students to use their own data and create their own problems?

- Are the students encouraged to use a variety of approaches to solve a problem?

- Are there assessment exercises that encourage students to estimate their answers and check their results?

- Is the science information given in the story problem and elicited in the answer correct?

- Is there opportunity for assessing skills (both in the use of science tools and in science thinking) through some exercises that call for hands-on activities?

- Are there exercises included in the overall assessment strategy that need to be carried out over time?

- Are there problems with purposely missing or mistaken information that ask students to find errors or critique the way the problem is set up?

- Are there opportunities for students to make up their own questions/problems or designs?

FIGURE 8-1
Questions to evaluate the quality of classroom assessment (NOTE. From "Assessing Science Learning in Elementary School: Why, What, and How?" by S. A. Raizen and J. S. Kaiser, 1989, *Phi Delta Kappan*, May, p. 721.)

PEER INTERACTION

Analyzing Teacher-Made Science Tests or Classroom Assessment Practices

Obtain a set of teacher-made tests or teacher plans for classroom assessment. Analyze the assessment instruments or practices according to the criteria discussed. What changes would you recommend?

ASSESSMENT STANDARDS

Reform movements in science education are currently active in many countries. The curriculum and assessment reform movement in the United Kingdom, the Pan-Canadian Science Project in Canada, and the National Science Education Standards in the United States have all defined scientific literacy standards for students. The latter encompass elaborate standards for assessment in science education. These cover five important areas:

- The consistency of assessments with the decisions they are designed to inform
- The assessment of both achievement and opportunity to learn science
- The match between the technical quality of the data collected and the consequences of the actions taken on the basis of these data
- The fairness of assessment practices
- The soundness of inferences made about student achievement and opportunity to learn (*National Research Council*, 1996, p. 5)

They emphasize that ideas about assessment have changed radically in the past few years, and that assessment and learning are "two sides of the same coin." The assessment standards define what teachers should teach and what students should learn. Assessments can be done in many formats, such as performances, portfolios, interviews, reports, and essays.

In this book, we are concerned with developing exemplary science teachers and will refer to the *National Science Education Standards* that relate to how teachers might develop and use assessments. Summarizing from the *Standards,* teachers should collect information about students continuously in order to improve their classroom practice, plan curricula, develop self-directed learners, report student progress, and research teaching practices (*National Research Council*, 1996, pp. 87–89).

AUTHENTIC ASSESSMENT

More authentic learning environments, such as those that result from constructivist teaching strategies, lead to more **authentic assessment**. This term, popularized by Grant Wiggins (1989), conveys the idea that assessments should engage students in applying knowledge and skills in the same

Assessment Standard A

Guideline: In assessments, the relationship between decisions and data is clear.

Assessment Standard C

Guideline: Assessment tasks must be authentic.

Authentic assessment means that tests should involve real-life tasks, performances, or challenges that replicate the problems faced by a scientist, historian, or expert in a particular field (Wiggins, 1989, p. 703).

way they are used in the "real world" outside school. Wiggins (1992) states, "I think what's going on is something more radical than rethinking testing. What we're really doing is rethinking our purposes" (p. 37). We are not only debating whether some assessment methods are superior to others, but rather *what is worth assessing.* We must use types of assessment that match the types of teaching and learning carried on in the classroom.

Two types of assessment are being especially promoted as supporting authentic learning. These are **performance** and **portfolio assessments.** Many other types of authentic assessment are detailed in this chapter as well.

Implementation of authentic assessment strategies means that teachers must recognize that assessment is an *integral part of teaching.* All types of assessment reflect the true purpose of instruction. Teachers must review their instructional practices to be certain they are in line with their assessment practices. They can also use assessment results to guide instructional decisions and plan curriculum modifications.

Performance Assessment

Performance or practical assessment provides a much more accurate picture of children's abilities to *understand and do science.* This assessment type ties in very well with a constructivist approach to learning, as it can truly reflect actual teaching and learning activities. In performance tests, questions are not of the type that require children to memorize definitions or formulas; instead, children are given authentic, real-world tasks to do using manipulatives, models, equipment, and practical objectives. Performance questions are practical activities—authentic situations in which children actually observe and manipulate objects, follow directions, design and carry out investigations, and are "performers." They are a valuable type of assessment for teachers following a constructivist style of teaching, as they provide children with a way of demonstrating what meaning they have made of the science concepts discussed in the classroom.

Performance tests are said to accommodate gender differences. Recent research indicates that performance tests are much fairer to girls than written tests, and that girls do as well or better than boys on them (The Scottish Office, 1993). Certain criteria should be followed when designing performance assessment instruments.

Performance Assessment Design Criteria

Designers of performance test items may wish to consider the following criteria, suggested by Wiggins (1992) as tools to guide the design process.

- What kinds of essential tasks, achievements, habits of mind, or other "masteries" are falling through the cracks of conventional tests?
- What are the core performances, roles, or situations that all students should encounter and be expected to master?
- What are the most salient and insightful discriminators in judging actual performances?

Assessments Standard A

Assessments must be consistent with the decisions they are designed to inform.

Performance assessment refers to a variety of hands-on experimental tasks and situations in which students are given opportunities to *demonstrate* their understanding and to *translate* their knowledge in a variety of contexts.

Portfolio assessment uses a collection of representative examples of a student's work.

Assessment Standard B

Achievement and opportunity to learn science must be assessed.

Assessment Standard E

The inferences made from assessments about student achievement and opportunity to learn must be sound.

Assessment Standard D

Guideline: Assessment tasks must be set in a variety of contexts, be engaging to students with different interests and experiences, and must not assume the perspective or experiences of a particular gender, racial, or ethnic group.

- Are a test's necessary constraints on help from others, access to resources, time to revise, test secrecy, and prior knowledge of standards authentic?
- Do our assessment tasks have sufficient depth and breadth to allow valid generalizations about overall student competence?
- Have we ensured that the test will not be corrupted by well-intentioned judges of student work?
- Who are the audiences for assessment information, and how should assessment be designed, conducted, and reported to accommodate the needs of each audience? (Wiggins, 1992, pp. 26–27)

Organization of Performance Assessment

Performance assessments can be organized in three ways: as *stations or circuits* in which children move from workstation to workstation, *set places* where children individually or in pairs design and carry out investigations, and *teacher demonstrations* in which the teacher performs and the students respond. Performance assessment in science could also include acting out or miming specific science concepts.

Investigations can assess many aspects of science, such as the *understanding and application of concepts, ability to design experiments,* and *problem-solving skills.* The area of performing experiments can be further broken down into such skills categories as observing, classifying, inferring, predicting, hypothesizing, controlling variables, measuring, recording data, interpreting data, and handling equipment.

It is important to note that, in some investigations, children actually have to define the problem before developing and carrying out a procedure. In others, there may be more than one right answer so that the emphasis in assessing performance is placed on the procedures, not the answers.

Careful planning for performance assessment activities is critical to their successful implementation. Teacher time must be taken into consideration. Do not rush into an extensive implementation of performance assessment for all science topics, but do it gradually as time permits. Phase in a few items at a time as preparation time and materials allow.

Setting Up Performance Stations

To prepare stations, it is first necessary to select the concepts or procedures that you wish to assess and then carefully design the problems and questions for each station. Place the procedures and questions and the relevant materials on tables or desks. Label each "Station 1," etc., and provide students with a package of answer sheets, one for each station activity. Have individual students circulate from one station to another at a teacher-given signal. (Hold a dry run with a few students in order to estimate an approximate time for doing each station.) It is good to have as many questions as there are students doing the stations, thus facilitating circulation. Performance station sheets for *grade 4* students studying *Cells* and *Sound* are shown in Figures 8-2 and 8-3.

Assessment Standard C

Guideline: For assessments to be valid the feature that is claimed to be measured must be actually measured.

We must emphasize that these categories or process skills are context dependent, and students do not necessarily perform at similar levels of ability in different contexts and investigations.

Assessment Standard A

Guideline: Assessments are deliberately designed.

Performance assessment can be used in a number of subject areas. Science is an excellent subject in which to begin.

STATION 1 SHEET

Station 1   **Animal or Plant Cells?**
(a) Place slide A in the microscope and focus. Observe the cells carefully.
Draw several of the cells in the space below.

(b) Are they plant cells or animal cells? (*Check* √ *one.*)   ___ plant   ___ animal

(c) Place slide B in the microscope and focus. Observe the cells carefully. Draw
several of the cells in the space below.

(d) Are they plant cells or animal cells? (*Check* √ *one.*)   ___ plant   ___ animal

(e) What is the difference between a plant cell and an animal cell?
_____
_____
_____

Tester's Comments: (help with focusing?)

FIGURE 8-2
Animal or plant cells?
(NOTE. From *Manitoba
Science Assessment 1994,*
by Manitoba Education and
Training, Winnipeg,
Manitoba, p. 10.)

The following are some station tasks our preservice teachers have
designed to accompany a unit on the *effects of water on rocks and the landscape* for *fourth-grade* children.

ACTIVITY STATION 1   Observe the different rocks on the table. See how
each rock has a different number attached to it with tape. Categorize
the rocks according to the following criteria:
– Little or no encounter with water
– Some encounter with water
– Lots of encounter with water

ACTIVITY STATION 2   Observe the pictures of landscapes on the table.
Choose one picture and write what you think would happen to the
landscape if a river were diverted through it. Then draw a diagram of
the new landscape.

ACTIVITY STATION 3   Note the clay and the large pile of paper confetti on
the table. Build a model to represent the erosion that would happen
when water brings down sediment from a mountain. After creating
your model with the confetti, draw and label a picture of it. (Students
should use the clay to create a mountain and the confetti to create the
sediment at the bottom of a river that starts on a mountain and ends in
the sea.)

Assessment Standard C

The technical quality of the data
collected is well matched to decisions
and actions taken on the basis of
their interpretation.

FIGURE 8-3
Ruler flick (NOTE. From *Manitoba Science Assessment, 1994*, by Manitoba Education and Training, Winnipeg, Manitoba, p. 12.)

Station 3   **Ruler Flick**
Look at the drawing below.

(a) Clamp the ruler so that 20 cm hangs out off the table. Pull down the end of the ruler quickly and release. What do you observe?

_____
_____

(b) What do you hear? _____
_____

(c) Change the clamp so that only 10 cm hangs out off the table. Pull down the end of the ruler quickly and release. What happened to the pitch of the sound?

_____
_____

(d) Why did this happen? Explain. _____
_____
_____

☀ **PEER INTERACTION**

Station Tasks

1. Discuss the tasks proposed by the preservice teachers. How would you improve or change these assessment tasks?
2. Design student procedure and performance sheets for your modified tasks.

Classroom management may be of prime concern to teachers who are beginning to use performance assessments in their classroom. Often teachers split their class into groups and have only one group doing the stations at a time. Berenson and Carter (1995) have some hints that may be of assistance:

- Set up four centers, one in each corner of the room. For classroom management purposes, students can be working on a written portion of the test while taking turns visiting the centers.

- Use student carrels or partitions to prevent students from imitating each other's work.

- Inform students that there is more than one right answer. Build in points for creativity and unique answers.

- Design several tasks that measure the same skills or concepts. Pass out the task cards to students at random.

- Keep a list of tasks with students' names and check students off over the course of a week or more (Berenson & Carter, 1995, p. 185).

Setting Up Performance Investigations

Special arrangements have to be made if this assessment technique is implemented. The assessor must be free to observe and listen to the students' comments. If the assessor is you, the classroom teacher, the rest of the class must be given an alternative activity so that you may concentrate on evaluating the investigation. An aid or a parent could be called upon to supervise the rest of the class while they are engaged in a self-directed activity.

Students are placed at a table singly or in pairs and are instructed to perform the task outlined on a sheet of paper. (If they are placed in pairs, the situation conforms more nearly to a natural class working situation. The assessment results will, of course, reflect the ability of the pair of students, not the individuals.) Students record their working details and results as instructed. The students' performance, including verbal comments, is observed by the assessor/teacher as the students are doing the investigations. The students' written comments are also considered in assessing their knowledge and understanding. Figures 8-4 and 8-5 show a student's instruction sheet and the assessor's recording sheet, respectively, for the topic "Soil Tests" for a *fourth-grade* unit on *Land and Water*.

For the "Soil Tests" investigation, students work in pairs and are provided with the following materials: three bags of soil, three funnels, filter paper, three beakers, a funnel stand, a timer, three measuring cups, a scoop, paper towels, and a pitcher of water. They are encouraged to discuss the problem and the various ways they might solve it before beginning the investigation. If necessary, the assessor is allowed to show them how to fold and use the filter paper and answer questions about other equipment.

The assessor observes and listens to students as they work and record observations on the comment sheet. The assessor has to make judgments as to whether the students use the inquiry skills successfully. For example, for the skill of observing in this investigation, it was important to note whether students paid attention to the details that were important to the success of the investigations. The use of other inquiry skills should also be assessed and noted on the assessor's sheet.

Assessment Standard B

Guideline: The opportunity-to-learn data focus on the most powerful indicators.

Assessment Standard B

Guideline: Equal attention must be given to assessment of opportunity to learn and to the assessment of student achievement.

FIGURE 8-4
Soil tests (student sheet)
(NOTE. From *Manitoba Science Assessment, 1994*, by Manitoba Education and Training, Winnipeg, Manitoba, p. 16.)

Investigation A. Soil Tests

1. Pretend you are a gardener. You wish to plant your flowers in a soil that will hold the water the longest.

   Your problem is to find out which soil holds the water the longest.

   You have equipment on the table to help you solve this problem. The three soil types are labelled.

   Study the 3 samples of soil and **predict** which soil would hold the water longest.

   Our prediction: Soil _____. Why do you think so?
   _____

2. Set up your investigation to find out the answer to the problem and record your data in the chart.

Soil Type	Result
A	
B	
C	

3. Which soil held the water longest? _____ Why did it do so?
   _____

Using Teacher Demonstrations to Assess Performance

A teacher demonstration can be used to illustrate a performance question in a situation where there is a lack of materials or where there are safety concerns relating to the equipment. One of our preservice teachers used the following demonstration as part of her unit assessment.

Objective. To have students explain the steps of the water cycle.

Materials. Electric kettle (or hot plate with tea kettle), ice cubes, metal tray, oven mitts, shallow pan.

Strategy. POE (predict, observe, and explain).

Procedure. I will practice the demonstration first and then perform the experiment myself for safety reasons. Before performing the experiment, I will ask students to predict what is going to happen to the ice in the tray. Also, I will ask them to infer if anything might happen to the outside of the tray. Then I will plug in the kettle and let it boil. With oven mitts I will place the metal tray full of ice in the steam of the kettle, but not directly over it. Then I will place the pan underneath the tray to catch the falling "rain." See Figure 8-6 (page 216). During the experiment, the students will draw and write their observations. Next, the students will describe and explain the stages of the water cycle—the rising of warm air, cooling of air to create water vapor reaching its dew point, and falling of "rain" or precipitation.

Investigation A. Soil Tests

Observation and Comment Sheet
Rate as poor or good.

Category	P	G	Comments
C.1 Worked co-operatively to design and do the investigation. 2			
C.2.a. Predicted 1 (#1 from student sheet)			
C.2.b. Controlled variables. 1			
C.2.c. Observed 1			
C.2.d. Measured (soils, water, time) 3			soils water time
C.2.e. Recorded data. 3 (#2 on student sheet)			
C.2.f. Interpreted data. 1			
C.2.g. Handled equipment. 1			
C.3.h. Understood the problem. 1			
C.3.i. Solved the problem 2 (#3 from student sheet)			
B. Understood the concept of absorption. 1			

Other comments:

FIGURE 8-5

Soil tests (tester sheet)
(NOTE. From *Manitoba
Science Assessment, 1994,*
by Manitoba Education and
Training, Winnipeg,
Manitoba, p. 17.)

Note: Numbers in each category in Figure 8-5 represent the marks allocated for each section.

 PEER INTERACTION

Using Performance Design Criteria

Using Wiggins's criteria, go back and evaluate the procedures and questions
you designed for Peer Interaction: Station Tasks (see page 212).

FIGURE 8-6
Water cycle simulation

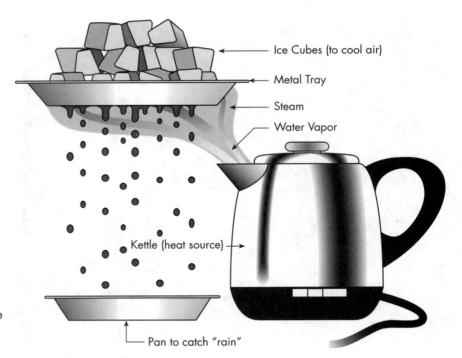

Ice Cubes (to cool air)

Metal Tray

Steam

Water Vapor

Kettle (heat source)

Pan to catch "rain"

The water vapor will reach its dew point, creating water droplets on the outside of the tray. These droplets fall down onto the pan like rain.

Portfolio Assessment

Teaching Standard C

Guideline: Guide students in self-assessment.

Many teachers collect chosen selections of students' work on a daily or weekly basis. These materials represent students' current abilities and diagnose student progress. Collected over a period of time, this work is gathered into folders called portfolios. Portfolios can help students to develop self-assessment abilities as they track their own progress and can show parents evidence of their children's growth and development.

Jasmine (1992) has identified four types of portfolios for assessment use.

Assessment Standard A

Guideline: Assessments have explicitly stated purposes.

- The *collection portfolio* is used to collect a wide variety of works that can be drawn from for specific assessment.
- The *student's showcase/display portfolio* includes the student's best work to show growth and development over time.
- The *teacher/student assessment portfolio* includes many of the copies selected from the collection portfolio, together with any necessary documentation for assessment. This might include anecdotal records, conference records, teacher-made tests, a self-evaluation, and student checklists.
- The *teacher resource portfolio* is a private portfolio for the teacher to keep any additional information or resources beneficial to each student (Jasmine, 1992).

Items for a science portfolio should be chosen conscientiously and deliberately. Kamen (1993) described a teacher, Virginia, who set aside some time each Friday for children to select their own best science work of the week. Virginia also made it a point to give students assignments that would lend themselves to portfolio inclusion. For instance, she planned lessons that required written work or drawings to illustrate science concepts or demonstrate an understanding of scientific ideas.

The items in a science portfolio may be very creative. They might include journal entries about science ideas and/or experiments, taped discussions with peers about science concepts, written reactions to new concepts, a science autobiography, original work with revised ideas showing mastery of concepts, creative science work (music, art, poetry, video, computer disk), or answers to open-ended science questions. Portfolios can also contain students' best homework (and reasons why they feel it is their best), explanations of what students feel they learned on a test, a letter to an absent friend explaining a science concept, reflections, and captions.

Portfolio Assessment Criteria

Portfolios may be used to illustrate and assess students' knowledge, understandings, skills, attitudes, and dispositions. Through portfolios, students can demonstrate their effort, progress, and achievement to their teacher, peers, and parents. Portfolios are useful to indicate current abilities and develop self-assessment abilities. The teacher may use portfolios for a summative report and/or a grade. Depending on the use of the portfolio, the teacher determines what he or she considers to be *evidence* of learning and *what will count as evidence.* Collins (1992a) outlines four classes of evidence:

- *Artifacts* might include journal records or illustrations a student has done, his or her records of an experiment, or a collection of newspaper stories dealing with the area studied.
- *Reproductions* might include photographs, cassettes, or videotapes.
- *Attestations* are documents about the portfolio owner written by someone else. This other person could be a classmate.
- *Productions* are those articles prepared especially for the portfolio— goal statements, reflections, and captions (summarized from Collins, 1992a, pp. 456–457).

Every piece in the portfolio should have a caption stating what it is, what evidence of learning is being documented, and why it is evidence. These captions allow learners to express what they have learned in their own words.

Student Self-Assessment

Portfolios encourage students to reflect upon their work. Students may write comments on their work after they have gathered it for a period of time. Over time, students will learn how to accurately assess their work, identify their best work, and be skillful in explaining why certain pieces should appear in the portfolio. In helping students ready their portfolios for

Assessment Standard C

Guideline: Students must have adequate opportunity to demonstrate their achievements.

Assessment Standard C

Guideline: Assessment tasks must be authentic.

parent nights, Hebert suggests that teachers can guide student reflections with the following questions:

- How has your work changed since last year (or last term)?
- What do you know about science that you didn't know at the beginning of the year?
- What would you like Mom and Dad to understand about your portfolio?
- Can you organize your work so that it will show what you understand? (Hebert, 1992, p. 61)

The popular use of portfolios in schools made our preservice teachers anxious to use them in their teaching. The following is a well-thought-out experience two preservice teachers developed.

8-1: Using Portfolios for *Grade 1* Children

Judy Horst, Cindy Ganz

First-grade science includes a theme called *People as Organisms.* For this topic, we used the portfolio to collect each child's discoveries. We had child partners assess portfolios. The guidelines for portfolio partners were as follows:

- Look closely at your partner's work sample.
- Write your name and today's date on the top of an index card.
- Write sentences that answer these questions:
  - What do you think the sample shows your partner learned?
  - What do you think your partner did well?
  - What do you think the sample shows your partner can do?

We devised a portfolio comment sheet (see Figure 8-7).We also devised a letter to send to parents, explaining the portfolio (see Figure 8-8).

Preservice Teacher Reflections

We used portfolios as part of the assessment of the science unit. The children included pictures they drew of themselves. They included the graphs comparing themselves to other students, thus bringing in mathematics concepts. The students incorporated taped conversations with their peers about their individual likes and dislikes. They used their school photographs to

Name _____   Date _____

Goals:

Student Comments:

Teacher Comments:

FIGURE 8-7
Portfolio comment sheet

emphasize what they learned about hair and eye color. They also used mold-ings of their feet to show how they integrated science with art.

All of these items lead children toward observing the progress of their own learning. If we had an opportunity to continue to document progress, we would consider noting areas where the student needs more work/help, and the students' responsibility for learning. Of all the items collected for a portfolio, we feel that the most insightful are the reflections and/or captions students wrote or dictated for each piece of work. We would stress the

Dear Parents,

Today your child is bringing home his/her science portfolio, reflecting progress in his/her learning. Included are the following items:

These baseline samples are examples of your child's work at the beginning of the school year. You can compare later work with these samples to see how your child has grown in mastery of science concepts. Attached to each work sample, you will find my comments, as well as evaluations and goals written by your child. Comments by their portfolios partners are also included. Please examine the portfolio with your child. When you are finished, return the entire portfolio to school.

Thank you.

Sincerely,

First-Grade Teacher

FIGURE 8-8
Early letter to parents to explain portfolio use

importance of these on every item students include in their portfolios. We suspect that students' initial reflections will always be sparse, but with feedback and experience, these reflections would become the most useful tools for teacher and students.

Most valuable for us to understand was using portfolio assessment to observe student's learning processes. The portfolio offers a comprehensive look at how a student is progressing. It is an effective way to see at a glance how the child is interacting with and processing new concepts. It may seem overwhelming to set up a portfolio system, but it is quite acceptable to start in a very small way and build on it over time. Some teachers use portfolios only for one subject area; others, for all areas or for integrated themes. It is ideal if the students put their completed work into their own collection portfolios and then decide, together with the teacher, which pieces should be included in the assessment portfolio and why.

Portfolios allow students to see for themselves how their ideas are progressing and how they are constantly grasping more sophisticated concepts. They also show students where they need to make improvements and what their individual weak spots are. Lastly, portfolios remove much of the pressure of peer competition for grades and allow students to focus on their own individual progress.

Concerns

Professional Development Standard A

Guideline: Science learning experiences for teachers must incorporate ongoing reflection on the process and outcomes of understanding science through inquiry.

Because of our limited opportunities to use portfolios over a long period of time, we have some concerns about using portfolios. How do portfolios work in large classrooms? How much time does it take to go through each portfolio with each child? How does a teacher best decide what to include or not include in a student's portfolio? Most parents are familiar with traditional assessment. Would parents still rely predominantly on letter grades? Portfolios take more organizational preparation and may not be the best assessment solution for everyone.

For those who see the potential and are willing to initiate portfolio use, we suggest you might be more successful if you first identify answers to the following questions on management suggested by Collins:

- For what purpose will the portfolio be used (self-reflection, grading, a narrative report on student progress, parent conferences, promotion to the next grade)?
- How much input will students have in deciding what is to be included in the portfolio?
- How often will the portfolio be reviewed and by whom?
- Which portfolio pieces are required and which are selected by students?
- Will work be produced alone or can it be a group portfolio?
- Where will the portfolio be kept?
- How much work will be included? (Collins, 1992b, pp. 25-27)

Finally, we suggest initiating portfolios gradually; the use of portfolios is an evolutionary process. Start small. As you begin to build a scheme to implement portfolio use, remember to plan for appropriate rubrics to assess student work.

RUBRICS FOR SCORING ASSESSMENT ITEMS

Many types of assessment, such as open-ended questions, performance tests, journals, and portfolios, depend on a greater degree of judgment than multiple-choice, true and false, or-fill-in-the-blank questions. The term *rubric,* often used to mean "scoring key," refers to the guidelines laid out for judging student work. McColskey and O'Sullivan (1993) suggest different ways to arrange the criteria against which student work will be judged.

Assessment Standard C

Guideline: Assessment tasks and methods of presenting them must provide data that are sufficiently stable to lead to the same decisions if used at different times.

Point System

A point system assigns points for certain features of the student's response. Open-ended questions are often scored with this approach because points can reflect partial as well as full credit for a response. For example, grade 3 students were given appropriate measuring equipment and asked to find out if stirring makes any difference in how fast sugar cubes and loose sugar dissolve. McColskey and O'Sullivan describe what the point system for their responses might look like for this performance activity:

4 points: If the response states that both types of sugar dissolve faster when stirred, but loose sugar still dissolves faster than cubes
3 points: If the response indicates that stirring made a difference but doesn't describe the relative difference (that loose sugar still dissolves faster)
2 points: If the response describes the relative speed (loose sugar dissolves faster) but not the effects of stirring or if the response just describes what happens (stirring makes sugar fall apart)
1 point: For incorrect responses
0 points: For no response (McColskey & O'Sullivan, 1993, p. 41)

Checklists

A checklist can also be used to indicate that a student has effectively completed the steps involved in a task or demonstration. Checklists can be applied to written work such as journals or to observable behavior. The following checklist could be used for the sugar-dissolving task:

______ 1. Loose sugar tested
______ 2. Sugar cubes tested
______ 3. Measurements done effectively
______ 4. Measurements problematic
______ 5. Problems in timing how fast sugar dissolved

_____ 6. Timed how fast sugar dissolved

_____ 7. Final answer consistent with evidence (McColskey & O'Sullivan, 1993, p. 42)

Students are given a check (√) for each criterion that applies. Different items on the checklist can be accorded different values.

Analytic Rating Scales

Rating scales describe performance along a continuum. An example follows:

> Student measurements in the investigation were inadequate, partially satisfactory, satisfactory, exemplary.

Focused Holistic Rating Scales

Rather than assigning separate scores for each important aspect of task performance, focused holistic ratings consider all the criteria simultaneously and result in a single summary rating or grade. This approach may be the most appropriate when the purpose is to provide students with an overall index of their performance on a task or product. For a performance test item on electricity, the scale might look as follows:

> *4 points:* Gives complete and acceptable answers to all questions; provides acceptable rationale; includes a complete and accurate diagram of a circuit with supporting evidence; demonstrates understanding of the concepts of electricity and conductivity; may use descriptive terms (conductor, flow, current, etc.).
>
> *3 points:* Gives fairly complete and acceptable answers to *most* questions; provides good answers, but rationale may be vague; includes a complete diagram of a circuit; shows understanding of the concept of electricity and conductivity; responds to explanation questions in an acceptable manner.
>
> *2 points:* Several incomplete or unsatisfactory answers; rationale is very limited; shows some understanding of the concept of electricity and conductivity; diagram of a circuit may be missing or incomplete.
>
> *1 point:* Very little response (diagram only or few answers); partial answers to a small number of questions, no rationale; does not include a diagram of a circuit; contains at least one correct answer (McColskey & O'Sullivan, 1993, p. 35, from California Assessment Program, Science Performance Field Test, Grade 6, 1990, California State Department of Education).

Assessment Standard B

Guideline: Equal attention must be given to assessment of opportunity to learn and to the assessment of student achievement.

☀ ADDITIONAL ASSESSMENT STRATEGIES

Even as both performance and portfolio assessment can aid teachers in assessing students' ongoing progress, other methodologies can provide additional continuous or culminating feedback. For a constructivist teacher, continuous or formative assessment is by far the most helpful kind because both the teacher and students receive more immediate feedback throughout the teaching and learning process. Culminating or summative assessment that is used for evaluative purposes focuses on levels of conceptual understanding that students have reached at the end of their unit of study.

Evaluation involves making value judgments based on the information provided by the process of assessment. Evaluation takes place when we summarize student progress in reports to principals and parents.

Continuous Assessment Strategies

Continuous assessment strategies need to be designed to fit in with the topic of a science unit, students' prior ideas, teachers' teaching styles, and students' learning styles. The following are lessons that Jacqueline, a preservice teacher, designed that allow for continuous assessment strategies to guide her instructional plans. For example, in developing a unit on *electricity* with *grade 4* students, Jacqueline tried a variety of nontraditional ways to assess her students' ideas about science concepts and her use of constructivist teaching practices.

Jacqueline's Lessons

Lesson 1

Objectives

In performing investigations, students should be able to do the following:

- Experiment with some materials that, when rubbed together, acquire an electric charge
- Observe the attraction of an uncharged object by a charged object
- Propose their personal theories as to why charged objects attract or repel
- Share their findings and personal theories during interactive whole group discussion

Lesson Activities

Set up four centers where student groups explore aspects of static electricity. In each center, students will experiment with fur, wool cloth, plastic combs, paper, and plastic wrap to see how objects might be attracted to each other or repelled. Direct students to note their findings, writing predictions, observations, and explanations in their science journals. When finished, ask student groups to discuss their findings and explain why they think some objects are attracted to each other and others repelled.

The lesson activities Jacqueline describes here are initial lesson activities only. As she considers the developing meanings the children construct, she will continue with suitable activities to help develop the lessons' objectives.

Assessment

Read children's *science journals* describing their personal thoughts and ideas about the investigation. Assess children's understanding of science concepts from their writings and drawings. Do not mark observations as right or wrong.

Lesson 2

Objectives

In performing the investigation, students should be able to do the following:

- Demonstrate through explanations and diagrams that they understand that like charges will repel each other
- Demonstrate through explanations and diagrams the circumstances under which attractions and repulsions occur

Lesson Activities

Conduct a teacher demonstration with balloons that have been rubbed with charged combs. Have students observe how the balloons repel each other. Have them suggest reasons for this repulsion. Hold a discussion about charged and uncharged objects. Record children's ideas on chart paper.

Set up the classroom so children can experiment with and manipulate the objects. Encourage children to test their predictions and then write about the results in their science journals. Remind the children that the ideas posted on the chart paper can be used to assist them with their writings.

Assessment

- Use *chart paper* to record the development of children's ideas. In subsequent lessons use the ongoing recordings on the chart as a means of self-assessment to see if the desired objectives are being understood by the children. The children may also use the chart paper as a form of reference when doing other activities.
- Set up a *performance assessment* with set places where children can demonstrate and explain how they can make the comb and the balloon attract and repel each other.

Lesson 3

Objectives

In performing this activity, students should be able to do two things:

- Depict how current electricity moves along a wire as in the simulation
- Compare and contrast static electricity and current electricity

Lesson Activities

Review the electric charges students observed in previous static electricity explorations. Ask students to identify other ways electricity might be "created."

Do a simulation of an electric circuit by asking children to hold hands with each other, using a pretend battery to complete the circuit. Have them pass squeezes along the circuit of hands to simulate how current electricity passes along a wire from a battery as in Figure 8-9. Have them compare static and current electricity.

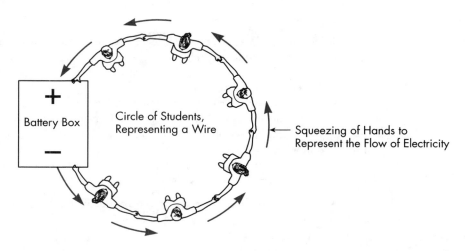

Battery Box

Circle of Students,
Representing a Wire

Squeezing of Hands to
Represent the Flow of Electricity

FIGURE 8-9
Simulation of an
electric current

Assessment

Conduct a *large group discussion* comparing current and static electricity. Ask students what is required to actually create an electric circuit. Responses will probably include a battery, wire, and light bulb. Then ask students what they observed that made static electricity. Specifically, ask students how they produced the electric charge.

Here you can evaluate the success of your simulation lesson. Make notes about the activity, including student comments and questions. Might there be a better way to introduce current electricity?

Lesson 4

Objective

In performing the investigation, students should be able to construct a simple circuit.

Lesson Activities

Have the children write a prediction in their journals as to how they could create an electrical current to light the bulb by using the available materials (light bulb, battery, and wires). Challenge the children to use the materials to construct an electrical circuit that can turn on the light bulb.

When all are successful, pose these questions to the group: "What would happen if both ends of the wire were held on the negative end of the battery? What would happen if both ends of the wire were held on the positive end of the battery?" Have them give reasons for their responses.

Assessment

For this assessment, the teacher could integrate science with creative drama. Have the children role-play in pairs. One person could play the role of an interviewer, while the other person plays the role of a scientist or inventor. The interviewer is to question the scientist as to how he or she made the electric current operate to power the light bulb. Some children may feel more comfortable expressing themselves to their peers in this informal setting. Make sure the partners have a chance to switch roles. The teacher can move about the classroom and monitor children, checking for individual understanding and making notes about responses. Questions asked could pose further problem(s) or extensions of the activity, including the following:

- What might you need to do to try to make the light bulb operate by a switch?
- What if you needed to light two bulbs? How might you do that?
- This type of role-playing can be an excellent preparation for *student-led conferences.* A science center could be set up at a student-led conference, and the children could explain to their parents how an electric circuit operates, using the materials from this lesson.

As you read through the following pages, you will recognize some of the strategies that Jacqueline used in her lessons. Many other assessment strategies are suggested to provide a diverse approach to assessment. Teachers have found many of the following assessment strategies helpful to monitor student progress through a science unit. Some can be used with the class as a whole to help guide your teaching, whereas other strategies are more useful for individual student guidance. You can also use these strategies to provide continuous feedback on the effectiveness of your teaching. Thus, these strategies can help guide you as to when to expand on a topic, reteach certain concepts, and take a break and revisit a topic later to promote a deeper understanding and positive attitudes.

Teaching Standard C

Guideline: Analyze assessment data to guide teaching.

Charting Children's Ideas

Display on a chart students' ideas that you glean from exploration activities. For an example, see Figure 8-10. Add students' ideas to the chart as the unit

FIGURE 8-10
Children's ideas about *Static Electricity*

Static electricity lifts or picks up objects.
Static electricity resides in matter.
Static electricity is like glue.
Static electricity is the result of two kinds of charges.
Static electricity gives me a shock.

progresses using colored pens so that students can easily see the development of their own ideas. Cross out those ideas that the students collectively agree to drop as learning progresses. Encourage students to reflect on their initial ideas and the progression of their ideas. Openly discuss with students the development of their ideas.

Personal Science Journals/Notebooks

Journal writing may be used as an assessment tool. Encourage students to write, record, and draw in their journals freely during and after each lesson. This type of record will provide both the teacher and the students with a sense of individual progress. To get started, you may wish to ask students to consider these questions:

- What is the problem we are investigating?
- What do you predict will happen?
- What did you do in this investigation?
- What did you observe happen in this investigation?
- What did you find out?
- How do these ideas fit in with what we already know or believe about (the topic)?
- What should we do now to find out more?

These writings should help students clarify their ideas and will also help you find out how students' meaning-making is progressing. Note two students' comments about their science classes in Figure 8-11.

Other ideas for journal items follow:

- Write a science autobiography that explains what science has been for you since the first grade.
- What are your feelings about science so far this year?
- Marc and Ana are absent today. Describe for them in words and pictures what you learned today in science so that Marc and Ana can learn today's lesson when they come back to school (Berenson & Carter, 1995, pp. 182–183).

Berenson and Carter also gave some hints to help teachers begin to use journal writing as an assessment method:

- Begin student journals with "writing with feeling" questions. These are perceived as less threatening since there are no right or wrong answers.
- Encourage students to write more words by discussing your expectations with the class or showing other students' writing as models.
- Respond to students in writing. For journals, it is not necessary to respond to all entries. Collect 5–10 journals a day for review, or ask students to select what entry they are particularly interested in having you read.

Teaching Standard C

Guideline: Guide students in self-assessment.

Teaching Standard D

Guideline: Design and manage the learning environment by engaging students in designing their own learning environment.

FIGURE 8-11
Examples of students'
journal entries

> *In class today we learned about force and machines. It is confusing trying to figure out what is the effort and the resistance of each machine but the teachers tried to make this clearer. When we worked in partners to understand better.*

In class today we learned about force and machines. It is confusing trying to figure out what is the effort and the resistance of each machine but the teachers tried to make this clearer. When we worked in partners to understand better.

> *Science class was interesting. Today we learned what a simple machine was, and it was different from what I had thought. I had a little bit of trouble understanding how a screw could be a machine, but understood better by the end of the lesson.*

Science class was interesting. Today we learned what a simple machine was, and it was different from what I had thought. I had a little bit of trouble understanding how a screw could be a machine, but understood better by the end of the lesson.

- Set a timer or have a specific time period set aside each day or week where students know they will be expected to write about science (Berenson & Carter, 1995, p. 183).

Anecdotal Records

Many teachers have found that keeping anecdotal records of individual students' comments, questions, and ideas helped document any growth and change in their ideas. One successful and not too time-consuming method used by a teacher was the recording of observations of students' behavior on stick-on notes while moving about the class (date the notes, put students' names on them, and place them in students' files at the end of the day or week).

Interviews or Conferences

Do not interview students during recess, after school, or during lunch break because they need time for personal leisure.

Short conferences or interviews with individual children or small groups of students are a good way to monitor children's meaning-making throughout the teaching of the unit. Students could be interviewed during regular periods while the rest of the class is writing in journals or engaged in science reading.

Most students enjoy being interviewed because they love getting the teacher's undivided attention. Some children feel more comfortable expressing themselves on a one-to-one basis, while others prefer to have one or two of their peers present. Keep notes on these meetings in students' science portfolios. Some sample questions follow:

- What do you know now about static electricity that you didn't know before you studied this unit?
- Explain how submarines work.
- How would you tell whether a pebble had come from a stream or a mountain?
- What are the similarities and differences between spiders and insects?

Berenson and Carter (1995) offer some suggestions about how to conduct interviews.

- Put students at ease. Conduct the interview as if it were a conversation. Explain to the students why you are interviewing them.
- Use neutral, reinforcing terms such as "I see, I hear what you're saying," and "I understand." Stay away from leading responses such as, "Good, that's right!" and "Excellent!" Remember to keep non-verbal clues as neutral as possible. Nod, maintain good eye contact, and restate what you think you have heard.
- Try not to lead the students or turn the interview into an instructional session, unless you want the interview to serve as remedial instruction.
- Plan a few basic questions that will allow you to gain understanding of students' ideas. Use probes to draw out students' ideas ("Can you tell me more about that?" "Can you explain your thinking?" "Where did your idea about this come from?").
- If possible, record the session so that you are not distracted from responding to and listening to student ideas (Berenson & Carter, 1995, p. 185).

Self- and Peer Assessment

You may find it useful to develop a simple system to encourage students to do some self-assessment so that they can take more responsibility for their own learning. Rudd and Gunstone (1993) have made considerable progress in encouraging young children to do this. They relate how a classroom teacher used questionnaires and concept maps as integral parts of the teaching/learning strategies, which were wholeheartedly accepted by the children. Grade 3 students prepared lessons for a grade 1 class, who in turn were asked to assess the grade 3 class's teaching efforts. This teacher's work revealed that the focus can be shifted from the teacher as assessor to the students themselves as assessors.

Teaching Standard C

Guideline: Use multiple assessment methods and systematically gather data about student understanding and ability.

Teaching Standard B

Guideline: To guide and facilitate learning, challenge students to accept and share responsibility for their own learning.

Teaching Standard C

Guideline: Guide students in self-assessment.

FIGURE 8-12
Children's self-assessment
sheet

Name _____ Date _____

1. How do I feel about this investigation?

_____

2. What was the most important thing I learned from this investigation?

_____

3. What was my favorite part of this investigation?

My least favorite part?

_____

4. Did anything in the investigation surprise me?

_____

5. Is there any other investigation that I would like to do now?

_____

Peer assessment has to be conducted in a nonthreatening environment.

One of our preservice teachers developed and used with her students the self-assessment questionnaire shown in Figure 8-12.

Try developing a system of peer assessment to be used in conjunction with cooperative group learning strategies. Have students reflect on their own and their peers' thinking patterns and their achievements during their investigations. Peer assessment has been used effectively to help assess students' participation in science investigations. See Figure 8-13 for a sample peer and self-assessment form.

Teaching Standard E

Guideline: To develop a community of science learners, enable students to have a significant voice in decisions about the content of their work and require students to take responsibility for the learning of all members of the community.

Teaching Standard E

Guideline: To develop a community of learners, nurture collaboration among students.

Projects and Reports

Many teachers have discovered that children benefit from participating in developing the criteria for assessing their reports or projects. A *fifth-grade* classroom group developed the following criteria:

- Knowledge and understanding of the problem
- Clarity of thinking
- Use of information
- Suitability of communication styles
- Evidence of conceptual development

Guide students to develop criteria as soon as the project/report has been assigned. This will not only help students understand and set clear goals and expectations for their work, but also help you as the teacher ascertain that students know what the project/report entails.

Peer Assessment

Rating Scale:	1. Never	2. Sometimes	3. Often	4. Always

My partner:

1. Shared the workload.

2. Helped me.

3. Was cooperative.

4. Suggested ideas.

5. Was reliable.

Comments:

Self-Assessment

Rating Scale:	1. Never	2. Sometimes	3. Often	4. Always

1. Shared my ideas.

2. I helped my partner.

3. I finished my work on time.

4. I cooperated with others.

5. I did my best.

6. I am happy with the end result.   Yes ____   No ____

7. I enjoy working in groups.   Yes ____   No ____

General comments:

FIGURE 8-13
Peer and self-assessment form

REFLECTIVE PRACTICE

Continuous Assessment Strategies

How would the continuous assessment strategies used with a grade 2 class differ from those used with a grade 6 class? Or would they?

Culminating Assessment Strategies

Culminating (or summative) assessment focuses on the conceptual ideas held by students at the end of a science unit. You may be able to use the same items or a variation of the items used at the beginning of the unit to elicit students' understandings of the topic. It is important that the focus be on questions related to *conceptual understanding,* not on rote learning. There are many ways to frame these questions. Questions that include diagrams or physical materials should form the bulk of the assessment. Questions answered as a part of *performance assessment* measures and those embedded in *science portfolios* have previously been described. However, alternative methods for both written and performance evaluations are also viable.

As you review the use of written assessment questions, remember that written answers can be a barrier for children who have difficulty with reading, writing, and spelling. Children's expressions of their understanding of science concepts can be assessed in ways that are not dependent on their reading and writing skills. For example, orally answering questions or making visual representations may acceptably illustrate an understanding of concepts in a unit of study. Science can be a great equalizer of children's abilities, especially for children whose proficiency in English is limited.

Concept Maps

This method can be especially effective with middle-school students and is described in chapter 3.

As a culminating assessment strategy, students can construct concept maps from a list of concepts. Give students concept labels and have them draw a concept map with linking words and examples.

The scoring of concept maps is idiosyncratic and can depend on the emphasis a teacher puts on the material. Normally, one would give a mark for each of the concepts correctly placed and for each correctly stated relationships.

Two examples follow; others can be easily constructed from the main concepts of any unit. Draw a concept map using the following labels:

1. Weather, prediction, heat, temperature, air movement, fronts, air pressure, relative humidity, moisture, clouds, dew point, precipitation
2. Forces, pushes and pulls, friction, balanced forces, unbalanced forces, gravity, weight

Assessment Standard B

Guideline: Achievement data collected focus on the science content that is most important for students to learn.

Concept maps for a unit, developed by the teacher, can be used as a basis for the development of questions. Sections or "arms" of the concept map can be selected and questions framed about those areas. In this way, one ensures that knowledge represented by the concept map is being tested. The concept map in Figure 8-14a has pre-unit and post-unit tests developed from it. The questions in Figure 8-14b, based on this concept map, could be used for exploring children's ideas at the beginning of a unit. The items for culminating assessment, also based on the concept map but dealing more specifically with the concepts studied, are shown in Figure 8-14c.

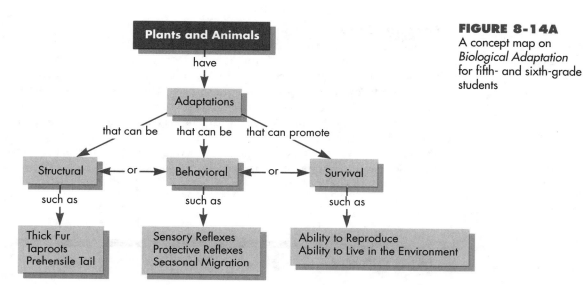

FIGURE 8-14A
A concept map on *Biological Adaptation* for fifth- and sixth-grade students

1. Hares and arctic foxes turn white in winter and brown in summer. How does this change help these animals survive? What do you think causes this change of color?

2. How are a wolf's teeth suited for the food it eats?

3. What are two different ways in which seeds are scattered?

4. What causes most ducks and geese to fly south in fall and return in the spring?

5. Look closely at the following pictures of birds (with different types of beaks) and infer what type of food they eat and where they would find it.

FIGURE 8-14B
Questions for exploring children's ideas on *Biological Adaptation*

1. Describe what an adaptation is, and give an example of a plant and an animal adaptation.

2. Name three structural adaptations of mammals that live in cold climates.

3. If you found a plant with very sharp thorns all along its stem, what would you infer about it?

4. Why is color so important to many animals' survival?

5. Describe two ways in which animals adapt to seasonal changes.

FIGURE 8-14C
Questions for cumulative assessment on *Biological Adaptation*

Concept Stories

A concept story is a story written in such a way as to incorporate a science concept or idea into a real-life situation. The story should demonstrate an understanding of that concept within the context in which it is presented. These stories can provide much insight into what meanings children have for the given concepts. Concept stories involve science concepts narrated in a story form. They combine science with language arts. Scoring of concept stories will depend on whether the concepts are correctly used in the story. The following case study describes one preservice teacher's experience using concept stories for culminating assessment purposes.

8-2: Using Concept Stories

April Horvath

The *grade 6* students had just completed a unit on *Weather*. In this unit, they had covered concepts such as *condensation, evaporation, molecules, water vapor, clouds, air pressure,* and *humidity*. I decided that I would use the concept story strategy to help assess students' understanding. I listed the foregoing concepts on the board so that the students could refer to them. The students were keen and motivated. Here are some samples of student responses:

These are students' first attempts at this type of assessment. Some relate to personal experience, while others are in the creative writing aspect.

One morning I went to look out the window. When I looked out the window I saw lots of condensation on it. Outside there was lots of swelling cumulus clouds in the sky. After a while I went outside. Then we got a shower. So then I went in to make a cup of tea. When I boiled the water, it evaporated into the air. That was called evaporation.

• • •

At a science place in the city my dad (who is a scientist) was doing some experiments. They were: boiling a kettle and experimenting on molecules and water vapor. He also was using a barometer to measure air pressure. I had lots of fun in the science lab.

• • •

The condensation was heavy on the windows because the temperature outside reached dew point. Also because it's so warm in here so when cold and warm meet it makes condensation.

• • •

Downstairs, Mrs. Discovery was over top a pot of boiling hot water with a tele-scope. 555,555.555 molecules are in this pot said Mrs Discovery. Look at that water vapor from the kettle exclaimed Mr. Discovery.

"The sky is full of Swelling Cumulous", said Julie. "I'm going to have a look at my experiment, the air pressure is very high, because the balloon is blown up."

"No evaporation is going to take place today, because it already took place last night. So it's going to rain today" said Mr. Discovery. "I love rain, I'm going to have a great day!" said Julie.

Preservice Teacher Reflections

My students were not familiar with this type of assessment. They were con-fused by the idea of stories being used in science. I asked them to use the words to show me that they knew what the words meant. I found that some students went to get out a textbook to find definitions for the words. Other students began to ask each other questions such as, "What are molecules?"

For the most part, it seemed as though each child had his or her own unique way of understanding these words. Although many of the things that the students said were similar, most of them used different words to describe what they knew.

Many of the students talked about seeing molecules in the air when you see steam. Other students seemed to understand that a special instrument was needed in order to see molecules. I could take the time to clarify the idea of "seeing" molecules with the students as a class in a discussion as part of a follow-up to this assessment.

Some of the students got so carried away with the writing of the story and being creative that they lost the focus of the activity, which was to show what they knew about weather-related concepts.

It is not always necessary to give a list of words that should be included in the story. Students can focus on the outcome of a particular situation based on the science concepts they have previously learned. Varying degrees of concept understanding may be reflected in their stories.

> Marks for concept stories should be based on using science concepts correctly as well as on creativity.

Labeled Diagrams

Drawings and labeled diagrams can provide much insight into children's thinking. Some children find it easier to explain themselves in this way. Some suggestions for science assignments are given here.

> Assessment Standard B
>
> **Guideline:** The opportunity-to-learn data focus on the most powerful indicators.

- Use a diagram to illustrate the water cycle. Label and explain your diagram.
- A feather is floating through the air. As it passes over a radiator, it suddenly begins to rise. Explain through a diagram why this might be happening.

- Use a diagram to show that you understand the difference between a parallel and a series circuit.
- Draw the forces acting on a ball being rolled down an incline.

One of our preservice teachers had just done several investigations in the unit *Physical and Chemical Changes* with *grade 5* children. They were then asked to draw diagrams to compare a physical change and a chemical change (and explain the difference). One student's diagrams (see Figure 8-15) reveal her general understanding.

Explanations Based on Situations

Having children explain the reasons for a situation will help you find out what meaning they have for the concepts involved. Here are some suggested questions.

FIGURE 8-15
Child's diagrams about
*Physical and Chemical
Changes*

FIGURE 8-16
Student trying to roller-skate
on an oil-soaked driveway

Some people squeeze oranges for their breakfast juice. Is squeezing an
orange to make orange juice a physical change or a chemical change?
Give your reasons.

Many people who wear glasses find that they often fog up when they
enter a warm room from the outdoors. Why does that happen?

Explanations Based on Pictures

Students can often relate to pictures or comic situations and are able to give
explanations for the situations represented. An example referring to the
concept of *friction* is presented in Figure 8-16.

Problem-Solving Questions

These types of questions will help you see whether students are able to
apply the newly acquired meanings they have for the concepts. Some suggestions follow:

Assessment Standard B

Achievement and opportunity to
learn science must be assessed.

A hunter is out in the woods in the middle of winter. It is very cold. He reaches
into his rucksack and pulls out a jar of jam with a metal lid. He tries and tries, but
he cannot open the lid. All he has with him are a pack of matches, a pot, and
some paper. Nearby is some fallen wood. Give a possible solution to the hunter's
problem.

•   •   •

A new factory moves into your small town. A few years later, the river in your
town turns brown and is very polluted. Some scientists state that the source of
the pollution is the new factory. This factory is important to the town, bringing
in jobs and money. Think about the problem and answer the following questions:

What might be the effects of the polluted water on the town?
What would you do?
What could the town do about the problem?

• • •

Suggest two methods for moving a piano onto the second floor of a house with a spiral stairway. Describe each method and draw diagrams.

• • •

You are a manager of a wildlife farm and wish to keep down the population of coyotes that are bothering some of the animals. Decide on a method that would do this without killing any animals.

Open-Ended Questions

Teaching Standard C

Guideline: Use multiple assessment methods and systematically gather data about student understanding and ability.

Open-ended questions are very useful in that students are given the opportunity to expand on their scientific ideas. Be sure to provide sufficient information so that they can respond in their own words. Use real-life examples such as those following.

A person walks into a room and turns on a switch. A few minutes go by, and the liquid in the thermometer begins to move down. Did the person turn on the heat or shut it off? Explain how you know this.

• • •

You are walking barefoot to a park on a hot summer day. There are a black paved path and a white sand trail leading to the park. Which one would you choose? Explain your answer and use diagrams if you like.

Multiple-Choice Questions

Assessment Standard A

Guideline: In assessments, the relationship between decisions and data is clear.

Multiple-choice questions should be used *sparingly*, and much time must go into their preparation. Because they allow only one right answer, they mirror a conception of science knowledge and understanding that is fundamentally in conflict with the canons of science, which hold that scientific knowledge is always tentative and open to change based on new evidence (Raizen & Kaiser, 1989). Construct or use questions that assess students' understanding of concepts, not verbal reasoning. One good way to develop the items is to use children's ideas about a concept that you have gathered previously. Some examples follow:

On a hot, clear day, you are at the lake and have just had a swim. You wish to dry your swimsuit quickly. Your cottage is air conditioned, with a temperature of 20°C. Outside the temperature is 30°C. Where would be the best place to put your suit to dry? *Explain* your answer.

a. On the white fence
b. Over the back of a black chair
c. Over the bathtub inside
d. On a clothesline
e. On the grass

• • •

A shadow is:

a. a trace of me.
b. a reflection or an image of me.
c. formed when I block the light.
d. part of me and follows me wherever I go.
e. my ghost.

   Explain your answer.

• • •

The paper clip sank because:

a. there are holes in it.
b. it is heavier than water.
c. of its shape.
d. it is made of metal.
e. the water was light.

   Explain your answer.

Creative Drama

Challenge students singly or in groups to act out appropriate science concepts. Often students who have difficulty expressing themselves orally or in a written form are able to show their understanding of concepts in creative drama or in mime. Some examples follow.

Have each group of students choose a topic from the *Electricity* unit and prepare a play/drama about it. Assess their performance on the accuracy of information, the effort put in, and the ability of the group to work together. Possible topics could include the following:

   How can we conserve electricity?
   How do electrons travel in a wire?
   What are some different ways of using electricity in homes?

• • •

One student can play the role of sugar and another student can play the role of water. "Sugar" and "water" can describe their life in lemonade to illustrate the solution process of sugar in water.

• • •

Pretend to be a particle of rock in a mountain and describe the journey to the sea.

• • •

Pretend you are a particle of matter. Show how you would behave inside a liquid, inside a solid, inside a gas.

• • •

With your group of children, illustrate one of the following:

The water cycle
Predator-prey relationships
Food webs or chains
Rotation and/or revolution of the earth

 PEER INTERACTION

Constructing Assessment Strategies

Select a science topic and develop both continuous and culminating assessment strategies, according to the needs of one topic and one age level of children.

Professional Development Standard A

Guideline: Science learning experiences for teachers must incorporate ongoing reflection on the process and outcomes of under-standing science through inquiry.

Professional Development Standard C

Guideline: Professional development activities must provide opportunities for teachers to learn and use various tools and techniques for self-reflection and collegial reflection, such as peer coaching, portfolios, and journals.

☼ TEACHER SELF-ASSESSMENT

An important aspect of assessment within a constructivist framework is teacher self-assessment. Thinking about one's own thinking and taking responsibility for one's own learning are critical aspects of the learning process. Teacher self-assessment also involves reflecting about current practices of assessment. It is imperative that you ask yourself what effect your assessment practices have on your students' achievement. One may develop a personalized questionnaire or use the excellent self-assessment questionnaire developed by McColskey and O'Sullivan (1993), as shown in Figure 8-17.

FIGURE 8-17
Teacher self-assessment questionnaire

Self-Assessment Questionnaire

1. List below, in your own terms, the four most important student outcomes that resulted from your science instruction last year. That is, what could students do well at the end of the year that they could not do well at the beginning of your instruction?
   i.
   ii.
   iii.
   iv.

2. Which of the following kinds of work did you require of students?
   _____ Listen to lectures
   _____ Take tests on text/lectures
   _____ Read textbooks
   _____ Take end-of-chapter tests
   _____ Design experiments
   _____ Talk with scientists
   _____ Solve problems in a team setting
   _____ Maintain journals of data collected
   _____ Do hands-on investigations
   _____ Make presentations to the class
   _____ Other: _____

3. In your science classes, on a typical day, how often were students engaged in and challenged by their work?

_____ All the time
_____ Very often (more than half the time)
_____ Often (about half the time)
_____ Somewhat often (less than half the time)
_____ Almost never

4. Think about the assessment methods represented by the grades in your gradebook. What might students infer about the purpose of science instruction from your choices about what is graded?

☼ CHAPTER REFLECTIONS

Changing assessment practices are a natural outcome of changing teaching and learning methods. No longer is learning equated with making exact replicas of teacher or textbook statements. Rather, children are encouraged to become independent learners and thinkers. Two main questions have to be asked when assessment methods are selected: Is what is being measured worth measuring? (If the item measures only a trivial objective, should it be replaced?) And what is the best technique for measuring an objective?

Assessment involves exploring children's many levels of meaning-making using a variety of strategies. Students' ages, experiences, and abilities as well as the topic determine the appropriate strategies to use. Although the performance assessment techniques take more initial time and effort, we encourage you to experiment with these, as we believe they can truly measure the essence of science.

With this chapter, we have concluded our four-phase Common Knowledge Construction Model. The next section of this text will focus on planning for teaching.

Questions for Reflective Inquiry

1. Describe the difference between science assessment and evaluation.

2. What are some of the current local, national, and international issues in assessment?

3. What might be the differences between science assessment within a constructivist and within a traditional framework?

4. Prepare a presentation you would make to a school parents' meeting explaining and defending the use of performance questions.

SUGGESTED READINGS

Berenson, S. B., & Carter, G. S. (1995). Changing assessment practices in science and mathematics. *School Science and Mathematics, 95*(4), 182–186.

Collins, A. (1992a). Portfolios for science education: Issues in purpose, structure, and authenticity. *Science Education, 76*(4), 451–463.

Collins, A. (1992b). Portfolios: Questions for design. *Science Scope, 15*(6), 25–27.

Wiggins, G. (1989). A true test: Toward more authentic and equitable assessment. *Phi Delta Kappan, 70*(9), 703–713.

Wiggins, G. (1992). Creating tests worth taking. *Educational Leadership, May,* 26–33.

PART THREE

PLANNING FOR TEACHING

In this section, we describe the multiple dimensions of science teaching and learning that we have to consider when planning for creating science lessons and units of study. We once again examine the considerations that teachers make as they work toward creating science experiences that promote scientific literacy for all students.

In chapter 9, we closely examine what "science for all" means and how to implement this objective. Specifically, we examine young children and science, multicultural science, girls and science, science for gifted learners, and science for special-needs students.

We explore the new technologies available in science education in chapter 10.

Two subsequent chapters complete this book. Chapter 11 summarizes the multiple voices influencing science education and details frameworks for unit and lesson planning. A sample unit planned by a preservice teacher completes this chapter. Reading the guidelines for reflective practice found in chapter 12 is an investment in your future professional growth.

Science for All Students

Reflective Inquiry

MICHELLE'S VOICE

I believe that science teachers need to take into account the needs of all students in their classes. Every student has his/her own individual needs. However, as teachers, we should reach all our students. I think it is difficult for teachers to do research on what these students need and then adapt their lessons to meet these needs because our time is limited. We have to continually be trying out different methods and strategies if we hope to reach all our students. Scientific literacy for all means a better country for all of us.

JOURNAL ACTIVITY

Meeting Needs of Students

What different student needs do you expect to have to meet in a typical classroom? Reflect on the kinds of adaptations for learning styles, cultural differences, achievement levels, or exceptionalities you may already have learned to consider in lesson planning.

At the end of her methods course in science, Michelle points out in her special project paper that teachers must be cognizant of the needs of all students. Michelle's goal is to develop a better America by educating children in science.

All students should be given the opportunity to become scientifically literate. Regardless of gender or age, ability or disability, we believe that all learners should have the same learning opportunities in science. The science community at large supports this same view. How can you, in your science planning, accommodate the instructional needs of a variety of learners? It will first be important for you to identify your learning population, analyze their learning needs, and then incorporate the teaching strategies to meet those needs.

Chapter 1 focused on the science standards that contribute to the development of a scientifically literate person. This chapter will discuss some of the often-neglected areas that directly involve the learner:

- Teaching science to young children
- Recognizing and respecting cultural differences of students
- Encouraging participation of girls in science
- Meeting the needs of special students

☀ YOUNG CHILDREN AND SCIENCE

Children in their early years of schooling should be taught science from a special perspective. We know that they learn through playing and exploring their environment. We can also take into account their natural curiosity and enthusiasm and plan age-appropriate activities accordingly. At the same time, we have to consider each child's own development, interests, and cultural background. A teacher cannot expect all children to learn the same things in the same way every day. The National Association for the Education of Young Children suggests that we consider the following factors in reviewing curricula for young children:

Does the curriculum

- promote interactive learning and encourage the child's construction of knowledge?
- encourage active learning and allow children to make meaningful choices?
- foster children's exploration and inquiry, rather than focus on "right" answers or "right" ways to complete a task?
- lead to conceptual understanding by helping children construct their own understanding in meaningful contexts?
- embody expectations that are realistic and attainable at this time, or could the children more and efficiently acquire the knowledge and skills later on?
- encourage development of positive feelings and dispositions toward learning while leading to acquisition of knowledge and skills?

- help achieve social, emotional, physical, and cognitive goals and promote democratic values?
- promote and encourage social interaction among children and adults? (Bredekamp & Rosegrant, 1992, p. 8)

This kind of science is grounded in the idea that children learn by doing. It advocates *interactive learning*—discourse among children and the teacher. Hands-on activities are an important part of a contemporary approach to teaching, but developing children's understanding through peer interactions and teacher conversations within a hands-on inquiry is even more powerful. In other words, physical play and manipulation are intrinsic elements of good science teaching at the early childhood level, but they must be grounded in active inquiry and social interaction.

In their book *The Young Child as Scientist*, Chaillé and Britain (1991) describe seven roles for the constructivist science teacher:

- Presenter
- Observer
- Question asker and problem poser
- Environment organizer
- Public relations coordinator
- Documenter of children's learning
- Theory builder (pp. 54–55)

Chaillé and Britain explain the last role by stating that in order to be responsive to children, teachers must build their own theories by cultivating their own understanding and interests as they interact with children. One important role of the teacher not mentioned is the notion of teacher as *"negotiator of meaning."* This aspect of teaching is critical, and if it is not emphasized, children are not challenged to voice and discuss their evolving ideas.

☀ REFLECTIVE PRACTICE

Roles of a Constructivist Teacher

Pick a suitable science topic for young children and "play out" what the teacher would say in each role identified. All of these roles for the teacher are very important.

Reardon (1993) suggests a method of getting young children to slow down to reflect and reconsider what they are exploring and investigating. She calls it "scientists' meetings"—gathering all the grade 1 children into a circle to discuss what they had been doing in science class. Here is how Reardon introduces these meetings in her own class:

> One way scientists find out what other scientists are working on and thinking about is by reading. Scientists write a lot, so there is lots to read. They write for magazines and journals; they write reports and letters. Of course, they talk to

Teaching Standard B

Guideline: To guide and facilitate learning, encourage and model the skills of scientific inquiry as well as the curiosity, openness to new ideas and data, and skepticism that characterize science.

Teaching Standard B

Guideline: To guide and facilitate learning, orchestrate discourse among students about scientific ideas.

Interesting objects in the classroom promote social interaction and foster inquiry and exploration.

each other, too. Another way they find out is by going to meetings. Sometimes the meetings are small, with just a few scientists who are working on the same kinds of things; sometimes there are big meetings of scientists from many countries. One or two scientists will report their work to a group, and the rest will listen, ask questions, talk, and argue about the ideas they hear.

Usually we'll have one or two scientists in our room discuss the work, but today we'll all talk around the circle and I'll be the recorder. First I want you to think about something you *did,* or something you *observed* or *noticed,* or something you *wonder* about. You may want to read what you wrote in your journal to help you remember. After you decide what you are going to share, write a letter "D" if it is something you did, an "O" if it's something you observed or noticed, and a "W" if it's something you wonder about. Then put your journal and pencil down and get ready to listen to the other scientists (Reardon, 1993, pp. 28–29).

In this example, children were encouraged to make each contribution short and focused. The teacher recorded everything and then read over all their contributions. A discussion followed, and children were then encouraged to decide what they would like to do next and with whom they would like to work. Reardon found these scientists' meetings critical to the children's construction of scientific knowledge.

Documenting children's learning is essential. Assessment practices for young children should be appropriate to their development. *Portfolios* and *performance assessments* give a much more accurate measure of their performance than pencil-and-paper worksheets because young children are not very good with symbols and depend on verbal instructions, which can be problematic if their listening skills are not well developed. Observation of children as they work reveals much about their knowledge and understanding. Anecdotal notes can be made of the critical observations. Interviews are also an excellent way to diagnose children's language development. In

Assessment Standard B

Achievement and opportunity to learn science must be assessed.

essence, assessment should be "authentic"—it should be part of and parallel to good teaching.

- When asked what Kate noticed about the rabbit, she said, "It's white." Anything else? "No."
- Next day, Kate remarked that the rabbit was "twitching its nose."
- Next lesson, after several children described the nest-making activities of the rabbit, Kate grasped my hand and said, "The rabbit is getting very fat. I think it is going to have babies."

Not only is it important to consider the age of children for enhancing scientific literacy, but it is paramount to also address cultural diversities in our classrooms so that we may reach all children.

☀ MULTICULTURAL SCIENCE EDUCATION

Atwater and Riley (1993), multicultural specialists on the American scene, emphasize that male and female students, exceptional students, and students who are members of diverse ethnic and cultural groups should have an *equal* chance to achieve academically in school. Atwater (1993) defines *multicultural science education* as a construct, a process, and an educational reform movement with a goal of providing equitable opportunities for culturally diverse student populations to learn quality science.

In preparing to consider cultural diversity in the school classroom today, a number of approaches are suggested:

- The *human relations approach,* which attempts to foster interpersonal relationships among members of different cultures in the classroom
- The *single-group studies approach,* which teaches the history, culture, and contributions of a single group in society
- The *multicultural approach,* which organizes the curriculum around perspectives of all ethnic groups within a country
- The *multicultural and social reconstructivist approach,* which combines the basic elements of the preceding approaches and deals with contemporary social and political issues in a multidisciplinary fashion (Sleuter, 1992, p. 19).

Unlike American multicultural or ethnic educators, who use the term *multicultural education,* their colleagues in Great Britain prefer to use the term *anti-racist.* Why is this so? Vance (1989) uses this term because he believes that children are growing up in a multicultural but racist society and "their school experience should lead them to appreciate the multicultural and racist origins and manifestations of knowledge; it must lead them to see beyond their own culture" (p. 107). This profound statement applies to school science education, where children should be taught early in life to appreciate the practice of science and technology by both men and women of various cultures. Watts (1992) reminds us that all children bring with them their own ideas of science, mediated through their own language,

A grade 1 teacher has been noting a particular child's progress in learning to observe. Here are her anecdotal notes made on a series of science activities.

Teaching Standard B

Guideline: To guide and facilitate learning, recognize and respond to student diversity and encourage all students to participate fully in science learning.

Teaching Standard E

Guideline: To develop a community of science learners, display and demand respect for diverse skills, ideas, and experiences of all students.

Teachers should plan activities that reflect the racially diverse backgrounds of the students.

and they interpret natural and scientific phenomena in terms of their own experiences, cultural norms, and values. Many children bring experiences of racism—either direct abuse or racist language from others. Unless teachers are prepared to acknowledge and address these ideas in their classrooms in such a way that each child feels valued, a comfortable environment for learning will not occur.

Hodson (1993) believes that we should be sensitive to those whose first language is not English and pay attention to scientific language use. Also, we should use content that takes into account the knowledge, beliefs, and experiences of children of other cultures. The third important consideration is that of learning styles. Different cultures have very different beliefs about how children should interact in the classroom. Other guidelines for the development of multicultural science education advocated by Hodson are summarized below:

Assessment Standard D

Guideline: Assessment tasks must be appropriately modified to accommodate the needs of students with physical disabilities, learning disabilities, or limited English proficiency.

- Review all curriculum materials for the purpose of identifying and replacing racially stereotyped material.
- Establish more democratic procedures, such as learner-driven teaching/learning methods, and more student control of curriculum content and assessment methods.
- Draw attention to ways in which scientific information is misused to underpin racist attitudes.
- Design curriculum materials that take material from a wide variety of cultures and countries.
- Include the contributions of non-Western and pre-Renaissance scientists.
- Emphasize the culturally specific nature of scientific practice.

- Acknowledge that science is a human activity and does not have an infallible method.
- Recognize that scientific and technological developments may bring benefits to some and problems to others.

Lesson and Unit Planning for Multicultural Science Teaching

All writers on multicultural science education seem to stress that curriculum materials should reflect the multicultural mix of society and should be global in nature, placing science in cultural, historical, social, political, environmental, and economic contexts. A series of science activities could be based on a story set in another part of the world and provide positive images of the people in the story. Through these activities, students can come to realize the international nature of science and the potential it has to overcome prejudice.

Helaine Selin (1993) states that while we are quick to recognize ethnic art and culture, we still look skeptically on non-Western scientific practices in medical and agricultural fields. This author has written a book called *Science across the Cultures* that lists over 800 books for educators on the scientific achievement of other cultures. In his 1993 article on science across the cultures, he discusses African geological history, archaeology, agriculture, architecture, and calendar and numeration systems. Native Americans also have a rich history, as documented in archaeological finds as well as agricultural, astronomical, and architectural traditions.

When planning and teaching science lessons, it may be useful to ask the following questions that Peacock has posed:

- Are the concepts to be studied relevant to all cultures?
- Are there specific activities that might motivate ethnic/minority students?
- Are similarities as well as differences examined?
- Is the contribution of other cultures stressed?
- Are community attitudes (for example, toward food, sex, dress) taken into consideration?
- Do the books/materials used reflect cultural diversity?
- Is stereotyping avoided?
- Are the origins of science in other cultures acknowledged?
- Are the practices of other cultures presented as backward/deprived? (modified from Peacock, 1992, p. 86)

See also the sample multicultural unit plan in Figure 9-1.

Stanley and Brickhouse (1994) state that an excessively narrow definition of science (that science is what Western scientists have produced during the last 200 years) is too limited in its perspectives and consequently detrimental to both science education and science. They suggest that discussions about the relative merits of Western science and the sciences of other cultures have the potential to be highly educative about science. If students can

Assessment Standard D

Guideline: Assessment tasks must be reviewed for the use of stereotypes, for assumptions that reflect the perspectives or experiences of a particular group or language that might be offensive to a particular group, and for other features that might distract students from the intended task.

FIGURE 9-1
Sample multicultural unit plan (NOTE. Adapted from *Science in Primary Schools: The Multicultural Dimension*, by A. Peacock, 1992, London: Macmillan, pp. 85–88.)

Sample Unit Plan Summary
Age of students: 9- to 10-year-old students
Time scale: 6–8 weeks, 2½ hours per week
Topic: Food

Investigative Skills:
• Observing and classifying
• Quantification of variables
• Formulating and testing of hypotheses
• Searching for patterns in the data

Concepts:
• Feeding, growth, and health
• Similarities and differences in food plants and animals
• Farming and waste disposal
• Changes that take place in cooking and preserving food

Activities:
• Bringing in a wide variety of breads and asking students to bring in their favorites for investigation
• Naming and labeling all the breads
• Baking leavened and unleavened breads
• Observing, measuring, describing a range of foods (for example, fruits and vegetables), their cooking and food value
• Measuring and describing changes in color, size, shape through cooking
• Using, testing, and designing cooking utensils made of different materials (woks, karahis, sufurias, various pots and pans)
• Growing seeds (mung beans, cress, coriander, fenugreek)

Scientific and Research Skills:
• Estimating and describing size, shape, weight, texture
• Recognizing and describing changes from unbaked to baked
• Predicting what will happen based on previous baking experience
• Naming unfamiliar breads, in all appropriate languages
• Following unfamiliar instructions for baking
• Using new sources of information (recipes, parents, community workers)

Multicultural Content:
• Learning what is the same and what is different about bread and baking in different cultures
• Stressing processes that are common in all cultures (preserving fresh food, using yeast cultures)
• Understanding how implied racism is avoided
  – By not stereotyping some tastes/foods as better/worse
  – By using community languages for naming breads
  – By discussing why some foods are unacceptable (say, animal fats for vegetarians)
  – By avoiding books that deal with only one kind of bread
  – By questioning culture-specific notions (such as three meals a day)

learn how the purposes of scientific inquiry have varied in other cultures and how science knowledge has been shaped by these needs, they will also learn that Western science is not universal.

PEER INTERACTION

Planning for Science That Is More Multicultural

Select any topic in a school science program and discuss how you would adapt it to make its objectives more appropriately multicultural.

☀ GIRLS AND SCIENCE

Another dimension in promoting scientific literacy for children is to provide more equal opportunities and expect equal achievement for female students in science. Gender differences in science and technology have received much press in the decade or so beginning with the book *The Missing Half* by Alison Kelly (1981). Current literature shows that mathematically gifted and scientifically gifted females are educated in a world that presents barriers to their success. Their lack of success has been related to many problems, such as parental and community expectations, teacher behavior toward girls in class, and sexism in textbooks.

Many enlightened parents and teachers are aware of these concerns and are trying to alleviate the problem. One such teacher did an exercise the other day with grade 5 and 6 students. The students were asked to draw a picture of a scientist. Before they handed the picture in, they were asked to name the scientist. This was to aid in the determination of the gender of the scientist. Of a total of 34 boys and girls, 80% drew male scientists. Only 1 boy drew a female scientist (he also drew a male scientist alongside). Several of their drawings are illustrated in Figure 9-2. The teacher was very distressed about the results, as she had deliberately encouraged girls' participation in science classes and had stressed feminine roles in science.

Other studies reveal similar results. Chambers (1983) recorded that *all the 8- and 9-years-old students* studied drew male scientists and, in a class of 32 9- to 10-year-old students, only 5 drawings (all by girls) were of female scientists. Concerning this situation, Pickford (1992) relates the interventions he undertook in his primary classroom in England. First, he gave his students a questionnaire with the overall heading "How do you feel when..." to which they responded by checking either sad, indifferent, or happy face symbols. The responses by all students to the questions on feelings toward science content and skills were positive. However, the differences occurred in the responses to those items dealing with *classroom methods*. Half of the girls marked the neutral face and a few were unhappy when having to *work with others*. The method he was using of having students *report their results* to the whole class also raised some negative responses.

FIGURE 9-2
Students' views of a scientist

Over a quarter (28%) of the girls were unhappy about this method, and less than one quarter of the girls felt happy about this activity. Only 14% of the boys were unhappy about having to report to the whole class. Pickford's last question, dealing with the writing of science reports, received a negative response from boys while girls found it more favorable.

Subsequently, Pickford used the following interventions:

Form friendship groups for working on science activities. These were effectively chosen by the children using a sociometric method which involved asking the children, "Write down the names of two people you would like to work with in science activities." The teacher then assigned children to work in groups with at least one person with whom they had identified.

Ask students to report back in small groups. This intervention was devised in response to the children's reluctance to report their group activities to the class as a whole. At the end of the practical sessions carried out in friendship groups, the class was divided into different groups (of no more than six) containing children who had carried out the full range of activities. Pickford encouraged the children to listen to each other's descriptions and then ask simple and supportive questions.

Use themes appealing to both girls and boys. Some teachers consider a space-based theme equally appealing to both boys and girls. For this reason, Pickford decided it would be an appropriate context for his attempts to improve girls' participation and attitudes toward science in the short term.

Present stories about women scientists. The presentation of stories about women scientists was intended to influence the stereotypical male images of scientists in the draw-a-scientist data.

Make science reports a group activity. The sharing of responsibility for a report of science activities was intended to improve attitudes about reporting in general. Children were encouraged to share writing tasks and to use a range of recording techniques, including drawing, charts, graphs, moving pictures, and models. Groups of approximately six children produced single science reports as small-scale classroom displays (adapted from Pickford, 1992, p. 23).

The effects of the interventions were interesting. In the friendship groups, many of the girls seemed more confident and actively involved in the investigations. The modification to the reporting-back method appeared to be the most successful of the interventions. It enabled all children to participate, rather than just a group spokesperson. The whole class preferred this type of reporting. Pickford's evidence from informal discussions suggested that the space-based theme as well as stories about women scientists were successful in improving the girls' attitudes about science.

The one intervention in which the results were more negative was the making of group reports. Some of the children showed impatience and intolerance toward others as they tried to work cooperatively. In a post-intervention survey using the same attitude questionnaire as at the outset of the project, Pickford noted that the girls' responses to the intervention strategies were positive.

Guidelines for Creating Gender Equity

A recent publication, *The Better Idea Book: A Resource Book on Gender, Culture, Science and Schools* (Canadian Teachers' Federation, 1992), has reviewed the problems females encounter in mathematics, science, and technology. This publication relates how girls are labeled by inference as collectively deficient for not recognizing the importance of mathematics, science,

Teaching Standard E

Guideline: To develop a community of science learners, enable students to have a significant voice in decisions about the content of their work and require students to take responsibility for the learning of all members of the community.

and technology and for lacking the confidence necessary to persevere and succeed. The following recommendations were made as a result of this study:

- Support for girls and math/science initiatives should not be undertaken solely on the basis of nationalistic economic fortunes.
- The biases of "science" need to be challenged within and without the discipline.
- The reality of the gender-biased classroom must be recognized before changes can be made.
- Schools must work to invent "girl-friendly" curricula and cultures that go well beyond avoiding overt gender bias.
- The responsibility for the development of gender-equitable education must be shared by both men and women inside and outside schools.
- Issues of greatest importance to girls and young women should not be avoided.
- Gender equity must become part of accountability at every level, which would require individual schools to track these outcomes as well.
- Research shows that gender bias in testing and the reformulation of biased tests must become part of all testing and accountability initiatives.
- Girls need a better idea of what to expect in the later school years in science- and mathematics-related programs.
- A profession that maintains an internal gender imbalance of power, roles, and responsibilities is unlikely to foster students free from gender stereotypes (summarized from Canadian Teachers' Federaton, 1992, pp. 59–60).

The criteria for determining whether your classroom is unbiased and equitable have recently been described by Allen (1995). Teachers should

Assessment Standard D

Guideline: Large-scale assessments must use statistical techniques to identify potential bias among subgroups.

As more girls are encouraged to engage in science inquiry, they may more confidently seek higher levels of scientific knowledge.

allow themselves to be observed by a peer or videotaped to ascertain whether they exhibit the following characteristics in their classroom teaching:

- Are female students given an equal amount of attention from the teacher?
- Do female students feel comfortable enough to ask *many* questions of the teacher?
- Is the class tension level comfortable and the discipline under control?
- Do female students appear fearful of being embarrassed when asking a question, or is a teacher or are male students sarcastic toward the answers given by female students? (Allen, 1995, p. 33)

After teachers have analyzed the results of their observations and reflections on their classroom teaching, Allen suggests that the following techniques be used to help prevent gender bias:

Be very open about the problems some girls may have in certain areas of math and science. It is important that female students understand that some of their problems result from the expectations of their abilities explicitly or implicitly intimated from birth to adulthood. Traditionally, female students have not been allowed the same freedom of exploration that males experience. Some decision making is not allowed in some households for females. Toys that female students traditionally play with differ from toys that males play with and may better promote an early understanding of structure, the laws of motion, and tools that facilitate the same. It is very important that female students realize that any conceptual problems they may have in developing a better understanding of science are not related to low intelligence or an inability to understand either math or science.

Females must be encouraged or required to ask questions. Female students are often trained by parents and expected by educators to be more submissive. If males ask questions, speak out of turn, debate with the teacher, or even argue, it is often culturally acceptable; but female students who behave in the same way may be labeled obnoxious, aggressive, or unfeminine. Therefore, females need to be encouraged to question and act more assertively. As teachers initiate classroom discussions from the beginning of the year, they should call on girls and question them during each lesson. When female students realize that they are expected to know answers, they will begin to ask questions before the teacher does!

Female students (as well as others) have to be exposed better to all integrated aspects of math and science, especially problem solving. The classroom teacher needs to start the year out by teaching many types of strategies for problem solving. If many, many examples are given to the class using these strategies, confidence will grow as will the comfort level of students in tackling problems. Once a foundation for

Teaching Standard B

Guideline: To guide and facilitate learning, recognize and respond to student diversity and encourage all students to participate fully in science learning.

problem solving is built, students can then be expected to show deviations in their strategies, which indicate cognitive growth and maturity. **Gender training for all classroom teachers should concentrate on the social and emotional development of female students in the math and science classrooms.** Any techniques that make females feel comfortable and successful should be used (summarized from Allen, 1995, pp. 44–45).

Teaching Standard D

Guideline: Design and manage the learning environment by engaging students in designing their own learning environment.

Another intervention explored in public education in recent years is that of setting up all-girl classes in science and mathematics. This situation has existed in private schools in North America and Great Britain for many years. Delamont (1994) traced the success of girls in single-sex schools in Great Britain, noting these schools have produced the majority of women scientists. They foster high achievement in and very positive attitudes toward science. There is no reason why these positive features cannot be initiated in public school systems. A large school division in a major Canadian city ("All-Girls Class," 1995) implemented a small project in September 1995 in which girls could choose to attend single-sex classrooms in mathematics and science beginning at grade 7, ages 12 and 13. This project had a successful year, and enrollment doubled for the 1996–1997 school year.

The lack of female and minority students in science is a serious concern in the United States. Females and minorities are underrepresented in science-related employment, as noted by Blake (1993). She notes that while the proficiency of 9-year-old boys and girls in all science except physical science is approximately the same, the performance gap becomes evident at age 13. Data from the same source indicated that girls have significantly less science experience than boys at comparable ages. To sum up our study, Blake suggests the following guidelines for structuring science activities that motivate and take into consideration the interests of all students:

- Choose activities that are free from sexual stereotyping.
- Spend instructional time on science activities every day.
- Design activities that will ease the stress of competition.
- Feature the use of simple science tools in your activities.
- Emphasize the practical applications of science and how it relates to students' lives.
- Include a wide variety of science topics and concepts in order to reduce anxiety.
- Present data on both males and females, whether the subjects are animals or humans, in all laboratory experiences.
- Give equal feedback to females, males, and minorities when working with science problems.
- Make a conscious effort to acknowledge the contributions of female and minority students and scientists to scientific observation (Blake, 1993, p. 34).

❋ SCIENCE FOR GIFTED LEARNERS

Gifted students are found in all schools and classrooms. Some teachers find them an extra burden to deal with because of the need to plan for extended activities. We hope that the following comments and suggestions provide some guidance for meaningful science programming for individuals or groups of students who have progressed beyond the expectations of a regular program at their grade level.

- Gifted students display their knowledge and skills in many different ways, ranging from high levels of performance on ordinary tasks and assignments to disruptive behavior when they are bored.
- Assessment to determine which students in a classroom are gifted can take various forms. The best judges of a student's abilities are often classroom teachers who have worked with him or her over a period of time. The collected, subjective impressions of a number of teachers can be a powerful indicator. Factors such as performance on tests, standardized test scores, and the quality of assignments can also certainly help confirm a teacher's assessment, but these objective indicators should not be relied on exclusively.
- Gifted students should not be excused from demonstrating achievement of curriculum objectives in the regular program. In fact, they should be encouraged to demonstrate their proficiency so that their exploration of more complex ideas and skills has some justification in the minds of their classmates. Gifted students do not necessarily automatically possess the knowledge or skills of the regular program, but they are likely to acquire them more quickly than other students. They are also likely to recognize relationships between ideas more readily. Their input in initial brainstorming sessions and in discussions can be invaluable.
- Special programming for gifted students should include a *high-interest approach* in which topics and activities are specially developed for these students and an *enrichment approach* in which the regular program is expanded, such as by using extensions to regular class topics. Other strategies that can be especially useful with gifted students are science fairs, science olympics, and problem-solving competitions.
- The difference between a gifted student's initial understanding and accepted scientific ideas may be less marked than with the regular student. The challenge for the teacher is to explore gifted students' understanding and challenge them to explore their ideas in many different ways.
- Encourage all students (but particularly gifted students) to *design their own investigations* to follow up on activities in the regular program. They can excel in this area if they are encouraged to do so.

Following are some examples of challenging problems for gifted students to pursue:

Teaching Standard D

Teachers of science design and manage learning environments that provide students with the time, space, and resources needed for learning science.

Teaching Standard D

Guideline: Design and manage the learning environment by structuring the time available so students are able to engage in extended investigations.

- Explain why we don't have a solar eclipse every month. (After examining the situation, very bright students may be able to explain that the cause is the tilted orbital plane of the moon. They will have to be able to consider the problem from a three-dimensional perspective.)
- What is the effect of joining two or more simple machines to make a complex machine? What is the effect of each of the simple machines that make up the complex machine? (Answers vary depending on the machines used and their combinations.)
- Is it possible to build a perpetual motion machine? Why? How? (No. For any machine to work there must be friction involved, and this friction would eventually slow down and stop the machine.)
- How are cold-blooded animals able to live through the changing seasons? (The temperature of their blood, which contains antifreeze-like ingredients, changes with the environment and prevents them from freezing and boiling. Also, in cold weather, their metabolism slows so that they can go for long periods without eating.)

Provide gifted students opportunities *to display and share their work* with the rest of the class. In terms of assessing their work, it is best to discuss with these students what they are going to attempt to do at the beginning of an investigation and whether they succeeded when they are finished. As with regular students, you should communicate to them your expectations as to meeting timelines, working effectively, using resources appropriately, and effectively reporting and presenting techniques and conclusions. Then use these criteria for assessment.

Teaching Standard B

Guideline: To guide and facilitate learning, challenge students to accept and share responsibility for their own learning.

Assessment Standard C

Guideline: Students must have adequate opportunity to demonstrate their achievements.

☼ SCIENCE FOR SPECIAL-NEEDS STUDENTS

Many research studies have examined the effects of various teaching strategies and curricula for students with disabilities. Special-needs students include children with learning disabilities; emotional or behavioral disorders; mild mental/cognitive disabilities; physical disabilities; visual, hearing, or speech and language impairments; and other health impairments including chronic diseases and traumatic brain injuries. After studying 66 research reports covering all these categories, Mastropieri and Scruggs (1992) found overwhelming support for the premise that science education was beneficial for these students because it helped them do the following:

- Expand their experiential backgrounds
- Learn skills and knowledge important for adult functioning
- Use concrete, hands-on learning activities
- Develop problem-solving and reasoning skills (adapted from Mastropieri & Scruggs, 1992, p. 378)

In addition, these authors believe that *science is the best subject area for mainstreaming students of all disability categories.*

Science can provide unique learning experiences and opportunities for students with disabilities. Patton (1995) states that the activity-oriented programs advocated by the current wave of educational reform—programs that cover fewer topics but in greater depth—are advantageous to special-needs students.

Atwood and Oldham (1985) also believe that the characteristics of a modern science program make it the best subject area for mainstreaming. They note that science education may have little emphasis in special education classrooms, perhaps because special education teachers have had little training in science. Although this may be true, with the movement toward more inclusive classrooms, it will be valuable for regular classroom teachers to make the necessary adjustments in their science teaching techniques to accommodate the various special needs in their classrooms. Mastropieri and Scruggs (1995) emphasize the following:

- Choose appropriate curriculum materials using activities-oriented approaches.
- Use effective teaching strategies with clear, structured presentations and activities that replicate and extend previous activities. Teacher enthusiasm, effective management strategies, and appropriate pace are critical.
- Incorporate tutoring and cooperative groups in the program.
- Use mnemonic strategies for aiding memory of scientific terms.
- Adapt specific science activities to the characteristics of student disabilities in the classroom.
- Use effective assessment procedures. Performance assessments have been shown to be more suitable for special-needs students than written tests (pp. 10–13).

 PEER INTERACTION

Science for All

Select one of the following situations for reflection and discussion.

1. Analyze a science lesson for gender equality. Observe a videotaped science lesson and analyze the interaction based on Allen's criteria. What recommendations for gender equality would you make after your analysis?

2. Examine a preschool program guide. Look for evidence of respect for young children's ideas related to science as well as the fostering of children's exploration and inquiry with a goal of conceptual understanding.

3. Describe the qualities of someone you perceive to be a gifted learner. Identify science activities that could accommodate the instructional needs of that learner.

Teaching Standard B

Guideline: To guide and facilitate learning, recognize and respond to student diversity and encourage all students to participate fully in science learning.

For the visually impaired, microscope images can be enhanced with a microprojector or on a video screen.

For students with limited motor skills, the Brock microscope operates well without breakable mirrors, bulbs, and focusing knobs.

Invent simple adaptations in the use of materials to facilitate specific disabilities. For example, a rope knotted at equal intervals could be used as a linear measuring device for visually impaired students or students who have difficulty with fine motor skills.

Assessment Standard D

Guideline: Assessment tasks must be appropriately modified to accommodate the needs of students with physical disabilities, learning disabilities, or limited English proficiency.

☀ CHAPTER REFLECTIONS

In this chapter, we have focused on the principles that develop scientific literacy for all students. We have further provided some guidelines for creating more equitable science learning experiences regardless of gender, cultural orientation, abilities, or disabilities. We have discussed classroom activities that teachers can use to conscientiously plan and adapt lessons to promote pluralistic ideas and equitable learning opportunities.

Questions for Reflective Inquiry

1. Select a topic and outline the modifications you might have to make to accommodate a special-needs child within the regular classroom.

2. What are your views on girls in science? What examples of gender bias can you remember from your school days? From your preservice teaching experiences?

SUGGESTED READINGS

Atwater, M. (1993). Multicultural science education: Assumptions and alternative views. *The Science Teacher, March,* 33–37.

Atwater, M., & Riley, J. (1993). Multicultural science education: Perspectives, definitions, and research agenda. *Science Education, 77*(6), 661–668.

Blake, S. (1993). Are you turning female and minority students away from science? *Science and Children, April,* 32–34.

Chambers, D. W. (1983). Stereotypical images of the scientist: The draw a scientist test. *Science Education, 67,* 255–265.

Hodson, D. (1993). In search of a rationale for multicultural science education. *Science Education, 77*(6), 685–711.

Mastropieri, M. A., & Scruggs, T. E. (1995). Teaching science to students with disabilities in general education settings. *Teaching Exceptional Children, Summer,* 10–13.

Selin, H. (1993). Science across cultures. *The Science Teacher, March,* 38–44.

Stanley, W. B., & Brickhouse, N. W. (1994). Multiculturalism, universalism, and science education. *Science Education, 78*(4), 387–398.

CHAPTER 10

Technology in Science

FOCUS QUESTIONS

1. What roles can technology play in science teaching and learning?

2. How can computer technology be integrated into science lessons?

3. What types of computer technology are readily adapted to the science classroom?

4. What do you know about using design technology in science teaching?

5. Name some science topics in which design technology can be readily incorporated.

Reflective Inquiry

ANDREA'S VOICE

A child can see a picture of a Bengal tiger, hear its roar, watch a video clip, see a map of its habitat—all with clicks of the mouse. Compare that experience to the traditional method of exposing students to the same information. Previously, a teacher would have had to read the information to the children, order a film to view and hear, and find maps that detail the tiger's habitat. I am truly excited by the possibilities that I have become aware of through this assignment. Because of my confidence, ability, and knowledge, I can now picture myself using multimedia materials in my classroom.

JOURNAL ACTIVITY

Computer Applications in Science

Discuss some of your experiences using the computer. Andrea gained confidence using the computer after she created a simple science activity as one of the assignments in her methods course. What are some ways you envision using a computer in science?

Today, faculties of education across North America have incorporated courses in computer literacy as part of their initial teacher preparation programs. Preservice teachers are becoming more comfortable using computers for word processing as well as for creating simple activities. One of the areas that preservice teachers focus on is learning to use multimedia programs such as *HyperStudio, HyperCard,* and *PowerPoint* to create simple science activities. They also surf the Internet to look for teaching materials in science. This chapter will describe some of the different possibilities of using computers to teach science.

✸ COMPUTER TECHNOLOGIES IN SCIENCE EDUCATION

Computers are a part of all of our lives, and children are no exception. In fact, increasingly, children are more often seen in front of a computer than a television set. (No wonder children often teach their teachers how to use the computer!) Our consumer sense tells us that computer use will only continue to grow and with it will come an ever-increasing use of computer technology in our classrooms. For example, *Safari Science Plus* is a program designed for children ages 6–8 who are fascinated by the wonders of science. In this program they explore a variety of scientific mysteries such as experiments with bubbles (known as "Bubbl-ology"), "Spy-Science," and trekking through the environment as "Eco-detectives."

In science education, computers can be used in a variety of ways. They continue to be utilized to stimulate content growth and develop science knowledge through software games. More recently, children are being taught to conduct research on the Internet and are learning the value of computers as organizational tools. For example, fourth-grade children affiliated with our own university summer programs were introduced to the development of multimedia programs and learned to use software for word processing, graphics, programming, and creating World Wide Web (WWW) homepages. They were taught *HyperCard* and *HyperStudio* multimedia programs as an aid in developing science activities. Teachers and students who use the foregoing programs find them to be user friendly. Since *HyperCard* is widely available, we will describe some of its basic principles so that you may be able to use this tool in developing science activities. Similar multimedia programs are available for Macintosh and other computer systems as well.

HyperCard: A Multimedia Program

The *HyperCard* program gives you the freedom of presenting science concepts in an interactive manner. You can use *QuickTime* movies, slides, clip art, prerecorded sounds, animation, and multiple graphics with *HyperCard*.

The basic elements of *HyperCard* are Stack, Field, Card, Button, Background, and Navigating tools. The cards in the stacks are composed of buttons, fields, and pictures. The buttons on the stacks are used to navigate

Teaching Standard D

Teachers of science design and manage learning environments that provide students with the time, space, and resources needed for learning science.

from one card to another or to execute other commands, such as playing sounds or animation. The buttons are enforced with *HyperCard* language called *HyperTalk*. By scripting with *HyperTalk*, you can issue specific commands to *HyperCard* so the program can be fully utilized. For example, to make a button that basically navigates from card to card, you need to insert the script: "Go to next card." Field in *HyperCard* is mainly used to carry text to accommodate theoretical meanings. By combining text, pictures, animation, and sound, we can construct a unique stack that can be used to teach our students. We refer to this personal stack as "HyperTeacher." There is no limit to what these *HyperCard* stacks can do. An example of a *HyperCard* stack developed by John Schrofel, a preservice teacher, is given in Figure 10-1. He used this stack to explore students' conceptions of as well as teach a lesson on tides.

John's students can learn about tides *from* hypertexts that John prepared. On the other hand, they can also use multimedia production tools to construct their own knowledge and learn to think *with* computers. Students can then represent their ideas and thoughts in their own hypertexts. It is this process that Salomon, Perkins, and Globerson (1991) refer to as learning *with* computers—forming an intellectual partnership with a computer. "When learners actively construct knowledge through multimedia, they acquire cognitive, metacognitive, and motivational advantages over those who merely attempt to absorb knowledge" (Jonassen, 1996, p. 193). When you learn how to create simple activities in science on a computer, you can confidently teach elementary students how to learn science *with* the computer.

Teaching Standard D

Guideline: Design and manage the learning environment by making the available science tools, materials, media, and technological resources accessible to students.

In multimedia presentations, text is organized and displayed in a nonsequential, nonlinear manner that is referred to as hypertext.

FIGURE 10-1
Tides: Sample cards from a *HyperCard* stack (NOTE. From John Schrofel. (1996).)

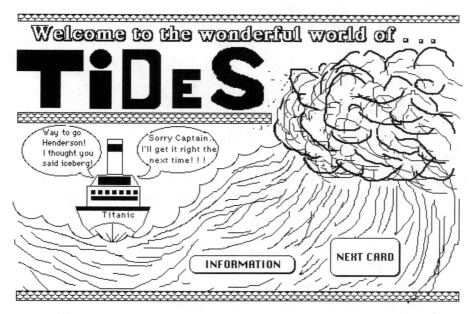

FIGURE 10-1
Continued

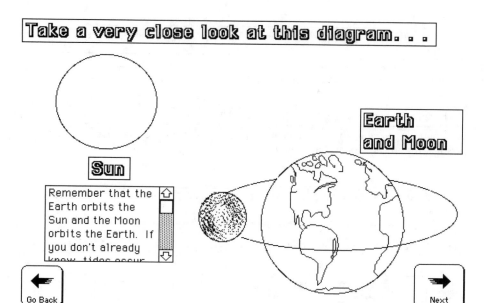

Answer the following questions:

1. Explain in complete sentences what you think TIDES are.

I think tides are movements of water in an ocean or other body of water that is affected by the rotation of the Earth.

2. What do you think will happen if: 1.) the moon was very close to the Earth? 2.) the sun was closer to the Earth? Explain.

1)   If the moon was very close to the Earth, I think there would be high tides because of the gravitational pull between the earth and moon.

2)   If the sun was closer to the Earth there would be high tides because the energy produced would cause the tides to be higher.

Once you have finished these questions you may go to the next card and continue.

FIGURE 10-1
Continued

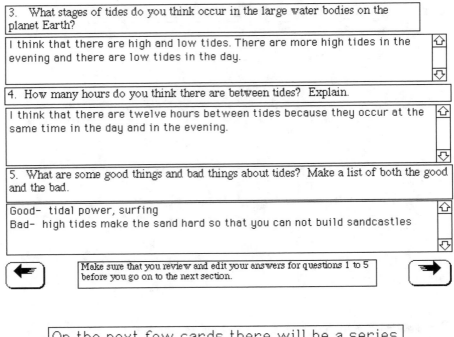

3.   What stages of tides do you think occur in the large water bodies on the planet Earth?

I think that there are high and low tides. There are more high tides in the evening and there are low tides in the day.

4.   How many hours do you think there are between tides? Explain.

I think that there are twelve hours between tides because they occur at the same time in the day and in the evening.

5.   What are some good things and bad things about tides? Make a list of both the good and the bad.

Good- tidal power, surfing
Bad- high tides make the sand hard so that you can not build sandcastles

Make sure that you review and edit your answers for questions 1 to 5 before you go on to the next section.

On the next few cards there will be a series of computer generated demonstrations showing you what happens when tides occur and what causes them. Pay careful attention to what goes on in the demonstrations because you will have to respond to a set of questions after you have evaluated what you have seen. Good Luck!

GO BACK

NEXT

FIGURE 10-1
Continued

FIGURE 10-1
Continued

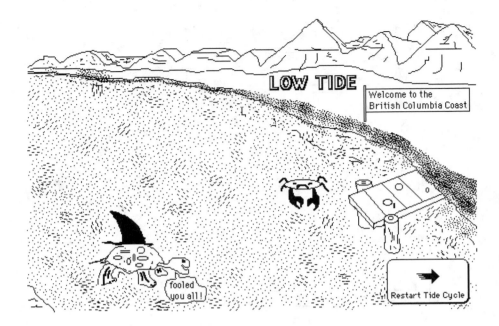

EVALUATION

1. Record in point form what you observed in the demonstration of the tide cycle. You will be able to refer to this record of data to help answer the questions that follow.

-high tide in the day and evening
-low tide in the day and evening

2. How many tides are there in a day? When do they take place? Remember to clearly share your ideas in complete sentences.

There are four tides in a day; two high tides in the day and two low tides in the night.

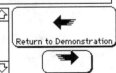

FIGURE 10-1
Continued

3. What factors in outer space have a direct impact on the tides on Earth? Remember
to state your ideas clearly in complete sentences.

I think that the moon affects the tides in that there is a gravitational pull
which causes high and low tides. The sun has no effect on the tides.

4.   Describe what you think happens to the water at high and low tides.
Explain your answer.

At high tide, the water is "pulled" onto the shore by the
gravitational pull from the moon. At low tide, the moon
rotates away and the water goes away from the shore
because there is no more gravitational pull.

Go Back

Continue

FIGURE 10-1
Continued

Compact Discs and Videodiscs

Multimedia presentations created from multimedia programs are stored in a
compact disc (CD) because a CD can store more data than a diskette. A CD
called *Anatomist* explores the details of human anatomy and allows you to
learn the parts of the human body in an innovative way. *EcoDisc* simulates a
real nature reserve and allows the learner to explore and experiment.

Videodiscs are basically the same as videotapes. Instead of storing a movie
on a tape, they store it on a big disc.

The Internet

The Internet is an information superhighway that can enhance learning. The
resources available for both students and teachers are limited only by the
ability of the explorer. We will briefly describe various aspects of using the
Internet, but the best way to learn how to use the Internet is to "surf" it.

Communication

Communication through the Internet with someone on the other end of
the network is done using *IRC (Internet Relay Chat)*. We have used *IRC* in
our teacher education program, in which preservice teachers reflect about a
constructivist science activity and carry on a discourse with their peers in
small groups. In a classroom rich with computers hooked to the network,
this type of science talk is possible. Upper elementary students will enjoy
learning science in this manner or communicating with scientists via the
electronic medium.

Teaching Standard D

Guideline: Design and manage the
learning environment by identifying
and using resources outside the
school.

Internet Tools

To be able to retrieve information from the Internet, *Gopher, Ftp, WWW, Netscape* or *Mosaic,* and *Telnet* are used. These tools can access an information server on the net, where you can view and/or download resource materials. *Gopher* is an information retrieval system and therefore described as the "surfer." *Ftp* stands for "file transfer protocol." It is used for downloading or uploading a file, a program, and scripts from another computer to yours and vice versa. To use *Ftp,* you have to know the specific *Ftp* sites. The *World Wide Web* (WWW) is a client-based Internet service. By using *HyperText MarkUp Language* (HTML) editor, a teacher can set up an information site for his or her resources such as pictures and documents, letting students or the general public around the globe view his or her work. *HTML* works under the "tagging technique" of text. It formats the text to allow Web clients to see what each text actually represents. *Netscape* or *Mosaic* can retrieve and display information on the Internet, making learning to surf the Internet easier and more attractive. *Telnet* is used for remote logging to another computer.

Preservice Teacher as Researcher (P-STAR) Conference Presentation: Internet for Science

It is phenomenal what the Internet can do. The Internet is like a multi-cultural community where people are connected by technology. Craig Milne, a preservice teacher, discussed the Internet as part of his science methods course presentation for our Faculty of Education. His written report follows:

> The Internet is a resource as a book is, except it is electronic. The Internet provides students with opportunities that were not even imaginable when I was attending public school. Students can now readily access more information in one school year than their grandparents would encounter in their entire lives. As books and periodicals become more expensive, the Internet will be a useful tool in fighting the ongoing budget wars. Science teachers now have almost unlimited resources available to them through the Internet. The advent of the interactive web site will give the teacher the opportunity to bring scientific concepts to life for their students. Students will be exposed to more ideas and opportunities to learn. Every teacher should be aware of the potential of the Internet, and the value it can provide students.
>
> The Internet is a fabulous tool to use in the science classroom. There are reference sites, as well as interactive sites, that can be used with an entire classroom, if the facilities exist. The key to using the Internet in the science classroom is being aware what is available on the Web. It is helpful to spend a few hours playing around the Internet, getting used to using the SEARCH, OPEN, and CLICK DIRECTED techniques. CLICK DIRECTED searching is quite simple for students to use. The information provided can be accessed by using the Yahoo! search engine. This is the simplest and most complete search engine available, as it works on a progressive narrowing down of the topic. My order of operation for this site was:

1. Click on Netscape.
2. Click on Directory.
3. Click on Yahoo!
4. Click on Science.
5. Click on Astronomy.
6. Click on Planets (I was now presented with a series of planet-specific sites to choose from.)
7. Click on Nine Planets.
8. Click on the location options.
9. Play around in the site, and have fun finding the information you require!

Other sites of interest on same topic:

- VIEWS OF THE SOLAR SYSTEM
  http://bang.lanl.gov/solarsys/
- PLANETARY FACT SHEETS
  http://nssac.gsfc.nasa.gov/planetary/planetfact.html (You can also access the NASA sites from this page.)

> A teacher should always be prepared to teach the lesson using conventional methods, as one may not always be able to access the sites one wants, or Internet server problems may be experienced.

When introducing the Internet to students, it is vital that they are actually able to see the format of the Internet server. It is of little value to give the students a list of commands to follow, without letting them see what the monitor looks like. By clearing away the students' desks, I was able to have them seated in a theater-like fashion, so all had a clear view of the monitor. The students took notes, outlining the various key commands and procedures to be followed to access the network. Students were then taken through the usage of various SEARCH commands, as well as "click-directed" searching.

Several students then approached the computer and searched for information on their respective planets, with their classmates coaching them when difficulties arose. The availability of information on each planet, complete with the latest NASA images, provided the students with a wealth of information on which to draw for their projects. The images were especially useful when the students were drawing their planets on poster paper. All said, the quality of the projects was vastly improved due to the amount of information available on the Internet. For example, Matt wanted to know the composition of the sun, not just how big it was. He also wanted to know how the sun works; what process is involved in creating such an enormous amount of heat. The information Matt found on the Internet was much more elaborate, and having images in full color also helped to create a better understanding of what the sun was, and what it did. As a result, Matt and his classmates were able to produce much more elaborate projects, and had a better grasp of their topics when asked questions.

Additional applications of the Internet in the science classroom are many if every student in the classroom has his/her own Internet station. In this situation, the students could be taken through various interactive Web sites as a group, resulting in a much more efficient use of the Internet. NASA, for example, has some fantastic sites developed specifically for interactive classroom usage. There are an abundance of sites available covering all aspects of science, be it biology, chemistry, or physics. The resources available for students will help open up worlds that would never have been imaginable a few years ago.

Another benefit of using the Internet is it helps students develop their computer skills. It is no secret that computers are playing a larger role in our lives everyday. Students need to have the skills on the various computer platforms if they want to survive in the world of the future.

Not every classroom or school is going to have the resources available to hook up to the Internet. Books and periodicals may remain the bread and butter for many schools. It is, however, necessary for schools to at least introduce students to the Internet and how to use it before they move on into the real world of business, post-secondary education, or the like.

Teachers must also be aware that they are using technology, and various networks have the propensity to shut down once in a while. The teacher should be prepared to continue lessons through more conventional means, should there be a problem with the computer or the network connections, or if the Web site is busy or not working.

Most of my students in grade 4 are very computer literate. They all have very well developed computer skills, and their abilities on the Internet are quite impressive. After 35 minutes of surfing, each student shared his or her findings of interesting Web sites. Then we surfed those sites together and decided on eight sites that connected to almost any science topic. This list of Web sites was copied by all students and saved onto their diskettes.

As a class, my students and I use the Internet at least twice a week for various searches. Computers and the Internet play a major role in the students' learning. My cooperating teacher and I are working on a class homepage. Once it is on the Net with our school's homepage, we will have the students create their own. They will incorporate still pictures and short video and audio excerpts to introduce themselves. Once all pages are finished, they will be on line and linked to our class homepage. I will have students demonstrate their science and technology works on their homepage to share with other students and educators from around the world who might be interested.

Here are North American sites that teachers can use as resources for science teaching at the elementary level:

American Sites for Science Investigations
http://WWW.minnetonka.K12.mn.us/support/science/tools/sciencecap.html

- ERIC Science Lesson
  gopher://ericir.syr.edu/11/Lesson/Science
- Elementary Science This Month
  http://1meWWW.mankato.msus.edu/ci.elem_sci.html
- 1995-96 Science Elementary Lessons
  http://WWW.voicenet.com/~mcdonald/lessons.html
- Elementary mini lessons
  http://WWW.npn.org/cyber.serv/AoneP/academy_one/teacher/cec/c
  ecsci/sci-elem.html

Canadian Sites for Science Investigations
http://www.sd68.nanaimo.bc.ca/schools/nroy/students.html

- Science Web
  http:scienceweb.dao.nrc.ca
  http:scienceweb.dao.nrc.ca/can/teach.html
- Safesites
  http://www.safesurf.com/sskwave.html

Teaching Standard F

Guideline: Actively participate in making decisions concerning the allocation of time and other resources to the science program.

- Bill Nye The Science Guy
  http://nye/abs.kcts.org/
- Canada's School Net
  http://schoolnet2.carleton.ca/
- Math/Science
  http://schoolnet2.carleton.ca/english/math_sci/
- Kids Web a Digital Library for School Kids
  http://WWW.npac.syr.edu/textbook/kidsweb/Virtual Frog
  http://george.1b1.gov/ITG.hm.pg.docs/dissect.html

Microcomputer-Based Laboratories (MBLs)

An MBL constitutes a technological system based on the principle of interfacing microcomputers with probe-ware and laboratory-ware. This computer system collects and graphically displays quantitative measurements such as temperature, light and sound intensities, pH, and velocity against real time. A promising feature of MBLs is that experimentation and experimental analysis occur simultaneously, thus minimizing laborious data collection efforts and providing more time for data analysis. Some science teachers use MBLs in their research as an instructional mode to enhance scientific attitudes in students.

According to Krajcik and Layman (1993), the MBL provides opportunities for asking and refining questions, making predictions, designing plans and/or experiments, collecting and analyzing data, debating ideas, communicating ideas and findings with others, drawing conclusions, and asking new questions. All of these attributes point to a constructivist approach to teaching and learning science. However, probes do not help students construct understanding about scientific concepts—a teacher must do that. If, for example, students use an MBL to monitor the temperature of physical systems, the teacher must help students analyze the MBL–produced graphs and science concepts involved in the activity.

Despite all the nice features of the MBL, a teacher must make a conscious effort to incorporate his or her knowledge of MBLs with students' conceptions. Before students can plan and design experiments, common knowledge between the teacher and the students must be achieved. Then information on the graph becomes clear. The tool only puts out graphs and information quickly; the interpretation of these belongs to the experimenter, the student. Nachmias and Linn (1987) show that without adequate theoretical reasoning, students usually tend to perceptually view and interpret the graphs they were able to produce by manipulating variables. The science process skills that enable problem solving may be enhanced as a result of MBLs (Friedler, Nachmias, & Linn, 1990). But the learning of science concepts depends on students' conceptual ecology and the teacher's teaching ecology. The overall effectiveness of MBLs depends on the teacher's understanding of how to use the new technology, personal knowledge of the concepts involved, and knowledge of how to help students link their MBL experiences with science concepts.

Teaching Standard E

Teachers of science develop communities of science learners that reflect the intellectual rigor of scientific inquiry and the attitudes and social values conducive to science learning.

Teaching Standard A

Guideline: Plan an inquiry-based program by selecting science content and adapting and designing curricula to meet the interests, knowledge, understanding, abilities, and experiences of students.

PSL (Personal Science Laboratory) Explorer is an IBM–based MBL program. Examples of some IBM-based MBLs programs are *Batteries and Bulbs, Heat and Temperature,* and *Reflection.*

Computer Simulations

In formally educating an individual, we strive to produce a knowledgeable, intelligent, skilled learner, capable of problem solving, with appreciation for all facets of life. Computers provide an enhanced teaching and learning opportunity to accomplish this. An example can be seen in a focused study of how computer simulations can enhance problem-solving skills.

BALANCE: A Predator-Prey Simulation —a computer biology simulations program published by Diversified Educational Enterprises and written by Rivers and Vockell (1987)—shows how an education instrument can produce an informed learner with problem-solving skills that can be translated to another areas.

BALANCE is a student-interactive simulation that explores the interrelated variables affecting predator-prey relationships. Students manipulate variables such as food supply, carrying capacity, environmental conditions, and external pressures. Tabular and graphic output illustrate the effects of the variables on the related population. The student develops problem-solving skills as well as tabulation, graphing, and interpretation skills. Students record data in a student laboratory guide, which provides realistic scenarios for exploration.

This program makes the student feel he or she is an ecology student actually studying a community. It is almost as if the student is doing fieldwork. This opportunity gives the student a greater understanding of scientific investigation. In this particular program, the student learns how to conduct scientific experiments that reflect real life. Rivers and Vockell found that students who used a guided computer simulation to cover course material had better problem-solving skills than those who covered the course material in the traditional manner.

Other examples of simulation programs are *A Field Trip to the Rainforest* (Mac-NET), *Coral Kingdom* (CD-ROM), and *Oceans Below* (Mac-CD-ROM).

Microworlds

Another representation of knowledge in a modern computer framework is through microworlds. Microworlds are conceptual frameworks that contain principles; they are not arranged in a didactic manner. This method of presentation allows students to learn principles independently. Microworlds give a more holistic view of subject material and are often closer to real life than a chapter of a textbook. Microworlds satisfy the need of students to think. Rather than merely state conceptions, they have implicit concepts constructed within them. The purpose of microworlds is to construct artificial realities, complete with underlying structures, constraints, and rules, that can be explored and manipulated by students.

Teaching Standard D

Guideline: Design and manage the learning environment by creating a setting for student work that is flexible and supportive of science inquiry.

Teaching Standard B

Guideline: To guide and facilitate learning, encourage and model the skills of scientific inquiry, as well as the curiosity, openness to new ideas and data, and skepticism that characterize science.

PEER INTERACTION

Computer Worlds

Create a simple hypermedia science activity for your students. Following is a
HyperCard example of an activity based on Newton's Third Law of Motion.

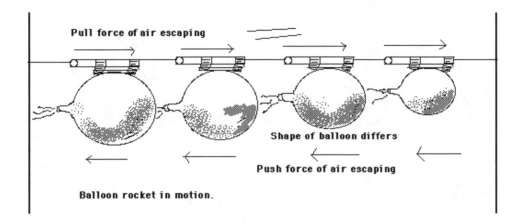

Balloon rocket in motion.

⊞ DESIGN TECHNOLOGY IN SCIENCE

For most people, technology means computers. Using computers for educational purposes is an example of educational technology, as is using videos,
overhead projectors, and nonprojected visuals like bulletin boards. Through
simulations and microworlds, computers also enable us to understand natural phenomena. As opposed to *educational technology, technology education*
allows us to use technology to better understand science principles or to
design, implement, and evaluate technological products.

Relationship Between Science and Technology

In science classes, teachers generally use technology to illustrate key science principles. For example, a teacher might use a pinhole camera to
help students learn how light travels in a straight path and why the pinhole
camera makes an inverted image. In this sense, we learn science concepts
using a technical device or a model of one. Learning science concepts is
the primary aim.

For a new relationship between science and technology, Raizen,
Sellwood, Todd, and Vickers (1995) draw innovative ideas from models
presented by Bybee and others (1989) and Layton (1993). These authors
"conceive of technology education as involving much more than 'using'
science to explain how devices work" (Raizen et al., 1995, p. 11). They

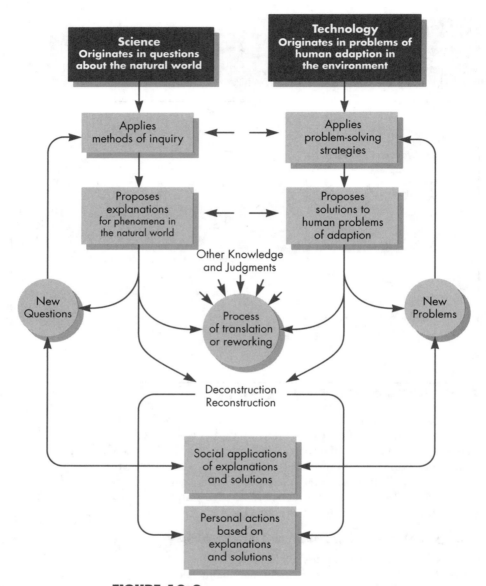

FIGURE 10-2
The relationship between science and technology and their connection to education goals (NOTE. From *Technology Education in the Classroom: Understanding the Designed World,* by S. Raizen, P. Sellwood, R. D. Todd, and M. Vickers, 1995, San Francisco: Jossey-Bass, Inc., Publishers, p. 12.)

suggest that we have students think about everyday or real-world problems from several perspectives (social sciences, mathematics, art, etc.), as illustrated in Figure 10-2, and design technology to implement possible solutions.

In this type of technology education—known as a design approach—the emphasis is on construction and utility of a product. Students are responsible for some decision making. They identify an everyday problem, set parameters within the available resources, devise their own design, learn the concepts that underlie the design, test and discuss the working of the device as well as its impact on society, and redesign as necessary. The design approach is compatible with a constructivist approach because children are encouraged to develop their own theory and it is community centered. For example, in the design of a boat, the child may ask, "How can I change the sails to catch the wind?" (Bottrill, 1995).

When added to science education, technology education will enhance critical, creative, and complex thinking skills in both subject areas (science and technology). For example, students can design and build different types of "bridges" according to local needs. What role does science play in the development and evaluation of technologies found both at home and at school? In other words, students should not only learn what to do, but they should also ask why it worked. This will lead students to see the usefulness of science concepts in the development of technologies.

Teaching Standard D

Guideline: Design and manage the learning environment by engaging students in designing their own learning environment.

The "Design Loop"

Dunn and Larson (1990) suggest that students may enter and exit at any point in the design process. The "design loop," taken from Raizen et al. (1995, p. 45), identifies a number of sequential concepts and activities (see Figure 10-3). The authors advise that these concepts and activities must be appropriate to the developmental level of a specific group of students. The elements of this design process are as follows.

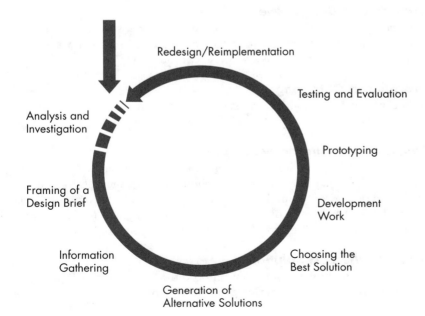

FIGURE 10-3
The "design loop" process model (NOTE. Reprinted with permission of *ties* Magazine, The College of New Jersey, Trenton, NJ 08650.)

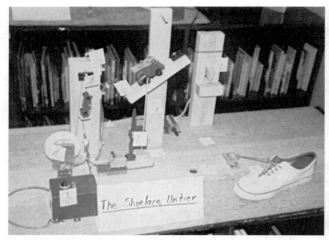

The Shoelace Untier (above) consists of 14 separate machines made up of electrical components that function in sequence to untie a shoelace.

The Dog Feeder (at right) is a complex machine consisting of 10 mechanical and electrical components that perform two separate operations; one dispenses dog food, the other dispenses water.

Analysis and Investigation

Choose a real-world problem. Analyze and investigate this problem to determine whether it warrants further study.

Framing of a Design Brief

How would the solution help the problem? What constraints are imposed on the development of the solution to the problem? Prepare a design brief or problem statement that answers these two questions.

Information Gathering

Gather information about the constraining factors in the development of a particular technology.

Generation of Alternative Solutions

Consider many possible solutions. Defer criticism of the alternatives at this point—it will prematurely narrow your choices. This stage calls for originality, flexibility, and self-confidence. Tell others of your ideas and imaginations. This will help you or your student (the designer) to clarify ideas. Other suggestions and improvements can be incorporated.

Choosing the Best Solution

From your many possible solutions, choose the one that best answers the questions in your design brief or problem statement. Does your solution

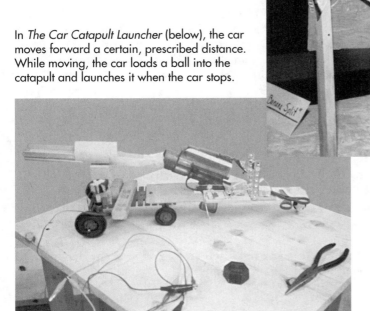

In *The Car Catapult Launcher* (below), the car moves forward a certain, prescribed distance. While moving, the car loads a ball into the catapult and launches it when the car stops.

The Banana Split Maker (above) can dispense a sliced banana, nuts, and fruit into a waiting bowl of ice cream represented by cotton wool in the photograph.

meet the criteria in your statement? Can you defend it in terms of the context in which the product will be designed?

Developmental Work

Develop the idea into a tangible device for solving the problem. Use sketches and color drawings before building—this allows you to visualize, compare, imagine, and negotiate. Create models using disposable materials. Give mathematical characterizations and draw technical drawings, as appropriate. The original design brief or problem statement will determine the foregoing steps and the final product.

Prototyping

After solving the functional problems and making decisions about size and material, create a real-size model or prototype. Appearance counts at this stage. Hence, use material that comes very close to the actual material.

Testing and Evaluation

Evaluate the solution against the criteria established in the design brief or problem statement. Assess the solution in terms of universal design character and needs.

Redesign and Reimplementation

Consider reworking the model to produce a finer solution or product.

This model involves critical and creative thinking. It is only a guide to the design process. When problem-solving skills are well developed, the design process becomes second nature.

To engage learners in design technology, consider assigning projects like the culminating activity one teacher used to have students translate and extend their understanding of problem solving. Having previously completed unit studies on electricity and forces and machines, students were asked to make a complex machine using at least eight simple machines that would solve a problem. Students chose their own problem, suggested possible solutions, explored these solutions, selected the best solution, and then designed a machine that solved the problem (see pages 282 and 283).

Managing a Design Project

Teaching Standard D

Guideline: Design and manage the learning environment by structuring the time available so students are able to engage in extended investigations.

The design process is an interplay between "active and reflective modes" (Sellwood, 1989, as cited in Raizen et al., 1995). For organizing and managing a design project, we need time, space, and resources (Bottrill, 1995).

Time

Time is required for action and reflection in each stage of the design loop. Hence, time spent on a design project must be justified in terms of the total learning value. Pay attention to these questions:

- How much time should be spent on a project and when?
- Will other class activities be suspended because of the project activity?
- What amount of time should be allocated to the tasks?
- Should it take place on consecutive days or be a weekly event?

Space

Decide where the design project should take place—in the classroom or elsewhere. Developing interpersonal relationships through collaborative learning is an essential aim of the design approach. Hence, space must be provided for group activity. The pertinent questions are the following:

- How will the room be organized?
- Where will each group work?
- Where will the materials and equipment be stored?
- How will semifinished work be stored?
- How will the groups of students be selected?

Resources

The equipment and materials can be shared. A wide variety of materials must be accessible, clearly labeled, and stored in containers. Potentially hazardous equipment such as saws, glue guns, and paper cutters should be handled carefully and stored in a safe place (Bottrill, 1995, p. 51).

A Teaching Model for Science and Technology

Understanding the designed world should be part of science education for all young people. Publications such as *A Nation at Risk* (National Commission on Excellence in Education, 1983), *Educating America for the 21st Century* (National Science Board Commission on Precollege Education in Mathematics, Science and Technology, 1983), *Science for All Americans* (American Association for the Advancement of Science [AAAS], 1989), *Benchmarks for Science Literacy* (AAAS, 1993), and *National Science Education Standards* (National Research Council, 1996) all recommend teaching science and technology as a primary goal for science education. Each of these reports suggests that responsible citizens should *know* as well as *use* science (Raizen et al., 1995). To help you make this a reality, study Figure 10-4. This teaching model will help you distinguish between science

Stages	Examples for Science	Examples for Technology
Invitation	Observe the natural world. Ask questions about the natural world. State possible hypothesis.	Observe the world made by humans. Recognize a human problem. Identify possible solutions.
Exploration, discovery, creativity	Engage in focused play. Look for information. Observe specific phenomena. Collect and organize data. Select appropriate resources. Design and conduct experiments. Engage in debate. Define parameters of an investigation.	Brainstorm possible alternatives. Experiment with materials. Design a model. Employ problem-solving strategies. Discuss solutions with others. Evaluate choices. Identify risks and consequences. Analyze data.
Proposing explanations and solutions	Communicate information and ideas. Construct a new explanation. Undergo evaluation by peers. Determine appropriate closure.	Construct and explain a model. Constructively review a solution. Express multiple answers/solutions. Integrate a solution with existing knowledge and experiences.
Taking action	Apply knowledge and skills. Share information and ideas. Ask new questions.	Make decisions. Transfer knowledge and skills. Develop products and promote ideas.

FIGURE 10-4
Teaching model (NOTE. From National Center for Improving Science Education (1995). *The High Stakes of High-School Science.* Washington, D.C.)

education for developing scientific knowledge and problem-solving science that utilizes design technology for its solutions.

REFLECTIVE PRACTICE

Design Technology Opportunities

Here is a list of design technology opportunities you or your students may want to try:

- A scale model of a dollhouse
- Musical instruments that produce sound
- New models for transportation
- Mobiles
- Intensive use of wheels
- Models of boats that support a certain amount of weight

Choose one of the above examples or find another design activity. Using a part of or the entire design loop, plan a detailed design activity.

CASE STUDY

10-1: Problem Solving in Design Technology for *Grade 6*

Ingmar Wenzel

Description

Problem solving is an integral part of design technology. Often design technology problems are a result of the human impact on the environment.

Uses

Design technology is designing, making, testing, and evaluating a product to efficiently influence and control the environment. Both the teacher and the students must be aware of environmental issues when considering both the type of problem being assessed, and the solution to the problem (i.e., will the finished product resolve the problem but create a negative impact on the environment?). The process of problem solving is not as easy as thinking that if the problem is solved, then the primary goal has been achieved. Students must also consider the possible ramifications of their design and end products. Students must become responsible for their own design.

Preservice Teacher Practice

I used this teaching technique with a *grade 6* class that had studied a unit on simple machines. I decided to incorporate a design technology lesson as an assessment strategy along with the written test I designed. Students were asked to design a complex machine with an intended purpose. The students' goals were:

1. To connect prior learned knowledge to design a complex machine that has an intended goal.
2. To use creative, divergent, and critical thinking skills.
3. To provide and consider other students' positive criticism and suggestions.
4. To evaluate their ideas.

The manner in which this activity proceeded differs slightly from the design line approach. Due to time constraints, and the lack of necessary materials at my disposal, I decided that the students would simply draw their complex machine, using the various simple machines previously studied, and describe it in a brief essay. The students were to set up a problem, generate one or several possible designs, and then plan how the design was to work. The criteria used for student assessment are as follows: idea originality; complexity of the design; thoroughness and detail of the drawing and the written material; proper use of knowledge on simple machines; and whether the designs could possibly work.

I decided to give students this open-ended approach to designing a complex machine based on their own ideas. Various references suggested that the teacher provide the necessary problem.

Children's Work

The students had approximately one week to design their machine and finish their essay and diagram. Many were very complex and well-designed. See Figures 10-5 and 10-6 for a sample of one student's work.

Personal Reflections

I was quite amazed at the complexity of some of the submitted reports. Many of the students put a great deal of effort in designing their own complex machine. From looking at the various entries, I was able to determine that these students did have a sound basic understanding of the scientific concepts concerning simple machines. The written component of the lesson proved to be valuable in explaining how these machines were intended to work. Many of the students were so enthusiastic about the activity, they asked for their assignments back so that they could make changes. They were independently assessing their own designs.

Feb 3 The Acme Mining Complex Eric

{What it's made of}

The Acme Mining Complex contains 4 wheel and axles, 7 gears, 2 pulley systems, 2 wedges, 2 levers, 23 inclined planes and 1 screw.

{How it works}

First, the truck with the digging claws digs a hole into the ground then the grabber arm on the end of the conveyor belt picks up all the rocks and puts them on the conveyor belt. then another grabber with a video camera mounted inside it lets the driver of the crane to see if its a diamond or if its just coal if its a diamond he will turn the gears which lowers the rope and then the diamond is grabbed by the grabbers on the crane and are put into a big bin. The crane is powered by a man who hits a piston and it pushes down on a lever and there is an air sack on the other end of the lever. Below the air sack there is a canister with coal in it and as the lever moves up the air sack is compressed sending steam up. Just before it leaves the sack boiling water is poured on the coal which produces the steam. The conveyor belt carries all the rocks that are not diamonds and sends them up an inclined plane and the they fall off the belt into the truck at the bottom. The conveyor belt is powered by an employee turning a wheel and axle with a gear on the end which makes the wheels pull the belt along. The truck with the grabbers on it is powered from the steam of the crane. The Acme mining complex is mobile. Cost: 1.3 million

FIGURE 10-5
Eric's work

☀ CHAPTER REFLECTIONS

In this chapter, we have provided you with fodder for looking toward the future and the integrative role computer technology will play in the classroom. Christopher Dede, a professor of information technology, argues that new technologies can help transform schools if they are used to support new models of teaching and learning, models that characterize sustained,

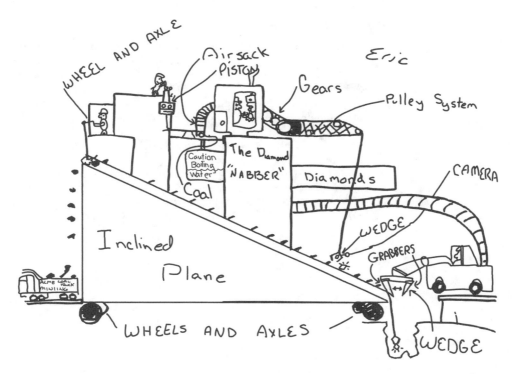

FIGURE 10-6
Continued

community-centered, constructivist classrooms for learner investigation, collaboration, and construction (O'Neil, 1995).

We have also introduced you to design technology in science. Conceptual models and practical examples of design technology in this chapter will give you sufficient motivation to develop ideas for designing technologies in your science class. When technology education in science is connected to children's worlds and their immediate surroundings, they will then see purpose in their learning.

Questions for Reflective Inquiry

1. Survey the Internet for science investigations. Download an investigation and share it with your peers.

2. What are some of the microworlds and computer simulations available to the elementary science teacher? Find out!

3. Building bridges, towers, and boats are common forms of design technology at the elementary level. What are other design technologies you could encourage your class to create? For example, how about designing a cart that is pulled by static electricity?

SUGGESTED READINGS

Bottrill, P. (1995). *Designing and learning in the elementary school.* Reston, VA: International Technology Education Association.

Dunn, S., & Larson, R. (1990). *Design technology: Children's engineering.* Washington, DC: Falmer Press.

Friedler, Y., Nachmias, R., & Linn, M. (1990). Learning scientific reasoning skills in microcomputer-based laboratories. *Journal of Research in Science Teaching, 27*(2), 173–191.

Jonassen, D. H. (1996). *Computers in the classroom: Mindtools for critical thinking.* Englewood Cliffs, NJ: Prentice-Hall.

O'Neil, J. (1995). Technology and schools: A conversation with Chris Dede. *Educational Leadership, October,* 7–12.

Raizen, S., Sellwood, P., Todd, R. D., & Vickers, M. (1995). *Technology education in the classroom. Understanding the designed world.* San Francisco: Jossey-Bass.

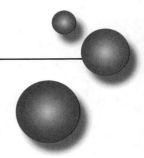

CHAPTER 11

Multiple Voices in Unit Planning

1. What are the many voices that have influenced science education reform?

2. How are these voices translated into considerations for unit planning?

3. What is a unit planning format that considers these voices?

4. From how many perspectives can science teaching be approached?

5. How can the "reflecting and assessing" phase of the Common Knowledge Construction Model be integrated into all of the lessons of a unit plan?

Reflective Inquiry

> **KIRSTEN'S VOICE**
> When planning my teaching unit on **Matter,** I tried to explore
> and research all of the aspects of science education that
> influence teaching and learning. Even though I was only
> planning for teaching grade 1, I knew that I needed to consider
> the multidisciplinary nature of science to meet the needs of all
> my learners.

JOURNAL ACTIVITY

Kirsten's Planning

Read the following pages in which Kirsten introduces her science unit. Reflect on the planning Kirsten has begun on Matter. Are there any aspects of her planning that surprise you? What value do you see in each aspect of her planning? What other considerations do you think Kirsten will need to make to complete her unit planning?

In her unit on *Matter*, Kirsten examines the nature of the learner and carries out extensive content analysis in terms of science subject knowledge as well as the historical, societal, and technological contexts of inquiry. She situates her lessons against this rich backdrop. Now, you might wonder why such an elaborate background is necessary for teaching elementary science. A rich foundation affords the possibility of approaching science from different perspectives. Let us briefly explore what background Kirsten has researched to develop her **content and pedagogical knowledge**.

Kirsten's Introduction to a *Grade 1* Unit on *Matter*

Nature of Students

The students in my grade 1 class come from a variety of socioeconomic and multicultural backgrounds. I also have several special-needs students and one ESL (English as a second language) student. I have designed this unit to be a meaningful and positive experience for all my students. Any of the activities can be easily modified to meet the needs of students with special needs.

Content Analysis

Matter is a term used to describe all the different substances in the universe. Solids, liquids, and gases are the three important states of matter, and most substances are found in at least one of these forms. During the course of this unit, the children will become aware that their world is made up of matter in three forms. The students will also experience the changing states of matter by participating, predicting, and observing during the various hands-on activities.

After students have explored, manipulated, and categorized objects around them into the three forms of matter, they will learn specific characteristics for each state. The planned activities will incorporate both individual and cooperative learning and will reflect a variety of learning strategies to explore children's conceptions and meaning-making.

What the children learn about the characteristics of solids, liquids, and gases will enable them to make sense of their world in a new light. They will be able to make simple predictions (based on what they have learned about solids, liquids, and gases) concerning the reversible and irreversible changes in matter.

By experiencing the activities of melting, evaporating, and freezing, the students will observe the changes in matter and come to understand that they can control aspects of their environment by manipulating solids, liquids, and gases. Not all matter in the world is specifically a liquid or a solid. Soft ice cream and pudding are a combination of both a liquid and a solid. The children will gain an understanding of the connections between the three states of matter.

Historical Context

The following historical discoveries were made during the human evolution of the understanding of matter. The specific scientists mentioned made contributions to the scientific ideas about solids, liquids, and gases.

Content knowledge refers to teacher knowledge of the subject matter. Remember that the learning tools, concept maps and Vee diagrams from chapter 3, can assist you in exploring and organizing this content knowledge.

"Pedagogical content knowledge" (Shulman, 1987) refers to the knowledge we need in order to teach the content of science, such as the nature of the learner and the nature of learning, as well as philosophical, historical, and sociological aspects of science.

Scientists' Understanding of Solids.

- During the 19th century, scientists came to the realization that most solids are composed of crystals.
- Toward the end of the 19th century, the study of modern atomic theory showed that crystals are made up of certain atomic arrangements.
- In 1912, the interior of a solid was investigated by x-rays.

Scientists' Understanding of Liquids. Archimedes (297–212 B.C.) stated the principle that floating objects or objects completely or partly submerged in a fluid have a certain amount of buoyancy or upthrust acting on them. The size of this upthrust is equal to the weight of the fluid that the object displaces. The denser the liquid, the easier an object floats in it.

Scientists' Understanding of Gases. Boyle (1627–1691) discovered that the volume of a fixed mass of gas is inversely proportional to the pressure if the temperature remains the same.

Charles (1746–1823) stated that the volume of a fixed mass of gas is directly proportional to the absolute temperature if the gas pressure remains the same.

Technological and Societal Context

Knowledge of the physical properties of matter (solids, liquids, and gases) has taught us how to cook, clothe ourselves, make tools, build shelters, sail the seas, and explore outer space. It is sometimes hard to believe that, through technology, man experimented with the smallest element of matter (the atom) to create a thermonuclear war.

The technological advances that our society is making every day concerning the properties of matter are somewhat overwhelming for a grade 1 child. How can I relate the technological and societal contexts to the everyday lives of my students? Through my unit, the students will learn that they can observe and control certain aspects of their environment by manipulating solids, liquids, and gases. I want my students to be able to relate their knowledge of matter to the community they live in and their environment. Changes in matter can help them understand cooking. When seasons come and go, the children will have an understanding of the melting, freezing, and evaporation that they observe around them. If my students know some of the properties of gases (odor, color, etc.), they may be able to recognize hazardous gases and protect themselves accordingly.

The knowledge my students acquire in this unit will act as a stepping stone to help them make sense of our society and the world around them.

☀ AN OVERVIEW FOR SCIENCE PLANNING

In Kirsten's science planning she has enriched her own science content background knowledge, identified the nature of her learners, and analyzed how she can make her unit on matter more meaningful for them. We

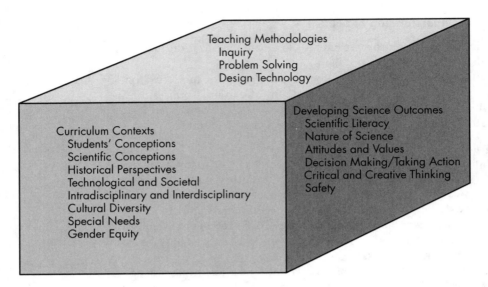

FIGURE 11-1
Dimensions of constructivist
science teaching

envision (and we hope you do too) that, as Kirsten continues to develop a
plan for her science unit, she will determine which teaching methodologies
and activities she will use to explore and categorize students' current
knowledge and conceptions, negotiate with her learners to develop
common meaning, translate and extend her learners' experiences and conceptions, and plan for continuous assessment of her students' growth.
These functions are at the core of our Common Knowledge Construction
Model. Planning for the specific teaching needs of individual students or
groups of students and incorporating science and technology to further
contextualize the teaching and learning experiences will also be important.
Careful planning is a key to good teaching.

To facilitate your planning, it may at first help you to see a visual
overview of the multidimensional nature of constructivist science teaching
and learning (see Figure 11-1). No dimension is separate, as science teaching and learning are integrative by nature. As you become more confident in
your science teaching and find success in developing strategies with your
students, you may want to expand the dimensions of this figure. Science
teaching is evolutional, as is all good teaching.

☀ REFLECTIVE PRACTICE

Voices Affecting Science Education
We are nearing the end of this book. We still need to look at unit planning.
What voices do you think influence the science we teach and how we help stu-
dents learn? How do these voices affect science education?

✴ MULTIPLE VOICES INFLUENCING SCIENCE EDUCATION

During the last three decades, science educators have been calling for the renewal of science education—for school sciences that characterize the social nature of the scientific enterprise (American Association for the Advancement of Science, 1989; Orpwood, 1984). The National Science Education Standards were recently developed for the express purpose that all students should achieve science literacy. The document states that many types of individuals (or voices) "will play a critical role in improving science education; teachers; science supervisors; curriculum developers; publishers; those who work in museums, zoos, and science centers; science educators; scientists and engineers across the nation; school administrators; school board members; parents; members of business and industry; and legislators and other public officials" (National Academy of Science, p. ix).

But what voices have driven these reforms? The worldwide communities of scholars and researchers that have influenced science education reform include historians and philosophers of science; sociologists; language specialists; proponents of science-technology-society connections; educational psychologists; multicultural science educators; advocates of gender equity; and constructivists. New models for science education have originated from all of their perspectives:

- *Historians and philosophers of science*—falsification of ideas in science (Popper, 1979), evolutionary changes (Toulmin, 1972), normal science and revolutionary paradigm shifts (Kuhn, 1970)
- *Sociologists*—internal convictions and persuasions: scientists' discourse (Latour & Woolgar, 1986); external convictions and persuasions: political economic analysis (Hodson, 1993)
- *Language specialists*—using the specialized language of science to make sense of the world and to make sense of and to one another; doing science—exploring the scientific process through the medium of language (Lemke, 1990; Sutton, 1992); "speak-on" science (Bruner, 1986)
- *Proponents of science-technology-society connections*—making the connections among science-technology-society relevant and accessible to all students (Bybee, 1986, 1994; Solomon & Aikenhead, 1994)
- *Educational psychologists*—cognitive structural wholes—person-world dichotomy (Ausubel, 1968; Piaget, 1973); person-world dialectical relationships (Marton, 1981, 1984); children's knowledge domains (Carey, 1985)
- *Multicultural science educators*—interpersonal relationships and learning styles as cultural factors (Atwater & Riley, 1993; Hodson, 1993; Keller, 1985)
- *Advocates of gender equity*—socially motivated feminism (Tuana, 1989), feminist oriented but includes social context as a critical feature

of scientific work (Longino, 1990), girls in science (Kelly, 1981), criteria for judging an unbiased classroom (Allen, 1995)

- *Constructivists*—children's science (Osborne & Freyberg, 1985); radical constructivism (Glasersfeld, 1989); common knowledge (Edwards & Mercer, 1987); students' ideas (Driver, Asoko, Leach, Mortimer, & Scott, 1994); relational conceptions (Ebenezer & Erickson, 1996); contexts of meanings (Bloom, 1992)

REFLECTIVE PRACTICE

The Most Influential Voices

1. Which of the foregoing voices in science education do you consider to have been most influential in changing science education in the past 10 years?
2. How can these voices be heard in your unit plan?

Teaching Standard A

Guideline: Plan an inquiry-based science program by developing a framework of yearlong and short-term goals for students.

Teaching Standard A

Teachers of science plan an inquiry-based science program for their students.

☀ CONSIDERATIONS FOR A UNIT OF STUDY IN SCIENCE

In chapters 1–10, we have been helping you to view science education from a number of perspectives. Now we are ready to put all these ideas together in tackling the task of lesson and unit planning.

Let us look back at Ron's approach to science teaching, described by him in chapter 4. He took the following steps to incorporate students' conceptions in his unit:

1. He researched the background of the unit topic in terms of the content from the curriculum guide and available resources.
2. He read reference books and science textbooks, looking for suitable activities. He carried out some of the experiments to judge their suitability.
3. He drew concept maps and Vee diagrams of the content of the unit.
4. He read key articles from the research literature that detailed children's understandings about the topic.
5. He gathered support for the unit, such as science supplies, and ordered videos, films, and computer software. He consulted with the librarian as to the supply of science reading books on the topic. Then he arranged for field trips or guest speakers.
6. He chose suitable strategies and activities to explore his students' ideas on the topic.

We admire how Ron went about developing his teaching plan with the guidance of his teacher educator. Ron's approach to science teaching incorporated multiple voices in science education. And, although Ron did not connect children's conceptions to historical and STS perspectives like Kirsten did, science teaching may be approached from different perspectives:

- Teaching may begin with *science concepts,* then translate these to personal and societal problems.
- Teaching may begin with *design technology* and the *why* questions may lead to examining science concepts.
- Teaching may originate from a *societal problem* and the science concepts may be studied within the context of the problem.
- Teaching may be situated within an *historical perspective* (studying the historical evolution of science concepts and their inventors).

The foregoing orientations can be easily represented in a unit of study. Underlying all of these perspectives is the consideration of children's conceptions from the first lesson to the end of a unit. What follows is a sample "multiple voice" unit plan on *current electricity* for the *fourth grade.* We suggest a basic unit plan outline and a lesson plan within the unit.

In a unit plan, identify intentions, prepare a set of lessons, write objectives, plan a sequence of activities, and prepare assessments. Intention(s) of the lesson may be based on students' conceptions, students' questions, a local science-related issue, historical development of a scientific idea, or something that was puzzling to the students. The set of lessons should be coherent and based on students' conceptions and curricular ideas, moving from simple to more complex ideas. Consider what science content standards will be covered in a set of lessons. Note that objectives must be operationally stated. The sequence of activities within a lesson must have a logical flow. Relationships between lessons must be established. Prepare activities to assess your students' ideas during or at the end of each lesson.

Preparing lessons based on students' conceptions is not all that easy. During the exploration phase, careful consideration should be given to choosing appropriate topic-related activities that are simple and related to students' experiences. The kinds of questions you should ask must be broad and should not lead to the right answers—you are simply asking for their ideas. In the constructing and negotiating lessons, activities must match students' ideas for clarifying or elaborating. Be a collaborative partner with your student in the scientific inquiry so that an authentic image of scientists at work is portrayed. Since students are constantly probed for their understandings, try to be an "intellectual friend" to your students.

We have outlined a detailed unit plan. When you are deeply engaged in writing your unit plan, many issues will surface. As you write, you will be able to clarify your ideas. You will experience the joys and pains of a curriculum developer and teacher-researcher. The unit will truly be yours!

✳ A UNIT FORMAT
Title of Unit
Select a unit of study in collaboration with your cooperating teacher.

Teaching Standard A

Guideline: Plan an inquiry-based program by selecting science content and adapting and designing curricula to meet the interests, knowledge, understanding, abilities, and experiences of students.

The unit plan presented in this chapter is based on the first approach. We have included this approach because science concepts become central to the study of a unit. Furthermore, this approach is not a drastic change from the way teaching traditionally occurs in science. However, we consider students' conceptions and also treat other orientations systematically—these are not options!

Unit planning provides you with a supportive framework and guidance in the complex task of preparing for teaching. It is important for you to have support from your science teacher educator, cooperating teacher, and peers as you work through this task. So find opportunities and time to dialogue with these individuals. Therein lies your strength!

Author(s)

Write your group members' names.

Curriculum

State the program(s) of science that you are using.

Grade Level

Indicate the grade level or age of children for which the unit is intended.

Nature of Students

Know your students. Ask yourself: "Whom will I be teaching?" Describe any special characteristics or considerations you need to make for the unit.

Purpose of Unit

What are the purposes of teaching this unit? Briefly describe.

Overview

Describe and justify major goals in the unit. What major ideas need to be developed or addressed? Your justification should reflect scientific knowledge, scientific attitudes, attitudes toward science, science-technology-society (STS) issues, and historical connections. The National Science Education Standards (National Research Council, 1996) and your district program guide should help you to determine the preceding goals.

Curricular Content Development

Science Content Knowledge

With the aid of theoretical diagrams, clearly discuss the scientific ideas that you wish to teach. This provides focus, organization, and an understanding of the entire topic or unit for both you and the children. Provide concept maps, Vee diagrams, and analogies that would help children to transverse the "zone of proximal development." Include proper references if you are copying experts' science ideas from books.

Historical Context

Situate your unit within historical and sociopolitical contexts. Identify the scientist(s) who contributed to the development of your unit's scientific ideas. For example, explore the questions: "How did William Gilbert investigate the properties of magnets? What were some of the social, cultural, and political influences in Gilbert's work?"

Technological and Societal Context of Inquiry

Identify technological and/or societal contexts in your unit. How do these contexts relate to your school community? Situate your unit within a local or global problem context. What technological products or processes are relevant to this unit? Grant students opportunities to become inventors.

Teaching and Learning Approaches

What teaching and learning approaches do you plan to use in this unit? For example, you might incorporate the following:

- Collaborative, reflective scientific inquiry in cooperative groups
- Experiments, discussions, argumentation, negotiation, social consensus
- Journal writing, drawing
- Representation of knowledge structures through concept and Vee mapping
- Mathematizing and symbolizing qualitative understandings with quantitative, mathematical problem solving
- Presentation of contextual historical problems
- Issue-centered approach to studying STS issues
- Multimedia computer technology (videodiscs, etc.)
- Problem solving and inventions as ways of exploring design technology

Teaching Standard A

Guideline: Plan an inquiry-based program by selecting teaching and assessment strategies.

Common Knowledge Construction Model
Phase I: Exploring and Categorizing

Exploration Activities. Design your initial activity(ies) to find out what ideas, meanings, understandings, views, and questions your students have about a natural phenomenon or a science-related issue. Describe activities and ways of exploring children's conceptions using the POE method, for example, or exploring children's views of an issue using TV/newspaper excerpts. Include key questions asked of children, materials, and procedures.

Categorization of Children's Ideas. Make sure you use children's ideas from initial activity(ies). Organize or categorize children's conceptions/views, providing examples of children's verbal, written, and pictorial responses.

Relating Children's Conceptions to Curricular Ideas. Present curricular ideas, teacher-made categories, and students' ideas in tabular format as follows:

The Common Knowledge Construction Model consists of four phases. Integration of or connections across all four phases of this teaching model are reflected in the unit on electricity that follows.

Curricular Ideas	Teacher-made Categories	Students' Ideas

In the chart, denote the following:

- Children's conceptions that make sense
- Children's conceptions that need to be explored further
- Additional curricular content—science or societal attitudes that need to be learned

Curricular ideas are experts' ideas presented in scope and sequence charts of a curricular document or in a textbook.

Teacher-made categories are teacher groupings of students' ideas.

Students' ideas are a sample of those revealed by the exploration activities.

Teacher Reflections. Reflect on what you have learned about your students and their ideas. Speculate about the sources of children's conceptions. Did they use analogies and metaphors? Relate your findings and students' conceptions to previous research findings on the same topic by quoting at least one research article in science education.

Direction for Subsequent Work. State general conclusions you make about directions for subsequent work.

Phase II: Constructing and Negotiating

Design lessons that are relevant to children's initial ideas:

1. The lessons/activities should help children develop strategies to confirm as well as expand upon their initial meanings that are appropriate because this gives them self-worth about their own knowledge. For example, if children state that electricity is "used up" or have a "source-consumer" model, develop the idea of electrical energy and transformation of energy from electrical energy to light and heat energy. Conservation of energy may be understood in this manner.

2. The lessons/activities should help the children develop strategies to clarify their own ideas. For example, if children have a "source-consumer" model for a simple circuit, develop the concept of electric current.

A constructing and negotiating meaning lesson format follows:

Title of Lesson. Write the title of your lesson. The title can be very creative and may be based on students' ideas or curricular ideas.

Students' Conceptions. Write at least one conception of students from the chart you prepared during the exploration phase. State how you will make children become aware of their ideas. For example, you may wish to display students' ideas on chart paper in your classroom. Point to this chart when you address one or more of their ideas.

Discussion. Write a statement of justification of students' conceptions and curricular ideas. For example, most students (8–12) believe that "Electricity, current, power, volts, energy, 'juice' or whatever, is stored in the source (battery) and flows to the load (light bulb) where it is consumed. The battery is usually seen as the active agent or 'giver' in this process, with the load regarded as the active agent, as a 'taker,' drawing what it needs from the battery" (Shipstone in Driver, Guesne, & Tiberghien, 1985, p. 35). Children should be able to understand that electrons do not flow 'out of' the battery, or 'into' the bulb. Electrons flow *through* all the devices that make up the circuit. Electrons flow from the negative part of the battery through the wire or foil to the bottom (or side) of the bulb, through the filament inside the bulb, and out the side (or bottom) and through the other piece of wire or foil to the positive part of the battery. The current then passes through the interior of the battery to complete the circuit (Hewitt, 1984).

Objectives. Objectives set the tone and must include specific action verbs. For example, begin each objective by stating that students will experience, measure, manipulate, build, classify, characterize, speculate, identify, verify, compare and contrast, hypothesize, predict, assess, etc. Do not use general terms like *understand, know,* and *explain* in objectives, for these are embedded in any educational objective.

Teaching and Learning Approaches. State the teaching and learning strategies you will use in this lesson: investigative activities, analogy, POE, journal writing, drawing diagrams, peer sharing, large group sharing, etc.

Materials and Resources. List the materials and resources you need for this activity. Items for an experimental or investigative activity such as chart paper, a journal, and books might be included.

Activities and Procedures. When you write the procedure for the lesson, imagine that you have a class of students. How will you organize the activities and students so that optimum learning will take place? This planning depends on the nature of learners, activities, subject matter, materials and resources, space, and time. Classroom management must be carefully considered to promote teacher-students interaction and peer science "doing" and talk. In other words, how will you engage students in classroom discourse during scientific inquiry?

Assessment. What is the outcome of this lesson? Have you accomplished your objectives for this lesson? How will you assess students' understandings?

Reflection. Based on your lesson plan, speculate on how the lesson will achieve what you have set out to do. Will the lesson motivate students to learn science concepts? Will students practice some of the processes of science (for example, learn to measure)? If you have an opportunity to teach, ask yourself the following questions: How did the lesson go? What was puzzling? Were there surprises? What would you do differently? How did the students respond to the lesson?

Phase III: Translating and Extending

- The lessons/activities should help children develop positive attitudes toward science, such as enthusiasm and motivation.
- The lessons/activities should help children develop scientific attitudes.
- The lessons/activities should also do some of the following:
  a. *Make historical connections;* for example, "How did Newton develop his ideas of light?"
  b. *Make STS connections.* A simple activity that explores inertia can result in further exploration of traveling in cars and the dangers of not wearing a seat belt. Students can explore how cars are tested for safety and even design safe ways to travel. They can also study the inventor and history of the seat belt and legislation on its mandatory use. Further study could be done on the controversy surrounding its use to save lives and on the use of airbags.
  c. *Be integrated with other subject areas.* A science unit on sound could easily result in making musical instruments, writing songs incorporating different sounds, performing a play, learning the mathematical units of sound, or exploring the sounds of instruments of different cultures.
  d. *Incorporate design technology.*

Teaching Standard B

Guideline: To guide and facilitate learning, encourage and model the skills of scientific inquiry, as well as the curiosity, openness to new ideas and data, and skepticism that characterize science.

Assessment integrates all four phases of the Common Knowledge Construction Model. We have operationalized this integration in the unit plan on electricity that follows.

Teaching Standard C

Teachers of science engage in ongoing assessment of their teaching and of student learning.

Teaching Standard C

Guideline: Use multiple assessment methods and systematically gather data about student understanding and ability.

Carry out your plan. Be flexible! Remember, science is not smooth and structured. Your unit will *evolve and change* as you continue to incorporate children's ideas. Remember to always check if the children have made meaningful connections to your activities as well as to teacher-students jointly planned activities.

Phase IV: Reflecting and Assessing

Assess as you go along. Have students gather or collect their notes in one journal; store concept maps, diagrams, etc., in an ongoing portfolio. Use this feedback to structure your lessons. Plan to assess each activity and the topic or unit according to the most appropriate method for the occasion. Select methods of assessment that will help children reflect on what they have learned and tie the concepts together. Some examples are student-teacher conferences, written questions, oral presentations, self-evaluations, peer evaluations, anecdotal records, and classroom charts.

Prepare specific culminating (end-of-unit) assessment activities and strategies for your unit. These may consist of performance activities such as investigations, art projects, or creative drama.

References

Create a bibliography that cites all references with page numbers.

A Unit Plan on Electricity

Current Electricity
Kelly Pruden

Kelly was assisted by her science teacher educator and an experienced elementary teacher, Mervin Haines, in preparing this unit. Kelly's original unit has undergone some revision before being included in this book.

Curriculum

Manitoba Education and Training Curriculum Guide: Grade 4

Grade Level

4

Nature of Students

In my practicum classroom, there are 27 students—14 girls and 13 boys. There are no special-needs students. The class is composed of students from various cultures, including three Asians and four Native Americans. The students generally work conscientiously and usually show much enthusiasm for and interest in science. They enjoy collaborative work settings where group and partner work are involved. They are also very keen to talk and share their ideas in class.

   The students are already aware that we will be learning about electricity in the near future, and they are looking forward to this!

Purpose of the Unit

The purpose of this unit is to explore and incorporate children's ideas about electricity. They will explore their predictions, ideas, and questions about electricity through hands-on activities, individual and group work, and class discussion. They will learn about current electricity through experiences that allow them to develop and clarify their conceptions as well as to explore the validity of their ideas.

   Students need to appreciate the everyday uses of electricity and make personal connections with the safety aspects and scientific concepts.

Overview

The development of scientific knowledge, scientific attitudes, attitudes toward science, and both science, technology, and society (STS) and historical connections is critical to science learning. Through the unit activities, all of these aspects will be covered. Students should be able to understand certain concepts about electricity, such as what an electric circuit is, how to put one together, and how electric current behaves.

   Encouraging students to develop attitudes such as objectivity, risk taking, creativity, accuracy, thoroughness, and curiosity in their learning experiences in the unit is important. For example, students will need to be objective when they observe and try to explain the phenomenon of a simple circuit. They will take risks when they make predictions such as those in the exploration phase. Here students will predict what they will need to make the bulb light. Creativity is also important because they will be writing stories about famous scientists who explored electricity. Accuracy may be emphasized as students draw diagrams of circuits. Students should be encouraged to research thoroughly the inventions related to electricity. Curiosity may be developed as students explore and manipulate materials, testing their ideas.

We want students to develop a positive and inquisitive attitude toward science learning in general. It is when students are interested and motivated that learning is likely to take place.

Students should realize the connections between what they are learning in science and its relationship to society and technology. For example, they will demonstrate an understanding of why electric power workers wear protective equipment when climbing electric power poles and repairing electric cables. They should be able to describe how electricity contributes to our everyday lives. Historical connections are also important, as they give us a link to the past.

Curricular Content Development

Science Content Knowledge

An electric circuit is the path of an electric current consisting of charges (electrons). The path is composed of voltage sources (dry cells, wet cells, generators) and conductors (connecting wires and filament in the light bulb). Voltage is the potential difference or the electrical pressure between

Kelly allows students to try to construct a simple circuit.

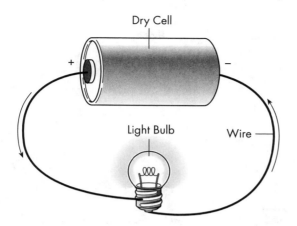

FIGURE 11-2
A closed circuit

the two ends of a battery that generates current. When a battery is connected to a wire, an electrical field is established. This field moves (nudges) the charges (electrons) that continue to be in random motion in a conductor.

If a circuit has a continuous flow of electricity through it, as in Figure 11-2, then it is called a *closed circuit.* An *open circuit* is one in which there is no current because the path is not continuous (as in Figure 11-3).

A *short circuit* is one in which the current crosses the normal path of the current and causes a fault in the circuit. The wires will become very hot and perhaps cause a fire. All homes have a fuse or circuit breaker to shut down the flow of electricity and prevent a fire when a short circuit occurs.

The conductor is the electric circuit, which is composed of materials that allow electric charges to easily pass through. For example, copper wire is a good conductor. Electrons move freely in the atomic network of the conductor, whereas protons are held in a somewhat fixed position within the nucleus of the atom. In fluids, the flow of an electric charge consists of negative and positive ions as well as electrons.

The opposite of *conductor* is *insulator.* The coating on a wire is an insulator.

Professional Development Standard A

Guideline: Science learning experiences for teachers must involve actively investigating phenomena that can be studied scientifically, interpreting results, and making sense of findings consistent with currently accepted scientific understanding.

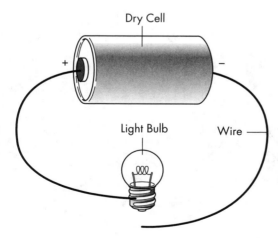

FIGURE 11-3
An open circuit

FIGURE 11-4
A series circuit

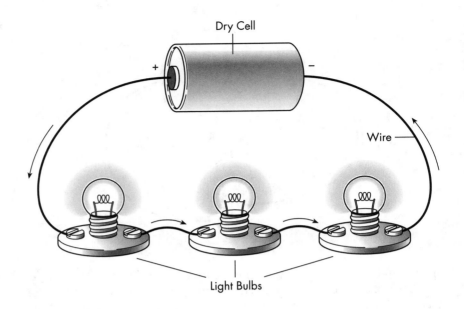

A *series circuit* has only one conducting pathway from the power source, with all the bulbs connected in a series as in Figure 11-4. If one bulb in the series circuit fails, the circuit will be broken and none of the bulbs will light. A *parallel circuit* has each bulb wired with separate conducting pathways from the battery (Figure 11-5). When one bulb fails in a parallel circuit, the remaining good bulbs will still light. Our homes are

FIGURE 11-5
A parallel circuit

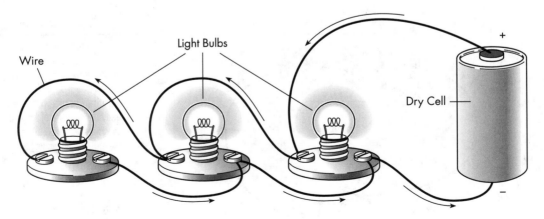

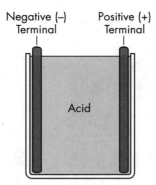

FIGURE 11-6
A wet cell from a battery

Negative (–)
Terminal

Positive (+)
Terminal

Acid

wired with parallel circuits. Some Christmas tree bulb sets are wired in a series circuit so that when one bulb fails, all the other bulbs go out.

For current to flow, negative electrical charges (electrons) must flow from the negative to the positive terminal in a circuit. Some batteries, such as car batteries, consist of cells containing an acid and two types of metal for the terminals (Figure 11-6). Negative charges will move to one metal terminal, leaving the other terminal positive. When the circuit is closed in this wet cell, the negative charge will flow across the wire and back to the positive terminal. There are also dry cells and batteries such as flashlight batteries that contain a damp paste and two different metal terminals, one of which is the outside casing (Figure 11-7).

A battery is made up of two or more cells connected with wires. Chemical energy in the battery is transformed into electric energy. This is why we say that a battery is a producer or supplier of electric energy that moves electric charges or electrons through a circuit.

FIGURE 11-7
Cross section of a dry cell

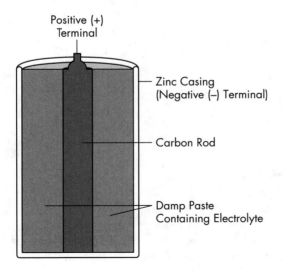

Positive (+)
Terminal

Zinc Casing
(Negative (–) Terminal)

Carbon Rod

Damp Paste
Containing Electrolyte

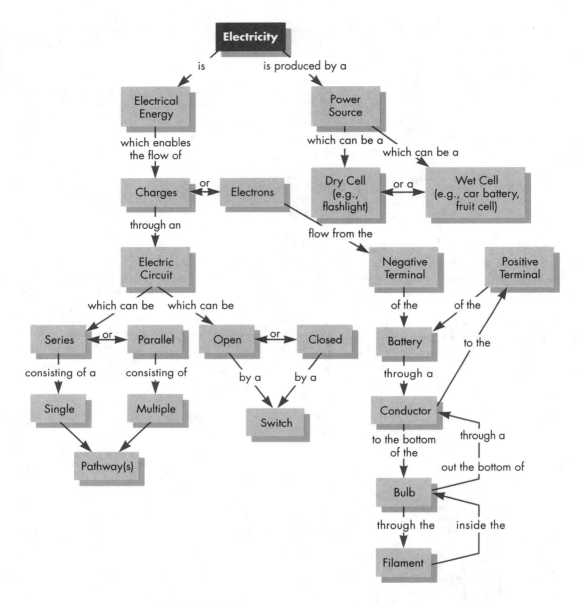

FIGURE 11-8

Concept map of *current electricity*

Professional Development Standard A

Guideline: Science learning experiences for teachers must build on teacher's current science understanding, ability, and attitudes.

I have drawn a concept map for the unit, which contains all the main concepts for the children to learn as well as the relationships among these concepts (Figure 11-8). Vee diagrams distinguish between series and parallel circuits (Figures 11-9a and 11-9b on page 312).

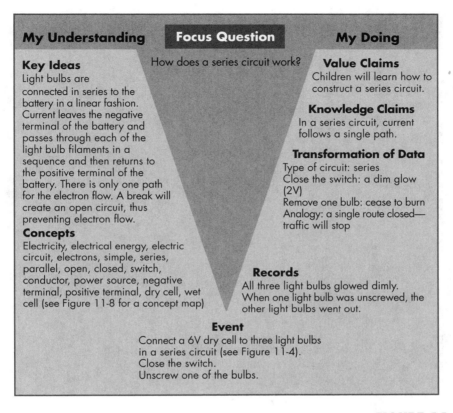

My Understanding   **Focus Question**   **My Doing**

Key Ideas
How does a series circuit work?

Light bulbs are connected in series to the battery in a linear fashion. Current leaves the negative terminal of the battery and passes through each of the light bulb filaments in a sequence and then returns to the positive terminal of the battery. There is only one path for the electron flow. A break will create an open circuit, thus preventing electron flow.

Concepts
Electricity, electrical energy, electric circuit, electrons, simple, series, parallel, open, closed, switch, conductor, power source, negative terminal, positive terminal, dry cell, wet cell (see Figure 11-8 for a concept map)

Value Claims
Children will learn how to construct a series circuit.

Knowledge Claims
In a series circuit, current follows a single path.

Transformation of Data
Type of circuit: series
Close the switch: a dim glow (2V)
Remove one bulb: cease to burn
Analogy: a single route closed—traffic will stop

Records
All three light bulbs glowed dimly. When one light bulb was unscrewed, the other light bulbs went out.

Event
Connect a 6V dry cell to three light bulbs in a series circuit (see Figure 11-4). Close the switch. Unscrew one of the bulbs.

FIGURE 11-9A
Vee diagram of a series circuit

Historical Context

Benjamin Franklin was an American diplomat, statesman, and amateur scientist who performed many electrical experiments. Franklin performed a risky experiment in 1752. He wanted to prove that lightning was a discharge of electricity from a cloud. To do this, he made a kite and attached a key to the end of the string. He waited for a thunderstorm and flew the kite up into the clouds. A spark passed along the wet string to the key, which he held by a dry silk thread, showing that the cloud was electrified and the electricity was passed along the string (Figure 11-10 on page 313). Franklin's experiment proved that electricity in the clouds caused thunder and lightning, but was very dangerous and should never be replicated.

Technological and Societal Context of Inquiry

Thomas Alva Edison (1847–1931) did much to develop the uses of electricity. He was the most productive inventor of his time, producing telegraph and telephone equipment, the first successful incandescent lamp bulb,

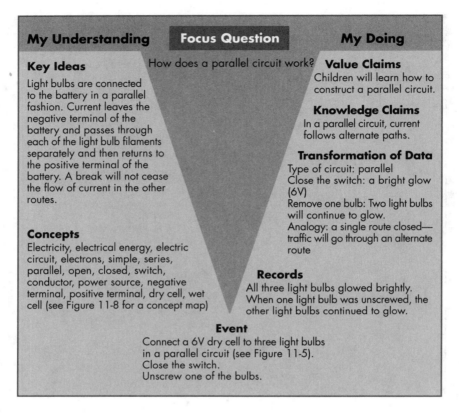

My Understanding

Key Ideas

Light bulbs are connected to the battery in a parallel fashion. Current leaves the negative terminal of the battery and passes through each of the light bulb filaments separately and then returns to the positive terminal of the battery. A break will not cease the flow of current in the other routes.

Concepts

Electricity, electrical energy, electric circuit, electrons, simple, series, parallel, open, closed, switch, conductor, power source, negative terminal, positive terminal, dry cell, wet cell (see Figure 11-8 for a concept map)

Focus Question

How does a parallel circuit work?

My Doing

Value Claims

Children will learn how to construct a parallel circuit.

Knowledge Claims

In a parallel circuit, current follows alternate paths.

Transformation of Data

Type of circuit: parallel
Close the switch: a bright glow (6V)
Remove one bulb: Two light bulbs will continue to glow.
Analogy: a single route closed—traffic will go through an alternate route

Records

All three light bulbs glowed brightly. When one light bulb was unscrewed, the other light bulbs continued to glow.

Event

Connect a 6V dry cell to three light bulbs in a parallel circuit (see Figure 11-5). Close the switch. Unscrew one of the bulbs.

FIGURE 11-9B
Vee diagram of a parallel circuit

and contributions to many others. In 1883, he invented the Edison effect lamp (Figure 11-11), which later was the basis of the radio tube.

The first electrical appliance to be operated in a home was the electric iron in 1882. In 1892–1893, the World's Columbian Exposition held in Chicago demonstrated several early versions of the kitchen appliances we use today. These were shown in the first "electric kitchen." In the early 1900s, electric coffeemakers, toasters, clothes washers, refrigerators, ranges, and vacuum cleaners were introduced and began to be widely used.

Many electrical appliances do not perform housework as such. For example, electric blankets, shavers, clocks, fans, and toothbrushes are all used to increase our comfort and aid our grooming needs.

For every electrical appliance, safety aspects need to be emphasized. Students can look at safety issues such as how to safely plug and unplug their boom boxes, lamps, classroom computers, and video games. As a society that depends so much on electricity, how could we function if we had no lamps, stoves, and vacuum cleaners? Together with my students, I would like to examine these possibilities.

FIGURE 11-10
Franklin's kite and cloud experiment, drawn by a student

Benjamin Franklin wanted to find out if lighting and electricity were the same thing so he flew a kite in a storm. The kite had a key on the string. The kite was hit by the lightning. Benjamin Franklin got a shock. He proved that electricity and lightning were the same after he made a lightning rod for houses. It saved many people's lives. Ben was happy.

Teaching and Learning Approaches

In any classroom, there is a diversity of teaching and learning styles. It is therefore important to incorporate a variety of teaching and learning strategies and to concentrate on each of the learning styles in order to be able to reach all students in the classroom. The following are some examples of teaching strategies that have been included in this unit.

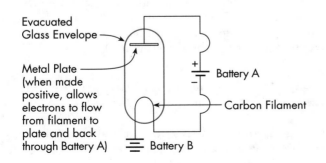

FIGURE 11-11
The Edison effect lamp

Hands-on Activities. These provide students with an opportunity to actually manipulate the materials they are learning about in class. For example, if students are learning about parallel circuits, give them an opportunity to construct them.

Journal Writing. Students record their observations, predictions, and explanations as well as depict their personal views in their science journals during and after science investigations. The journals provide a record of progress and a form of communication for both students and the teacher. Many of the lessons will incorporate journal writing, such as lesson 4, in which series circuits are explored.

Teacher and Student Negotiation. Both teachers and students are encouraged to negotiate ideas with each other to help clarify or expand upon them. This process helps students feel that their conceptions are valid and their ideas are meaningful.

Common Knowledge Construction Model

Phase I: Exploring and Categorizing

Exploring and categorizing students' ideas is the first phase of the Common Knowledge Construction Model (see chapter 5). Children's ideas are explored so that both teacher and students become aware of what the children already know from experience or the ideas children might advance when they later observe an event. Children's ideas are then categorized so that the teacher has a manageable set of ideas from which to develop lessons for the topic.

Exploration Activity. To begin with, we will use a simple activity to systematically explore children's ideas. We need a starting point and therefore want to see how the students will mentally construct a simple circuit to make the light bulb glow.

Students are given a worksheet indicating that they are given one battery, one wire, and one bulb. They are asked what they would do to light the bulb. The students have a space to write their responses as well as a space to draw a diagram of what they would do (Figure 11-12).

Categorizing Children's Conceptions. I collected the students' responses and organized them into the following categories.

1. **The wire gets connected to both the bulb and the battery in a linear fashion.** *Student example:* "First you conected [connected] the wire to the bulb. Then you touch the wire to the battery."

FIGURE 11-12
Student worksheet

" *Electricity — Exploration* " 1

You are given the following materials:
battery , one wire , one bulb

WRITE WHAT YOU WOULD DO TO LIGHT
THE BULB.
I would take the wire and tuch
one end to the battery. I would
take the other end and tuch
it to the bulb (I hope it works.)

DRAW WHAT YOU WOULD DO TO LIGHT
THE BULB

2. **The wire must go around the bulb and touch both sides of the battery.** *Student examples:* "You would take a bulb and fold the wire around the bulb. Then take the wire and make it touch the battery."

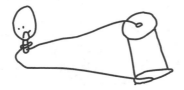

"Take the battery and the wire. Put one end of the wire and put it at the top. Then take the other side of the wire and put it at the bottom. Put the bulb anywhere on the wire."

"I would put one end of the wire on the battery, and then I would wrap the wire around the bulb twice. then I would put the other end of the wire on the other end of the battery."

"I would take the bulb and the wire and wrap the wire around the bottom of the light. Then I would take the other end of the wire and touch it to the positive side, then take the bottom of the bulb and touch it to the negative side."

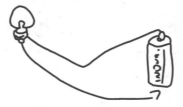

3. **The wire and the bulb must touch the battery. One end of the wire goes under the bulb and onto the battery.** *Student examples:* "I would put the wire on the battery and bulb on the battery and put the other end of the wire under the bulb on the battery."

"I will take the battery and put one end of the wire on the bottom and the other side on the top. I'll put the light on the top of wire and battery."

"Take the bulb and battery. Put the bulb on the positive. make sure the wire touches the bulb. Put the next piece on the negative and then the bulb should light up."

4. **The wire must be connected to both ends of the battery and both terminals on the bulb.** *Student examples:* "Take a piece of wire and put on the positive on the battery. Put the bottom of the light on the negative and the wire on the side."

"I would put one wire to the side of the light bulb and put the other end of the wire on the positive of the battery and put the bottom of the light bulb on the negative."

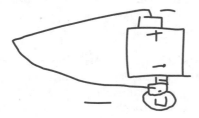

"Put one side of the wire on the negative side and put the other side on the bulb. Put the top on the positive side."

"I will take the wire and the bulb and take the wire and twist it around the bulb and put the bulb on the battery and take the other side of the wire and put it on the end of the battery."

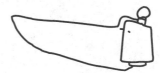

5. **The wire must touch both ends of the battery. It also must be connected to both terminals on the bulb, but not be shorted across the battery.** *Student example:* "Take the wire. Put one end on the bottom and one on the top and at the top bend the wire a little and touch it on the bottom and on the side of the bulb."

Relating Children's Conceptions to Curricular Ideas. The children had many good ideas but, except for category 4, they had not accurately described how to light the bulb. I arranged the curricular ideas in a table (Table 11-1), along with my teacher-made categories and a corresponding example of students' ideas.

Teacher Reflections. Of the students' ideas explored for the purpose of this unit, several showed a unipolar model in their drawings (category 1). One student explained the circuit in this manner: "First you connect the wire to the bulb. Then you touch the wire to the battery." He did not

TABLE 11-1

Curricular Ideas, Teacher-made Categories, and Children's Conceptions About How to Light a Bulb

Curricular Ideas	Teacher-made Categories	Students' Ideas
A dry cell can be a source of electricity. The path through a bulb, cell, and their connecting wires is called a circuit.	1. The wires gets connected to both the bulb and the battery in a linear fashion. 2. The wire must go round the bulb and touch both sides of the battery. 3. The wire and the bulb must touch the battery. One end of the wire goes under the bulb and onto the battery. 4. The wire must be connected to both ends of the battery and both terminals on the bulb. 5. The wire must touch both ends of the battery. It (the wire) must also be connected to both terminals on the bulb, but not be shorted across the battery.	"First you connect the wire to the bulb. Then you touch the wire to the battery." "You would take the bulb and fold the wire around the bulb. Then take the wire and make it touch the battery. On both sides." "I would put the wire on the battery and bulb on the battery and put the other end of the wire under the bulb on the battery." "Take a piece of wire and place it on the positive on the battery. Put the bottom of the light on the negative and the wire on the side." "Take the wire. Put one end on the bottom and one on the top and at the top bend the wire a little and touch it on the bottom and on the side of the bulb."

understand that the circuit must be connected in a circular form and to certain points on the battery and bulb.

Another group of students saw the need to connect the wire to both ends of the battery but not to both points of terminals on the bulb (category 2).

A few students wrapped the wire around the bulb and placed the tip of the bulb on the battery to make a complete circuit (category 3).

One student showed considerable insight (category 5). In reality, he would have had to use two wires to accomplish what he drew. His arrangement would not have lit because he made a short circuit with the second wire across the battery.

Only a few students in category 4 were able to place their wire correctly.

Relating Children's Ideas to Previous Studies. Much research has been carried out on students' ideas about simple electric circuits. Driver, Squires, Rushworth, & Wood-Robinson (1994) report some very interesting results from earlier research done by Osborne and Freyberg (1985) and others. Young children as well as high school and college physics students hold several alternative explanatory models of a simple circuit (Figure 11-13). Note that our students were not asked to indicate the direction of the current or to explain the flow of charges (electrons) that constitutes current.

Through the initial exploratory lesson, students were able to communicate in writing as well as by drawing their ideas about a simple circuit using

Professional Development Standard B

Professional development for teachers of science requires integrating knowledge of science, learning, pedagogy, and student; it also requires applying that knowledge to science teaching.

Note that our students were given only one wire. It is better to give them a light bulb, a 1.5V battery, and a number of connecting wires. Have students arrange the given materials to light the bulb. Have them draw as well as explain their arrangements. Ask students to propose their answers to the question: "How does the bulb light?" This question will enable students to theorize about the mechanism of the simple circuit.

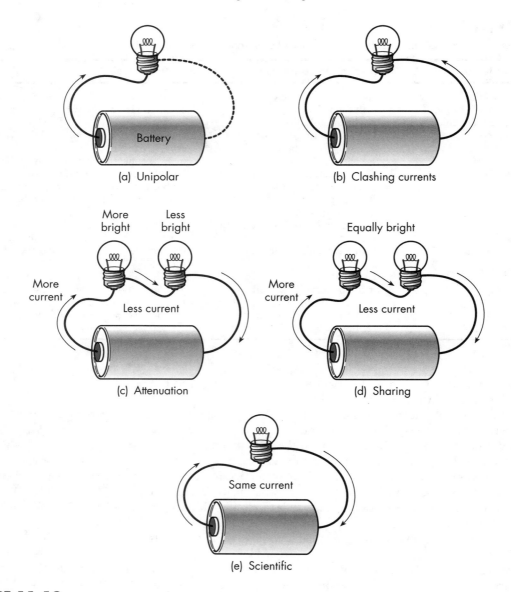

(a) Unipolar

(b) Clashing currents

More bright   Less bright

More current   Less current

(c) Attenuation

Equally bright

More current   Less current

(d) Sharing

Same current

(e) Scientific

FIGURE 11-13

Students' alternative models of electric circuits (NOTE. Adapted from Driver, R., Squires, A., Rushworth, P., & Wood-Robinson, V. (1994). *Making sense of secondary science: Research into children's ideas*. London: Routledge.)

one dry cell, one bulb, and one wire. In future lessons they will be encouraged to explore hands-on activities and discuss their findings. It is vital to allow students to share their ideas and conceptions as well as see the validity of their responses via a multiple-voice approach to learning.

Directions for Subsequent Work. We found that only 4 of the 27 students had clearly described the correct way to connect the cell and bulb with one wire (category 4). Based on the students' conceptions and how they related to the curricular ideas, I decided on the following lesson sequence:

Lesson 1: Simple circuits (a) with one wire, (b) with two wires
Lesson 2: Single cell with switch
Lesson 3: Light bulbs and dry cells. How does an electrical charge pass through them? Analogy and animation.
Lesson 4: Series circuits (a) with multiple dry cells, (b) with multiple light bulbs
Lesson 5: Parallel circuits (a) with multiple dry cells, (b) with multiple light bulbs
Lesson 6: Comparing series and parallel circuits using analogies
Lesson 7: Electricity in our community (STS)
Lesson 8: History of electricity
Lesson 9: Electrical safety
Lesson 10: Electricity in other cultures
Lesson 11: Electricity and design technology
Culminating Assessment: written test and performance-based test

Phase II: Constructing and Negotiating

Constructing and negotiating meaning is the second phase of the Common Knowledge Construction Model. In this phase, we will develop lessons to clarify the students' ideas elicited in the exploration phase. In the exploration phase, students were asked to conceptualize how they would put together a circuit using a dry cell, a bulb, and one wire.

Two mini-lessons are developed for lesson 1 to follow through with the exploration activities. Students will be required to manipulate and assemble materials to make the light bulb glow. The first lesson gives students one wire for the circuit, whereas the second mini-lesson gives them two wires.

A Simple Circuit

Lesson 1

Students' Conceptions

"I would put the wire on the battery and put the other end of the wire under the bulb and the battery."

Discussion

The students will learn how to create a simple circuit using (a) one wire and (b) two wires. This is an important lesson. The students will be able to experience the reality of producing a simple circuit because the bulb will light when the circuit is correctly made. They will be able to evaluate the accuracy of their predictions.

Objectives

Students should be able to do the following:

1. Construct a simple circuit using (a) one wire, one bulb, and a dry cell.
2. Draw and describe a simple circuit (with one wire) in their science journals.
3. Construct a simple circuit using (b) two wires, one bulb, and one dry cell.
4. Draw and describe a simple circuit (with two wires) in their science journals.

Teaching and Learning Approaches

Partner work, large group sharing, teacher-student demonstration, drawing and labeling diagrams, teacher-student negotiation

Materials/Resources

Bulbs, wires, and dry cells for partners, science journals, chart paper

Activities and Procedures

MINI-LESSON A: SIMPLE CIRCUIT WITH ONE WIRE

Partner activity

1. In *partners,* have students put together a simple working circuit with one wire.
2. Have students draw and record in their science journals what they did to construct the simple circuit.

Large group sharing

3. Allow for *large group sharing,* where students show what they did to construct their simple circuit.

Teacher-student construction and negotiation of meaning

4. The teacher should record ideas and statements given by students so they can be *discussed and negotiated.*

Teacher-student demonstration

5. The *teacher* should now demonstrate, with the help of the *students* who have made a successful working circuit.
6. Students should confirm this with a *partner,* and then *on their own.*
7. Once all the students have been successful, draw a diagram (see Figure 11-14) on large chart paper, asking students for input as you draw.
8. The students should copy this labeled diagram in their science journals and compare it to their earlier drawings.

MINI-LESSON B: SIMPLE CIRCUIT WITH TWO WIRES

Partner work

1. In *partners,* have students put together a simple circuit with two wires.

FIGURE 11-14
Simple circuit with one wire

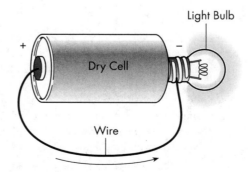

Light Bulb

Dry Cell

Wire

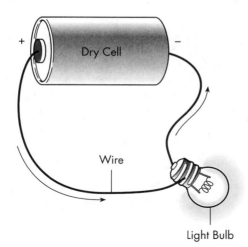

FIGURE 11-15
Simple circuit with two wires

2. Have students draw and record what they did to construct the simple circuit.
3.–8. Follow the same steps as in mini-lesson 1. With students' help, draw a diagram similar to that in Figure 11-15.

Teacher-student construction and negotiation of meaning, teacher-student demonstration

Assessment

1. The teacher should assess lesson 1 through observing the students as they do the activities and reading their journal entries.
2. Have students compare the simple circuits with one wire with the circuit with two wires. Why do they both work? Are there any advantages/disadvantages to each circuit? Describe them.

Reflection

Students are able to extend their learning from the exploration activity to this lesson, where they actually participate in the circuit making. They should now be prepared to move on to the next lesson, where they will make a switch. Before this next lesson, the teacher must be certain that each child knows how to make a simple circuit.

Simple Circuit With a Switch

Lesson 2

Discussion

This lesson is an extension of lesson 1

By now, students should know how to make a simple circuit. By adding a switch to the circuit, a connection to everyday life will be made. The switch will enable students to understand the importance of switches for appliances and lights.

Objectives

Students should be able to do the following:

1. Construct a simple circuit that includes a switch.
2. Describe how a simple circuit is affected by a switch.
3. Identify at least 10 items that use switches to control electricity flow and record them in their journals.

Translating and extending

Teaching and Learning Approaches

Small group activity, drawing and labeling diagrams, large group sharing

Materials/Resources

Bulbs, wires, dry cells, switches for each group, science journals, chart paper

Activities and Procedures

Small group activity

Large group sharing

Criteria: correct labels, spelling, representation of proper connections and direction of current

This activity will give the teacher an opportunity to assess students' ideas.

Constructing and negotiating meaning

1. In small *groups of three,* have students set up their own single-cell circuit, including a switch.
2. Have the *group* draw a labeled diagram of its circuit on chart paper.
3. Have each *group* come up to the front and share its diagrams.
4. Both the *teacher and the students* will comment on each group's drawings and negotiate meanings.
5. Students will make labeled drawings in their journals, similar to Figure 11-16.

Assessment

1. Assessment will take place by observing students at work, their chart presentations, and their journal entries. Students can be asked to make a simple circuit with a switch if the teacher wishes to check each student's ability.
2. Ask students to identify at least five items that use switches to control electricity flow in the school. Have them record these in their journals.

FIGURE 11-16
Simple circuit with a switch

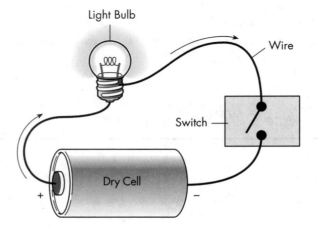

Reflection

Students will begin to see how electricity is omnipresent in their everyday lives. They learned that every time they use a switch, they control electricity flow.

Mechanism of the Simple Circuit

Lesson 3

Students' Conceptions

Students often think of the battery as the "giver" and the light bulb as the "receiver" of electricity. The battery "delivers" or the light bulb "takes" according to its "needs." In other words, students view the battery as the *source* and the light bulb as the *consumer* (Driver, Squires, Rushwood, & Wood-Ronbinson, 1994, p. 121).

Discussion

Through this constructing and negotiating lesson, students will be able to understand the production of electrical energy and how it is transformed into heat and light as well as the mechanism of the circuit (how electric current passes through the devices). They will discuss, explore, verbalize, write, and create so as to form and rework conceptions about how electricity works. By actually looking "inside" the circuit and through analogies, they will have the opportunity to visualize the path that an electric current takes.

Objectives

Students should be able to do the following:

1. Draw a labeled diagram of the structure of a light bulb.
2. Draw a labeled diagram of the structure of the inside of a dry cell.
3. Communicate (verbally and in writing) how the filament of a light bulb and the parts of a dry cell are components of a circuit.
4. Discuss electrical energy including the concept of conservation of energy—transformation of one form to another. In an electric circuit, the energy transformations are chemical ⇒ electricity ⇒ light and some heat.
5. Trace the path of an electric current through a dry cell, connecting wire, and light bulb.
6. Construct wet cells.
7. Compare and contrast dry and wet cells.

Teaching and Learning Approaches

Teacher demonstrations, large group observations and discussion, drawing and labeling diagrams, analogy, group investigation

This is a vital lesson on the concepts of electrical energy and current. Students will also learn the parts of a light bulb and a dry cell. This lesson will take a few class periods. Students must understand how electricity works before they can understand further components of the unit.

Introduce analogies carefully, especially if students have not experienced analogies before.

Materials/Resources

Various broken light bulbs and bisected dry cells for teacher demonstrations; safety gloves and apron for the teacher; fruits; fruit juices; vegetables; paper clips; strips of iron, copper, and zinc; two wires; a small quartz clock; small light bulb; science journals; chart paper

Activities and Procedures

MINI-LESSON A: ELECTRICAL ENERGY

Have students set up simple circuits and ask them to observe how the supply of electrical energy is used in a circuit by a light bulb to create light.

MINI-LESSON B: LIGHT BULBS

1. The teacher will pose several questions to get students thinking about how electricity works. For example: "How do you think electricity works? Why do we connect the dry cell to the bulb? Why must the wire touch the dry cell? Do you think there is something inside the dry cell to create electricity? Do you think there is something inside the bulb to create electricity? What does the filament inside the bulb do? What role does the connecting wire play?"
2. Students should record their ideas in their journals.
3. Next, have students gather around the teacher to observe the insides of various broken light bulbs held by the teacher. Do not allow students to touch the broken bulbs. Have students describe what they see.
4. With students' help, draw a diagram of the inside of a light bulb on the chart paper. Label the parts and trace the path of the current (see Figure 11-17).
5. Have students copy the labeled diagram in their journals.

MINI-LESSON C: DRY CELLS

1. Discuss the responses students made in their journals to the questions the teacher posed about dry cells.
2. Have the whole class observe the insides of various dry cells as the teacher holds them.

Children's source-consumer model is similar to the concept of electrical energy rather than the idea of current. Since we must start from children's ideas, it is better to start from the concept of electrical energy before introducing the idea of current.

Exploring students' ideas

Teacher demonstration

Teacher demonstration

FIGURE 11-17
Light bulb (charges flow through the filament in the bulb)

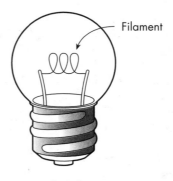

Filament

Light Bulb

TABLE 11-2

The Water Analogy—Comparing the Flow of Water in a Closed System of Pipes to the Flow of an Electric Charge

Water and Pump System	Electrical Circuit System
Pump	Battery
Pipes	Wires
Faucet	Switch
Operating device when the water is flowing	Light bulb
• A break in a water pipe results in water spilling from the pipe.	• A break in an electric circuit results in a complete stop in the flow of electricity.
• When you open the faucet, the water starts to flow.	• When you open the switch, the flow of charges (current) stops.
• When you close the faucet, the water stops flowing.	• When you close the switch, the charges flow, or there is current.

3. Discuss and name the dry cell parts and have students suggest the path of the current (refer to Figure 11-7 on page 309).
4. Explain the flow of current using the water analogy. Have students study the analogy chart (see Table 11-2) and discuss where the analogy breaks down. (If students haven't studied analogies before, prepare them with some literary similes and metaphors.)
5. Show a simple circuit.
6. If possible, show a computer simulation of the electricity flowing through the dry cell, wires, and bulb (must be at children's level).
7. With the students' help, draw a large diagram of the path of the current through the dry cell and around a circuit that includes a light bulb. Have them draw it in their journals.

Use of computer simulation for constructing and negotiating meaning

Constructing and negotiating meaning

MINI-LESSON D: **A WET CELL**

Have students make batteries with fruit (pineapple, banana, orange, lemon, etc.), fruit juices (orange juice, grape juice, tomato juice, coconut juice, etc.), vegetables (potatoes, turnips, squash, bell peppers, etc.), and different metals. A light bulb, a small quartz clock, or your tongue can be used to close the circuit (see the arrangement in Figure 11-18). Have students work in small groups and compare the group results.

Compare the acid in the fruit, fruit juices, and vegetables to the acid in a car battery.

When you place the ends of the metals on your tongue, you will feel a slight tingle and experience a metallic taste. This indicates an electric circuit.

Assessment

1. Have students identify the principal components of a circuit and how electricity is generated.
2. Ask them to compare the workings of a dry cell and a wet cell (lemon cell).
3. Together with students, identify all concepts (see Figure 11-8 on page 310). Have students make a concept map.

Group inquiry and discussion

FIGURE 11-18
Two types of fruit wet cells

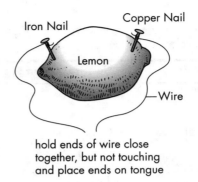

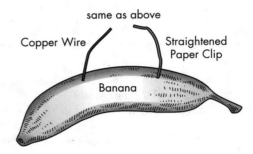

Reflection

After completing the lesson, students should understand the mechanism of the simple circuit or how electricity works. This is a prerequisite to further lessons.

Series Circuits (a) With Multiple Dry Cells, (b) With Multiple Light Bulbs

Lesson 4

Students' Conceptions

Students need to be able to articulate the components of a circuit and how a circuit functions before they tackle series circuits. Review the path of a circuit with a concept map.

Objectives

Students should be able to do the following:

1. Predict the various ways that a series circuit can be hooked up to (a) several dry cells, (b) several light bulbs.
2. Construct a series circuit with (a) several dry cells, (b) several light bulbs.

3. Discuss the function of series circuits.
4. Add the concept of series to their concept map.

Discussion

Don't rush the study of these different kinds of series circuits. Be sure they have time to try out each type several times.

Teaching and Learning Approaches

Small group work, student demonstrations, class discussions, activities, POE strategy.

Materials/Resources

Three to four dry cells per group, three to four bulbs per group, six to eight wires per group, science journals, chart paper

Activities and Procedures

MINI-LESSON A: MULTIPLE DRY CELLS

1. Form small groups and have students predict what would happen if there were three or four dry cells hooked up *end to end* in a circuit and one bulb.
2. Have students record their predictions in their journals and give reasons for their answers.
3. Have students test their predictions.
4. Have students show their results and explain what happened, giving reasons for their explanations.
5. Discuss the meaning of the word *series* and how it applies to this type of circuit. Have students draw a series circuit in their journals (Figure 11-19).

POE activity in small groups, student demonstrations, constructing and negotiating meaning

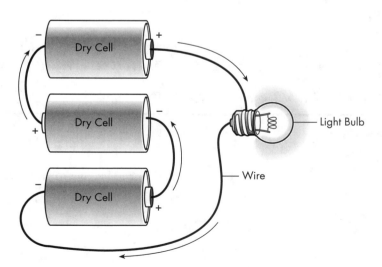

FIGURE 11-19
Series circuit with three dry cells

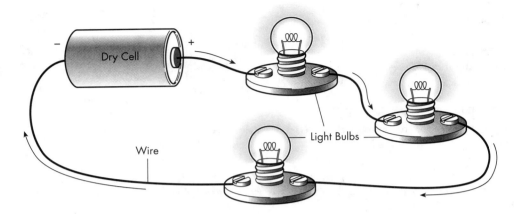

FIGURE 11-20
Series circuit with three bulbs

POE small group activity

MINI-LESSON B: **MULTIPLE LIGHT BULBS**

1. Ask students in small groups to predict, observe, and explain what would happen if you had one dry cell and multiple bulbs in a circuit, as in Figure 11-20.
2. Have students unscrew one light bulb and note what happens. Have them infer the reason why the other bulbs do not light.

Assessment

Have students describe each type of series circuit in their journals and list its advantages. What might be the purpose for making each type?

Reflection

A series circuit is the basic type of simple circuit. Allow students to become very familiar with this type and the functions of the multiple bulb and multiple dry cell types.

Parallel Circuits With (a) Multiple Dry Cells and (b) Multiple Light Bulbs

Lesson 5

Discussion

Students need to make different kinds of parallel circuits in order to see their advantages over series circuits.

Objectives

Students should be able to do the following:

1. Predict the various ways that a parallel circuit can be hooked up to (a) several dry cells and (b) several light bulbs.
2. Construct a parallel circuit with (a) several dry cells and (b) several light bulbs.
3. Discuss the function of the different kinds of parallel circuits.
4. Add the concept of parallel to their concept map.

Teaching and Learning Approaches

Small group work, student demonstrations, class discussions, POE activities, analogy charts

Materials/Resources

Three to four dry cells per group, three to four bulbs per group, six to eight wires per group, science journals, chart paper

Activities and Procedures

MINI-LESSON A: MULTIPLE DRY CELLS

1. Ask students to predict in small groups what would happen if you had multiple dry cells and one bulb hooked up, as in Figure 11-21.
2. Discuss the meaning of the word *parallel* and point out how the two sets of wires hooking up the dry series are parallel to each other.
3. Have students record their predictions in their journals and then have them set up this type of circuit.
4. Have some of the groups demonstrate their circuits and discuss the results. If the light bulb has blown, have them suggest the reason why.

POE activity, student demonstrations, constructing and negotiating meaning

MINI-LESSON B: MULTIPLE LIGHT BULBS

1. Have students in small groups devise a circuit in which three or four light bulbs are hooked up in parallel fashion (see Figure 11-22), as were the dry cells in Figure 11-21.
2. When they are successful, have students unscrew one bulb and note what happens. Compare this to what happened when using a series circuit.

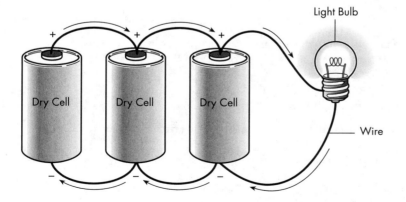

FIGURE 11-21
A parallel circuit with multiple dry cells and one light bulb

FIGURE 11-22
A parallel circuit with one
dry cell and multiple bulbs

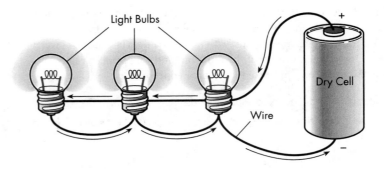

FIGURE 11-22
A parallel circuit with one dry cell and multiple bulbs

3. Have students answer the following question in their journals: What are the advantages of having (a) dry cells in parallel circuits and (b) light bulbs in parallel circuits?

Assessment

Use your observations of the students as they work and their journal entries as measures of their understanding.

Reflection

1. By the end of this lesson, the differences between series and parallel circuits should be more clear to most of the students.
2. Have students write a poem using the concepts of series and parallel circuits.

Comparing Series and Parallel Circuits Using Analogies

Lesson 6

Discussion

Introduce these pictorial analogies carefully, especially if students have not experienced this type of analogy before.

Objectives

Students should be able to do the following:

1. Use analogies to describe series and parallel circuits and the purposes of each type.
2. Compare and contrast series and parallel circuits.

Teaching and Learning Approaches

Large group work, chart work

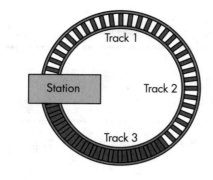

FIGURE 11-23
Railroad track analogy
for a series circuit (NOTE.
From *Journeys in Science*,
by J. A. Shymanski,
N. Romance, D. Yore, and
P. Beugger. Reproduced with
the permission of Prentice
Hall Canada, Inc. Copyright
©1989.)

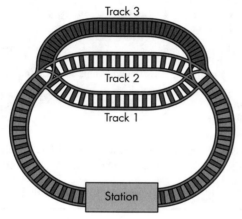

FIGURE 11-24
Railroad track analogy
for a parallel circuit (NOTE.
From *Journeys in Science*,
by J. A. Shymanski,
N. Romance, D. Yore, and
P. Beugger. Reproduced with
the permission of Prentice
Hall Canada, Inc. Copyright
©1989.)

Materials/Resources

Chart paper, science journals

Activities and Procedures

1. Show students charts detailing two railroad track analogies to help them
   understand the difference between series and parallel circuits, as illustrated in
   Figures 11-23 and 11-24. Ask students what each aspect of the railroad
   tracks represents. How does this compare to how the circuits function?

   *Constructing and negotiating
   meaning using analogies*

2. Help your students, working as one large group, to construct analogy charts
   like Tables 11-3 and 11-4.

   *Constructing and negotiating
   meaning through analogy mapping*

TABLE 11-3
Analogy Chart Comparing a Railroad Track to a Series Circuit

Railroad track compared to	Series circuit
Station compared to	Power source (battery or dry cell)
Sections of track compared to	Light bulbs
??????????	Wires
Trains have to run one after the other	Flow of current through light bulbs

TABLE 11-4
Analogy Chart Comparing a Railroad Track to a Parallel Circuit

Railroad track compared to	Parallel circuit
Station compared to	Power source (battery or dry cells)
Sections of track compared to	Light bulbs
??????????	Wires
Trains can run on parallel tracks	Flow of current through light bulbs

Constructing and negotiating meaning

3. Have students discuss how useful the analogies were in helping them understand the difference between series and parallel circuits and then write down their comments in their journals.
4. Using students' input, make a large chart comparing the similarities and differences between series and parallel circuits.

Assessment

1. Use the students' discussion and their journals as evidence of their understanding.
2. Have students draw a comic about the concepts of series and parallel circuits.

Reflection

Refer to chapter 6 for a discussion on analogies.

Using analogies has its advantages and disadvantages. The problems usually occur when the differences or "nonfit" between the actual subject and the analogy are recognized.

Phase III: Translating and Extending
The third phase of the Common Knowledge Construction Model is translating and extending. In this phase, we are looking at making connections from electricity to our everyday use of technology. We also want to consider historical and safety issues as well as perspectives from various cultures. Lessons 7–11 will allow students to translate and extend their personal knowledge from previous lessons.

Electricity in Our Community (STS)

Lesson 7
Discussion

We will be extending the students' knowledge of series and parallel circuits to applications in the school and at home.

Objectives

Students should be able to do the following: Make verbal and written connections between various types of circuits (simple, series, and parallel circuits) and electrical appliances/machines at home and in school.

Teaching and Learning Approaches

Student discussion of applied electrical matters with an electrician, STS connections, writing of brief reports in small groups

Materials/Resources

Guest speaker (electrician)

Activities and Procedures

1. A guest speaker, an electrician, will speak to the class about circuits in the school and the home and such innovations in electricity as circuit breakers, dimmers, etc.
2. Have students prepare at least two questions to ask the speaker.
3. After the speaker has departed, ask students to report on the new knowledge they gained from the session.
4. The teacher will record all their comments on a large sheet of chart paper.

Use of community resources (the electrician can be a parent) and STS

Assessment

1. Students will be assessed on the quality of their questions.
2. Students will write a letter to their parent/guardian telling what they learned about household electricity from the lesson. Have them return the letter with a parent's or guardian's signature and comments.

History of Electricity

Lesson 8

Discussion

Students will learn about the history of electricity so that they can see how it has developed over the years. It is important not only to teach modern ideas about and uses of electricity, but also to show students how the concept was first discovered. Students should learn who was involved and how electricity was harnessed for our use today.

Objectives

Students should be able to do the following: Write an illustrated research report about the major influences (Franklin and Edison) on electricity as we know it today.

Science history

Teaching and Learning Approaches

Library research, computer-based learning (the Internet), small group work, communication through traditional or interactive electronic multimedia research reports.

Materials/Resources

Library resources; computers (Internet facilities); software such as *HyperStudio, HyperCard, PowerPoint*; chart paper

Library research

STS and history of science

Activities and Procedures

1. Have students research in the library famous scientists who studied electricity.
2. Have students use materials from power companies.
3. Have students look for information on the Internet.
4. In small groups, have students write traditional or electronic research reports.

Children enjoy presenting their reports in the multimedia format.

5. Have students present their reports to their peers at a "science meeting." Encourage students to ask questions.

Assessment

Criteria for the written and the oral report will be outlined for students. The quality and understanding of the new knowledge gained in writing the reports and the oral presentation will be used as aspects of the assessment.

Electrical Safety

Lesson 9

Discussion

Students will be introduced to the safety aspects of electricity. This is an extremely important lesson, and you may wish to consider teaching it nearer the beginning of the unit. Because the children have been working with low-voltage dry cells in the classroom, they may not be as cautious with other, higher-strength ones outside the classroom. It is therefore extremely important to review electrical safety with your students.

Objectives

Students should be able to do the following: Identify safe and unsafe electrical situations at school and at home.

Teaching and Learning Approaches

Whole class brainstorming, viewing a movie/film, whole class discussion, quizzes

Materials/Resources

Film/movie, books on electrical safety, pictures/posters of safe and unsafe situations

Activities and Procedures

1. Have students suggest safety precautions for electricity, and record them on a chart.   **Exploring children's ideas**
2. Have students watch a movie/film/computer program on electrical safety.
3. Discuss the salient safety issues presented in the movie and connect these to students' initial ideas.
4. Also obtain materials that local power companies have designed for the schools. Group students and arrange that they present their safety knowledge in some literary, dramatic, artistic, or musical form.   **STS connections**

Assessment

1. Have students work in groups of three to write and perform a song (rap, rock, etc.) about electrical safety.
2. Have students draw a comic, make a poster for their school, or make a newspaper, radio, or TV ad on electrical safety.

Reflection

Students should understand why electrical safety issues are important in and out of the classroom. For example, if students are using electrical equipment during an experiment or at home, they should know how to pull out the plug when they are finished.

Electricity in Other Cultures

Lesson 10

Discussion

Most of the students will probably be aware only of American/European issues about electricity. They need to be exposed to how other cultures produce and use electricity. They need to look at the lifestyles of other cultures in a nonbiased fashion and to respect other cultures' use of alternative energy sources.

Objectives

Students should be able to do the following:

1. Collect data through reading and interviews.
2. Demonstrate an appreciation and understanding of how other cultures use electricity.

Teaching and Learning Approaches

Whole class discussion, interviews, Internet and library research, small group report writing and sharing

Materials/Resources

Library resources, human resources, Internet facilities

Activities and Procedures

Exploring children's ideas

1. The whole class will engage in a discussion led by the teacher. The teacher will ask questions such as, "Do you think all cultures in the world see and use electricity in the same ways that we do? How could we find out?"
2. After a preliminary discussion to see what students know about other cultures' electrical power production and use, have them choose a culture to research and report on. Have students try to infer how environmental conditions and societal customs have influenced the production and use of electricity.
3. Students will research and share their reports in small groups. At the end of the presentations, the teacher should try to draw together all the ideas about the role of electricity in different cultures.

Assessment

Ask each student to write down three ideas about electricity that they learned from their peers during the sharing (and that differ from the ideas in their own report). The students should hand this paper in.

Reflection

Through this lesson, students will have acquired an understanding and appreciation of how various cultures produce and use electricity. What can we learn from other cultures about conserving electrical energy?

Electricity—Design Technology

Lesson 11

Discussion

It is important that students use the concepts of electricity to construct electrical devices such as fans, flashlights, and heating devices. Students may also be asked to design a model house and wire a room. Lessons 7–10 may be substituted for this project.

Objectives

Students should be able to do the following: Design an electrical device or wire their model house to demonstrate their knowledge about series and parallel circuits.

Teaching and Learning Approaches

Designing a brief, planning a design, calculating the cost, sharing the ideas about the product with the class, constructing the device, testing the device, patenting and marketing the device

Refer to chapter 10 for details about design technology.

Materials/Resources

Electrical equipment from your home, junkyard, stores, human resources (discuss with peers, friends, relatives)

Activities and Procedures

1. The teacher will present a challenge to students for designing a new product or improving existing products or processes.
2. In small groups, have students brainstorm ideas to make electrical devices.
3. Record the groups' ideas, no matter how unusual or impossible.
4. Have small groups of students prepare a design brief. The teacher should evaluate the brief and discuss with the groups the safety issues, relevance of their device, cost of materials and resources, and marketing plans for the product.
5. Students will develop a plan for the design of the product using colored and well-defined diagrams.
6. Students will share their plan with the teacher and their peers. The peers should give feedback at this point.
7. Students should collect materials, and construct and test their devices.
8. Have students bring the devices to class and show them to the rest of the students at a "science meeting."
9. Have students find procedures to patent and market their products.

The design may be graphically produced using appropriate software.

Assessment

Assessment will be based on the design brief, their graphical plan, peer feedback, the appearance and usefulness of the product, and the environmental suitability of the product.

Reflection

This project will take many days to complete. Students may start the project after lesson 6. This can be an in-class project. This project will develop the engineering ability of the students.

Phase IV: Assessing and Reflecting
Students will be given a performance and a written test about electricity. Ongoing assessment will also be used for final evaluation.

Performance Test. From the materials provided (wires, light bulbs, dry cells, switches), construct and draw a labeled diagram of the following: simple circuit, series circuit, parallel circuit—30 points. (Criteria: 5 points for the construction of each type of circuit; 5 points for each labeled diagram)

Written Test.

1. Draw a concept map or write a concept story correctly using the following concepts: circuit, series circuit, parallel circuit, positive terminal, negative terminal, electricity, switch, light bulb, wire, dry cell—10 points (Criteria: 1 point for each concept correctly used)

2. Explain how electricity works in a simple circuit. Write a short paragraph and draw a labeled diagram to illustrate your ideas—10 points. (Criteria: 6 points for the paragraph if scientifically correct, and 4 points for the diagram if drawn and labeled correctly)

3. Name a scientist who explored electricity or developed an invention using electricity. Write a short paragraph describing this discovery—10 points. (Criteria: 2 points for naming the scientist and 3 points for accurately describing the work)

Term Work. Take into account all of the assessment measures for the 10 lessons, including those for lessons 7–10. Allot each student 4 points for each lesson—40 points total.

Design Technology Project. Assign 25 points for this project.

Portfolio. Assign 25 points for student portfolios on electricity.

Overall Mark. 150 points

References
Include complete references.

☀ CHAPTER REFLECTIONS

In this chapter, based on the National Science Education Standards (National Research Council, 1996) and a constructivist perspective, we have suggested a format for unit planning that incorporates multiple voices affecting science. A basic outline for planning a unit and lesson was presented, followed by a unit on current electricity by a preservice teacher. Since you are learning to teach science in your science methods course, we expect you to keep detailed, written records of all your planning and teaching of a science unit. Let your students' ideas inspire and guide your teaching, and do not feel you have to stick firmly to your preplanned written outline when you actually teach. In the next chapter, we will hear the voices of practicing teachers relate stories of professional growth and development.

Questions for Reflective Inquiry

1. Observe a science class in action. What science education voices do you hear? Does the teacher deal with scientific objectivity in this class?

2. Prepare and teach a unit that reflects multiple voices in science. What are the students' attitudes and dispositions in your science classes? Support your claims with examples.

SUGGESTED READINGS

Driver, R., Squires, A., Rushworth, P., & Wood-Robinson, V. (1994). *Making sense of secondary science*. London: Routledge.

Osborne, R., & Freyberg, P. (1985). *Learning in science: The implications of children's science*. New York: Heinemann.

Webster Division. (1974). *Batteries and bulbs*. St. Louis: McGraw-Hill.

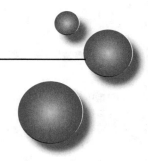

CHAPTER 12

Transformation From Student to Professional Teacher

FOCUS QUESTIONS

1. What does professional growth mean to you?
2. What does it mean for a teacher to be a reflective practitioner?
3. How can a classroom teacher integrate research about teaching and learning with everyday classroom lessons?
4. What are the important elements and stages of the professional growth of teachers?
5. What are the guiding principles for professional growth?

Reflective Inquiry

KEN'S VOICE

*Professional growth is an inherent part of our job as science educators. In order for teachers to offer students the highest quality education in science, **we must be dynamic, rather than static in our approach.** No teacher ever stops learning or growing professionally if he or she is a teacher of merit. When you think you know it all, you stop growing as a professional.*

JOURNAL ACTIVITY

Your Professional Development

1. Reflect on your professional development from the point of view of your university/college experiences in the courses you have taken.

2. What evidences of professional development did you see during your practicum/preservice teaching experiences?

When you finish this course, you probably will have completed your preservice science education program. This phase is only the beginning of a long, continuous professional practice and inquiry. You will be leaving your university or college, a zone of relative comfort, and facing the complexities of the classroom. Teaching is a complex phenomenon, and learning to teach is developmental. It takes time and constant effort. Continual personal reflection is necessary to become an effective teacher. Risk taking, openness, flexibility, collegiality, mutual trust, and commitment to the task of inquiry are characteristics of learning to teach science.

Many professional opportunities and challenges await you. What are they? What are the successes and joys, struggles and pains of professional development?

☀ PROFESSIONAL GROWTH
What Is Professional Growth?

Professional growth means many things to practicing teachers. Consider their voices.

KEN'S VOICE

*Professional growth means different things to me, personally. First, it means **being responsible to our customers—the students**. As the students of today face a challenging job market horizon, it is our responsibility to give them the tools they will need to not only compete, but to succeed. We are responsible for giving them that chance. Professional growth also rejuvenates our interest. As we progress through our careers, we need to develop **new skills and interests** to keep our minds fresh!*

MARY-ANN'S VOICE

*Professional growth is a process a teacher continually goes through **to learn new teaching techniques, update curriculum knowledge, and become aware of contemporary changes in education and how to implement these changes in the classroom.** To me personally, it means an opportunity to improve my teaching methods and increase my knowledge and awareness of new changes in education; for example, cooperative learning, new mathematics curriculum, employability skills, and education office (department) policy changes.*

BARBARA'S VOICE

*Professional growth describes **the growth of individuals and professional learning enriched through in-services, visitations,***

reading, and team planning. *To me personally, professional growth means learning more about student interaction, teacher-student relations, content area knowledge, and relating to students' expertise.*

These practicing teachers have all taught for over 10 years and are well established and recognized as leaders in their schools and school district. They recognize that the significant aspects of professional development include the beliefs that it is a *continuous process* and an *inherent part of their profession* and that they be willing to respond to a survey about professional development.

They observe as well that professional growth keeps them personally stimulated and interested in their changing profession. Even more important, they believe that professional growth enables them to provide their students with the highest quality education in science. These teachers feel responsible to their students, who will be building future careers. To these teachers, professional development becomes a personal initiative and responsibility.

Professional Development Standard C

Professional development for teachers of science requires building understanding and ability for lifelong learning.

Attitudes Toward Professional Growth

Teachers' voices speak out loud and clear about the positive aspects of professional growth. Some of their comments are follow.

MARY-ANN'S VOICE

I get to hear updated information on in-services, equipment, and science events. I pass this information on to my colleagues.

ALAN'S VOICE

The interpersonal relationships enjoyed through professional development activities have to be considered a positive aspect. Also, the knowledge gained is of use and value.

DENISE'S VOICE

I have a better knowledge of how and what to teach. I learn ways of expanding the curriculum and children's experiences. I have a firm belief in hands-on teaching. I know where to look for information, pictures, guests, etc. I have warm feelings of seeing teacher friends at in-services. I have a greater belief in my own contributions.

KEN'S VOICE

I have an expanded knowledge base, an increased exposure/acceptance as a leadership source, more confidence as a public speaker and a contributor. In addition, I can use this professional experience for my resume.

SOPHIA'S VOICE

My self-confidence has skyrocketed. I realize I've become a very good salesperson.

BARBARA'S VOICE

Professional development keeps up the interest—keeps me trying new things, and I become dynamic, not stagnant.

SHIRLEY'S VOICE

The number one way it has helped has been in the communication with peers struggling to implement an effective program. It has also made it possible for me to access some of the most current and relevant materials.

The teachers express the *benefits* of professional growth in that their teaching has improved as a result of the activities in which they have been involved. Also, they report that professional activities somehow energize and motivate them to go back to the daily work in the classroom with fresh ideas and renewed energy.

When teachers were asked specifically, "What can you see as the possible *negative aspects* of professional development?" some expressed the frustrations and stress of trying to keep up to date, whereas others had specific comments on types of workshops and in-services. Some of their comments follow.

MARY-ANN'S VOICE

I dislike being given half-day or one-day "crash" courses and being expected to implement these new ideas immediately. Many professional development activities are run by nonteachers. I have learned that these presenters are usually out of touch with the reality of the classroom. I'd much rather be taught by other teachers. They have much more credibility and realistic expectations.

DENISE'S VOICE

Before there is growth, there is generally some stress. Everything generally takes lots of time. Sometimes, when too many things happen in our lives at one time, it can cause stress.

SOPHIA'S VOICE

You spend too much of your time trying out your wonderful ideas, and other subjects suffer.

KEN'S VOICE

> *Continued dependence on you as a leader is hard. Other teachers come to accept the fact that you will lead. Time commitment— overindulgence in committees—can take away from recreational/ relaxation pursuits and classroom energy and responsibility.*

Generally, these teachers view professional growth and reflective practice in a very positive light, as enhancing their performance in the classroom and contributing to the educational community at large. The problems of time commitment, stress, and continued dependence on them as leaders remain.

Not only did our experienced teachers discuss what professional growth means to them, but they also focused on how it can be attained. They suggest the following activities:

- Take both science and professional courses at the university or college.
- Have informal talks and sharing sessions with other teachers.
- Observe other teachers in their classrooms.
- Read current literature (professional journals and books).
- Attend after-school, noon, and daylong in-services in the school or district or outside the district in subjects such as these:
  - Studying the curriculum
  - Training in new curriculum thrusts
  - Expanding computer knowledge
  - Learning about portfolio assessments
  - Studying cooperative learning
- Plan a project or in-service.
- Work on school committees to organize events such as science fairs or science "olympics."
- Serve as a science coordinator within a school.
- Attend meetings of these coordinators to form a district leadership team.
- Reflect on who you are as a person, learner, and teacher.
- Participate in professional organizations.
- Participate in university/school collaborative projects.
- Initiate collaborative projects.

Professional Development Standard C

Guideline: Professional development activities must provide opportunities to know and have access to existing research and experiential knowledge.

Professional Development Standard C

Guideline: Professional development activities must provide opportunities to learn and use the skills of research to generate new knowledge about science and the teaching and learning of science.

✸ THE TEACHER AS A REFLECTIVE PRACTITIONER

A program coordinator articulates her views about the concept and values of professional growth.

LESLIE'S VOICE

> *Professional growth is a reflective process. It is ongoing and continuous as one continues to learn, implement new ideas, and monitor student growth and development.*

Professional Development Standard C

Guideline: Professional development activities must provide regular, frequent opportunities for individual and collegial examination and reflection on classroom and institutional practice.

Professional growth is clarification and validation of my philosophy of teaching and learning; reflection on links between philosophy and appropriate practice; analysis of new ideas as to how they fit with what I currently understand. Are these ideas consistent with what I believe? If I modify my practice, what is the student response? If after considerable refinement and reflection the idea can be incorporated, then it becomes part of professional practice.

Teacher educators' and researchers' conceptions of reflective practice are similar to those the excerpt suggests. A reflective practice is based on the knowledge constructed through a teacher's personal, practical experience. Shulman (1986) aptly showed the difference between a craft and a profession:

> The professional holds knowledge, not only of how—the capacity for skilled performance—but of what and why. The teacher is not only a master of procedure but also of content and rationale, and capable of explaining why something is done. The teacher is capable of reflection leading to self-knowledge, the metacognitive awareness that distinguishes draftsman from architect, bookkeeper from auditor. A professional is capable not only of practicing and understanding his craft, but of communicating decisions and actions to others (Shulman, 1986, p. 13).

Thus, professional growth is the development of a teacher into a proficient craftsperson, a reflective practitioner, generator, and disseminator of knowledge for further discourse. The teachers whom we surveyed mostly talked about the craft of teaching. Knowing how to carry out reflective practice is even more important.

Ginsburg and Clift (1990) define reflection as the systematic and concerted synthesis of theory and practice. Many believe that reflection is an ongoing process that enables teachers to continually learn from their own experiences by considering alternative interpretations of situations, generating and evaluating goals, and examining experiences in light of alternative goals and hypotheses.

Grimmett, MacKinnon, Erickson, and Reicken (1990) concur with many of the ideas the foregoing science teachers raise about professional growth. As well these science teacher educators ask three questions: (a) What is being reflected on? (b) How is the reflective process engaged? (c) What is the purpose of reflection? They indicate three distinct perspectives on reflection: contemplation leading to the application of research findings to practice (applying theory to practice), deliberation among competing views of teaching (discussing different views of teaching), and reconstruction of experience (examining one's own experience).

Currently, all three perspectives are evident in teacher practice. Seeing merit in the last of these three perspectives, Clarke (1994) points out that engaging in a reflective practice intentionally makes certain aspects of your practice problematic so that you may gain new insights into that practice. It is a conversation with yourself carried on within your problem setting. When you openly and actively converse with your social context, you are generating knowledge-in-action (Erickson, 1991; Feiman-Nemser & Buchman, 1986). Based on Donald Schön's work (1983, 1987), Clarke explains, "Knowledge-in-action is the raw material on which reflection operates" (p. 148). You may act on the problem while you are carrying out the reflection (reflection-in-action). On the other hand, you may plan a course of action after much thought and deliberation when the activity is over (reflection-on-action).

When you engage in professional practice, you will shift from traditional classroom practices. Initially, you may base your reflections on imitating or "cloning" other teachers. Later, you will shape your reflections on your own practice by probing your own beliefs and making those explicit. We encourage you to reflect about your practice to become an empowered (independent and autonomous) teacher. If you tend to replicate other teachers, you will evolve into a *repetitive practitioner*! Reflecting on your practice as a whole rather than particular aspects is defining a practice that is uniquely yours. The reflective practice Clarke emphasizes occurs when the teacher engages in systematic classroom research.

☼ THE TEACHER AS A CLASSROOM-BASED RESEARCHER

Professional development of a teacher is a long process, beginning with preservice teaching. Even at that stage, research into teaching practice can take place. Many of the lesson and unit plans used in this book are examples of collaborative research among our preservice teachers, our practicing teachers, and their teacher educators. Classroom-based research is where you and your students meet to learn science. It is a great setting for your development of science content knowledge because the children are real and the classroom is real. It is a valid context in which you grow as a professional.

Fortunately, many teachers no longer view research with suspicion, but realize that teaching is a dynamic, evolving profession. They understand that not only are they expected to keep up with the literature pertinent to their practice, attend courses and workshops, and engage in professional dialogue with their colleagues, but they are beginning to accept the idea that they are able to do research in their classrooms. When you undertake classroom-based research, you generate knowledge useful to you as a teacher. You begin to question your views about learning and subject them to further analysis, interpretations, and revisions. Since you personally own your research and its findings, you may be excited to share your experiences with colleagues or with those engaged in university projects. Note the comments of one of our experienced teachers who participated in a collaborative research effort on assessment:

Professional Development Standard B

Guideline: Learning experiences for teachers of science must use inquiry, reflection, interpretation of research, modeling, and guided practice to build understanding and skill in science teaching.

Teacher and students doing chromatography research in their classroom.

DENISE'S VOICE

I learned to speak and share ideas effectively. Then I had to gain confidence in myself—that I did have some good ideas, and I had to learn to say those ideas in such a way that I would be heard and my ideas would be tried by my colleagues.

Improving their teaching strategies and teaching units over time is a goal of many reflective teachers. Teachers can address concerns about their teaching in "action" research, which Kemmis and McTaggart (1982) state "provides a way of thinking systematically about what happens in the school or classroom, implementing action where improvements are thought to be possible, and monitoring and evaluating the effects of the action with a view to continuing the improvement" (p. 5). The International Reading Association (1989) states that action research can serve at least the following 12 purposes:

- Helps solve classroom problems
- Encourages effective change
- Revitalizes teachers
- Empowers teachers to make decisions in their classrooms
- Identifies effective teaching and learning methods
- Promotes reflective teaching
- Verifies what methods work
- Promotes ownership of effective practices
- Widens the range of teachers' professional skills
- Provides a connection between instructional methods and results

- Helps teachers apply research findings to their classroom
- Enables teachers to become change agents

With regard to action research, it may seem too early for you to think about this issue as you prepare for teaching. So many components of your new work as a novice teacher must be addressed during the first three or more years. Action research might seem beyond your capability. But the components of new work may be examined in an empathetic environment when you establish collaborative relationships with your colleagues and teacher educators.

Collaborative Relationships

Classroom-based research can be an effective tool for developing collaboration among colleagues. Collaboration between university researchers and teachers in classroom-based collaborative teaching and research projects is an initiative recommended by Ebenezer and Erickson (1996). They argue that this collaboration is a responsibility of the educational research community and curriculum developers. Such an approach should begin to blur the boundaries between the researched and the researcher and should enrich the practices of both.

Throughout the world there are collaborative action research groups where practicing teachers, preservice teachers, and teacher educators are actively engaged in researching teaching and learning. Projects consist of personal reflection on teaching, narrative inquiries, and storying about personal practical knowledge. While some groups focus on personal practice, others are engaged in assessing students' conceptions of science concepts and reflecting about how best to incorporate them into science lessons using multiple strategies such as analogy mapping, classroom discourse, and hypermedia.

These are only a few examples of classroom-based collaborative projects. If your educational community has a classroom-based collaborative research group, we recommend that you join this group. A collaborative action research group will provide you with a forum for the exchange of ideas. If there is no such group, create one. The exchange of ideas will promote reflection and develop both a language of professional knowledge and classroom inquiry. It will encourage open communication and criticism among collaborators to achieve professional growth and improved practice.

Collaboration and Leadership

Saranson (1990) emphasizes that teacher development and enhanced professionalism must be undertaken along with developments in curriculum, assessment, leadership, and school organization. In other words, when you are a practicing classroom teacher, you will have opportunities to work as a curriculum planner, mentor, peer observer, coach, and leader. Saranson reminds you that you should systematically consider the professional development part of all of these. It must be your personal agenda! For example,

Professional Development Standard C

Guideline: Professional development activities must provide opportunities for teachers to receive feedback about their teaching and to understand, analyze, and apply that feedback to improve their practice.

Professional Development Standard A

Guideline: Science learning experiences for teachers must encourage and support teachers in their efforts to collaborate.

the teachers who responded to the survey described at the beginning of this chapter hold leadership positions in science or mathematics in their schools. They meet regularly with program coordinators as part of the school district organization to discuss innovations and plan adaptations and modifications of these innovations within their schools. They also take part in collaborative research programs in conjunction with a local university and/or ministry of education. Read the following teacher's comments about her role:

DENISE'S VOICE

It's always fun to work on any professional development committee. So many great ideas evolve from working with others. I have enjoyed working on the math leadership committee with Cheryl, the program coordinator, and planning special math weeks for the school.... It also has been a pleasure to work with Leslie, the other program coordinator, on various science-related in-services. Both of these professionals have the knack of making people want to try new ideas and extend themselves. As a result of their support and encouragement I have been able to try additional science- and math-related activities that are beneficial to our school, the university, and another school division.

☀ ELEMENTS AND STAGES OF PROFESSIONAL GROWTH

Essential Elements: Support and Time

Why do some teachers involve themselves in professional development responsibilities while others plug along from day to day in the grind of the classroom? Personal qualities doubtless contribute, but the climate of the school and school district have much to do with how far teachers will extend themselves beyond their classrooms. One teacher emphasizes that *two elements must be present to support teachers* in their professional growth. Without this support, it is very difficult for teachers to go it alone. These elements are as follows:

Administrative support. When teachers want to try different things, it is important that they feel supported and that their efforts be encouraged.
Time. With so many changes occurring, it is of utmost importance that teachers be given time to attend workshops or observe other teachers to assist their learning.

For teachers to successfully strive for professional excellence, a strong support mechanism within the school and administration is essential. Notice what the same teacher emphasizes:

DENISE'S VOICE

Up to about eight years ago, I had always done special things in my classroom and had helped on many committees within the school. Somehow, these things were expected and never recognized—no notes of thanks or "good job." Once we had exceptional P.D. leaders and once school leaders (principals) realized that staff members needed these pats on the back more often than [at] evaluation time, teachers felt more fulfilled and were even willing to go the extra 10 miles. It is at that time that all concerned—students, staff, administration, etc., really benefit.

The "pats on the back" by administrators are one form of collegiality. Hargreaves (1994) recognizes collaboration and collegiality as important factors in promoting professional growth. Two different forms exist—collaborative culture and collaborative collegiality. In collaborative cultures, collaborative working relationships between teachers and their colleagues tend to be spontaneous, voluntary, development oriented, pervasive across time and space, and unpredictable. They can build confidence in the teachers who are able to interact knowledgeably with innovations. On the other hand, contrived collegiality that is imposed on teachers in order to implement a new program, encourage team planning, or promote peer coaching may not have the desired results. Hargreaves found that two of the major consequences of contrived collegiality were inflexibility and inefficiency.

Some of the teachers state that the *time* taken up with professional development activities may have in some way hindered their classroom science teaching. They express their concerns as follows:

> **Professional Development Standard C**
>
> **Guideline:** Professional development activities must provide opportunities for teachers to learn and use various tools and techniques for self-reflection and collegial reflection, such as peer coaching, portfolios, and journals.

ALAN'S VOICE

Finding time for professional development in a busy schedule is always a factor. One must be willing to give up personal time in many cases.

SHIRLEY'S VOICE

There are several professional development activities in many areas and I cannot possibly attend them all because of the time and energy demands of the classroom.

MARY-ANN'S VOICE

Some of my responsibilities (as science coordinator within the school)—science orders, equipment inventory, searching for equipment, etc.—have taken up valuable time I could have used to prepare my lessons.

Time for professional development must be built into the school calendar so that teachers do not feel pulled in all directions, as did these teachers.

Stages in Professional Growth

No two teachers view professional growth in identical ways. However, for most it means a gradual shift in focus from their classroom performance to learning about innovations that would improve their students' ability to learn. Teachers' concerns are thus transferred from their survival in the classroom to providing an attractive and productive learning environment for their students. Many teachers were able to go a step further in sharing new ideas with other teachers and providing leadership. One teacher expresses this well.

KEN'S VOICE

There were many stages of professional growth in my teaching career. When I began as a teacher, my primary objective was to learn the curriculum and my focus was on my classroom performance. As I gained experience, I became more involved in committee work for a variety of reasons. First, you had a responsibility to improve the quality of your teaching. Second, it was important to develop contacts with colleagues. As an experienced teacher, you wish to continue contributing and to provide leadership when you feel confident that you have skills to offer.

According to this teacher, there is a *learning stage* and then a *sharing stage*. His first concern is on learning the curriculum, with a focus on classroom performance. As he gained experience, he became involved in committee work, then went on to provide leadership. The following developmental stages in this teacher's professional growth occurred:

1. Learning university theory
2. Engaging in classroom practice
3. Serving on professional organizations and committees
4. Participating in leadership committees and study groups
5. Facilitating change with colleagues

✸ CHAPTER REFLECTIONS

This chapter focused on professional growth by highlighting the voices of practicing teachers. As you begin your life as a classroom teacher, you will find that opportunities for professional growth are many and diverse. The responsibility for initiating and carrying out professional responsibilities and reflections is yours. Consider the following as guiding principles for professional growth.

The National Science Teachers Association (NSTA) is a large, powerful organization that is committed to improving science education from pre-K through college. NSTA holds one national and three regional conferences per year. These conferences are well attended, and many teachers play leadership roles by presenting workshops and papers and serving on committees. NSTA also provides NASA Educational Workshops for Elementary School Teachers (NEWEST). NSTA publishes *Science and Children*, a teacher journal that has many useful activities. NSTA publishes curriculum units, supplementary activities, and posters.

- Approach science education studies taking into account your personal beliefs, attitudes, understandings, and values about teaching and learning.
- Explore teaching and learning in a variety of contexts and make these explicit.
- Understand that knowledge is personally constructed and socially negotiated.
- Understand that learning may take several forms: It may be content and context dependent and thus relational; it may be evolutionary as a result of prior knowledge interacting with new ideas; it may be revolutionary, with new ideas replacing old ideas.
- Realize that your personal teaching style will be a fusion of your personal conceptions and socially constructed knowledge.
- Learn to take risks and be open-minded and flexible in adopting alternative ways of teaching and learning.
- Know that it takes time to develop a practical philosophy of teaching and learning. Be ready to encounter conceptual conflicts and painful times as you develop this personal philosophy.
- Learn the importance of reflective inquiry so that the problems of teaching will be evident and the solutions may be pondered.
- Research the ways to solve the problems in teaching and develop a rich repertoire of strategies for solving classroom dilemmas.

Adopting the foregoing guiding principles is important for developing a practical philosophy of teaching and for professional growth. Only when you believe in and practice sound principles of teaching can you implement these in the classroom. These principles will become actualized and integrated with other components of your professional work when you become an active, collaborative partner with colleagues and teacher educators in the inquiry of teaching and learning.

Questions for Reflective Inquiry

1. How can you as a new teacher maintain a successful balance between commitments within and without the classroom?

2. What are the critical aspects of your professional growth that you will emphasize during the first few years of your teaching?

SUGGESTED READINGS

Bell, B. (1994). Editorial. *International Journal of Science Education, 16*(5), 493–495.
Clandinin, D. J. (1989). Developing rhythm in teaching: The narrative study of a beginning teacher's personal practical knowledge of classrooms. *Curriculum Inquiry, 19*(2), 121–141.

Clarke, A. (1994). Student-teacher reflection: Developing and defining a practice that is uniquely one's own. *International Journal of Science Education, 16*(5), 497–509.

Connelly, F. M., & Clandinin, D. J. (1988). *Teachers as curriculum planners: Narratives of experience.* New York: Teachers College Press.

Erickson, G. (1991). Collaborative inquiry and the professional development of science teachers. *Journal of Educational Thought, 25*(3), 228–245.

Grimmett, P. P., MacKinnon, A. M., Erickson, G. L., & Rieken, T. J. (1990). Reflective practice in teacher education. In R. T. Cliff, W. R. Houston, & M. Pugach (Eds.), *Encouraging reflective practice in education.* New York: Teachers College Press.

Gunstone, R. F., Slattery, M., Baird, J. R., & Northfield, J. R. (1993). A case study exploration of development in preservice science teachers. *Science Education, 77*(1), 47–73.

Hargreaves, A. (1994). *Changing teachers, changing times.* New York: Teachers College Press.

MacKinnon, A., & Erickson, G. (1988). Taking Schön's ideas to a science teaching practicum. In P. Grimmett and G. Erickson (Eds.), *Reflection in Teacher Education* (pp. 113–137). New York: Teachers College Press.

Schön, D. A. (1987). *Educating the reflective practitioner.* San Francisco: Jossey-Bass.

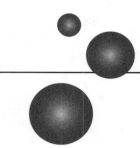

APPENDIX A

Managing Cooperative Learning

DEVELOP CLEAR RULES AND PROCEDURES

Establish rules for group behavior with the help of the class. The rules should include such things as listening carefully to each other without interrupting, giving everyone a chance to participate, getting everyone's opinion before making decisions, and working quietly, keeping on task.

GROUP FORMATION

Generally, teacher-selected heterogeneous groups work best. Cross-cultural and language acquisition are best served when groups are heterogeneous. Students need to know that they are expected to learn to get along and communicate effectively with people they may consider different from themselves. Specific groups usually last as long as a project or specific study unit is completed. You may organize groups by randomly assigning students from the class list or according to specific criteria, such as making sure you have one top student and one lower ability student in each group, separating friends, or having both sexes in each group.

INITIAL ACTIVITIES

Cooperative group skills are learned over a period of time, through a series of activities. Students first need to get to know and trust one another. Coelho (1994) suggests the following activities:

Group Introductions—All about Names. Interview a partner, asking her such questions as:
- What's your given name? How do you pronounce it?
- What's your family name? How do you pronounce it?
- Do you have a nickname? Can you tell me anything about the meaning of your name or about names in your culture?

Then reverse the procedure, with the other partner being interviewed. Then introduce your partner to the rest of the group.

Exploring Commonalities. Ask students to find out, by brainstorming, what everyone in the group has in common. Have groups report their findings.

Identifying the Group. Have the students by discussion and negotiation determine a name and logo for the group. You may wish to establish a few guidelines and have students give a reason for their choice.

Bulletin Board. A bulletin board with the name and logo of each group and space for the groups' materials to be posted may be created.

Cooperative Activities. Simple problems or puzzles may be given to the groups to break the ice and initiate group processes. Students need to learn group interaction skills such as the following:
- Making sure everyone has an equal chance to speak
- Learning how to encourage everyone's participation
- Keeping on task
- Listening to others
- Praising contributions of others (adapted from Coelho, 1994, pp. 52–64)

CONDUCTING THE LESSON

1. As soon as groups have gone through the introductory stages, introduce the lesson. The teacher should explain the *purpose of the lesson, give directions for the lesson,* and *explain the criteria for success.* Oral and visual instructions are usually necessary. Students should be instructed to discuss the directions for the lesson with each other and then seek further explanation from the teacher, if necessary. Then they should clarify their group's goal. Group roles are often assigned to each member. You may wish to select an appropriate role for each member from the following list described by Putnam (1997).

   Recorder. Documents the work of the group, takes notes, writes answers

   Reader. Reads the written material, reads the answer for the group

   Summarizer. Recapitulates what has been decided in the group, summarizes the ideas shared

   Encourager. Reinforces group members for performing well or staying on task, instills strength of purpose, invites members to participate

   Courier. Brings materials to the group, carries messages or assignments to their destinations

Checker. Makes certain that everyone is on task, agrees with the answer, understands the assignment, discussion, or answer

Interrogator. Challenges group members to defend their answers and to avoid superficial responses or to explore a matter more deeply

Manager. Ensures directions are followed, organizes the group process, makes sure the group is ready to report its answer or turn in the work

Time Keeper. Watches time and keeps the group on task and moving forward

Voice Control Technician. Monitors the noise level in the group and indicates when the students need to quiet down

Equalizer. Makes sure all group members are treated fairly and courteously, that they have opportunities to participate and derive benefit from the group work (Putnam, 1997, p. 66)

A simpler structure for young children might include the following roles:

Communicator. Responsible for consulting with the teacher and reporting back to the group; helps plan how to communicate the group's findings to the class

Manager. Responsible for listing and organizing the supplies needed and for picking up and returning them to the supply cupboard

Tracker. Responsible for planning how the activity can be organized and monitoring progress

Checker. Responsible for making sure the team understands the problem and focuses on how to solve it; checks to be sure the problem has been solved

Coach. Responsible for encouraging all team members to participate; helps team members work together

2. Have each group carry out the activity and record its findings. Monitor the activities of the groups to see that the job descriptions have not overpowered the purpose of the science activity.

3. Conduct a reporting session to allow each group to explain its activity and the nature of its results.

4. Have each team member reflect on the activity in his/her science journal.

ASSESSMENT

You should apply the same sound assessment techniques to cooperative learning that you would to other types of science activities (see chapter 8 of this book). Be sure to evaluate *individual success.* Even when students have learned together, the best way to determine what each student knows is to give each student an individual assessment. Putnam (1997) states that "... the only justification for grading students as a group is when the specific purpose of the group is to promote interdependence, when a project or presentation requires some type of group evaluation ... and when the activity is set up to allow thoughtful and critical group input and editing" (p. 182).

Individual students can be assessed on the basis of quizzes and tests, notebooks, journals, learning logs, reports, portfolios, etc. They can also be given participation points for their contribution to the group effort.

REFERENCES

Coelho, E. (1994). *Learning together in the multicultural classroom.* Markham, Ontario, Canada: The Pippin Teacher's Library.

Putnam, J. (1997). *Cooperative learning in diverse classrooms.* Columbus, OH: Merrill.

APPENDIX B

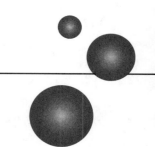

Using Discrepant Events
in Science Lessons

Discrepant events can be excellent stimulators and motivators in science lessons. When the puzzling event occurs, students want to find out the "how comes" and "whys." Discrepant events often create a strong feeling in the observer. This is the time to capitalize on the curiosity of students to help them *construct and negotiate meaning*. Discrepant events must be carefully planned and designed as part of a teaching sequence. They must fit in with the content of the unit. An excellent source for discrepant events can be found in *Teaching Science to Children: An Integrated Approach* by Alfred Friedl (1986).

Care must be taken to initiate the discrepant event and then to allow the students time to puzzle about the results. Friedl (1986) states that three general steps should be employed:

1. Set up the discrepant event. An example is to place a coin under an upright clear glass tumbler so that you can see it from the side of the glass. Then pour water into the glass and notice what happens. The coin has disappeared!
2. Involve students in solving the discrepancy. Encourage them to repeat the activity, pouring the water slowly and then quickly to see if it makes any difference. Then observe the coin from all angles. Have students suggest solutions and try out other activities.
3. Resolve the discrepancy. Because this activity would be an excellent introduction to the bending (refraction) of light, other activities with a light box could be performed in which the bending of light in different

mediums is observed. In the case of the discrepant event just done, the explanation is that the light travels through several different media (glass, water, and glass again) and is bent so much that the light from the coin does not reach the outside of the glass tumbler.

REFERENCE

Friedl, A. E. (1986). *Teaching science to children: An integrated approach.* New York: Random House.

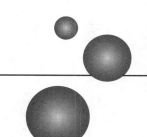

APPENDIX C

Science Safety: Everyone's Responsibility

Program Standard D of *National Science Education Standards* (National Research Council, 1996, p. 218) specifies that "the K–12 science program must give access to appropriate and sufficient resources, including quality teachers, time, materials and equipment, adequate and safe space, and the community." Safety in the science class is in the hands of the administrator, the teacher, and the students. The administration has indirect responsibility, the teacher has direct responsibility, and the student has personal responsibility. In this section, we will examine each of these individual's responsibilities and also offer suggestions for safety in the science class that include everything from keeping animals to storing and using equipment. Your curriculum documents will also list safety rules.

WHAT CAN ADMINISTRATORS DO?

Administrators should be responsible for the following:

- Providing sufficient space for science
- Supplying safe equipment
- Supplying information and resources through an ongoing school science safety committee in the school and in-service education
- Maintaining the general upkeep of the science facilities
- Conducting safety audits once a year and repairing or replacing substandard equipment
- Identifying people within the school who are qualified to administer first aid

WHAT CAN TEACHERS DO?

Teachers should be responsible for the following:

- Developing and enforcing a set of safety rules for every group of children
- Charting and posting safety rules in class so that everyone can see; children can take part in this activity to help them remember as well as obey the rules that they have developed
- Setting an example (being a role model) for children
- Handing out proper equipment, materials, and supplies to children
- Carefully observing the actions of the children when they are engaged in science investigations; never leave them without adult supervision
- Doing a "safety audit" of the classroom by taking inventory, checking the equipment for damage, and developing emergency lists (emergency phone numbers and parents' phone numbers at home and work)
- Developing contingency plans—safety checklists and a first-aid kit for class (cultivate a "what-if?"/defensive science approach)
- Developing and teaching a safety unit
- Reviewing the rules before each science activity
- Notifying the principal/parents in writing if planning an out-of-the-ordinary experience or excursion
- Maintaining a list of students with allergies, contact lenses, corrective medical devices, and other special needs

WHAT CAN STUDENTS DO?

The students should be responsible for the following:

- Being aware of safety procedures so that they follow them naturally
- Being aware of possible hazards in the surroundings
- Being alert and taking things seriously—this means no fooling around
- Knowing the location of first-aid equipment (first-aid box, fire blanket, and fire extinguishers)
- Knowing the different procedures to escape fire hazards
- Wearing appropriate clothes during science investigations
- Wearing goggles if necessary
- Keeping long hair tied back and leaving jewelry at home
- Reporting any unsafe situations to the teacher right away

SOME SPECIFIC CAUTIONS
Animal Care

Before introducing animals into the classroom, review the policy of the school or local school district. When keeping animals, the teacher should think of the safety of students and the animals. The housing must be spacious and sanitary, and disposal of the animal must be humane. Egg incubation must be allowed only if a home can be found for the chicks. Venomous creatures should not be kept. If animals are brought to the classroom, they should be checked by a veterinarian and given rabies shots. If an animal dies, the cage should be disinfected to prevent the spread of any diseases. The children should wash their hands after handling an animal to prevent spreading disease. Animals should be handled properly to teach children to have a reverence for all animal life forms.

Place aquariums away from direct sunlight because the glass can crack and algae will grow very quickly. Empty the aquarium before moving it because a filled aquarium can be very heavy and it can break. To empty a tank, do not use the mouth suction method, as the water may be contaminated; empty it by dipping with a cup or pitcher. Dying or dead fish should not be handled with bare hands—use gloves.

Plant Care

Poisonous seeds or other parts of such plants as poison ivy, poison oak, or poison sumac should not be brought into the science room. Plants grown with insecticides and pesticides may be harmful to children if they are exposed to them in excessive amounts, as may bread molds and spores. When handling plants, the children should be reminded not to put anything in their mouths. Some plants such as foxglove, castor bean, and dieffenbachia, and some fungi have parts that are poisonous if eaten. Children should also wash their hands after handling plants, as insecticides can be transferred from plant leaves to hand to mouth.

Heat and Electricity

Open flames, such as candles, must be used cautiously. Have access to a fire extinguisher, bucket of sand, first-aid kit, and fire blanket. Students should only be allowed to used controlled voltages such as dry cells and low-voltage batteries (no more than six volts).

Chemicals and Glassware

Keep all chemicals out of children's reach. Store in closed containers in a locked area. Know the risks and hazards involved as well as first-aid measures. Common household chemicals such as aerosols and cleaners should be handled with care.

Use plastic, unbreakable wares if possible. If glassware is used, caution children about handling it carefully. Check glass for splits and cracks. If glass breaks, the teacher should clean up the mess. Never pick up broken glass with bare fingers. The bigger pieces can be collected using plasticine, and the glass slivers can be gathered using a damp cloth.

SUGGESTED READINGS

An excellent set of safety suggestions and procedures is available from the National Science Teachers Association (NSTA, Arlington, VA.)

An excellent book on animals in the classroom is recommended: Kramer, D. C. (1989). *Animals in the classroom.* New York: Addison-Wesley.

REFERENCES

INTRODUCTION

Clarke, A. (1994). Student-teacher reflection: Developing and defining a practice that is uniquely one's own. *International Journal of Science Education, 16*(5), 497–509.

Connelly, F. M., & Clandinen, D. J. (1988). *Teachers as curriculum planners.* New York: Teachers College Press.

Erickson, F. (1986). Qualitative methods in research on teaching. In M. Wittrock (Ed.), *Handbook of research on teaching* (3rd ed., pp. 119–161) New York: MacMillan.

Erickson, G., Mayer-Smith, J., Rodriguez, A., Chin, P., & Mitchell, I. (1994). Perspectives on learning to teach science: Insights and dilemmas from a collaborative practicum project. *International Journal of Science Education, 16*(5), 585–597.

Feiman-Nemser, S. (1986). The cultures of teaching. In M. Wittrock (Ed.), Handbook of research on teaching (3rd ed., pp. 505–526) New York: MacMillan.

Gunstone, R. F., Slattery, M., Baird, J. R., & Northfield, J. R. (1993). A case study exploration of development in preservice science teachers. *Science Education, 77*(1), 47–73.

Kagan, D. M. (1992). Professional growth among preservice teachers. *Review of Educational Research, 62*(2), 129–169.

Stofflett, R. T. (1994). The accommodation of science pedagogical knowledge: The application of conceptual change constructs to teacher education. *Journal of Research in Science Teaching, 31*(8), 787–810.

CHAPTER 1   CONCEPTIONS OF SCIENCE

American Association for the Advancement of Science (1989). *Project 2061 Science for All Americans.* Washington, D.C.: The American Association for the Advancement of Science Inc.

American Association for the Advancement of Science (1993). *Benchmarks for science literacy.* Washington, D.C.: The American Association for the Advancement of Science Inc.

Bodner, G. M. (1986). Constructivism: A theory of knowledge. *The Journal of Chemical Education, 63*(10), 873–877.

Carnegie Forum on Education and the Economy (1986). *A nation prepared: Teachers for the 21st Century.* The report of the Task Force on Teaching as a Profession. New York: Carnegie Corporation of New York.

Duschl, R. A. (1988). Abandoning the scientistic legacy of science education. *Science Education, 72*(1), 51–62.

Jenkins, E. (1991). The history of science in British schools: Retrospect and prospect. In M. R. Matthews (Ed.). *History, philosophy, and science teaching: Selected readings,* 33–41. Toronto, ON: OISE Press.

Kelly G. J., Carlsen W. S., & Cunningham, C. M. (1993). Science education in sociocultural context: Perspectives from the sociology of science. *Science Education, 77*(2), 207–220.

Kuhn, T. (1962, 1970 2nd Ed.). *The structure of scientific revolutions.* Chicago: University of Chicago Press.

Latour, B. (1987). *Science in action.* Cambridge: Harvard University Press.

Longino, H. (1990). *Science as social knowledge: Values and objectivity in scientific inquiry.* Princeton, NJ: Princeton University Press.

Martin, R., & Brouwer, W. (1993). Exploring personal science. *Science Education, 77*(4), 441–459.

Mendeleev, D. I. (1905, 3rd ed.) *Principles of chemistry.* London: Longmans.

National Commission on Excellence in Education (1983). *A nation at risk: The imperative for educational reform.* Washington, D.C.: U.S. Department of Education.

National Research Council. (1996). *National Science Education Standards.* Washington, D.C.: National Academy Press.

Pearson, K. (1892/1951). *The grammar of science.* London: J. M. Dent and Sons Ltd.

Raizen, S. A., Sellwood, P., Todd, R. D., & Vickers, M. (1995). *Technology education in the classroom.* San Francisco, CA: Jossey-Bass Publishers.

Shrödinger, E. (1958). *Mind and matter.* Cambridge: Cambridge University Press.

Williams, H., & Stinner, A. (1996). *Teaching science in the secondary school: A modern perspective.* Winnipeg MB: University of Manitoba Press.

CHAPTER 2   CONCEPTIONS OF SCIENCE TEACHING AND LEARNING

Ausubel, D. P. (1968). *Educational psychology.* New York: Holt, Rinehart and Winston.

Bodner, G. M. (1986). Constructivism: A theory of knowledge. *The Journal of Chemical Education, 63*(10), 873–877.

Driver, R., & Erickson, G. (1983). Theories in action: Some theoretical and empirical issues in the study of students' conceptual frameworks in science. *Studies in Science Education, 10,* 37–60.

Driver, R., Asoko, H., Leach, J., Mortimer, E., & Scott, P. (1994). Constructing scientific knowledge in the classroom. *Educational Researcher, 23*(7), 5-12.

Edwards, D., & Mercer, N. (1987). *Common knowledge: The development of understanding in the classroom.* London: Methuen.

Gilbert, J. K., & Watts, D. M. (1983). Concepts, misconceptions and alternative conceptions: Changing perspectives in science education. *Studies in Science Education, 10,* 61–98.

Glasersfeld, E. von (1989). Cognition, construction of knowledge, and teaching. *Synthese, 80,* 121–140.

Karplus, R. (1977). *Science teaching and the development of reasoning.* Berkeley, CA: University of California.

National Research Council (1996). National science education standards. Washington, DC: National Academy Press.

O'Loughlin, M. (1992). Rethinking science education: Beyond Piagetian constructivism toward a sociocultural model of teaching and learning. *Journal of Research in Science Teaching, 29*(8), 791–820.

Osborne, R., & Freyberg, P. (1985). *Learning in science.* London: Heinemann.

Piaget, J. (1973). *The children's conception of the world.* St. Albans: Paladin.

Renner, J. (1982). The power of purpose. *Science Education, 66*(5), 709–716.

CHAPTER 3 STRUCTURING SCIENCE KNOWLEDGE

Ausubel, D. P. (1968). *Educational psychology.* New York: Holt, Rinehart and Winston.

Ausubel, D. P., Novak, J. D., & Hanesian, H. (1978). *Educational psychology: A cognitive view.* New York: Holt, Rinehart and Winston.

Briscoe, C. (1993). *Building contexts for learning and generating knowledge: Students' use of language in a small group concept mapping activity.* Paper presented at the Annual Convention of the American Educational Research Association (AERA), Atlanta, GA.

Cross, A. (1992). Pictorial concept maps—putting us in the picture. *Primary Science Review, 21,* 26–28.

Ebenezer, J. V. (1992). Making chemistry learning more meaningful. *Journal of Chemical Education, 69,* 464–467.

Jonassen, D. H. (1996). *Computers in the classroom: Mindtools for critical thinking.* Englewood Cliffs, NJ: Prentice Hall.

Kilshaw, M. (1990). Using concept maps. *Primary Science Review, 12,* 34–36.

Leith, S. (1988). Using concept mapping as an aid to unit planning. In P. Holborn, M. Wideen, & I. Andrews (Eds.), *Becoming a teacher.* Toronto: Kagan & Woo.

Metcalfe, H., Williams, J., & Castka, J. (1974). *Modern chemistry.* New York: Holt, Rinehart & Winston.

Novak, J. D. (1978). An alternative to Piagetian psychology for science and mathematics education. *Studies in Science Education, 5,* 1–30.

Novak, J. (1991). Clarify with concept maps. *The Science Teacher, October,* 45–49.

Novak, J. D., & Gowin, D. B. (1984). *Learning how to learn.* Cambridge: Cambridge University Press.

Pines, A. L. (1985). Toward a taxonomy of conceptual relations and the implications for the evaluation of cognitive structures. In L. H. T. West & A. L. Pines (Eds.), *Cognitive structure and conceptual change* (pp. 101–116). Orlando, FL: Academic Press.

Roth, M., & Verechaka, G. (1993). Plotting a course with Vee maps. *Science and Children, 30*(1), 24–27.

CHAPTER 4 CONSTRUCTING COMMON KNOWLEDGE

Ausubel, D. P. (1968). *Educational psychology.* New York: Holt, Rinehart and Winston.

Bar, V. (1986). *The development of the concept of evaporation.* Jerusalem: The Amos de Shalit Science Teaching Centre, Hebrew University.

Bloom, J. W. (1992). The development of scientific knowledge in elementary school children: A context of meaning perspective. *Science Education, 76*(4), 399–413.

Borghi, L., De Ambrosis, A., Massara, C. I., Grossi, M. G., & Zoppi, D. (1988). Knowledge of air: A study of children aged between 6 and 8. *International Journal of Science Education, 10*(2), 179–188.

Bruner, J. (1986). *Actual minds, possible worlds.* Cambridge, MA: Harvard University Press.

Carey, S. (1985). *Conceptual change in childhood.* Cambridge, MA: MIT Press.

di Sessa, A. (1988). Knowledge in pieces. In G. Forman & P. Pufall (Eds.), *Constructivism in the computer age.* Hillsdale, NJ: Erlbaum.

Driver, R. (1985). Beyond appearances: The conversation of matter under physical and chemical transformations. In R. Driver, E. Guesne, & A. Tiberghien (Eds.), *Children's ideas in science.* Milton Keynes: Open University Press.

Driver, R., & Easley, J. (1978). Pupils and paradigms: A review of the literature related to concept development in adolescent science students. *Studies in Science Education, 5,* 61–84.

Driver, R., Squires, A., Rushworth, P., & Wood-Robinson, V. (1994). *Making sense of secondary science: Research into children's ideas.* London: Routledge.

Ebenezer, J., & Erickson, G. (1996). Chemistry students' conceptions of solubility: A phenomenography. *Science Education, 80*(2), 181–201.

Edwards, D., & Mercer, N. (1987). *Common knowledge: The development of understanding in the classroom.* London: Methuen.

Gabel, D. L. (1989). Let us go back to nature study. *Journal of Chemical Education, 66*(9), 727–729.

Gilbert, J., Osborne, R., & Fensham, P. (1982). Children's science and its consequences for teaching. *Science Education, 66*(4), 625–627.

Gilbert, J. K., & Watts, D. M. (1983). Concepts, misconceptions and alternative conceptions: Changing perspectives in science education. *Studies in Science Education, 10,* 61–98.

Guesne, E. (1985). Light. In R. Driver, E. Guesne, & A. Tiberghien (Eds.), *Children's ideas about science.* Milton Keynes: Open University Press.

Hawkins, D. (1978). Critical barriers in science learning. *Outlook, 29,* 3–22.

Helm, H. (1980). Misconceptions in physics amongst South African students. *Physics Education, 15,* 92–105.

Hills, G. (1989). Students' untutored beliefs about natural phenomena: Primitive science or common sense? *Science Education, 73*(2), 155–186.

Leboutet-Barrell, L. (1976). Concepts of mechanics among young people. *Physics Education, 20,* 462–465.

Marton, F. (1981). Phenomenography—describing conceptions of the world around us. *Instructional Science, 10,* 177–200.

Novak, J. (1977). *A theory of education.* Ithaca, NY: Cornell University Press.

Osborne, R. (1983). Modifying children's ideas about electric current. *Research in Science and Technology 1*(1), 73–82.

Piaget, J. (1973). *The child's conception of the world.* St. Albans: Paladin.

Prieto, T., Blanco, A., & Rodriguez, A. (1989). The ideas of 11- to 14-year-old students about the nature of solutions. *International Journal of Science Education, 11*(4), 451–463.

Rowell, J. A., Dawson, C. J., & Lyndon, H. (1990). Changing misconceptions: A challenge to science education. *International Journal of Science Education 12*(2), 167–175.

Russell, T., & Watts, D. (1989). *Growth.* Primary SPACE Project, Research Report. Liverpool: Liverpool University Press.

Säljö, R. (1988). Learning in educational settings: Methods of inquiry. In P. Ramsden, *Improving learning: New perspectives.* Great Britain: Kogan Page.

Shipstone, D. M. (1984). A study of children's understanding of electricity in simple DC circuits. *European Journal of Science Education 6*(2), 185–198.

Smith, C., Carey, S., & Wiser, M. (1984). A case study of the development of size, weight, and density. *Cognition, 21,* 177–237.

Stavy, R., & Stachel, D. (1984). *Children's ideas about "solid" and "liquid."* Israeli Science Teaching Centre, School of Education, Tel Aviv University.

Stavy, R., & Wax, N. (1989). Children's conceptions of plants as living things. *Human Development 32,* 88–94.

Vygotsky, L. (1978). *Mind in society: The development of higher psychological process-es.* Cambridge, MA: Harvard University Press.

Watts, D. M., & Gilbert, J. K. (1985). *Appraising the understanding of science concepts: Light.* Guildford, England: Department of Educational Studies, University of Surrey.

CHAPTER 5 EXPLORING AND CATEGORIZING

Erickson, G. (1992). Some suggestions for running an interpretive discussion. *[SI]²Network, 5*(1). Vancouver, BC: University of British Columbia.

Jones, B., & Lynch, P. (1987). Children's conceptions of the earth, sun, and moon. *International Journal of Science Education, 9*(1), 43–53.

National Research Council (1996). *National Science Education Standards.* Washington DC: National Academy Press.

White, R., & Gunstone, R. (1992). *Probing understanding.* New York: Falmer Press.

Wurtak, L. (1990). *Young children's conceptions of living and nonliving objects: Implications for teaching.* Unpublished master's thesis, University of Manitoba, Winnepeg, Manitoba, Canada.

CHAPTER 6 CONSTRUCTING AND NEGOTIATING

Barnes, D. (1988). Oral language and learning. In S. Hynds & D. Rubin (Eds.), *Perspectives on talk and learning.* Urbana, IL: NCTE.

Blough, D., & Berman, J. (1991). Twenty ways to liven up learning logs. *Learning,* July/August, 64–65.

Edwards, P. R. (1991/1992). Using dialectical journals to teach thinking skills. *Journal of Reading, 35*(4), 312–316.

Ellis, K. (1980). *Thomas Edison—Genius of electricity.* Bath: The Pitman Press.

Emmitt, M., & Pollock, J. (1991). *Language and learning.* Melbourne, Australia: OUP.

Erickson, G. (1992). Some suggestions for running an interpretive discussion. *[SI]²Network , 5*(1). Vancouver, BC: University of British Columbia.

Good, R., & Smith, M. (1987). How do we make students better problem solvers? *The Science Teacher, 54,* 31–36.

Howard, V. A. (1988). Thinking on paper: A philosopher's look at writing. In V. A. Howard (Ed.), *Varieties of thinking: Essays from Harvard's Philosophy of Education Research Center.* New York: Routledge.

Johnson, D. W., Johnson, R. T., & Holubec, E. J. (1993). *Cooperation in the class-room* (6th ed.). Edina, MN: Interaction Books.

Johnson, D. W. & Johnson, R. T. (1989). *Cooperation and competition: Theory and research.* Edina, MN: Interaction Books.

Kagan, D., Ozment, S., & Turner, F. M. (1987). *The western heritage.* (Vol. II). (3rd ed.). New York: Macmillan.

Kuhn, K., & Aguirré, J. (1987). A case study—On the journal method—A method designed to enable the implementation of constructivist teaching in the classroom. In J. D. Novak (Ed.), *Proceedings of The Second International Seminar: Misconceptions and educational strategies in science and mathematics Vol.II.* (pp. 262–274). Ithaca, NY: Cornell University.

National Research Council (1996). *National science education standards.* Washington, DC: National Academy Press.

Pizzini, E., Abell, S., & Shephardson, D. (1988). Rethinking thinking in the science classroom. *The Science Teacher, 55*(9), 22–25.

Pradl, G. M., & Mayher, J. S. (1985). Reinvigorating learning through writing. *Educational Leadership, 42*(5), 4–8.

Roth, K. J. (1991). Reading science texts for conceptual change. In C. M. Santa & D. E. Alverman (Eds.), *Science learning: Processes and applications* (pp. 48–63). Newark, DE: International Reading Association.

Sanders, A. (1985). Learning logs: A communication strategy for all subject areas. *Educational Leadership, 42*(5), 7.

Santa, C. M., & Havens, L. T. (1991). Learning through writing. In C. M. Santa & D. E. Alvermann (Eds.), *Science learning: Processes and applications* (pp.122–133). Newark, DE: International Reading Association.

Slavin, R. E. (1995). *Cooperative learning* (2nd ed.). Boston: Allyn & Bacon.

Slavin, R. E. (1990). *Cooperative learning theory, research and practice.* Englewood Cliffs, NJ: Prentice Hall.

Scott, J. (Ed.). (1993). *Science language and links.* Portsmouth, NH: Heinemann.

Sutton, C. (1992). *Words, science and learning.* Philadelphia: Open University Press.

Tompkins, G. E., & Hoskisson, K. (1991). *Language arts: Content and teaching strategies* (2nd ed.). New York: Merrill.

Treagust, D. F. (1993). The evolution of an approach for using analogies in teaching and learning science. *Research in Science Education, 23,* 293–301.

CHAPTER 7   TRANSLATING AND EXTENDING

Aikenhead, G. S. (1980). *Science in social issues: Implications for teaching.* Ottawa, Ontario: Science Council of Canada.

Aikenhead, G. S. (1987). High-school graduates' beliefs about science-technology-society III. The characteristics and limitations of scientific knowledge. *Science Education, 71*(2), 459–487.

Aikenhead, G. S. (1988). An analysis of four ways of assessing student beliefs about STS topics. *Journal of Research in Science Teaching, 25*(8), 607–629.

American Association for the Advancement of Science. (1989). *Project 2061: Science for all Americans.* Washington, DC: American Association for the Advancement of Science.

Arons, A. (1981). Thinking, reasoning and understanding in introductory physics courses. *The Physics Teacher 19,* 166–172.

Bruner, J. (1966). *Toward a theory of instruction.* Cambridge, MA: Harvard Press.

Bybee, R. W. (1985). *NSTA Yearbook: Science Technology Society.* Washington, DC: National Science Teachers Association.

Cross, B. (1992). A balancing act. *Science and Children, 29,* 16–17.

Cutcliffe, S. (1989). The STS curriculum: What have we learned in twenty years? *Science-Technology-Society & Human Values, 15*(31), 360–372.

di Sessa, A. (1988). Knowledge in pieces. In G. Forman & P. Pufall (Eds.), *Constructivism in the computer age.* Hillsdale, NJ: Erlbaum.

Driver, R. (1989). Students' conceptions and learning in science. *International Journal of Science Education, 11,* 481–490.

Ebenezer, J., & Landry, A. (1994). Fostering common knowledge through problem solving. *The Manitoba Teacher, 35*(2), 13–23.

Ebenezer, J. V., & Zoller, U. (1993). The no change in high school students' attitudes toward science in a period of change: A probe into the case of British Columbia. *School Science and Mathematics, 93*(2), 96–102.

Fensham, P. J. (1988). Approaches to the teaching of STS in science education. *International Journal of Science Education, 10*(4), 346–356.

Good, R., & Smith, M. (1987). How do we make students better problem solvers? *The Science Teacher, 54,* 31–36.

Hofstein, A., Aikenhead, G., & Riquarts, K. (1988). Discussions over STS at the fourth IOSTE symposium. *International Journal of Science Education, 10*(4), 357–366.

Jackson, K. F. (1985). *The art of solving problems.* New York: St. Martin Press.

Kanis, I. B. (1990). Improving the elementary school curriculum—Science education for the twenty-first century. *The Science Teachers Bulletin, 8*(30), 23–26.

Orpwood, G. (1984). *Science for every student: Educating Canadians for tomorrow's world.* Ottawa: Science Council of Canada.

Pizzini, E. L., Shephardson, D. P., & Abell, S. K. (1989). A rationale for and the development of a problem solving model of instruction in science education. *Science Education, 73,* 523–534.

Reif, F. (1981). Teaching of problem solving—a scientific approach. *The Physics Teacher, 19,* 310–316.

Rutherford, F. J., & Ahlgren, A. (1990). *Science for all Americans.* New York: Oxford Press.

Solomon, J. (1988). Science technology and society courses: Tools for thinking about social issues. *International Journal of Science Education, 10*(4), 379–387.

Streitberger, H. E. (1978). Levers: How we got levers. *Science and Children, 15,* 9–12.

Verstraete, L. (1990). *Issue-centred STS (Science-Technology-Society) in the elementary classroom: A case study.* Unpublished master's thesis, University of Manitoba, Winnipeg, Manitoba, Canada.

Vygotsky, L. (1976). Play and its role in the mental development of the child. In J. S. Bruner, A. Jolly, & K. Sylva (Eds.), Play. New York: Penguin.

Waks, L. J., & Barachi, B. A. (1992). STS in U.S. school science: Perception of selected leaders and their implications for STS education. *Science Education, 76*(1), 79–90.

Yager, R. E. (1984). Defining the discipline of science education. *Science Education, 68*(1), 35–37.

Yager, R. E., et al. (1988). Assessing the impact of STS instruction in 4–9 science in five domains. ERIC 292641, SE 048985.

Zoller, U. (1987). Problem solving and decision-making in science-technology-environment-society (STES) education. In R. Riquarts (Ed.), *Proceedings of the 4th international symposium on world trends in science and technology education* (pp. 562–569).

CHAPTER 8   REFLECTING AND ASSESSING

Berenson, S. B., & Carter, G. S. (1995). Changing assessment practices in science and mathematics. *School Science and Mathematics, 95*(4), 182–186.

Collins, A. (1992a). Portfolios for science education: Issues in purpose, structure, and authenticity. *Science Education, 76*(4), 451–463.

Collins, A. (1992b). Portfolios: Questions for design. *Science Education, 15*(6), 25–27.

Hebert, E. A. (1992). Portfolios invite reflection—from students and staff. *Educational Leadership, May,* 58–61.

Jasmine, J. (1992). *Portfolio assessment for your whole language classroom.* Huntington Beach, CA: Teacher Created Materials.

Kamen, M. (1993). *A teacher's process of implementing authentic assessment in an elementary science classroom*. Paper presented at the annual meeting of the National Association for Research in Science Teaching, Atlanta, GA.

McColskey, W., & O'Sullivan, R. (1993). *How to assess student performance in science: Going beyond multiple-choice tests*. Greensboro, NC: SouthEastern Regional Vision for Education.

Murphy, S. (1994). Writing portfolios in K–12 schools: Implications for linguistically diverse students. In L. Black, D. Daiker, J. Sommers, & G. Stygall (Eds.), *New directions in portfolio assessment*. Portsmouth, NH: Heinemann.

National Research Council (1996). *National science education standards*. Washington, DC: National Academy Press.

Raizen, S. A., & Kaiser, J. S. (1989). Assessing science learning in elementary school: Why, what, and how? *Phi Delta Kappan, May,* 718–722.

Rudd, T. J., & Gunstone, R. F. (1993). *Developing self-assessment skills in grade 3 science and technology: The importance of longitudinal studies in learning*. Paper presented at the annual meeting of the National Association for Research in Science Teaching, Atlanta, GA.

Science: Assessment of achievement program. (1993). Edinburgh: The Scottish Office.

Wiggins, G. (1989). A true test: Toward more authentic and equitable assessment. *Phi Delta Kappan, 70*(9), 703–713.

Wiggins, G. (1992). Creating tests worth taking. *Educational Leadership, May,* 26–33.

CHAPTER 9 SCIENCE FOR ALL STUDENTS

Allen, D. (1995). Encouraging success in female students. *Gifted Children Today, March/April,* 44–45.

All-girls class sets sights on math and sciences. (1995, April 19). *Winnepeg Free Press,* p. B1.

Atwater, M. (1993). Multicultural science education: Assumptions and alternative views. *The Science Teacher, March,* 33–37.

Atwater, M., & Riley, J. (1993). Multicultural science education: Perspectives, definitions, and research agenda. *Science Education, 77*(6), 661-668.

Atwood, R. K., & Oldham, B. R. (1985). Teacher's perceptions of mainstreaming in an inquiry-oriented elementary science program. *Science Education, 69*(5), 619–624.

Blake, S. (1993). Are you turning female and minority students away from science? *Science and Children, April,* 32–34.

Bredekamp, S., & Rosegrant, T. (Eds.). (1992). *Reaching potentials: Appropriate curriculum and assessment for young children: Vol. 1*. Washington: National Association for the Education of Young Children.

Canadian Teachers' Federation. (1992). *The better idea book: A resource book on gender, science and schools*. Ottawa, Canada.

Chaillé, C., & Britain, L. (1991). *The young child as scientist: A constructivist approach to early childhood education*. New York: HarperCollins.

Chambers, D. W. (1983). Stereotypical images of the scientist: The draw a scientist test. *Science Education, 67,* 255–265.

Delamont, S. (1994). Accentuating the positive: Refocussing the research on girls and science. *Studies in Science Education, 23,* 59–74.

Hodson, D. (1993). In search of a rationale for multicultural science education. *Science Education, 77*(6), 685–711.

Kelly, A. (Ed.). (1981). *The missing half*. Manchester, England: Manchester University Press.

Mastropieri, M. A., & Scruggs, T. E. (1992). Science for students with disabilities. *Review of Educational Research, 62*(4), 377–411.

Mastropieri, M. A., & Scruggs, T. E. (1995). Teaching science to students with disabilities in general education settings. *Teaching Exceptional Children, Summer,* 10–13.

Patton, J. R. (1995). Teaching science to students with special needs. *Teaching Exceptional Children,* Summer, 4–6.

Peacock, A. (1992). Planning science lessons with a multicultural dimension. In A. Peacock (Ed.) *Science in primary schools: The multicultural dimension*. London: Routledge.

Pickford, T. (1992). Girls and science: The effect of some interventions. *Primary Science Review, 25,* 22–24.

Reardon, J. (1997). Developing a community of scientists. In W. Saul, J. Reardon, A. Schmidt, C. Pearce, D. Blackwood, & M. Bird (Eds.). *Science workshop: A whole language approach*. Upper Saddle River, NJ: Prentice Hall.

Selin, H. (1993). Science across cultures. *The Science Teacher, March,* 38–44.

Sleuter, C. E. (1992). What is multicultural education? *Kappa Delta Gamma Record, 29*(1), 4–8.

Stanley, W. B., & Brickhouse, N. W. (1994). Multiculturalism, universalism, and science education. *Science Education, 78*(4), 387–398.

Vance, M. (1989). Biology teaching in a racist society. In D. Gill & L. Levidow (Eds.), *Anti-racist science teaching*. London: Free Association Books.

Watts, M. (1992). Questions of policy: Some lost opportunities in the making of primary science. In A. Peacock (Ed.), *Science in primary schools: The multicultural dimension*. London: Routledge.

CHAPTER 10 TECHNOLOGY IN SCIENCE

American Association for the Advancement of Science. (1989). *Science for all Americans*. Washington, DC: American Association for the Advancement of Science.

American Association for the Advancement of Science. (1993). *Benchmarks for science literacy*. Washington, DC: American Association for the Advancement of Science.

Bottrill, P. (1995). *Designing and learning in the elementary school*. Reston, VA: International Technology Education Association.

Bybee, R. W., et al. (1989). *Science and technology education for the elementary years: Frameworks for curriculum and instruction*. Andover, MA.: The NETWORK, Inc., National Center for Improving Science Education.

Dunn, S., & Larson, R. (1990). *Design technology: Children's engineering*. Washington, DC: Falmer Press.

Friedler, Y., Nachmias, R., & Linn, M. (1990). Learning scientific reasoning skills in microcomputer-based laboratories. *Journal of Research in Science Teaching, 27*(2), 173–191.

Jonassen, D. H. (1996). *Computers in the classroom: Mindtools for critical thinking*. Englewood Cliffs, NJ: Prentice-Hall.

Krajcik, J. S., & Layman, J. W. (1993). Microcomputer-based laboratories in the science classroom. In NARST News: Research matters—to the science teacher. *National Association for Research in Science Teaching, 35*(1), 3–6.

Layton, D. (1993). *Technology's challenge to science education: Cathedral, quarry, or company store*. Buckingham, England: Open University Press.

Nachmias, R., & Linn, M. (1987). Evaluations of science laboratory data: The role of computer-presented information. *Journal of Research in Science Teaching, 24*(5), 491–506.

National Commission on Excellence in Education. (1983). *A nation at risk: The imperative for educational reform*. Washington, DC: U.S. Department of Education.

National Research Council. (1996). *National science education standards*. Washington, DC: National Academy Press.

National Science Board Commission on Precollege Education in Mathematics, Science and Technology. (1983). *Educating America for the 21st century*. Washington, DC: National Science Foundation.

O'Neil, J. (1995). Technology and schools: A conversation with Chris Dede. *Educational Leadership, October*, 7–12.

Raizen, S., Sellwood, P., Todd, R. D., & Vickers, M. (1995). *Technology education in the classroom. Understanding the designed world*. San Francisco: Jossey-Bass.

Rivers, R., & Vockell, E. (1987). Computer simulations to stimulate scientific problem solving. *Journal of Research in Science Teaching, 24*(5), 403–415.

Salomon, G., Perkins, D. N., & Globerson, T. (1991). Partners in cognition: Extending human intelligence with intelligent technologies. *Educational Researcher, 20*(3), 2–9.

Sellwood, P. M. (1989). Progression and development for the practical curriculum. In *National project: Practical problem solving, 5-13, Standing Conference on Schools, Science and Technology, Department of Trade and Industry*. London: Department of Trade and Industry.

CHAPTER 11   MULTIPLE VOICES IN UNIT PLANNING

Allen, D. (1995). Encouraging success in female students. *Gifted Children Today, March/April 1995*, 44–45.

American Association for the Advancement of Science. (1989). *Project 2061: Science for all Americans*. Washington, DC.

Atwater, M. M., & Riley, J. P. (1993). Multicultural science education: Perspectives, definitions, and research agenda. *Science Education, 77*(6), 661–668.

Ausubel, D. P. (1968). *Educational psychology*. New York: Holt, Rinehart and Winston.

Bloom, J. W. (1992). The development of scientific knowledge in elementary school children: A context of meaning perspective. *Science Education, 76*(4), 399–413.

Bruner, J. (1986). *Actual minds, possible worlds*. Cambridge, MA: Harvard University Press.

Bybee, R. (Ed.). (1986). *Science-technology-society. 1986 NSTA yearbook*. Washington, DC: National Science Teachers Association.

Bybee, R. W. (Ed.). (1994). *Reforming science education: Social perspectives and personal reflections*. New York: Teachers College Press.

Carey, S. (1985). Cognitive science and science instruction. *American Psychologist, 41*(10), 1123–1130.

Driver, R., Asoko, H., Leach, J., Mortimer, E., & Scott, P. (1994). Constructing scientific knowledge in the classroom. *Educational Researcher, 23*(7), 5–12.

Driver, R., Squires, A., Rushworth, P., & Wood-Robinson, V. (1994). *Making sense of secondary science: Research into children's ideas.* London: Routledge.

Ebenezer, J., & Erickson, G. (1996). Chemistry students' conceptions of solubility: A phenomenography. *Science Education, 80*(2), 181–201.

Edwards, D., & Mercer, N. (1987). *Common knowledge: The development of understanding in the classroom.* London: Methuen.

Glasersfeld, E. von (1989). Cognition, construction of knowledge, and teaching. *Synthese, 80,* 121–140.

Hewitt, P. (1984). *Conceptual physics: A new introduction to your environment.* (2nd ed.). Boston: Little Brown.

Hodson, D. (1993). In search of a rationale for multicultural science education. *Science Education 77*(6), 685–711.

Keller, E. F. (1985). *Reflections on gender and science.* New Haven, CT: Yale University Press.

Kelly, A. (1981) (Ed.). *The missing half.* Manchester, England: Manchester University Press.

Kuhn, T. (1970). *The structure of scientific revolutions* (2nd ed.). Chicago: University of Chicago Press.

Latour, B., & Woolgar, S. (1986). *Laboratory life: The construction of scientific facts* (2nd ed.). Princeton, NJ: Princeton University Press.

Lemke, J. L. (1990). *Talking science: Language, learning, and values.* Norwood, NJ: Ablex.

Longino, H. (1990). *Science as social knowledge: Values and objectivity in scientific inquiry.* Princeton, NJ: Princeton University Press.

Marton, F. (1981). Phenomenography—describing conceptions of the world around us. *Instructional Science, 10,* 177–200.

Marton, F. (1984). Towards a psychology beyond the individual. In K. M. J. Lagerspectz & P. Niemi (Eds.), *Psychology in the 1990's.* Amsterdam: North Holland.

National Research Council of the National Academy of Science. (1996). *National science education standards.* Washington, DC: National Academy Press.

Orpwood, G. (1984). *Science for every student: Educating Canadians for tomorrow's world.* Ottawa: Science Council of Canada.

Osborne, R., & Freyberg, P. (1985). *Learning in science: The implications of children's science.* New York: Heinemann.

Piaget, J. (1973). *The child's conception of the world.* St. Albans: Paladin.

Popper, K. (1979). *Objective knowledge: An evolutionary approach.* Oxford: Clarendon Press.

Shipstone, D. (1985). Electricity in simple circuits. R. Driver, E. Guesne, & A. Tiberghien (Eds.), *Children's ideas in science.*

Solomon, J., & Aikenhead, G. (Eds.). (1994). *STS Education: International perspectives on reform.* New York: Teachers College Press.

Sutton, C. (1992). *Words, science, and learning.* Philadelphia: Oxford University Press.

Toulmin, S. (1972). *Human understanding: An inquiry into the aims of science.* Princeton, NJ: Princeton University Press.

Tuana, N. (Ed.). (1989). *Feminism and science.* Bloomington, IN: Indiana University Press.

CHAPTER 12   TRANSFORMATION FROM STUDENT TO PROFESSIONAL TEACHER

Clarke, A. (1994). Student-teacher reflection: Developing and defining a practice that is uniquely one's own. *International Journal of Science Education, 16*(5), 497–509.

Ebenezer, J. V., & Erickson, G. (1996). Chemistry students' conceptions of solubility: A phenomenography. *Science Education, 80*(2), 181–201.

Erickson, G. (1991). Collaborative inquiry and the professional development of science teachers. *Journal of Educational Thought, 25*(3), 228–245.

Feiman-Nemser, S., & Buchman, M. (1986). The first year of teacher preparation: Transition to pedagogical thinking? *Journal of Curriculum Studies, 18,* 239-256.

Ginsburg, M., & Clift, R. (1990). The hidden curriculum of preservice teacher education. In R. Huston (Ed.), *Handbook of research on teacher education.* New York: Macmillan.

Grimmett, P. P., MacKinnon, A. M., Erickson, G. L., & Riecken, T. J. (1990). Reflective practice in teacher education. In R. T. Cliff, W. R. Houston, & M. Pugach (Eds.), *Encouraging reflective practice in education.* New York: Teachers College Press.

Hargreaves, A. (1994). *Changing teachers, changing times.* New York: Teachers College Press.

International Reading Association. (1989). *Journal of Reading, 33*(3), 216–218.

Kemmis S., & McTaggart, R. (1982). *The action research planner.* Victoria, Australia: Deakin University.

Saranson, S. (1990). *The predictable failure of educational reform.* San Francisco: Jossey-Bass.

Schön, D. A. (1983). *The reflective practitioner: How professionals think in action.* New York: Basic Books.

Schön, D. A. (1987). *Educating the reflective practitioner.* San Francisco: Jossey-Bass.

Shulman, L. (1986). Those who understand: Knowledge growth in teaching. *Educational Researcher, 15*(2), 4–14.

INDEX

379

ABOUT THE AUTHORS

Jazlin Ebenezer, shown on the right in the photo below, is assistant professor at the Faculty of Education, University of Manitoba, Winnipeg, Canada. Her experience includes teaching science curriculum and instruction to preservice teachers at various levels during their certification year. At the graduate level, she teaches "The Study of Teaching." Jazlin conducts classroom-based, action-oriented collaborative research, which is supported by the Social Sciences and Humanities Research Council of Canada. Her research program focuses on preservice teachers' voices, attitudes, and conceptualizations; students' perceptions of science concepts and incorporating their ideas into science lesson sequences; environmental ethics and sustainable living; and electronic multimedia within a constructivist framework. She

has authored and co-authored a number of articles both in scholarly and professional journals and has presented papers in Russia, South Africa, America, and Canada. She carries out ongoing research with universities in Cape Town, South Africa. At the Manitoba Ministry of Education and Training, she is involved with the decision-making processes of science and chemistry curriculum development and implementation.

Sylvia Connor (Leith) is a recently retired science education professor from the University of Manitoba, Winnipeg, Canada. Her particular areas of interest are children's conceptual understanding and curriculum development and assessment. She has worked on curriculum and assessment projects for the province of Manitoba, the Ontario Institute for the Study of Education, the Assessment of Performance Unit in England, and the Science: Assessment of Achievement Program in Scotland, as well as on a special assessment project for the Scottish Education Department. Since retirement she has pursued her interests by doing contracts in science assessment and curriculum development for the province of Manitoba.